CULTURAL HERITAGE AND CONTEMPORARY CHANGE
SERIES I. CULTURE AND VALUES, VOL. 4

General Editor
George F. McLean

RELATIONS

BETWEEN CULTURES

Edited by

GEORGE F. McLEAN

and

JOHN KROMKOWSKI

THE COUNCIL FOR RESEARCH IN VALUES AND PHILOSOPHY

Library of Congress Cataloging-in-Publication

Relations between cultures / edited by George F. McLean and John
Kromkowski.
Includes bibliographical references and index
1. Pluralism (Social sciences) 2. Ethnicity. 3. Nationalism. 4. Ethnic
relations. 5. Culture conflict. 6. Consensus (Social sciences)
I. McLean, George F. II. Kromkowski, John, 1939- .
JC330.R45 1991
303.48'2--dc20
91-58118
CIP
ISBN 1-56518-009-7
ISBN 1-56518-008-9(pbk.)

ACKNOWLEDGEMENT

Deep appreciation is extended to the authors of this study whose generous effort and rich wisdom realized the investigation which this volume reflects.

Acknowledgement is made to: The University of Texas Press for permission to cite from the *Royal Commentaries of the Incas*; to Macmillan Publishers for permission to cite M. Buber, *Between Man and Man*; to the Paulist Press for permission to quote from *The Cloud of Unknowing*, ed. J. Walsh; to Harvard University Press for the tables reprinted by permission of the publishers from *The Harvard Encyclopedia of Ethnic Groups in America*, Stephan Thernstrom, editor, Cambridge, Mass.: The Belknap Press of Harvard University University Press, Copyright c 1980 by the President and Fellows of Harvard College; and to The University of Notre Dame Press for permission to include tables from Philip Rosen, *The Neglected Dimension: Ethnicity in American Life*, copyright 1980.

Appreciation is extended as well to Mrs. B. Kennedy and Mrs. Linda Perez for their work in preparing the manuscript, to the James A. McLeans for their support in the realization of this project, and to The Catholic University of America for some support toward editing this volume.

TABLE OF CONTENTS

PREFACE

At the end of this century, when all had predicted that a new universalism would have rendered cultural diversity and ethnic sensibilities a past irrelevancy, problems centering upon relations between cultures seem to be more alive than ever. In part, this may be due to the fact that, by intensifying commercial and political interchange between hitherto separated peoples, modern civilization has intensified as well the potential for clashes of cultures. More deeply, however, the universalizing trends of modern life, by threatening to depersonalize individuals and peoples, have forced them to return to their cultural roots in order to find their sense of personal and national identity and hence the basis for their freedom and dignity.

Indeed, it may be more true to say that the pervasive development of the appreciation of the person has generated, in turn, an appreciation of what persons, through their various cultures, can create. This has opened a renewed search for ways in which the creativity of diverse cultures can be stimulated and interrelated. It can be expected that the new expressions of human meaning will set the directions for life in the XXIst century.

The inter-disciplinary and cross-cultural team of scholars which undertook the present study of these issues interwove discussion, research, writing and redrafting. Their aim was not only separately to present their discrete insights, but to enable all to take into account, test and respond to the perspectives of the others. Hence, this volume has its cohesion not only through an external logic that links its multiple chapters, but through the internal dynamic by which they were generated in mutual interaction among scholars from a broad range of disciplines and cultures. These invistigations are continued in the subsequent volumes: *Urbanization and Values*, *The Place of the Person in Social Life*, and others to follow.

The Introduction by John Kromkowski to the present volume opens up the terrain of the study. He extends the horizons of community existence beyond factors of place to those of socio-political interaction, beyond personal identity to that of the community in which the person lives, beyond continuity through time to the living of a tradition, and beyond sharing with others to participation in the divine ground. In these terms complementarity and conflict in our basic human project take on their real drama and constitute a major challenge to any who would understand and respond to present problems and hope to live more fully.

The Prologue by Paul Peachey clarifies the challenge entailed in combining community as a given with such creative human initiative. In this the goal must be to develop a world in which the many cultures and communities not only can survive, but can prosper in jointly proclaiming new dimensions of mankind's God-given and hence god-like potential. This is the challenge to which this study responds in three Parts.

Part I concerns the nature of cultures and their interrelations. G. McLean in Chapter I studies the nature of culture as a living process of human creativity developing through time and providing a basis for interaction with other peoples. V. Manimali employs phenomenological and Indian insights to identify the roots of culture in the communitary nature of the person in Chapter II. G.J. Wanjohi in Chapter III illustrates ways in which relevant philosophical content is embedded and communicated through the proverbs of his people, the Gikuyu of Kenya.

Profs. A. Gallo and L. Molina in Chapter IV contribute a substantive study of the nature of ethnic group identity and alienation, illustrated by the multiple peoples of Guatemala. John Kromkowski carries out an analogous study of the development of ethnic group consciousness in the United States in Chapter V. Prof. T.I. Oiserman of the Soviet Union in Chapter VI draws upon the resources of Marxist philosophy to relate culture to labor and the structures of modern production, which he describes as a second nature deriving from human activity.

Part II concerns the processes of interaction between cultures and the conflicts which these generate. Chen Na in Chapter VII illustrates how these tensions can arise even between generations within the same culture as the younger Chinese generation calls for more opportunities for self expression in a culture which has always prized harmony. This can be excruciatingly exacerbated through the stress which modern scientifically structured systems place upon unity and conformity. Focusing upon the issue of language in Chapter VIII, E. Baltazar describes the cultural dilemmas faced by nations with four, ten or more regional languages as they confront the needs of modern education and intercommunication.

In many circumstances cultural tensions are the effect of past empire building with which we must deal in the present and the future. Prof. P. Roosevelt provides some background in Chapter IX on the differing approaches of pre- and post-revolutionary Russia in coping with the problem of a plurality of peoples, and hence of cultures, within a single national unity--a problem of ever increasing and more explosive urgency. R. Hozven in Chapter X illustrates the problem implied by the impact of Western cultures upon the cultures of the Southern Hemisphere. His masterful depth analysis of Garcilaso de la Vega's *Royal Commentaries of the Incas* identifies the successive levels and interchanges of self-understanding and mutual misunderstanding, of critique and resistance, which were involved in the effort of one culture to adapt and survive under the force of an alien supervening colonizing culture. J. Asike carries out a similar study in Chapter XI regarding the implications of the colonial period for modern Africa, while Prof. Atomate Epas-Ngan (Chapter XII) describes the recent efforts of new African nations to develop successively in terms of their cultural roots, of socialist ideologies, and of democratic institutions.

The set of chapters in this second part regard then the experience of China and the Philippines, Eastern Europe, Africa and Latin America. When complemented by the earlier chapters of Profs. Gallo and Molina and of Kromkowski on Central and North America, respectively, they constitute a world-wide survey of the problems of the relation between cultures in its various modalities. These derive from colonial and/or imperial domination, free immigration or imposed international gerrymandering, or simply clashes between generations in times of rapid and radical change.

Part III proceeds to search for ways of responding to this complex problematic of relations between cultures. G. McLean in Chapter XIII proposes that a metaphysical foundation for facing the problem is to be found in the nature of the person as received or as gift, understood as implying a new, positive and creative sense of tolerance. J. Kuczynski in Chapter XIV attempts to build a universalism upon an enriched Marxist socio-economic theory. Another Polish scholar, K. Turek, follows with a pair of deftly nuanced and tightly reasoned chapters. The first identifies the advances of science as a process of unifying vision (Chapter XV). But Chapter XVI goes further to identify the added human dimension which escapes the processes of scientific universalization. This is precisely the area of freedom and creativity which at once both grounds and expresses personal and cultural identity (Chapter XVI). It is about this that people are passionately concerned; it is in these terms that they set the ultimate goals which profoundly shape their lives as individuals and as peoples.

It would appear then that the developing interrelation between cultures, rather than imposing a progressively depersonalizing, univocous and universal civilization, may provide the broadened horizon needed for a more personal reappropriation and renewal of one's own culture. This was the conclusion which the Chapter of E. Baltazar drew from the vision of Pierre Teilhard de Chardin. Ways in which this might be implemented through education is the burden of Chapter XVII by T. Ready. He suggests that much new and important content for a contemporary natural law ethic is to be found in the requirement for a proper operation of cultures and for intercultural harmony. This involves the classical notion of deep commitment and concern for the well-being of others, but does so in ways that enable the moral imagination to translate general laws into concrete moral and social imperatives. Some religious foundations for this, already intimated in Chapter XIII, are indicated by J. Price in Chapter XVIII. He shows how cross-cultural studies can help to identify both the full significance of the deepest religious insights proper to a culture and the deeply shared insights of a common humanity.

The Epilogue by K. Schmitz brings together a number of these themes in a searching analysis of the requirements for relations between cultures in our day. He points out the dangers of abstract and univocous leveling in the search for universal values and common structures. He illustrates thereby the need for the development of concrete cultural universals which are rich with the achievements of the many cultures and pregnant with promise for future creativity. Indeed, it is his tantalizing suggestion that the points of cultural interaction--from neighborhood to world federations--may be the points at which needed, but as yet unknown, dimensions of what it means to be human can become manifest in new human inventions. Here, to echo President John F. Kennedy, God's work will truly be man's own.

The Discussions summarize a number of the issues brought up during the group interchanges on specific chapters and are cross-referenced thereto.

George F. McLean, Secretary
The Council for Research in Values and Philosophy
Cardinal Station, P.O. Box 261, Washington, D.C. 20064
Tel.: 202/319-5636; fax (#3): 202/319-6089

INTRODUCTION

The difficulty experienced by people of different cultures in living together would appear to be one of the major problems of our day. It appears in terms of language in Canada and Belgium; of religion in Ireland and India; of the colonial and Indian populations in Central and South America; of diverse ethnic groups in the Balkans and in Africa; and of the very diversified immigrant populations in North America, the Southern cone and elsewhere. In all these areas--and most others besides--where people of quite different cultures live in fairly close proximity, the key to a life of personal dignity and social peace is their ability, both as individuals and as members of groups, to relate in a positive manner to those who are different.

The problem, of course, is not new; it echoes through ancient biblical narratives as well as the accounts of the fall of the Roman empire. Some factors, however, make it a particularly urgent problem in our day. First, where different tribes constituted essentially different peoples which in the past could live in relative juxtaposition to others, today this is no longer possible. The development of large national entities has united the destiny of multiple peoples, as for example in Yugoslavia or Nigeria; the development of modern means of communication, production and commerce binds them into ever more intense interaction and interdependence. Hence, the possibilities of peace and progress now depend upon the ability of these different peoples to cooperate with, and mutually to promote, those with whom their national destiny has come to be intertwined.

The Nature of Community

Niemeyer's treatment of the problem of collective or communal existence suggests a fruitful path of analysis. The type of social entity, cultural phenomena and person-group experience signified by the words nationality and ethnicity appears to be related to Niemeyer's discussion of "the something that endures in a succession of generations, tends to produce representative rulers, engenders power for common action in history, and fosters an inner energy of change and creativeness."

This common perspective of consciousness renders possible a broad and deep area in which actions and language symbols are commonly understood: a rich soil of taken-for-granted assumptions, associations and references enabling persons to communicate by gestures, hints, signs, or even silently, and to act toward, and with, each other with a great economy of decision-energy. On this soil grow common aspirations, the "agreed-upon objects of love" to which Augustine pointed. On it also develop unwritten but highly effective structures, the patterns of custom, conventional judgments, and the do's and don't's usually more strictly obeyed than written statutes. Above all, here flowers confidence, the assurance with which a person moves among his fellow beings, knowing what to expect and on what grounds to engage in cooperative efforts.

All this, however, is confined to a *limes*, a spatial boundary. The definition of this boundary with precision may not be possible, but there are areas beyond which a particular order does not obtain. Within the *limes*, however, there is a world of familiarity to which every one of its members "belongs." In other words, there is something like a "whole" of which as a single person one feels a "part," moving among other "parts" like oneself. The whole structure of meaning and familiarity makes for the possibility of public friendship which Aristotle treats in the *Nicomachean Ethics* as basic openness and benevolence towards all other "parts," even though they not be of one's personal acquaintance. But this entire world of familiarity and conventionality stands in existential tension toward the highest ranking truth which elicits the public effort at justice. The confinement of this order to a certain area circumscribed by a *limes,* and to certain persons who are its bearers within this geographical boundary, attaches the order of consciousness to a corporeal and material matrix. Thus, there is always the possibility of destroying the entire order by destroying the matrix, and for this reason it makes perfect sense to say that a realm *exists.*

For the commonly held truths at the top of this structure, we shall propose the term "myth," stipulating that the meaning of the word in this context shall not be that of a historical variant of order, namely the "cosmological myth" or order that prevailed, as Frankfort put it, "before philosophy." Rather, myth in this context applies to any set of symbols through which a multitude of people, living together, symbolically secure the transparency of life and awareness of participation in the divine ground. In this sense one would have to say that no realm, ancient or modern, is without its myth. Philosophy as noetic consciousness of participation has made a difference in the quality of life, but no realm has ever been founded by a philosopher or been held together merely by syllogistic propositions. In countries in which the "barbarism of reflection" is widespread by means of instruction, the underlying myths are no longer symbolized by express celebrations and they are hardly recognizable. Such countries resort, on their festival occasions, to phrases and slogans derived from analytical thought rather than to restatements of their myth.

All the same, even there the myth is effective in what most persons take for granted, in tacit assumptions about reality and the meaning of life, about God, man and nature. Such assumptions are held by the average person, not in syllogistic, but rather in mythical form. The average American, for instance, takes for granted that each "individual" has a soul, a claim to personal dignity, and an independent mind; he distinguishes "time" from "eternity"; he attributes authority to "the people," but also to "the law"; he believes in an enduring "Constitution"; he pledges allegiance to a "nation under God"--all this in the uncritical ways of myths. If it were not for the myth, the mutual comprehensibility of actions and language symbols among the "parts" would atrophy after a while, and in place of familiarity and confident communication there would arise the universal assumption of hostility which prevails, for instance, in desert life. In the course of time, a myth that is not supported by appropriate cultic celebrations may suffer a decline and recede far into the subconscious. All the same, there is a decisive difference between that kind of weakening and the total collapse of the myth, from which results an opaqueness of life that befalls men as a major disaster.[1]

The Grounds of Community and Conflict

Niemeyer's discussion of the problem of naming the social reality that endures in the succession of generations, produces rules, and engenders common action that is energetic, creative and changing raises a parallel if not identical problematic. Niemeyer illustrates the issue and elaborates the following resolution:

There is a plethora of imprecise designations for that which politically 'exists': nation, society, community, people, country, state. For the purposes of political theory illuminating the order of existence from within, fairly precise terms have been developed and one may argue that that is all that is required. Men, however, have lived not in one political order but in a number of them 'existing' side by side, and the phenomenon of this multifarious 'existence' has seemed to defy logic and comprehension, although it is a salient experience. For this reason we believe that theoretical concepts acknowledging a mystery at this point come closer to whatever insight we may gain. We should like to examine four such concepts dealing with the problem of a collective or communal 'existence.'

The Egyptians had a mythical term that symbolized the otherwise unexplainable fact of political existence: the *ka*. According to Henri Frankfort the closest approximation of this word is 'vital force,' something impersonal which is capable of being present or not being present.[1] In hieroglyphs, only the king's *ka* is pictured, never that of a commoner, although the commoner is supposed to derive his *ka* from the king. The *ka* supports man on earth as well as in the beyond; it is 'the experience of power in its direct relation to man'; it is through the *ka* that one can achieve something. One pyramid text reveals that Re, the god, is the *ka* of the king, while the subjects say: 'My *ka* belongs to the king, my *ka* derives from the king, the king makes my *ka*, the king is my *ka*.' The community, in other words, is equated with a vital energy noticeable in every one of its members, which goes back to the king and ultimately to the god Re, where its why and how remains shrouded in mystery.

Ibn Khaldun in his *Muqaddimah*[2] coined a concept better left untranslated: '*asabiyah*' which, according to Wehr's *Dictionary of Modern Written Arabic* (1961) means: 'nervousness, nervosity; . . . zealous partisanship, bigotry, fanaticism; party spirit, team spirit, esprit de corps; tribal solidarity, racialism, clannishness, tribalism, national consciousness, nationalism.' In Ibn Khaldun, '*asabiyah* connotes a political whole that appears on the historical scene, moves through various stages (bedouin life, sedentary life, decline) from small beginnings to optimal strength and through weakness to ultimate extinction. '*Asabiyah* is often translated as 'community consciousness' but obviously implies much more--namely, the concrete and unique identity of a political whole, its 'existence' with its aspects of vitality and morality, a concept of common consciousness which still embraces the phenomenal aspects of birth, health, sickness, and demise. A similar concept is Vico's *mente eroica*, the 'heroic mind' that animates patricians to band together in society for the preservation of the common good; a 'mind' which, however, then wanders from the patricians to the people and eventually to the monarch, so that there is a continuing identity through a variety of constitutions. The eventual decline, according to Vico, comes not from constitutional changes but through the loss of the tension between that 'mind' and God, resulting in a spiritual self-centered 'barbarism of reflection' which leads to 'dissolution' and 'madness that wastes the substance of society' at which point people lose their 'arms and language.' Vico, like Ibn Khaldun, sees the identity of a political whole as a continuing consciousness or 'mind,' but finds that this 'mind' has something like a life cycle.

The fourth concept is Bodin's sovereignty, the 'highest and perpetual power to command over citizens and subjects,' which power he assumes to be 'above the law,' though subject to natural law. Bodin has often been described as advocating absolutism or even worse. No such advocacy can be read into this concept of sovereignty. He states explicitly that it is not the power of anyone who holds governmental office, but rather that which underlies all official powers. Sovereignty is not a possession of either the prince or the people; it is the concept for a whole that cannot be possessed but only imputed either to the prince or to the people or both. Prince and people are both concepts of succession: one cannot identify 'the people' with a numerically definite multitude existing at any given time, or 'the prince' with a particular king alone. The king never dies nor do the people. Bodin's sovereignty connotes a continuing identity, the "existence" of a community that is prior to human laws and entails powers of obligation. Each person wielding political command then is but a keeper of the perpetual sovereignty which is not diminished by any specific power it confers on these keepers and which continues to "exist" beyond their particular person. Bodin, too, was aware of the law of vitality of political entities, but his concept on the whole is closer to the Egyptian *ka* than to Ibn Khaldun's *'asabiyah* or Vico's *mente eroica.*

All four concepts reflect the ultimately mysterious character of what modern usage calls "society," the mystery stemming from its continuity in time, its relative independence from human volition and personalities, and its proneness to decay. The four concepts also agree in assuming that political existence is some kind of participation in the divine ground; that the vitality of a political whole has something to do with this; that "there is no power except from God"; and that the appearance of political entities is attributable to Providence. Such overtones are missing in the current concept "society," with its attending association with causal "factors" and its pretense to complete analytical knowability of the object. All the same, modern language offers no ready substitute, so that for the time being we must be content with having circumscribed what it is that begs a name and having indicated why this something seems to be partly knowable, partly ineffable. Along this road it may be possible to push a little farther.[2]

Niemeyer goes on to argue that these four concepts assume that political existence is participation in the divine ground and that community thus abiding in time 'imitates eternity', i.e., transcends its individual members in the succession of generations united to the highest and best element, "united in a common transparency of being."

Niemeyer reminds us, however, that community has its

"irrational" dimension, its opaque "forces" and "patterns" which, though incapable of transparency in themselves, still abide in time and are passed from generation to generation.

They are the habits, customs, conventional standards of approval and disapproval, prejudices, superstitions, property relations, gradations of respectability and other "ways of doing things." Such norms, as Bergson has pointed out, operate through unorganized pressures to which people respond unreflectively. Each obedient response itself adds to the pressures on others, so that psychic and customary patterns are the most tenacious and ubiquitous manifestations through which a political community distinguishes itself. While customs are distinctly evident to the point of being "picturesque," they are incapable of that transparency of being which provides meaning to existence and action. The transparency of being can reside only in what Yeats has called the "eternity of race," the commonly acknowledged truth regarding God, nature, man, and society. The psychic and social patterns can resist or defy the "eternity of race" or conform themselves to it, so that a community's habits stand in unceasing tension toward the "eternity of race," the name of this tension being justice. Where habits and customs drift away and develop in terms of their own impulsive causality, the community will eventually lose its reason for being and finally, as Vico has reminded us, lose its language and arms, too.

There is also a tension between the "eternity of race" and the "eternity of soul," as Aristotle indicated by his distinction between the "good citizen" and the "good man". Under normal circumstances, the "eternity of race" seems to be accorded higher rank, in all probability because it is thought out much more carefully than anything that a single individual can work out in his lifetime, but also because one cannot have a community on everyday notice by critical individuals. On occasion, however, an outstandingly sensitive person experiences what Bergson has called an opening of the soul and attains insights into reality and moral order beyond those underlying the community. His life then manifests a quality that attracts people for whom the previously accepted truths all of a sudden become opaque, a new transparency appears, and the "eternity of soul" confronts the "etrnity of race" with an authoritative: "You have heard it said . . . but I say to you!" These are the words of Jesus, but they also characterize a situation that obtained when Xenophanes confronted Homer and Hesiod, Socrates, Athens, and Siddhartha Gautama Brahmanism, a tension which Bergson has explored in his *Two Sources of Morality and Religion*, and Jaeger in his *Theology of the Early Greek Philosophers*. It is not the tension of man's irrationality toward the "eternity" of his consciousness, but rather the confrontation of rationality

with higher rationality in a mode of gentle persuasion, resulting not in disobedient subordination but in supersession
of the lower by the higher authority and a "leap" in the level
of existence.[3]

Finally, the development in recent decades of greater sensitivity to
the person, and hence group and cultural identity, gives new importance
to its recognition and promotion, just as its denial or repression is rendered increasingly less tolerable. This underlines the need to come to a
better understanding of the nature of cultural identities and symbol
systems, of their significance, and of the possibilities of their positive
interrelation.

The Study of Cultural Conflict and Complementarity

There is need then for a study of the nature of complementarity
versus conflict as regards the relation between cultures. This must search
out implications for the development of conditions which promote a
positive realization and expression of cultural values in a way that is
harmonious and complementary to those of others with whom we live.

It would appear to require: (a) continued reflection, (b) scholars
from such different disciplines as philosophy, anthropology and politics,
(c) with an opportunity, in order to refine personal insights through
writing, to discuss the problem critically, in depth and in its multiple
dimensions with persons from different cultures, and (d) in the light of
such intensive discussion to draft and gradually shape a volume which
reflects the discoveries of the group.

This volume, *The Relation Between Cultures*, represents the end of
one phase of inquiry, reflection and clarification and the beginning of
another process--extending this dialogue and discussing its problematics
and findings. The reader is invited into the study which produced this
international, intercultural and interdisciplinary corpus. The ongoing
character of the project, the dialogue it aspires to provoke and the problematics contained in this collection must be underscored.

Complexity and pluraformity must be acknowledged as a basic
feature of the reality we share as a common humanity. As curious persons in search of wisdom, insight, explanation and knowledge, the amazing variety and interaction of cultures invite us to think through our
cultural legacies and the accounts of other cultures, as well as other
forms of systematic symbolization of reality. The search for ways of
knowing which simultaneously are parsimonious and profound is a life-
long quest. The reach of that quest across ages and languages has been
lengthened by this collaboration of scholars each of whom was forced to
draw deeply from the wellspring and foundation of his or her experiences and disciplined research. This scholarly enterprise and the dialogue,
extended through the publication of this volume, cannot be reduced to a
recipe for action, nor does it compose a completely orchestrated score
which can be replicated. It aims rather to be sensitive to deep values and

aspirations, insightful regarding structures and conflicts, provocative of new paths and catalytic for creative action.

In an era when the expansion of cultural horizons is discussed in terms of the critique of the Eurocentric canon, with its lists of books reflecting a particular set of ethnicities, serious philosophic and pheno- menogical probing of cultural-ethnic identity, change and unity is im- perative. Simplistic formulation of the question only exposes the crisis. This volume and the extension it invites from its readers initiates a ther- apy that is well beyond the critique of Eurocentrism and ethnocentrism. In many respects this collection probes the grounds for the analysis of cultures and philosophically clarifies the experience of understanding culture.

The authors have avoided the close-grained anecdotal material that have plagued ethnographic and ethnological inquiries. The broader can- vasses of epistemology, change and unity are ever-present, though the specific inquiries are not forced into interchangeable logarithms. Reality is not a crossword puzzle. At bottom these explanations of cultural reali- ty and the relation between cultures offer an opportunity to learn about the ways in which persons experience, understand and change the worlds of meaning they inherited and will bequeath to others.

This study points to such interesting themes as identity, conflict and cultural cooperation. It reveals diverse methods and approaches: the literary and philosophic; the scientific and inductive; the hermeneutical and theological. Moreover, it indicates that these themes and methods are woven inextricably into the symbolization of order and relation between persons that constitutes a tradition. Finally, it illustrates the dialogue among persons whose openness to the search for convergence and an- alogies among cultures suggests the possibility of new levels of cultural synthesis.

Such inquiry transcends variety, yet maintains the integrity of diversity among peoples and cultures. This reconfiguration of the rela- tion between cultures spans earlier formulation of the problematic and the simpler paradigms of cultural distinctions and difference expressed in such emblematic form as Old World-New World; First-Second-Third World; Modern-Traditional; Ancient-Modern; Ancient-Medieval-Re- naissance-Modern; EasternWestern; Humanistic-Scientific; Mythic-Phil- osophic-Historic; Primitive-Technological and Eurocentric. The range of representation from nominal culture-geographical forms such as Ameri- can, Asian, European and African seems less significant in light of the variety of local realities that constitute governmental orders on the vari- ous continents and even the planetary ecumene. These have been brought into being by the movement of peoples within and between these con- ventional, but hardly meaningful, stereotypic designations that have posed as relevant ways of aggregating human diversity as well as geo- political realities.

The field of exploration arrayed in this volume is a moving prob- lematic. For example, though the number of living languages appears to be declining, the rise of literary languages has increased. Simultaneously, the inter-pollination of world views fostered by the exchange of scholars and the incorporation of persons from various ethnic and cultural experiences into national and international academic discourse suggests a growing need for cultural research, for analysis of traditions and for multicultural literacy. We are all experiencing a magnificent crisis of growth. This study is a propaedeutic to a much fuller range of cultural analysis and interpretation regarding symbolization about the primordial reality which constitutes the human condition.

The gods and nature, the human plethos and social order appear to be the constants which occur in many forms and languages. To understand the relation between cultures is to trace their dissimilarity to their origin and their implications. Resolving conflict among cultures is immensely more complicated. No doubt imaginary worlds of harmonious order can be hoped for. Such willful incantations, critiques of cultural orders and recipes for cultural change and cooperation have been proposed. These programs exist alongside of, within, or more usually at the margin of, existential societies and historical forms of culture. Such programs and persons, be they ideologues, philosophers or philomythos, propose alternate pathways to expressing the mystery of shared experience--the *cultus* which bonds participants of a society to each other, to other gods and to nature.

The bold, yet beginning, steps taken in these chapters can move the reader toward a multi-cultural competency which becomes a necessity as one recognizes the imperative of living in the global village. This volume should help us all to think globally and to act locally. It is an irony of the moment, however, that universities generally prepare persons to act globally and to think within their cultural boundaries; these chapters have been written from another perspective.

The task of researchers and teachers should be to attune themselves and those who would listen to the causes and consequences of the action deposited in the various traditions. To recover the tradition of various cultures and to explore ways of critically clarifying and expressing the efficacy of one's cultural legacies are the twin missions of the researcher-teacher, that is, he or she must give us roots as well as wings! In this fashion the formation of multi-cultural competency will be grounded in more real possibilities of equivalence and convergence than the current extremes of cultures in fragmented isolation, of cultures destroyed through the progressive action of totalitarian homogenization, and of cultures ignored, neglected and consequently withering for lack of renewal through critique and social practice.

The public discussion of the relation between cultures indicates that this concern is an intellectual and political problem. William Pfaff's penetrating essay, "Moral Reasoning," warns of the cultural relativism of post-modernism which claims that universal principles and liberal, rationalist efforts to discover truths are not credible. Pfaff reports that reason has become pluralized, and reality indeterminate, while regimes of knowledge which create warrants for action have become tenets of post-modern academics. This quandary does not dissolve into the intramural-ism of academic schools, but bursts forth in political action where, so to speak, power makes truth. In this regard the problematic of this study intersects with Pfaff's concern about moral reasoning. From what ground can one claim to speak truth to power if the academic arena has not probed the reality of cultural variety? Pfaff's therapy was to visit Delphi, the cultural ground of his tradition. The normative thrust of his finding is captured in the following report:

> A visit to Delphi, in Greece, is a sobering experience. The statues and images from the Archaic period, before the 6th century B.C., wear stylized, idealized, half-smiles, seductive but undifferentiated. In the classical period the faces become increasingly individual, self-conscious; they become moral persons. They offer the shock of recognizing an individual across 25 centuries.
>
> They speak as well. There are the classical texts, which we have, but at Delphi itself, incised at the entrance to the Temple of Apollo, were two very modern injunctions: 'Know thyself,' and 'Nothing in Excess.' We still fail to know ourselves and still are victims of our excess, but it seems undeniable that we still live in a continuity of intelligence and moral responsibility that began with Greek rationalism. To cut ourselves off from this means cutting ourselves off not only from a usable past but from our essential quality as a society. The possibility that this could actually happen is what is most troubling about the whole affair of the universities.[4]

Like Pfaff, the participants in this study through ten meetings probed their traditions. Their engagement in dialogue which is brought together in this volume suggests that one need not be pessimistic and troubled about universities that probe traditions in search of convergence and equivalence. Perhaps the parsimony of two truths: "Know thyself" and "Nothing to Excess" will not satisfy the passion for truth in knowing and doing that prompted the transformation and conquest of cultures induced and propelled by modernization. That such excesses have destroyed persons and cultures and provoke subsequent traditionalist revivals is now patently clear. Rethinking the entire problematic of the relation between cultures is the task at hand. Deep insight into primordial reality, based upon the phenomenology of cultures, philosophical anthropologies and comparative analysis of cultural symbolization, is proposed in this volume. Its hope is that these insights will catalyze further inquiry and your own reformulation. The intellectual and political stakes are enormous, for nothing short of a reconstruction of theory is needed in order to shape an agenda for the realization and expression of cultural values in harmonious and complementary ways.

John Kromkowski
The Catholic University of America
Washington, D.C.

NOTES

1. Gerhart Niemeyer, *Between Nothingness and Paradise* (Baton Rouge, La.: Louisiana State Univ., 1971), pp. 190-91.
2. *Ibid.*, pp. 181-83.
3. *Ibid.*, pp. 186-87.
4. William Pfaff, "Moral Reasoning," *Baltimore Sun*, December, 1988.

COMMUNITY: THE CONCEPTUAL CONFUSION

PAUL PEACHEY

As this century advances the meeting of peoples and the interpenetration of cultures have progressively intensified. The convening of this seminar, with participants from the five continents, is the illustration closest to hand. Not only are diverse cultures and peoples meeting, but one can also speak realistically of an emerging global civilization. Indeed, the inter-cultural seminar as a mode of academic work is already a global cultural trait. Despite the enormous diversity of cultures, disciplines, and perspectives represented, its members can undertake their task with relative ease. Were they suddenly compelled to live together in the full round of daily living, however, difficulties would quickly emerge.

In the Preface, G. McLean has identified the two poles between which lies our task, as well as the problem confronting humankind today. On the one hand, we are all caught in the ethnocentrism which appears inherent in our human condition. Thus, as in the case of the ancient Greeks, we attach "to the term civilization an exclusivist connotation such that the cultural identity of peoples begins to imply cultural alienation between peoples."[1] Such "exclusivism," since time immemorial, has made "man a wolf to man." On the other hand, there is the road leading to "the homogenization of life implicit in its modernizing rationalization." This could be offered as "the price of progress" or the "means of social peace," but thus "to reject one's cultural heritage would be to lose the depth of one's human sensibilities--a spiritual type of mental lobotomy."[2]

This summons us to "a less exclusivist sense of culture," to the use of any particular culture as "more bridge than barrier(s)." But there precisely lies the difficulty. Our needs for identity, for attachment, for security are microcosmic: family, kin, community. Microcosms, however, are not self-sufficient; whether for sustenance or security, the macro-order is mandatory. As history shows, however, it is attainable only at great cost. Moreover, the two orders, the micro and the macro, appear often to clash in the requirements they entail. Thus historians long ago observed that as civilization expands, local cultures decline. The explosion of macro-systems of human interaction since the eighteenth century revolutions, both industrial and political, has provoked a resounding dirge over the decline of community.

Culture and community are closely linked, indeed partly overlapping, concepts. Communities generate cultures, while cultures are matrices within which communities are formed. Cultures, to be sure, are broader in scope than communities. A culture or cultural area may embrace many communities, and thus within cultural areas particular communities may develop sub-cultures. Particularly when they reach sufficient size, cultures may harbor quasi-imperialistic impulses vis-a-vis lesser configurations. Accordingly, cultural conflict is hardly a rare phenomenon, and often is waged via conflict between communities.

Ethnicity and Culture Conflict

The conflict of cultures appears as an inevitable corollary of the growth of societies and civilizations. In the modern era such growth has crystallized on the level of the nation-state. In exceptional instances, though these have been regarded as prototypical, ethnicity became embodied in nation-states. Even so, regional and local variations in language and culture were inevitable. More typically, the hundred and fifty-odd nation-states, in which the human population is now organized, are multi-ethnic in character. For the most part, nation-states are artificial constructs; to a considerable extent interstate boundaries are geopolitical accidents, within which political domination has been achieved by the ideological appeal of nationalism.

The conflict of cultures occurs, then, on two levels; one internally within multi-ethnic nation-state societies; the other, between such nations. While we expect ethnic diversity to increase with state size--one might think of India or the Soviet Union--communal conflict can be acute in smaller states as well, as is testified by Ireland and Lebanon. Frequently, of course, intra- and inter-social levels of ethnic or communal conflict are tangled, as in the two latter examples just cited.

The success of nation-building depends on the upward transfer of loyalties from lesser or micro groups to the nation-state, and thus on the relativization of the claims of the lesser ethnic groupings and subcultures within the national boundaries. Nationalism operates in a dual manner: it both presupposes and produces a relativization of lesser loyalties. Hence, forced nationalization and modernization can lead to reaction or to revitalization of ethnic groups or cultural particularities.

Within multi-ethnic societies, shifts in relative power among ethnic groups can generate conflicts. In Belgium, e.g., a higher birthrate in the Flemish population than among the Walloons eventually had territorial consequences, severely disturbing an earlier equilibrium. In the United States, advances by the black population, both federally and popularly supported during the 1960s, evoked a "new ethnicity" among population groups most directly impacted economically and ecologically by such advances.[3] In other societies, such as India, ethnicity typically is territorially grounded. In the United States, though ethnic groups are distributed differentially, they possess no territorial claims. Immigrant aspirations and concern for transfer of immigrant loyalties to the new fatherland gave birth to the "melting pot" theme in American culture. While this ideal was highly successful on the plane of political loyalty, ethnic particularities did not "melt," at least, not in the short-run. Ethnic culture and consciousness persist, reinforced, to be sure, by such numerous other factors as economics, religion and language.

Moreover, as theoretical discussions around the "new ethnicity" showed, more was at stake than the presumed temporary survival of old-world or non-Western cultures. Prior to the ethnic renewal, ethnicity already had been defined as a new cultural form, generated in the American context.[4] What was at stake was also the achievement and maintenance of personal and social identity in a society which increasingly was dissolving communal solidarities.

Community: the Problem of "Conceptual Stretching"

The problem of communal solidarity in American society had long been the focus of community studies as a specialty within sociology, enriched by borrowings from anthropology. However, given the specialization, fragmentation, and pluralism characteristic of the American scene, little crossover between the older tradition and exponents of the new ethnicity occurred. Community studies deal above all with territoriality; ethnicity with descent, and thus ultimately with kinship. The interplay, and sometimes conflict, of kinship and locality, however, is an ancient problem in social development, of which little account was taken in these recent developments.[5]

It is not our task here to describe, much less to evaluate, either ethnic or community studies. Having noted the importance of the problem of community in the meeting of cultures, I shall outline a problem that plagues the concept of community, a problem that must be taken into account in a discussion of the meeting of cultures. The concept of community suffers from what Giovanni Sartori, in another context, calls "conceptual stretching;" that is, as communities have grown in scope and complexity, the concept has been stretched accordingly. Specifically, according to many researchers, the basis of "community" shifted increasingly from "locality" to "interest." This semantic shift is both ironic and confusing--ironic, because it was against the interest-based modalities of Toennies's *Gesellschaft*[6] that the sociological concept of community first received its classic formulation; confusing, because, to put the matter colloquially, the term now mixes apples and oranges. "Locality" clearly having lost out to "interest," the problem is whether the two modes of social affiliation can be grasped in the same concept?

The community concept, however, has undergone "stretching" before. Deriving from the Latin *communitias*, it carries more than two thousand years of conceptual residue. The root of the term was *moenia*, a defensive wall (cf. French *mur*, English *mural*). Appended with the preposition *com*, the term signifies those within the walled settlement.[8] In a sense, the concept thus parallels somewhat the Greek *polis*, the society that lifted the Greek from the "idiocy" of a pre-political vegetative existence to full humanness.[7] Thus, etymologically it might be argued that our trouble begins with the modern sociological definition. For the modern sociological usage apparently shifts the axis of the concept from the original political level back to a pre-political or naturalistic level. In any case, a history of the evolution of the concept of community over the millennia remains a desideratum.

Community: "Unwilled" versus "Natural Interdependence"

Meanwhile, in the contemporary context, community came to signify the mode of solidarity which preceded, and which survives precariously at the margins of large-scale modern social configurations. In traditional societies, "communal" forms of interdependence dominate; in modern societies, "associational" types. In the former, the communal, to follow Max Weber,[8] the participants in a relationship feel that they "belong together." In the latter, the associational, what transpires is merely the "mutual adjustment of interests." The family is prototypical of the one: the market of the other.

Community, then, refers to "that order of social coherence which develops on the basis of natural interdependence." The natural "includes all those attributes that one had inherited collectively, into which one has grown and been born, and through which one has grown together with others; . . . as soon as other than natural facts provide the social ferment, human associations take on a non-communal character."[9]

The critical variable, according to Norbert Elias, is the human will. Elias complains that failure adequately to distinguish the "willed" and the "unwilled" in human relations has "shrouded" our terminology in a "voluntaristic twilight." Our terms:

> blur the distinction between human bonds that can be made and unmade at will by those concerned, and human bonds which cannot be made and unmade at will. . . . Although it is certainly possible for men to bind themselves to each other with due deliberation and their own choice, the whole groundwork of interdependencies which bind people to each other at a given developmental phase has not been planned or willed by those who form it and are bound by it.[10]

Communion versus Community

The communal/associational contrast cannot simply be equated with the willed and the unwilled for both modes doubtless contain both of these elements. In fact, at this juncture we uncover a second source of confusion, that between "communion" and "community." Herman Schmalenbach, who drew this distinction, thereby replaced the Toennies/Weber dichotomy by a trichotomy. The concept of "communion," he argues, though radically different from community, is often mistaken for it. Not only is community a natural given; it is also an "association constituted in the unconscious. Community, as an organic and natural coalescence, precedes emotional recognition of it by its members. Feelings are simply subsequent forms of experience at the levels of consciousness. They are *products* of community." The case of human communion, however, "is radically different. Emotional experiences are the very stuff of the relationship. They are, in fact, their basis. Jubilant followers who swarm around a leader"[11] are an example. Church and sect exemplify the distinction here drawn between community and communion: the institutional order of the church parallels the "natural" basis of community, while the sect is rooted in the subjective experiences of the members.[12]

Being rooted in feelings, communions are by nature "precarious and unstable." Indeed, they "always tend to become transformed into societal or communal structures." Today marriage and religious ties are among the most important forms of communion, though friendship serves as the "clearest model." Schmalenbach thus summarized the three categories: "The members of community, then, are originally interdependent. The parts of a society are originally apart. The comrades of a communion have, in the first instance, no joint interest. Communions develop only as members meet or when a community is already formed."[13]

Why this second confusion between "communion" and "community"? The reasons seem ready at hand. On the surface, family ties appear prototypical of the qualities of personal warmth and intimacy. But this is hardly correct, for a family is "where they have to take you in." Friendship, on the other hand, constitutes a qualitatively different order, an order based on spiritual affinity. Siblings, once grown, may have little in common-- their interests, friendships, and affiliations may lie elsewhere, yet their blood tie persists for that is something "communal", given, rooted in "nature," if you will, in the "realm of necessity." Friendship, on the other hand, contains a much stronger volitional element, and belongs, as it were, to "realm of freedom." Siblings may also be friends, but not necessarily so.

Mediating Structures

The *Gemeinschaft/Gesellschaft* pair, of course, was not intended to obviate a detailed social taxonomy. The Gesellschaft is constituted by an infinite variety of social formations--hence the concepts of "social pluralism" and "pluralist societies." Some of these formations have recently been described as "mediating structures"[14] providing linkages between our private communal worlds and the remote and frigid macro structures of modern societies. Students of local life, for their part, see "networks" as taking up the slack of declining neighborhoods. Social networks are the self-made ego-based communal surrogates that we assemble in delocalized societies.[15] Much of the "communion" of which Schmalenbach wrote is doubtless realized in networks. Nonetheless, as we have seen, communion is not community, and it is the sustenance of community that is the problem in the modern world.

Renewing Community

Broadly speaking, societal modernization entails three fundamental processes of social reconstruction: (1) the establishment of a macro order, in terms of contemporary expectations, the nation-state and the corresponding institutions; (2) the reconstitution of the communal base; and (3) the configuration of the intervening social space. The psychological correlates of these processes have not yet fully played themselves out. Even less are they fully understood.

The concept of community has been applied at all three levels, and perhaps not without justification. For while that concept often is made to refer to local societies, it is also used with reference to qualities thought to appear variably in all social configurations. Thus, I may refer to Alexandria, Virginia, as my "community," but I may also have a sense of community as an American citizen. These two sensibilities, however, vary independently so that I may be attached to one while alienated from the other.

Here we are dealing only with the conceptual problem. Between the "unwilled" ascriptive solidarities of kinship and place and the "willed" and achieved affiliations in the macro domain runs a profound qualitative ravine. Yet as social formations evolved over time the concept of community has been "stretched" to cover both, leading to endless confusion. Nonetheless this conceptual problem is symptomatic rather than idiosyncratic. The growth of a global civilization confronts us with differentiations and complexities that vastly exceed the simple dichotomies of traditional language. In effect, to apply the term "community" to ties of blood and place, as well as to those of interest groups, professions, states and groups of states is to reenact Babel. Researchers can substitute or invent concepts on an *ad hoc* basis, and in this manner, within the scope of the inquiry, some clarity can be realized. But perhaps only history can solve the problem of everyday language.

Finally, to return to our initial point, "liberals" tend to lose patience with the primordial solidarities of kinship and place. "Conservatives," on the other hand, seem more vulnerable to the blandishments of retribalization. Beyond some indeterminate point, the weakening of micro level primordial solidarity, leads to rootlessness, and hence possibly to emotional overload at the nation-state level. It is true that at this stage in world history "nation-building" remains an unfinished task for many peoples. Even so, nation-states today carry an excess of emotional freight, not only, as commonly assumed, because of a lack in supranational institutions, but also because of communal voids at infra-national levels.[16] Since human reality is in part conceptually constructed, conceptual clarification must remain high on our agenda.

The Catholic University of America
  Washington, D.C.

NOTES

1. See ch. I, above, p. 17.

2. *Ibid.*, p. 22.

3. J. Kromkowski, ch. V.

4. N. Glazer, D. P. Moynihan, *Beyond the Melting Pot* (Cambridge, Mass: M.I.T. Press, 1963).

5. F. de Coulanges, *The Ancient City* (Garden City: Doubleday Anchor, 1956).

6. F. Toennies, *Community and Society* (New York: Harper Torch-

book, 1957; original German edition, 1887)

7. W. Jaeger, *Paideia: The Ideals of Greek Culture* (New York: Oxford, 1985); Hannah Arendt, *The Human Condition* (Garden City: Doubleday Anchor, 1959).

8. M. Weber, *The Theory of Social and Economic Organization* (New York: Free Press Paperback, 1947), p. 136.

9. H. Schmalenbach, "The Sociological Category of Communion," in *Theories of Society*, T. Parsons et al., eds. (New York: Free Press of Glencoe, 1961), pp. 331-347.

10. N. Elias, "Toward a Theory of Communities," in *The Sociology of Community*, C. Bell & H. Newby, eds. (London: Frank Cass & Co., 1947).

11. Schmalenbach, *op. cit.*, p. 335.

12. Cf. E. Troeltsch, *The Social Teachings of the Christian Churches* (New York: Harper Torchbooks, 1960).

13. Schmalenbach, *op. cit.*, p. 339.

14. P. Berger and R. Neuhaus, *Mediating Structures.*

15. Cf. E. Litwak, *Helping the Elderly: The Complementary Roles of Informal Networks and Formal Systems* (New York: Guilford Press, 1985).

16. Cf. K. Deutsch, *Nationalism and its Alternatives* (New York: A.A. Knopf, 1969).

PART I

CULTURAL IDENTITY

AND

CULTURAL PLURALISM

CHAPTER I

MEETING OF CULTURES

MEETING OF PEOPLES

GEORGE F. McLEAN*

The study of the meeting of cultures is a study in the practical order, for what meets are not ideas or ideals, but people in action. Such meetings are not solely physical phenomena, collisions of bodies under the tug of gravity like rocks tumbling down a mountain side. Rather, they are meetings of persons as they themselves decide to act and as they orient that action. Hence, it would seem helpful to include in a study of the meeting of cultures an investigation of the self which decides to act and directs his or her action.

Further, contrary to the myth of the isolated, totally independent and self-made person, the evidence presented in the Chapter of Dr. Kromkowski suggests strongly that the one who acts is increasingly sensitive to being a member of an ethnic group, and that to varying degrees this membership is a component of one's sense of identity. As integral to the sense of self, which is at the root of all processes of self-determination, this affects the understanding of one's relations to others, one's choice of values and the direction of one's actions.

The components of this group identity are many. A 1973 symposium sponsored by the Social Science Research Council (SSRC)[1] on ethnic identity identified six criteria: (1) emphasis upon ancestral and cultural origins, (2) sense of cultural and social distinctiveness, (3) place in a broader system of social relations by which the distinctiveness of the group can be appreciated, (4) transcendence of kin or locality group, (5) adaptation of ethnic categories for strategic purposes, and (6) the character of ethnic categories as emblematic and bearers of cultural content. In the chapter of Prof. A. Gallo these features are listed more succinctly.

The person and the group then are the concrete units; their culture is a more formal factor, a basic set of mind and heart, not to mention of institutions and other artifacts. Hence, while it is persons in groups which meet, the self-identity of its members, the sense of identity of the group—and hence all interaction between groups—is specified essentially, though not exclusively, by their culture. The present chapter concerns this cultural dimension of group identity and interaction. It will proceed in four steps: I. the nature of culture, II. the origin of a cultural tradition, III. a living tradition, and IV. the meeting of cultures.

THE NATURE OF CULTURE

Etymologically, the term culture derives from the Latin term for tilling or cultivating the land. Cicero and other Latin authors used it for the cultivation of the soul or mind (*cultura animi*), for just as even good land when left without cultivation will produce only disordered vegetation of little value, so the human spirit will not achieve its proper results unless trained.[2] This sense corresponds most closely to the Greek term for education (*paideia*) as the development of character, taste and judgment, and to the German term "formation" (*Bildung*).[3]

Here, the focus is upon the creative capacity of the human spirit: its ability to work as artist, not only in the restricted sense of producing purely aesthetic objects, but in the more involved sense of shaping all dimensions of life, material and spiritual, economic and political. The result is a whole person characterized by unity and truth, goodness and beauty, and encouraged to share fully in the meaning and value of life. The capacity to do so cannot be taught, although it may be enhanced by education. More recent phenomenological and hermeneutic inquiries suggest that, at its base, culture is a renewal, a reliving of one's own origination in an attitude of profound appreciation.[4] This may lead us beyond self and other, beyond identity and diversity, in order to comprehend both; this will be taken up below.

By attending more to the object, culture can be traced to the terms *civis,* or citizen, and civilization.[5] These reflect the need for a person to belong to a social group or community in order for the human spirit to produce its proper results. The community brings to the person the resources of the tradition, the *tradita* or past wisdom and productions of the human spirit, thereby facilitating comprehension. By enriching the mind with examples of values which have been identified in the past, it teaches and inspires one to produce something analogous. For G.F. Klemm this more objective sense of cultures is composite in character.[6] For the social sciences Tyler defined this classically as "that complex whole which includes knowledge, belief, art, morals, law, customs and any other capabilities and habits required by man as a member of society."[7]

Each particular complex or culture is specific to one people; a person who shares in this is a *civis* or citizen and belongs to a civilization. For the more restricted Greek world in which this term was developed, others (aliens) were those who did not speak the Greek tongue; they were "barbaroi" for their speech sounded like mere babel. Though at first this meant simply non-Greek, its negative manner of expression easily lent itself to, perhaps reflected, and certainly favored, a negative axiological connotation, which indeed soon became the primary meaning of the word 'barbarian'. By reverse implication it attached to the term 'civilization' an exclusivist connotation, such that the cultural identity of peoples began to imply cultural alienation between peoples. Today, as communication increases and more widely differentiated peoples enter into ever greater interaction and mutual dependence, we reap an ever more bitter harvest of this connotation. A less exclusivist sense of culture must be a priority task.

THE ORIGIN OF A CULTURAL TRADITION

The first SSRC criterion for ethnic group identity is emphasis upon origins, both ancestral and cultural. In this the power of shared physical origins and common ancestors is not to be underestimated. This is experienced personally in the bond one feels to a brother, sister or cousin and in the response one feels impelled to make to their needs. It reaches out in varying degrees to those who share a common lineage or race, as is suggested in the term "brother" or "sister" among blacks. Just after the "Six-day War" Rabbi Richard Rubenstein[7] described vividly how, though he had been theoretically ambiguous about much of the support for the development of the State of Israel, once the lives of his people were again in danger he experienced a deep visceral concern and a willingness to put all his resources at their disposition. True, the proximity and horror of the holocaust made this particularly vivid, but most groups have experienced in their history massacres and the slow grinding physical toll of suppression. This is reflected, e.g., in the range of statistics regarding blacks and hispanics in North America who begin with abnormally high rates of infant mortality, pass through low rates of education and income and end with a correspondingly low level of life expectancy. Though difficult to measure, the deep subconscious sense of threat would appear to be a powerful element in the sense of identity of these groups and hence in their interaction with others.

Our concern here is not simply with physical bonds, but especially with the related human consciousness and patterns of will, and with the way in which these are shaped or configured. In these there are similarities to animals as well as important differences. The animal's knowledge is bound strictly to, and conditioned by, its physical environment, with which it is thereby enabled to live in harmony. Human knowledge, however, is not thus bound, for the person can understand these conditions reflectively; one can hold them up, as it were, for inspection, possess them, question them and work freely toward guiding and transforming them by making clothing, building shelter and producing food. Despite this essential difference there remains an important analogy. Where animal life is necessarily synchronized with its physical surroundings, human life is lived freely with, and in terms of, other persons who also are self-conscious and free agents. Absolute knowledge without regard to conditions of time and place is not possible because we are not absolute. Indeed, even if such knowledge were possible it would not be of interest for we exist in relation to others and that relationship reflects both our own and their conscious and free dispositions.

In analyzing the import of this conscious life with others the approach of phenomenologists working in terms of human intentionality can be particularly helpful. They point out that our consciousness always has been relational, that it always has been a "consciousness of." John Caputo[9] traces this to the period before birth when life begins in and with the rhythm of the life of the mother. The first sense of motion is of her motion; the first sense of sound is of her heartbeat. Upon birth the infant begins to recognize parents and siblings with whom he or she is fully "at home" and at peace, able to trust and on that basis able, not merely to learn survival techniques, but to grow in self-confidence and self-expression. Progressively, the infant learns forms of behavior and modes of communication with others. This is extended by games with peers and interaction with relatives and neighbors. Coming alive is a process of growing with, and in relation to others from whom, especially with language, one receives a pattern for conceiving and categorizing nature and a scheme of values for appreciating and responding to others. We are born then not into a chaotic field of primal physical and even personal forces, but into both a cosmos and especially a community which is intricately coordinated and delicately delineated.

To this it is important to add time and history. For whatever be the basic possibilities which flow from being human, through time the various peoples have configured their conscious and social life in marvelously different manners. Each people has had its own experience of life among themselves, in interaction with nature and with other peoples. Each has made its own response to the challenges of life and drawn therefrom its own lessons regarding what promotes and what destroys life in its many dimensions. Here, it is important to note the type of question that is being answered. It is not merely one of tactical adjustments in response to temporary threats; nor is it a pragmatic question of appropriate means. Rather, the question is what we wish to realize above and through any and all such expediencies. What is taking place then is more fundamental: it is the progressive uncovering of the meaning of life and of the values which are worthy of commitment.[10]

In this the individual and collective will of a people is central. What a people finds true in terms of its appreciation of meaning and value is accepted and reaffirmed; what is discovered to be degrading and destructive tends to be disavowed, rejected and discouraged. Thus, tradition differs from history. It is not all that has happened in the past, for that would include the bad as well as the good: a Simon Legree as well as an Abraham Lincoln. Only Lincoln, however, has been chosen as the example of what the country stands for and what it wishes to hand on to subsequent generations. Tradition, then, is what has been accepted and embraced, affirmed and cultivated, promoted and passed on.

It might be noted that Lincoln could be effective in his decisions only in the context of a long mobilization of anti-slavery opinion throughout the world and the support and even ultimate sacrifice of great numbers of lives. Nonetheless, it is Lincoln, rather than General Grant or any of the thousands of Civil War dead, who stands out. In him there was the special balance of vision, moral courage and practical accomplishment that constitutes a classic affirmation of the content of his culture. Like the Parthenon in Greek architecture and the Declaration of the Rights of Man in the Enlightenment, the lives of such heroes as Gandhi, Martin Luther King and Mother Theresa--without military, police or political power--solely by their balanced realization of the virtues of their people.

Finally, it is perhaps not so much the historical Lincoln who has become part of the cultural tradition of his country. For the historical Lincoln was a man of his time: troubled, confused and tentative. In contrast, the Lincoln of the American tradition, enshrined in the Lincoln Memorial, is bigger than life. He is the Great Emancipator, repository of all our aspirations of freedom and equality, inspiration of all our efforts, judge of our failures, and ultimate court of appeal above and beyond legislature and legal system. It is the Lincoln of symbol and myth--based upon history, but drawn beyond history in the hearts and minds of his countrymen--who symbolizes meaning and value which he appreciated only dimly. As such he has become an essential component of a living tradition, and hence a touchstone for the culture of the nation.

In sum the cultural dimension in the life of a community is the context of its consciousness and of learning. The content of this context is derived from the experience of the people and hence constitutes its particular expression of the meaning and value of human life. The lives of saints and heroes, as particularly powerful and indeed classic expressions of that sense of life, become symbols of the virtualities of their cultural tradition, recall the members of the group to ever new awareness of its beauty, evoke creative expressions of its transforming power, and constitute norms for future action.[11]

A LIVING TRADITION

In this light the first SSRC criterion for ethnic groups as "past oriented" may need reassessment or reinterpretation, particularly inasmuch as our present sense of time is often that of a simple succession of ever fleeting moments without lasting duration. When the past is considered simply as no longer and hence as non-existent, to be oriented thereto is to be oriented to nothingness or to the void. If the past is seen as a series of facts, each with its detailed concreteness, to be "past-oriented" is to be trapped in a pattern of circumstances which no longer obtain and a pattern of action which today can be only ineffectual and inappropriate, if not unjust or even tyrranical.

In reality what we have seen is that cultural traditions differ from history precisely in being not a series of concrete facts, but the effect of human consciousness and freedom as people respond to history, draw out its lessons and progressively articulate a sense of the meaning of life which is distinctive to their people.

Such a classical model is not chronologically distant from us in the past, and hence in need of being drawn forward artificially. Rather it lives and acts now in our lives which it inspires and judges. Through time it is the timeless dimension of history. Rather than needing to reconstruct it, we belong to it, just as it belongs to us. The continuity of such a tradition consists then in its being nothing less than the ultimate community of human striving. Seen in this light, human understanding is implemented less by individual acts of subjectivity, than by our situatedness in a tradition that fuses both past and present.

To assert the continuing reality and significance of what has emerged in the past does not deny, but rather implies, the vital and possibly perduring significance of novelty, that is, of the new reality which is taking place today and tomorrow. It is essential to protect and promote the creative human consciousness in its exploration and ever new articulation of truth and meaning, as well as the free human will in shaping its response to goodness and value. Because these take place progressively and only in concrete circumstances, ethics as the application of tradition cannot be merely abstract theoretical knowledge of laws or factual historical material from the past. It must concern human institutions and attitudes which change; it must provide rules which guide but do not determine moral consciousness, thereby enabling it to respond appropriately in changing circumstances.

In this ethics differs in two ways from techné. The latter is governed by a fully articulated idea which it repeats in detail. In contrast, because in acting the subject not only makes the object but realizes him or herself as well, the ethical evaluation of the appropriateness of an action always must include the subject as well as the object. Hence, it cannot be decided abstractly, but must take account of the concrete exercise of human freedom. Secondly, these concrete and adapted applications of the law are not escapes from the law: they do not diminish or compromise law. Rather, if human life is truly free and creative any prior articulation of a law must be imperfect for it could not yet express all that a free and creative human spirit can devise. Thus, in guiding the application of one's cultural heritage ethical laws are not diminished, but perfected as human freedom shapes the present according to the culture's sense of what is just and good. For in so doing it creates more of what is meant by justice and goodness; it extends and enriches moral knowledge.[12]

Living the tradition then is not simply repeating the past but unfolding its values and meanings which have been discovered through the lived experience of a people. All are given special possibilities by this lode of past experience and, under penalty of being unfaithful to their tradition, all are challenged both to unfold its possibilities and implications for appropriate human life in the circumstances of their day and to build toward a yet more adequate future.

THE MEETING OF CULTURES

The above suggests a notable shift of goals--especially from Plato, but in a sense from Aristotle as well--and thus a real step beyond the Greek tradition of Socratic search for clear principles for public life. It suggests that the search is not for a pattern of Platonic ideas or ideals separated from human life. Nor would the search be to develop a pattern of principles or virtues articulated prior to action, in relation to which pattern all applications would be merely a subsequent and accidental part of understanding. The goal here is not to determined what is right in general, but what is good in the concrete, and hence in the situation. This is not a matter of mere expediency; by completing what the general law omits it constitutes the very perfection of the law.

In this Aristotle notes the importance of two virtues. One is prudence (*phronesis*) which, in the light of the normative discoveries about appropriate human action contained in the tradition, through thoughtful reflection discovers the appropriate means in the circumstances. What we are now more aware of than before, however, is that in most countries such circumstances include a plurality of groups with which we must interact. Indeed, even our self-determination includes a sense of self which to a significant degree is constituted by positive and contrasting relations to other groups.

In this situation of coexistence with other cultural groups another virtue identified by Aristotle, namely, sagacity (*sunesis*) takes on new importance. One can choose the proper means in today's pluri-ethnic circumstances only if one takes account adequately of other groups. In turn, this can be done only if one puts oneself in their circumstances, shares their concerns and undergoes their situation with them. In contrast, Aristotle describes as truly "terrible" the power of the one who is capable of understanding the situation but lacks orientation to moral ends or concern for the good of the other.[13] Perhaps Hobbes[14] described too well such an attitude, encoded in one major contemporary ideology, when he wrote that man is a wolf to man.

How can this be overcome, how can *sunesis* as a positive attitude of care and concern for the welfare of others be achieved? Would not all that has been said above about cultural identity preclude such cross-cultural openness and mutual understanding and concern? Are not fundamentalism, intellectual Balkanization, ethnic or communal strife, and even genocide the predictable--even the experienced--results of the intensification of ethnic consciousness? Is it not time then to turn away from this road, and to accept the homogenization of life implicit in its modernizing rationalization, not only merely as the price of progress, but as the means of social peace?

On the other hand, if what was said in the second section above be valid, to reject one's cultural heritage would be to close off the full dimensions of one's human sensibilities--a spiritual type of mental lobotomy. Further, to sever the next generation from its sense of meaning and value would be to produce a generation that would be, not merely alienated and empty, but manipulative, "terrible" and terrifying. Fortunately, the fact that ethnic sensibility has increased with, and perhaps in response to, modernization suggests that in any case there is little chance for eventual disappearance of cultural consciousness. Certainly, a different approach is needed.

This would begin from the notion of an horizon as all that can be seen from the vantage point of one's cultural tradition. The fact that we have been born and raised in this family, neighborhood and cultural group and that this shapes our vision and gives it an horizon needs to be recognized and accepted. However, an horizon is not a barrier or separation, for it consists of what has been discovered in the past about the goals and meaning of human life and action, as well as a sense of the time in which I stand and of the life project in which I am engaged. It is a fertile ground filled with experience, custom and tradition as this comes into the present and, through the present, passes into the future.[15] It is then more bridge than barrier, more opportunity than opposition. It might be compared to a telescopic lens ground by the assembled experience of one's predecessors. Through this, the person is enabled to see far and to interpret with refined sensibility.

Rather than destroy such a lens, it is important to be as fully aware of it as possible, to take attentive account of its special characteristics, features and situatedness, and then to make expert use of it. How is this to be done--how can it enable us to relate to other cultures--if our horizon bespeaks all that can be seen from *within* that cultural perspective?

First, it must be noted that the human mind is in principle transcendent. Though it recognizes realities, it is not captivated by them; instead it evaluates them as being good or less so, as being able to be improved upon or not worth improving. In other words, the human person is not simply an animal possessed by its environment; the person possesses its knowledge in such wise that one can compare and evaluate objects. In brief, the person transcends particular objects, seeing them in terms of a broader sense of truth--one wants to know more--and of good--one wants to improve.

Second, as larger nation states are developed, as travel and immigration increase and as competition and communication intensify, increasingly one is impacted by other groups who live, interpret and evaluate differently. It becomes progressively clearer that one's own culture is not the only one possible.

Third, this could lead to a rejection of others; often it has resulted in considering others as inferior or even as non persons. It is especially the religious sense within the various cultures that can help to free people from this feeling of being absolute. Understanding themselves as subordinate to God and only a partial manifestation of His truth and power opens in principle the possibility of recognizing that others too are reflections of the divine perfection and as such our own brothers and sisters.

In all three of the above ways religion can contribute to a sense of our own situatedness as a first step toward openness, for if we can realize that we are not the sole bearers of truth then we can have a questioning attitude. Rather than simply following through with our previous ideas until a change is forced upon us, true openness or sensitivity to new meaning requires a willingness continually to revise our initial projection or expectation of meaning, our horizon. This is neither neutrality as regards the meaning of the tradition, nor an abandonment of passionate concern regarding action towards the future. To be aware of our own horizon and to adjust it in dialogue with others is to make it work for us in discovering those new implications of our tradition which are required for our times.

The logical structure of this process is to found in the dialectic of question and answer. A question of whether it is this or that is required in order to give our attention direction, without which no meaningful answer could be given or received. This requires that the answer not be settled or determined; progress or discovery requires openness. But this is not simple lack of determination; it has a specific direction that orients our attention and sensitizes us to significant evidence.

Because such discovery depends upon the questions, the art of discovery is the art of questioning. Consequently, in working with other groups our efforts at finding the answers should be not to suppress their questions, but to reinforce and unfold them. To the degree that their probability is intensified they can serve as a searchlight to bring out new meaning. Thus, in contrast to opinion which suppresses questions, and to arguing which searches out the weakness of the others' argument, conversation as dialogue is a mutual and cooperative search for truth. Through eliminating errors and working out a common meaning truth is progressively unveiled.[16]

Because of the dynamic character of being emerging into time, the horizon is never definitively fixed. At each step a new dimension of the potentialities of a cultural tradition are opened to understanding, for its meaning lives with the consciousness, not of its originators, but of the many members of the group living through history and with others. Through the dialectic of questioning between the horizons of various groups the ability of all is intensified for questioning one's own heritage and receiving answers that are ever new.[17]

In all of this one's attitude requires close attention. If one's goal is simply to develop new horizons for the emergence of one's own mind, our goal could be to achieve absolute advance knowledge and thereby absolute dominion over other groups. This would lock us into a prejudice that is fixed, closed in the past, and unable to allow for the life of the present or the horizons of others. In this way powerful new insights become with time deadening ideologies, prejudgments which suppress freedom and cooperation.

In contrast, an authentic attitude of openness appreciates the nature of our finiteness and on this basis is both respectful of the past, open to others and thereby able to discern appropriate paths for the future. This openness consists not merely in receptivity to new information, but in a recognition of our historical, situated and hence limited vision. Escape from the limitations of vision which have deceived us and held us captive is to be found then, not through those who are well integrated into our culture and social structures, for dialogue with those of similar horizons opens one only to a limited degree. Real liberation from our most basic limitations and deceptions comes only with a conscious effort to take account of the horizons of those who differ notably, whether as another ethnic group, as a distinct culture intermingled with our own, or--still more definitively--as living on the margins of all of these societies and integrated into none.

Such openness is directed primarily, not to others as persons who are to be surveyed objectively or obeyed unquestioningly, but to ourselves. It opens our horizons, extends our ability to listen to others, and assimilates the implications of their answers for changes in our own positions. In other words, it is an acknowledgement that our cultural heritage has something new to say to us. The characteristic hermeneutic attitude of effective historical consciousness is then not methodological sureness, but openness or readiness for experience.[18] For those who adopt this stance, their cultural heritage is not closed, but the basis of a life that is ever new, more inclusive and more rich.

The Catholic University of America
Washington, D.C.

NOTES

*See Discussions II and III.

1. Anya Peterson Royce, *Ethnic Identity: Strategies of Diversity* (Bloomington: Indiana Univ. Press, 1982), pp. 24-27.

2. V. Mathieu, "Cultura" in *Enciclopedia Filosofica* (Firenze: Sansoni, 1967). II, 207-210; and Raymond Williams, "Culture and Civilization," *Encyclopedia of Philosophy* (New York: Macmillan, 1967), II, 273-276, and *Culture and Society* (London, 1958).

3. Tonnelat, "Kultur" in *Civilisation, le mot et l'idée* (Paris: Centre International de Synthese), II.

4. V. Mathieu, *ibid.*

5. V. Mathieu, "Civilta," *ibid.*, I, 1437-1439.

6. G.F. Klemm, *Allgemein Culturgeschicht de Menschheit* (Leipzig, 1843-52), x.

7. E.B. Tylor, *Primitive Culture* (London, 1871), VII, p. 7.

8. Richard L. Rubenstein, Remarks at CUA Workshop, June, 1964; see also his "God After the Death of God," in G. McLean, ed., *Religion in Contemporary Thought* (New York: Alba House, 1973), pp. 297-310.

9. John Caputo, "A Knowledge of Moral Sensibility: Moral Emotion," in Frederick E. Ellrod, George F. McLean, David Schindler, and Jesse A. Mann, eds. *Act and Agent: Philosophical Foundations for Moral Education and Character Development* (Washington, D.C.: Univ. Press of America, 1986).

10. Hans-Georg Gadamer, *Truth and Method* (New York: Crossroads, 1975), pp. 245-53.

11. *Ibid.*, pp. 254-58, 278-79.
12. *Ibid.*, pp. 281-86.
13. *Ibid.*, p. 289.
14. Hobbes
15. Gadamer, pp. 261-264.
16. *Ibid.*, pp. 325-32.
17. *Ibid.*, pp. 335-40.
18. *Ibid.*, pp. 324-25.

CHAPTER II

PERSON, COMMUNITY AND CULTURE

VARGHESE MANIMALA*

In analyzing the relation between cultures the two basic units to bear in mind are *person* and *community*. We are all implicitly aware of ethnic persons and ethnic communities. All our behaviors from ordinary food habits to the highest expressions of the spirit, e.g., religion, are colored by our personality and by the community to which we belong. Undoubtedly, persons and unions of persons or communities exert great influence in creating and handing on culture. Each person or community adds to or detracts from the culture in which it belongs. From birth to death a person is united with others on the concrete emotional and ideological levels of existence. This leads to the awareness of self and of others which, with its consequent actions, lead to the full growth of one's personality.

Our approach will be largely phenomenological and descriptive; at the same time we shall make references to the conclusions of such sciences as psychology, sociology and anthropology. References to Indian thought and circumstances will be made where applicable.

INDIVIDUAL, PERSON AND PERSONALITY

Jacques Maritain and certain other philosophers held as a principle: "The individual exists for the society, but the society exists for the person." If one distinguishes between individual and person a special dignity is ascribed to the person, beyond that possessed by an individual as such. This can be seen in the animal kingdom where there are many individuals but no persons. Carrying over this distinction to the realm of human beings, we speak in the same sense of 'individuals' when concerned primarily with a single individual with human nature--to whom of course, a certain dignity cannot be denied insofar as all humans are spiritual subjects. We will speak of a 'person', however, when considering the uniqueness, the incomparability and therefore the irreplaceability of the individual. According to Paul Tournier, "the whole difference between an individual and a person is that the individual associates, whereas the person communicates."[1]

The term individual has the sense of belonging to a group without involving any specific identity; it can be thought of as non-relational. The individual is understood not merely as possessing a complete nature of a particular kind, but as having a particular existence. There is an innate tendency for the individual to assert oneself and to strive towards one's own fulfillment. As an individual one stands 'separate' or distinct from all else. One asserts one's independence, even if in a limited manner, and cannot be absorbed or subsumed under another. Further, the note of self-consciousness can be added to the human individual; indeed, some consider this the special note of 'person'. These notions so overlap the notion of person that it is difficult to think of either individuals or persons exclusively without one involving the either.

With these preliminary remarks let us enter directly into an analysis of the person in order to understand its depth and meaning, and the way in which it is related to culture. Etymologically we can trace the meaning of this term to the Etruscan *Phersu* which evidently denoted a mask or the wearer of the mask at festivals in honor of P(h)ersephone. As the Etruscans were influential in the development of the Roman theater, Persephone's mask came to be known among the Romans by the adjective: *persona.* Later this came to signify any mask, especially those used in theaters. To this Etruscan word the Romans fused one of their own words, *personare,* which means "sounding or speaking through," because the mask was that through which the voice of the goddess or the character was heard. Thus, from the very beginning, the mask not only had visual and acoustic functions or properties, but was used also to represent a personage. The term was easily transferred from the device to the theatrical role or dramatic character represented through it.[2] Gradually the term was used to indicate the concrete character of a real personage, and not merely a dramatic role. In the philosophical sense it came to mean a human substance in its properly and distinctively human individuality.

The Greeks had a word with a meaning similar to that of the Latin *persona,* meaning, the word *prósopon (pro-sop-on),* whose central part meant 'to see' and 'to be seen'. The Greek term easily passes over into the "look" or "countenance" of someone, which is also ambiguous. Here the element of difference comes forward, for we recognize each other most easily by our countenances or faces. This distinctiveness points to the uniqueness already associated with the Latin notion of a dramatic character *(dramatis personae);* indeed, a variant of the Greek word: *"prosopéion'* means "mask." More importantly, the Greeks used the word *prosopon* periphrastically *(tò sòn prósopon),* i.e., as a roundabout way of speaking in the second person: to say "person" is to say "thou." It is a direct form of address meaning "I and Thou," "you and me." It means: "face to face" *(katà prósopon),* or a direct encounter with nothing between, just as the usual setting for intimacy is a *tête-à-tête.*[3]

The Greeks attached great importance to the face, which according to Aristotle is had only by humans and no other animal.[4] Thus, hidden within the Greek term for person *(prosopon)* is the sense that only human beings have faces or structures that shows forth meaning. It is transparent with the innocent, concealing with the devious, glowing with the joyful, grieving with the sad, indifferent with the bored. A person's face is a signature of the character within; one cannot disengage the face from a certain interiority.[5]

Having analyzed the etymological and linguistic meaning of the term person, much remains to be investigated, for the term person has many layers of meaning. On the surface it means any human being, but on a deeper level it points to a uniqueness which cannot be interchanged or counted. The person is an individual being endowed with a nature that is incommunicable. In the visible world only human beings exist as persons. They alone are designated by their own proper names, appear as subjects of all statements and are the carriers of all attributes. The capacity for spiritual self-consciousness and its corresponding self-determination belong essentially and solely to the notion of the person; thus the unborn child is a person.[6]

In ordinary parlance the term "personal" connotes privacy. "Don't ask about it, it is very personal to me," has a ring of being intimate and secretive to oneself. This indicates that the person is a unique centre and that access to a person is access to a certain privileged intimacy. Dignity, uniqueness and intimacy cling to the meaning of the person. In contrast to this the term *personality*, as we often use it, suggests the opposite meaning. When we use the expression she or he "has a lot of personality," we intend to make a compliment, namely, that one creates a pleasing or striking impression upon first meeting. Such "personal charm" stands to intimacy as surface to depth.[7]

From this follows also the idea of the mystery of person. Speaking of the 'unspeakables', Wittgenstein remarks: "There are, indeed, things that cannot be put into words. They make themselves manifest. They are what is mystical."[8] Herein also falls the mystery of the human person. The person is important in a way that other things are not, but what gives this personal value? It is not something a person has done; for we demand human rights for people regardless of their ability, race, color, talent, or achievement simply because they are human beings. Man is mysterious because his nature is a bundle of paradoxes: he is individual yet social, unified yet diversified, complete and yet incomplete, incommunicable yet communicating, objectively self-contained yet transcending himself. He is a person with his own rights and in his own right, yet responsible for and to others.[9]

This paradoxical and mysterious aspect makes the person a fascinating object of study by poet and dramatist, philosopher and psychologist, sociologist and anthropologist. One has to fight against the tendency to treat persons as objects, or to reduce them to logical or language games. The human person may have to be subjected to scientific study, but this is to be done with utmost respect to the person and with humility. The person is mystery, not in the sense of being 'totally unknown' to us, but in the sense that we do not know *what* one is. The distinction of Gabriel Marcel between *problem* and *mystery* will be helpful here.[10] He sees problem as capable of being known objectively, whereas a mystery is subjectively encountered. A problem, being objective, can be solved by means of intellectual analysis, observation or experiment; a mystery, being 'subjective' in the sense that the self is involved in it, cannot be solved by any objective approach. A problem, we may say, is based upon our ignorance in the matter; hence it is solved or 'disappears' when we come to know what we did not know about it. In contrast, a mystery is based upon our intuitive sense of certainty rather than upon ignorance. Thus, in mystery there is an 'openness' which is closed only be fanaticism or dogmatism which are contrary to understanding, for it not only arises out of ignorance but results in further ignorance.

Just as man is a mystery to himself, so the 'other' is a mystery to him. Knowledge of the other is based not on perception or inference, but upon 'meeting' the other as a 'Thou'. Martin Buber has analyzed this "I-Thou" relationship in detail, and we shall refer to it later. For him, it is this I-Thou relation and communication which constitutes the I and the Thou.

Personality

Thus far we have been concerned with the analysis of the term 'person'. Though the terms person and personality are used almost synonymously we can perceive a certain distinction between them. Personality in the empirical-psychological sense is the 'wholeness', the structural integrity, of a person's spiritual tendencies and permanent inclinations. Insofar as these provide the foundation for the individual style of value judgments and convictions, the words "personality" and "character" very often are used in practically the same sense. As there are different functions performed by the person we can speak of various levels of personality: the higher functions to a great extent being influenced and conditioned by the lower (e.g., subconscious). Also, functions of the lower levels can be influenced by the higher, so that the various levels exert a mutual influence upon one another. But it should be noted that in spite of their being conditioned by the lower, in the order of existence the higher levels of 'spiritual life' differ and have their own special functions (e.g., thinking and willing). While normally the I-relationship of the different experiences fit together into a structual whole, this unity of personality can be greatly upset in certain forms of mental derangement (e.g., split personality).

Sometimes we use the expression: "he/she is quite a person" (of course, here the obvious reference is to the personality) if one has original ideas and strong convictions. We feel this even more if that person displays great courage and forcefulness in carrying out his/her convictions and goals. The powers of understanding and choice of behavior seem to characterize a personality. A great sense of self-identity and a well ordered form of relationship to others seem to make one a 'person'. Where one's powers and habits are highly developed and harmoniously integrated we attibute a high measure of personality. Even though a truly harmonious, all-embracing and perfect development of all aspects of the personality is hardly ever possible, it is still in accordance with the dignity of the person to strive for a certain full development of the psychological personality and especially towards the absolute values of the morally good and the norms of an ethical personality.[11]

In this context it should be noted that, though personality is dynamic, there is an enduring sense of personal identity. Each person has historicity, a unique place in the time-flow. The remark: "I wasn't myself today," does not mean that one is a different person, but merely that today's actions and feelings were not part of one's usual personality pattern. In turn, this implies a recognition of identity. In the same manner we do not change pronouns when we change verbs--the "I" is the same in "I went," "I go," "I shall go." The metabolic cycle may replace all the matter in our bodies every seven years, but still we remain the same persons. I am still responsible for the acts which I committed years ago. Chaucer, Dante, Milton and other writers might have taken many years to complete their works, but we do not attribute these works to other persons.[12]

The distinction between person and personality helps us to see how the abnormalities of amnesia and multiple personality do not invalidate this position, which is confirmed further by psychoanalytic and other studies of personality development from infancy through adulthood. The same person may have different habit systems and associations which at least potentially are identifiable by a particular person as his/her own. In this context we can understand the concepts of traditional philosophy: subsistent self, spiritual self, etc. Perhaps, the term 'spirit' may characterize man better than any other term, for among its characteristics are universality, freedom, historicity, responsibility and transcendence.[13]

Person as Relational

Just as a human person cannot be understood in isolation, a person's growth cannt be assured except in a human community. The very value of the human person we speak of is relational, i.e., there should be somebody to recognize my worth. If one's own inherent qualities are such that one is good for others and brings out the best in them, then one is good in oneself. Although a hypocrite or a fake may occasionally spark a response, in the long run his/her artificial qualities are laid bare; only a person of genuine worth evokes consistent responses from others.

A person should not be approached purely on utilitarian grounds. One is of value because one is good not for others but in himself/herself. Doctors or rescuers struggle to save a person's life not for remuneration or fame, but because of a conviction that a human being is worth keeping alive. The value of a human life is measured in terms not on productivity, but of the potential of each person to become whatever one may make of oneself; yet in this process one both uses and is useful to others. Deep in the heart of every human being there is a feeling of intrinsic dignity. Often obscured by slavery, neglect, war and poverty, but still it is there. Every person has rights which are inalienable and the constitution of every country vows to protect these rights of its citizens.

Persons stand in a hierarchy of relations. To the physical universe the person is related as a master, predicting and controlling through scientific understanding, and making it serve one's pursuit of other goals. To one's fellowman the person is related as a confrere, a fellow voyager on life's sea engaged in cooperative pursuit of mutual goals. To oneself the person is an identical subject, integrated within oneself, the author of one's own activities, with a sense of one's own history, responsibility and destiny. Lastly one is related to the Supreme Being in ways which manifest themselves in the diverse phenomena of religion as human experience. Moreover, one is constantly adjusting to a changing universe so that this integration is not a static mosaic, but an orderly series of dynamic processes. A perfect person would have well ordered relationships with all reality, and would be able habitually to respond to each being in proper proportion with due regard to others and to oneself. Of course, one can only approach such perfection to this life; no one person can encompass all possible relations, whether of knowledge, dominance or aesthetic appreciation. One mark of greatness is the ability to accept one's limitations while striving to maximize one's potentialities to the fullest.[14]

Individual Self in Indian Philosophies

Before we proceed to analyze the concept of community, it may be appropriate to describe in brief the concept of the individual self or 'person' in Indian Philosophies.[15] Though one never doubts the existence of one's own 'self', being asked to describe its structure or nature can place one in a quandary. In the first stage of the dialectical dynamism of human existence the individual has not yet awakened to his/her individuality or personal existence. At this level the individual prefers anonymity to personal distinction, "loses" oneself among the "many," and reckons oneself merely as one of them. No personal decision is exercised, nor does one assume personal responsibility for one's decisions; rather, these are borrowed from others and one's actions are governed by public opinion. By thus depriving oneself of personal freedom one enjoys almost a sense of tranquility and security which one is afraid to lose. This is the state of human "fallenness"; according to Heidegger, it is marked by curiosity, idle talk and ambiguity.

The antithesis of this anonymous existence is the stage of being in which the individual develops a craving to distinguish him/herself from others in everything so as to be recognized as "exceptional." Conflict with others becomes inevitable, barely concealing dictatorial domination of one over the many. The third stage is that of synthesis between anonymous existence (thesis) and extreme self-assertion (antithesis); here the individual recognizes and respects other's freedom while exercising his/her own. Conflict may not be completely ruled out at this stage, but neither is compromise absent; it is a stage of "loving struggle" where each individual maintains his/her own freedom by granting it to others as well.

These three stages of the dialectic of personal existence may be regarded as arising out of three constituents (*gunas*) of human personality which Sankhya's system describes as *sattva, rajas* and *tamas. Tamas* is the principle of inertia and infatuation (*moha*); its predominance over other constituents in human personality naturally reduces one to a life of anonymity and passive submission to others; one gives oneself over to sensory pleasures completely and is dominated by senses (*indriyas*). *Rajas* is the principle of activity and of the ego; its domination over the other constituents leads one towards an extreme form to self-assertion and domination over others; the *rajasik* person dwells in *ahamkara* (egoity) more than in the senses and is prepared to give up sensory pleasures if such sacrifice is necessary to fulfill the craving for distinction and fame. *Sattva* (goodness) is the principle of knowledge and equanimity; its predominance over the other two constituents gives proper perspective to one's relation to the world. The *sattvik* person acts from the standpoint of *buddhi* (intellect) the course of the action to be pursued for one's own good as well as for that of others; the person who dwells in *buddhi* is not controlled or hindered either by *indriyas* or by *ahamkara*.

The movement of the individual from the senses to *ahamkara* and from *ahamkara* to *buddhi* is thus a dialectial movement proceeding through 'opposites' towards a synthesis. This dialectical psychological movement of human existence receives a cosmic ontological interpretation in the *Sankhya* system, whereby *buddhi, ahakara* and the *indriyas* are not distinguished from each other depending upon the predominance of one *guna* over the others, but are regarded as the successive stages of *prakritic* evolution and involution.

There are various ways to conceive human destiny beyond the level of moral existence; namely, as the realization of the passive individual soul (*parusa*), the Universal Being (*Brahman*) or personal God (*Isvara*). In all these instances, however, what is sought is a spiritual status of being transcending the "transitoriness" of all that is in the world. A sense of 'vacuity'pervades one's whole existence, and this "nothing-ness" of all that is, is disclosed in the mood of dread--especially in the phenomenon of death. This inevitable, gruesome prospect of the annihilation of one's being-in-the-world necessitates the quest for an eternal, transcendent status which will be unaffected by death.

The transcendent subjectivity of the self is described differently by the Hindu philosophical systems, depending upon the metaphysical framework of each system. Broadly, there are two views: the first describes transcendent subjectivity as "objectless" or as being its own object; here no duality is experienced. The second view regards it as capable of being in relation to "an object," namely, to *Brahman* or *Isvara*; here the subject and *Brahman* remain distinct. The former view is held by the Sankhya, Nyaya-Vaisesika and Advaita systems, while the latter view is helf by the Visisstadvaita and Dvaita systems of philosophy. Even in the latter view, however, this "object" is itself so "united" with the subject as to be its inner ground; hence there can be no strict "dualism" between them. These systems maintain that the transcendent subjectivity of the self is other than the principle of egoity (*ahamkara*), which is the cause of "exclusive" subjectivity. Ramanuja regards the self as *ahampadartha* or the spiritual subject of experience. It is not the product of *avidya* (ignorance), and hence its reality is not confined to that of the body; it is distinct from *ahamkara* which is born of *avidya* connected with the body and is the seat of pride.

The self is capable of three kinds of subjectivity: the "exclusive," the "inclusive" and the "transcendent." The self is egoistic and practical in its exclusive subjectivity; it seeks to rise above the ego-centric limitations and becomes altruistic and philosophical in its "inclusive" subjectivity; finally, it seeks to transcend this ethical level of being and becomes "spiritual" in its metaphysical and "transcendent" subjectivity.

COMMUNITY

In our analysis we found that persons are relational beings: one is constitued a person because of one's manifold relations. Phenomenology and existentialism hold that the self is essentially in a world-with-other-selves. The world (*Welt*) of man is a with-world (*Mitwelt*): to-be-in-the-world is to-be-with-others (*Dasein ist Mitdasein*). One cannot escape this aspect of one's existence; any account of the meaning of self necessarily includes a description of relations with other selves. As significant content of intentionality the other self is not "outside" the acts of self-consciousness of the intending self, but immediately present in a relationship of meaning.[16] Gabriel Marcel has expressed this aspect of personality in his philosophy as the richly real "presence of persons." So long as one remains shut up in one's own self, wether through philosophical abstraction or pathological egotism, the self remains unattuned to the real presence of the other and is unawakened to the full presence of reality. This is the reason why Marcel says that the essential characteristic of the person is openness or availability (*disponibilité*). We must "avail" ourselves of the full rich presence of persons, and allow that presence into our thoughts. For Marcel existence is always intersubjective and it is in intersubjectivity (*intersubjectivité*) that a person reaches full development. "To encounter someone is not merely to cross his path but to be, for the moment at least, near *to* or *with* him. To use the term I have often used before, it means a being co-present."[17].

A person can have two attitudes: availability (*disponibilité*) and unavailability (*indisponibilité*); which Marcel prefers to translate as "handy" and "unhandy." The unavailable person is incapable of responding to calls made upon him/her by life--unable to sympathize with other people or imagine their situation. The person remains shut up in the petty circle of his private experience, which forms a kind of hard shell round him through which he is incapable of breaking. They are 'unhandy' from this point of view and unavailable from the point of view of others. For the second person or thou there is a presence of persons, a being with, and belonging to, each other. Cultivating in fidelity the "we" which I and thou create implies disposability (*disponibilité*). This is characterized by a readiness to respond, an openness, a kind of "being at hand" or at the service of others, a welcome. One who possesses this quality makes oneself available to others for instant communion because he or she is "uncluttered by a sense of his/her own importance."[18]

Speaking in the same vein Martin Buber says that man stands always in an I-Thou relationship. According to Buber two fundamental attitudes or postures are to be found in all human experience: the *personal* and the *functional*, or the world of "I-Thou" and of "I-It" relations. The "I" in these two worlds is not the same because "the primary I-Thou can only be spoken with the whole being; the primary I-It can never be spoken with the "whole being."[19] The fundamental difference between these attitudes is not determined by the object with which the "I" relates, but rather by the *manner* in which the "I" relates oneself to the object. As Maurice Friedman explains: "I-Thou is the primary word of relation; it is characterized by mutuality, directness, presentness, intensity and ineffability. I-It is the primary word of experiencing and using. It takes place *within* man and not between him and the world; hence it is entirely subjective and lacking in mutuality. I-Thou and I-It cut across our ordinary distinctions and focus our attention, not upon individual objects and their causal connections, but upon relations *between* things, the *dazwischen* (the "there-in-between").[20]

Buber believes that the only way to exercise a genuine existence is by engaging in a truly interpersonal relationship with the other. Only by concentrating my total being on the interests and needs of the other can I effect that perfect mutual relationship which results in genuinely existential living. For Buber life is *between* persons and not *in* them. One lives in the spirit only to the extent that one is responsive to the Thou. There can never be an I in itself and in isolation; it is always an I which faces a Thou in a truly personal relationship. The world of I-Thou always establishes relations, whereas the I-It world is one of experience. In the I-It world one regards living things, works of art and other persons as objects of experience which one judges, uses and classifies. In the I-Thou world another person, a living thing or a work of art can speak to us and we can establish relation with it.

Six qualities or characteristics might be listed for the I-Thou world: (1) In contrast to the I-It world, the whole of one's being is involved and one is conscious of meeting the whole. (2) Meeting a Thou involves an exclusiveness, a sacrificing of other possibilities to the demands of this particular relation. Though other things exist, they do so in the light of the Thou. (3) The I-Thou relation is direct; the Thou is an end in itself and no mediation of sense, idea or fancy is necessary. (4) While the I-It world is only of the past, the I-Thou world deals with the present. (5) What is prevalent in the I-Thou world is not *eros*, but *agape*. (6) The I-Thou relation involves genuine response and responsibility, for there is mutual obligation, pledge, promise, and loyal bonds. The I of the I-Thou world is the loyal self, "pledged to the other in bonds of covenant, one who has exchanged vows of fidelity, one who has claims upon the other and, at the same time, puts himself under claim."[21]

Buber criticizes two aberrations of our age: individualism and collectivism. "Individualism understands only a part of man, collectivism understands man only as a part, neither advances to the wholeness of man or to man as a whole. Individualism sees man only in relation to himself, but collectivism does not see man at all; it sees only 'society'."[22] While modern individualism fails completely because it understands only a part of the person, collectivism does no better: in actuality one is just as solitary in a collectivism as in individualism. Buber asserts that in a collectivity one is *not* a person. The collective promises to give one security in the "whole" and promises to take care of one's every need. But in so doing, it prevents one from being a person, for it does not allow one to commune with other human beings. Hence, the solitariness which one sought to escape in an individualism becomes magnified in a collectivity; instead of overcoming isolation a collectivity "overwhelms and numbs it."

> Collectivism is not a binding but a bundling together, armed and equipped in common, with only as much life from man to man as will inflame the marching step. But community, growing community, is the being no longer side by side but *with* one another of a multitude of persons. And this multitude, though it also moves towards one goal, yet experiences everywhere a turning to, a dynamic facing of, the other, a flowing from I and Thou. Collectivity is based on an organized atrophy of personal existence, community on its increase and confirmation in life lived towards one another.[23]

Buber's alternative to individualism and collectivism is *community*, the existence of man with man. Only when the individual knows the other in all his otherness has he broken through his own solitude in a strict and transforming meeting. As Ernest Breisach remarks:

> Buber's new community grows out of the free decision of authentic persons. The new community must be established without destroying the personal independence which man has achieved by centuries of struggle. Community must be based on the mutual recognition of the individual person which in turn demands free persons working together in voluntary cooperation.[24]

Community, according to Buber, is built on what he calls the sphere of the *Between*. He insists that this is not a fantasy or fiction. The "between" is a reality that needs constant working out anew; it is not something inert, permanent and changeless. Rather it is ever recreated whenever two human beings meet. Buber explains:

> The fundamental fact of human existence is man with man. What is peculiarly characteristic of the human world is, above all, that something takes place between one being and another, the like of which can be found nowhere in nature. . . . It is rooted in one being turning to another, as this particular other being, in order to communicate with it in a sphere which is common to them but which reaches beyond

the special sphere of each. I call this sphere which is established with existence of man as man but which is conceptually still uncomprehended, the sphere of 'between'.[25]

In the meeting of two individuals I and Thou there is an essential remainder which is common to both of them, but which reaches out beyond the special sphere of each. This remainder is the basic reality, the 'sphere of the between' (*das Zwischenmenschliche*).

We may call this "between" the sphere of the "we." In the meeting of the I and Thou (or 'thous') a transcendence is realized, namely a going beyond the personal level of existence of each. This level is required in order for community to exist. Though it is not individually in the 'I' or 'you', potentially it is in both. This potentiality is actuated when we have the courage to transcend the limits of being merely oneself in order to be with others. To be in a community we have to combine what Paul Tillich calls "the courage to be oneself and the courage to be a part."

> The section of reality in which one participates immediately is the community to which one belongs. Through it and only through it participation in the world as a whole and in all its parts is mediated. Therefore he who has the courage to be as a part has the courage to affirm himself as a part of the community in which he participates.[26]

In man there is a tendency towards egocentricity, which does not stand in obvious harmony with man's openness to the world. On the contrary, there is an inherent tendency in the ego to adhere to one's own purposes, conceptions and customs. Thus, one has a tendency not only to break into the open, but also toward a certain self-enclosure. When a person breaks into the open the ego is always involved. A person can overcome his self-centredness and attain his destiny, not by rejecting his ego, but by incorporating it into the larger totality, the context of a unified world and unified humanity. One's destiny cannot be attained for oneself alone, but only with other persons; hence, the unity of the world is built together with others. This mutuality of human destiny is a basis for human community. In one and the same community many individuals seek fulfillment. Their individual paths differ as do their roles and contributions within their groups. Nevertheless, they have a common goal and are brought together in the one community.[27] To live in community implies then two tensions: to be an individual and to be a member of the community.

Phenomenological inquiry into the self as essentially being-with-other-selves and enriched by their existential evocation is consistent with the empirical evidence from cultural anthropology: of the need to understand the person as in community with others. As human survival individually and as a species requires prescribed patterns of behavior and relationship, the human being is always in a moral community. Just as this unity constituted persons as persons, so it constitutes them as moral beings of a particular kind as determined by the rational intention which forms the relationship.[28]

A community requires a unifying idea or purpose, but this alone is not enough, for even a club has a purpose. A community is based more upon a unity of love and mutual concern; in this it transcends a society which is primarily a legal structure or 'organization'. With the sense of community often there has developed an emotional aversion to legal structures as if in some way endangering its inner union.

The existential foundation of every community is communion or a common participation in some good, which it strives to preserve or increase. A feeling of togetherness is only the first requirement for a community in the full sense for if there is to be, not just a mass of men, but a true community a merely emotional attitude will not suffice. There must exist also such spiritual values as mutual respect and love, or at least some regard for the personal worth of others. Further, the need for legal structure with true authority may also flow from the essence of community, since otherwise the effective pursuit of its goal cannot be guaranteed. Thus, the moral bonds which preserve a community and assure beneficial cooperation by its members are bonds, not only of love but also of justice.

Building Up the Community

In order to build up a community it is important to bear in mind certain important values connected with the human person, namely, uniqueness, dignity and intimacy. Each person is unique: though there were, are and will be millions of human beings, not a single one will be repeated. This points to the great dignity of the human person who must be treated not as a thing or as merely useful to my purpose, but as of infinite value in him or herself. This is being lost in the face of wars, nuclear devices, racial discrimination, domination over others, communalism and religious fanaticism. The uniqueness of the individual is a basis not for opposition, but for cooperation in the struggle to move ahead, in spite of failures, towards the creation of a better humanity. Hobbes once said: "Homo homini lupus," men are wolves unto each other; a character in Sartre's play "No Exit" declares: "Hell is other people." Though there may be some truth in such statements when humanity is considered from a negative point of view, the person still has the capacity to transcend oneself to a level of active pro-existence, that is, existence lived for others.

This level of existence can be arrived at and lived only through a sense of *intimacy* and trust. In order to grasp the meaning of intimacy, others must be distinguished from *privacy* and *familiarity*.[29] Privacy is the effort to block another from knowing something about us. Essentially it is a negative term, derived from the Latin words *privo* and *privatus* which were used in such expressions as "withdrawn from public life," "delivered from something or someone," and "stripped of office." Though today its meaning is more positive, it is still defensive. The term "familiarity" designates knowledge that comes about gradually through the accumulation of details about a thing or a person, leading us to expect a pattern of behaviour. The Latin word from which it is derived (*famulus, familiaris*, meaning "servant": *familia* meaning "a household") carries with it the connotations of subordination and of the ordinary or common place, which are still adumbrated in the term today. In its reference to what is ordinary and everyday the term familiarity shares a reference to surface; thus we may become familiar with a person's behaviour without coming to know him intimately.

In contrast, *intimacy* designates a relation of some depth between persons. The term is derived from Latin words that associate inwardness with depth: the adverbs *intus*, and *inter*, meaning "in the midst of" and "within," carry connotations of depth. The inward depth is built up through the comparative *interior*, meaning "inner, nearer, more deeply," and the superlative *intimus* meaning "inmost, most profound, most hidden and secret." Intimacy is not violated privacy--the familiarity which often breeds contempt--it will not be present in the relation between one who dominates and one who is dominated, for genuine intimacy cannot be forced. It is offered by a person in trust that the offer will be received by another with respect, and on the basis of a certain mutual integrity and openness. Intimacy arises with the circle of giving and receiving, it is not without a certain risk of self-rejection inseparable from the generosity of the gift of self. Intimacy is possible only through self-disclosure, and full intimacy calls for shared self-disclosure.

This disclosure brings persons together in a closeness that reaches beyond formalities for, although individual features and social roles usually play a part in setting the tone and character of the relationship and continue to be recognized within it, nevertheless intimacy transcends these forms. It is rooted in the unique *being present* of a person, and consists in sustained wonder in this sheer presence. Its principal mark is *attentiveness to this presence*. Sometimes intimacy may dawn upon persons so suddenly that they wonder how it happened. At times people find it hard to express intimacy adequately in words and may resort to non-verbal signs, for intimacy may surprise us too deeply for anything but wordless joy or grief--or it may consist of a felt shared presence that is all but ineffable. Analogously, *trust* is also required for intimacy between human persons. On this level of human intimacy public scrutiny or empirical testing is not possible for persons are considered worthy of belief and commitment. We do not seek to learn about another person through intimacy: if we gain any knowledge here it is only accidental. Rather, we simply acknowledge being attuned with another personal presence. The self we come to know in, and through, intimacy is just this presencing.

In order to build up community and culture we need a delicate blend of privacy and intimacy. Privacy should not become the ruling consideration in our relationship with others. Temporary withdrawal from others in order to recoup oneself for better relationship may be necessary, but privacy should not be a means to individualism. In our modern technocratic culture there is great stress upon individualism and a tendency to be lost in the crowd and to avoid responsibilty. We need to fight these tendencies in order to develop a personal and the interpersonal culture.

Community in Indian Thought

Before we proceed to analyse the relations between person, community and culture, a brief reference to the concept of community in the Indian thought may be in place. Except in Buddhism and later Jainism we do not find a systematic discussion of community. In Buddhism there are three refuges ('pillars') which the monks are supposed to avow: *Buddham saranam gachami; dharman (dhammam) saranam gachami; sangam saranam gachami*: I take refuge in the Buddha; I take refuge in the law; I take refuge in the community." This is the community of the disciples of the Buddha; but the ordinary folk could associate with the monks and had free access to the monastery. Even before the settled communities of monks, there were wandering 'sannyasins', called *parivrajakas*, who occasionally came together to share the 'same roof', at least during monsoon time. Once a settled form of community (in the relgious sense) developed, it had a minimal structural form. The Buddha bound his monks by two vows: celibacy and the simple life; surprisingly there was no vow of obedience. He told his disciples: "let dharma be your principle and truth be your guide." No one was to be lord over another; in the community one could question, dissent, and even break away from the group. Compassion and respect for one another was to reign in the community.

Later religious communities in Hinduism have the buddhistic community as their progenitor. Sankara found his communities to counteract the influence of monastic buddhism. But as with any human institution, rivalry and individualism of the monks often mocked monastic life.

For building a true community the buddhist notion of compassion is very useful. It has three essential characteristics: sensitivity, openness and intimacy.[30] If we are sensitive to the needs of the other and open to his or her person and values we can build a community based upon genuine human values. Later Buddhism advocated the ideal of *bodhisativa*, meaning a person of 'realization' who exists for the sake of others. A *bodhisativa* has realised the nullity of existence in this world. Though he could enter into *nirvana* (let us translate it as 'liberation'), he does not do so because the vast majority of the people have not come to this 'realization' and he sees it as his responsibility to help them. In ordinary terms we can say that a *bodhisativa* is a selfless person committed to the liberation of others: he is truly altruistic.

RELATION BETWEEN PERSON, COMMUNITY AND CULTURE

It is not difficult to perceive that person, community and culture are interrelated. The concept of culture and how it is transmitted were analysed in an earlier chapter. Culture comes from the Latin word *colere* "to cultivate." Originally it meant: (1) cultivation and development of human powers beyond their natural state (culture as spiritual formation). The ancient world and the Middle Ages called this *'humanitas,' 'civilitas'*. In the seventeenth and eighteenth centuries the concept of culture was expanded and came to mean: (2) that which one adds to nature either in oneself or in other objects. Accordingly, while nature designates that which one is born with or is given from outside of oneself and without one's cooperation (facticity), culture includes everything that is the result of the person's conscious and free activity. Culture finds its proper end in the completion and perfection of the person's nature. A cultural activity which is contrary to one's nature is not true, but merely apparent or false culture.

Depending upon whether a particular cultural activity is directed immediately to the human person and his/her perfection, or to objects which exist independently of one, a distinction is made between personal culture (language, community life, morality, religion, etc.) and material culture (technology, art, etc.). Most cultural activities actually include both areas. Mere external, material culture is called civilization; its task is to serve as a foundation and pre-supposition for inner, spiritual culture. Culture results only from the cooperation of many individuals in the human community; from the contributions of the different national cultures there arises a common human culture.[31]

What is the role of persons and community in building up culture and its transformation? The individual person is the 'initiator' of culture; the community is the locus wherein this culture is built. In the building of a culture certain persons may be called upon to play a vital role. If these individuals act with responsibility and a broader vision, i.e., with a view towards the good of the whole of mankind, they will bring about a great transformation in cultures. If they insulate their community or society from all external influences and build up their society on communal lines the chance of conflict between cultures devlops, for when a community becomes culturally "inward looking" persons in the community develop a narrow cultural puritanism and pride.

As culture is related primarily to attitude, a mere growth in technology, material advancement or affluence need not indicate a corresponding growth in culture; instead there can exist what is called a cultural lag. The so-called superiority of culture is a myth. Every culture is unique, and different cultures can cooperate for the growth of a human culture which assures multiplicity in unity.

CONCLUSION

In this paper it has been our endeavor to analyse the nature of the human person and of community, and their relationship to culture. Our analysis revealed the greatness of the human person, one's uniqueness and value, and at the same time the interpersonal character of human nature. Since a person is relational and is always called upon to act responsibly towards one's fellow human beings a call to community is built into one's nature. The more deeply one realizes this call and actualizes it the more human one becomes. As a member of a special community one builds up a culture and lives in it; one contributes to, and profits from, the culture of the community.

When the society becomes communally minded or oppresses other communities the individual should protest and uphold the great human values. Sometimes religious fanaticism, sectarian values, regionalism, narrow linguistic consciousness, minority feelings, etc., can cloud the vision of leaders who then may set up a culture which misleads the members of the community. Communalistic and fanatical slogans have greater appeal because they cater to the 'lower self' of man. Hence, we must guard against the process of dehumanization and aim at building communities established on the worth of the human person through intimacy, compassion and a life dedicated to the total liberation of mankind. Such a vision will attune us with every person on earth whether near or far--the whole of creation.

Vijnana Nilayam
Janimpet, Eluru
A.P., India

NOTES

*See Discussion I.

1. Hans Urs Von Balthasar, "On the Concept of Person", trans. Peter Verhalen, *Communio*, 13 (1986), p. 18. See also Paul Tournier, *The Meaning of Persons* (New York: Harper & Row, Publishers, 1957), p. 129.

2. Cf. Kenneth L. Schmitz, "The Geography of the Human Person," *Communio*, 13 (1986), p. 29; also Balthasar, "Concept of Person", p. 20.

3. Cf. Schmitz, "Georgraphy of the Person", pp. 29-30.

4. Cf. Aristotle, *Historia Animalium*, 491, b9-11.

5. Cf. Schmitz, "Georgraphy of the Person", pp. 30-31. We could go further into details of the history of the word 'person' and its application in Biblical and dogmatic theology. Though this would be fruitful, for our present purpose it is not necessary.

6. Cf. Walter Brugger and Kenneth Baker, *Philosophical Dictionary* (Washington: Gonzaga University Press, 1974), p. 302.

7. Schmitz, "Geography of the Person", p. 28.

8. Ludwig Wittgenstein, *Tractatus Logico-Philosophicus*, 6, 522.

9. James E. Royce, *Man and Meaning* (New York: McGraw Hill Book Company, 1969), p. 212.

10. His two volume work, *The Mystery of Being:* Vol. I, *Reflection and Mystery*, trans. G. Frazer; Vol. II, *Faith and Reality*, trans. R. Hague (Chicago: Henry Regnery Company, 1951) deals at length on this theme. We can make only a reference to it here.

11. Cf. Royce, *Man and Meaning*, pp. 214-215; and also Brugger

Baker, *Philosophical Dictionary*, p. 304.

12. Cf. Royce, *Man and Meaning*, p. 216.

13. *Ibid.* p. 219.

14. *Ibid.* pp. 220-221.

15. I use the term 'philosophies' purposely as in India there is not only one form of philosophizing, but many. There is a highly monistic form of philosophy (e.g., Sankara) as well as a dualistic form (e.g., Madhava); there are also highly mystical forms of philosophy as well as gross materialisms. For my analysis of the Indian concept of the person I base myself principally upon: Srinivasan, *Studies in East-West Philosophy* (Delhi: Arnold-Heineman, 1974), pp. 12-22.

16. Shannon M. Jordan, "The Moral Community and Persons," *Philosophy Today*, 30 (1986), p. 11.

17. Gabriel Marcel, *Creative Fidelity*, trans. Robert Rosthal (New York: Farrar, Strauss and Giroux, 1964), p. 12. Also cf. Francis J. Lescoe, *Existentialism With or Without God* (New York: Alba House, 1974), pp. 102-104.

18. Cf. Marcel, *Being and Having*, trans. Katherine Farrer (New York: Harper & Row, 1965), p. 201; *Creative Fidelity*, pp. 38-39; Lescoe, *Existentialism*, pp. 104-105.

19. Cf. Martin Buber, *I and Thou*, trans. Walter Kaufmann (New York: Charles Scribner's Sons, 1970), p. 31.

20. Cf. Maurice Friedman, *Martin Buber: The Life of Dialogue* (New York: Harper & Row, 1960), p. 57; Lescoe, *Existentialism*, pp. 158-159.

21. Cf. Buber, *I and Thou*, pp. 8, 76; Lescoe, *Existentialism*, pp. 160-161.

22. Buber, *Between Man and Man*, trans. Ronald Gregor Smith (New York: Macmillan, 1966), pp. 200, 202.

23. Cf. *Ibid.*, pp. 31-32; Lescoe, *Existentialism*, pp. 152-153.

24. Ernest Breisach, *Introduction to Modern Existentialism* (New York: Grove Press, 1962), p. 168; cf. Buber, *Between Man and Man*, pp. 201-202; Lescoe, *Existentialism*, pp. 153-154.

25. Buber, *Between Man and Man*, p. 203.

26. Paul Tillich, *The Courage To Be* (New Haven: Yale University Press, 1972), p. 91.

27. Cf. Wolfhart Pannenberg, *What is Man?*, trans. Duane A. Priebe (Philadelphia: Fortress Press, 1972), pp. 55-56.

28. Cf. M. Jordan, "Moral Community and Persons", pp. 113-115.

29. For a detailed analysis of these concepts cf. Schmitz, "Geography of the Human Person," pp. 40-48.

30. For an excellent discussion of the notion of compassion cf. David Brandon, *Zen in the Art of Helping* (London: Routledge & Kegan Paul, 1979), pp. 47-61.

31. Cf. Brugger and Baker, *Philosophical Dictionary*, pp. 81-83.

CHAPTER III

THE PHILOSOPHY OF GIKUYU PROVERBS

AND OTHER SAYINGS

WITH PARTICULAR REFERENCE TO ETHICS

G.J. WANJOHI

INTRODUCTION

Proverbs are a literary genre of many languages. This is especially true of the non-written languages or those which have been so for a long time. Space does not allow me to enlarge on the nature, form, genesis and function of proverbs. Suffice it to say that a proverb is a statement arrived at inductively (and thus universal) whose function is to state a case in the most succinct manner. Another quality of a proverb is its symbolic character. This aspect helps to separate a proverb from other universal but literal statements. However, there exist in many languages, including the Gikuyu language, a considerable number of well known-literal sayings which are classified as proverbs. In my estimation these sayings are not proverbs properly speaking, since they lack universal and symbolic character.

A proverb is like a joke: either you grasp it right away or you don't grasp it at all. The reason for this is that the truth enunciated in proverbs is intuitively grasped. This is interesting in that here the economy of form and expression issues in economy of apprehension, appropriation.

Among the Gikuyu of Kenya, whose literacy is less than one hundred years old, proverbs abound. In fact, one can say that they have a proverb for almost every occasion. They use them to express their ideas on the supernatural as well as on cooperation, diligence, generosity, honesty, laziness, wealth, poverty, etc. The proverbs the Gikuyu people employ can be taken as a fairly accurate manifestation of their world-view and their way of life--in a word, of their culture.

CONTENT

As might be expected, moral teaching among the Gikuyu is accomplished through proverbs. But before showing how that is so we shall try to answer a fundamental question: Do Gikuyu proverbs contain or express any philosophy? In my view, they do, as I shall attempt to show.

The heated debate which has been going on for over two decades on the status of African philosophy has helped to reach an important conclusion: regardless of the loftiness of the subject matter in which it engages, a thought is not philosophical unless it adopts a critical and reflective attitude towards that subject matter. In other words, the locus of philosophical thinking is to be found not at the level of object language, but at the metalinguistic level. On the basis of this view of philosophy, Gikuyu proverbs express a philosophy. This can be illustrated by three such proverbs:

> 1. *Thiiri utarihagwo no wa urogi.* (The only debt which must not be paid is the one of poisoning someone.)[1]
>
> 2. *Ngia itari thiiri ti ngia.* (A poor person without debts is not poor.)[2]
>
> 3. *Kuriha thiiri gutiiriragwo.* (One does not regret having paid one's debts.)[3]

As I will argue, all three proverbs engage in a metalanguage about morality and consequently are philosophical.

The message in the first proverb is that whereas it is obligatory to pay one's debts (object language), there are some debts which ought not to be paid--those having to do with immoral matters or actions (metalanguage). The conclusion reached in the independent clause of the last sentence presupposes a critical and reflective stance as to what is moral or immoral. The proverb says that even though in itself paying debts is good, there are circumstances which would make it non-obligatory and even immoral. Let me illustrate this concretely. X promises to pay Y $100 if he poisons (murders) Z. Y goes ahead and murders Z, and so X supposedly owes him $100. The proverb is telling us that X is not obliged to pay Y $100 because the matter surrounding the debt is an immoral one. The ability to see things this way betokens a philosophical attitude on the part of the people, namely, the Gikuyu who employ the proverb.

Since a proverb is symbolic, we can subtitute "keeping a promise" for "paying one's debts" and the same reasoning will follow. (If King Herod had been aware of the Gikuyu proverb here under discussion and were willing to conform to it, the head of John the Baptist might have been spared.)

Now let us proceed to the second proverb. The metalinguistic interpretation involved here is very interesting. At the object language level, to be poor means to lack money, property or children. But one can have all these things on loan and pretend that one is rich. But the actual owner can come and take away all of them, leaving the borrower-pretender empty-handed. Experience teaches us that if one is used to a high standard of living, to fall from this standard makes one feel humiliated. This will not happen to a poor man who is used to having little. For him it can be said that his poverty (in material things) constitutes his riches (peace of mind, since he has no creditors to worry about).

The ability to see that it is not the possession of things *per se* which makes one rich but the *circumstances* in which they are possessed or not possessed, certainly implies metalinguistic and therefore philosophical, thought.

Now we come to the third proverb which says that one does not regret having paid one's debts. Here we shall inquire first concerning the sources of regret. These are mainly two. One of these is occasioned by having acted stupidly, and leads the person to exclaim, "I wish I had not been so foolish"! The other type of regret comes from having committed a moral fault such as stealing, assaulting another person, lying, etc., and may lead one to pay a heavy penalty. The first kind of regret can be called epistemological and the second moral.

Having paid one's debts can cause neither an epistemological nor a moral regret. This is so because one is quite certain of what one is doing: that it is the correct and right thing. In order to pay the debt one may have to sacrifice in order to meet one's obligation, for one does not believe in "stealing from Peter to pay Paul." If, as a result of discharging one's debts, one is made fun of by those who do not believe in debt-paying, one will not thereby feel sorry because one knows that one has acted correctly, justly and morally. In virtue of its symbolic character, this proverb can be generalized to mean that one does not regret having done the right thing, whatever that might be.

Is this proverb uttering something philosophical? In my estimation it is, in as much as it is saying more than just that it is good to pay one's debts. What the proverb adds is that it is good to pay one's debts regardless of whether this hurts or not or causes one to become an object of ridicule. I contend that for thought to be able to see this far it must be operating at a metalinguistic, reflective and critical level, and therefore is philosophical.

Form

As is apparent, the subject matter of Gikuyu proverbs is interesting enough. Even more interesting, I find, is the form in which these proverbs express moral ideas, namely in terms of an apparent contradiction. I shall first give examples of pairs of some such proverbs. Afterwards I shall proceed to indicate how the seeming contradiction can be resolved.

Pairs of Seemingly Contradictory Proverbs

1. *Mwitwari ndari haaro.*
   (He who sticks to his affairs avoids trouble.)[4]

1. (a) *Muria wike akuuaqa wike*
   (He who eats alone dies alone.)[5]

2. *Gukira kuri nqaatho.*
   (To keep silence is praiseworthy.)[6]

2. (a) *Gukira ni guthuurana.*
   (To keep silence is to hate each other.)[7]

3. *Kamuingi koyaga ndiri.*
   (Many people can lift a mortar.)[8]

3 (a) *Mathanwa me kiondo kimwe matiagaga gukomorania* (Axes which are in the same basket are bound to knock each other.)[9]

4. *Kiara kimwe gitiuragaga ndaa.*
(One finger cannot kill a louse.)[10]

4 (a) *Hiti cia huura imwe ni cio ithuraine,*
(Hyenas of the same lair hate each other.)[11]

As a way of resolving the apparent contradiction involved in the first pair of contraries, let me observe that it is good and ethical to keep to oneself and avoid interfering with other people's business (1). In so doing a climate of peace and harmony is created for the benefit of all. However, too much keeping to oneself, too much individualism, failure to look around and bring help to those who might need it is evil or unethical (1a).

The lesson to draw from what has just been said is that there are times when we should keep to ourselves and refrain from meddling in other people's affairs. There are also times when remaining enclosed in ourselves will be detrimental, not only to others but to ourselves as well. To know the times and the circumstances in which to "interfere" or not to interfere with other people's affairs calls for the virtue of prudence. In many Gikuyu proverbs this virtue is often alluded to, though not explicitly named. The same kind of interpretation can be offered for the second pair of proverbs referring to the keeping of silence. I would like to suggest that the apparent paradox contained in the first two pairs of proverbs is resolvable with reference to the virtue of prudence.

The apparent contradiction in the last two pairs of proverbs can be summarized by saying that it is *both good and bad* for people to come together, to co-operate. The resolution of this contradiction proves to be rather subtle.

Among the theories proposed by social philosophers regarding the origin of human society there is one (to which I subscribe) which says that this was brought about by the individual human being's inability to be sufficient to himself physically or otherwise. The effect of different individuals coming together was not only to overcome an individual's weakness, but to enable each individual to specialize in a given task, thus realizing man's potentialities more fully. But for this double advantage a price has to be paid: the friction and the inconveniences of living together. Perhaps even worse is the tendency of society, even the most democratic one, to tamper (whether consciously or unconsciously) with the freedom of the individual. This happens especially through the bureaucratic system the society is forced by its very nature to set up. The action of society in depriving an individual of his freedom or limiting it unduly is deplorable; equally to be decried is the individual's attempt to destroy the society by one's antisocial actions and attitudes. It cannot be gainsaid that a tension exists between society and the individual.

The last two pairs of opposed proverbs and others like them highlight the individual-society tension. The apparent contradiction in these proverbs is to be understood in terms of the strained relationship between the individual and society. The important message of these proverbs is that living with others is a necessary evil which requires sacrifice, compromise and accomodation. Here, too, the role of prudence cannot be underestimated. The important place occupied by prudence in the Gikuyu proverbs bearing on morality points to the idea that for the Gikuyu people the right or good action, that is to say, virtue, is the mean between the two extremes of deficiency and excess.

Two such proverbs superbly illustrate this position:

1. *Kuuma ti kuuma ta ihiga, na kuororoa ti kuororoa ta maai.* (To be hard is not to be as hard as a stone, and to be soft is not to be as soft as water.)[12]

2. *Muihwa ndahooyaga na ndaimagwo.* (A nephew on the side of one's sister does not beg, and if he begs he is not refused.)[13]

Since the meaning of these proverbs is quite obvious, I shall give only a short exegesis of each. For the first proverb let us take the example of a father and mother vis-à-vis their son. The father believes that in order to discipline his son, he must never make any concession to him, he must always say no to him. In terms of the proverb under consideration, this particular father can be said to be as hard as a stone. This is not virtuous. As for the mother, she may be the type who believes that in order to show that she loves her son she must always grant whatever he asks. This mother can be said to be as soft as water. This is not virtuous, either. In the one as well as in the other case, virtue would consist in allowing the boy occasional concessions and in not bowing to some of his demands. This would depend, of course, on the nature of these demands and the circumstances. In both cases prudence has to be the guiding principle.

Let me interpret the second proverb in the following manner. For a self-respecting person living among his own, it is not good (virtuous) to be begging or asking for things, since one's relatives ought to be attentive enough to notice and provide whatever is needed. Should they fail in this, however, the person can explicitly express his/her needs or beg. In that case the request should be granted because it was not wrong to make it, given the circumstances. The part played by prudence in these two proverbs is unmistakable.

The emphasis on virtue as a mean and of the role of prudence in Gikuyu proverbs dealing with morals is very much reminiscent of Aristotle. There is no indication of any intercourse between the Aristotle of the third century B.C. and the Gikuyu people whose recorded history goes back to only the early sixteenth century A.D. However, there is one common denominator between the two: reason. It does not matter in which age or epoch man lives. So long as he is a rational animal he will be guided more or less by reason and will tend to see and do things in nearly the same way.

Conclusion

From what has just been said, the statement that the Gikuyu morality is founded on reason should not come as a surprise. This statement is supported by the analysis of the word *"kihooto"* which has both epistemological and moral meanings. As will be pointed out, these meanings are identifiable one with the other.

At the epistemological level the word *"kihooto"* (noun and adjective) carries the meaning of reason, reasonable, rational, rationality, truth, truthful, etc. These senses are expressed by such sayings (but not proverbs properly speaking, as I have already shown) as the following:

1. *Muingatwo na njuguma niacookaoa, no muingatwo na ki hooto ndacookaoa.* (The one chased away with a club comes back, but the one chased away with reason/truth does not come back.)[14]

2. *Kihooto kiunaga uta mugeete.* (Reason/truth breaks a taut bow.)[15]

3. *Kihooto kiringaga ruui ruiyuru.* (Reason/truth fords a flooded river.)[16]

At the level of morals the term *"kihooto"* (which again functions as a noun and as an adjective) conveys the ideas of right, just, fair, etc. Two examples will help bring out these senses:

1. *Gutua ciira na kihooto.* (To judge a case justly/fairly.)

2. *Ugwo weeka ti kihooto.* (What you have done is not right/fitting.)

The epistemological and moral senses of "kihooto" are identified in the saying (again not a proverb): *"Uugi ni kihooto.* (Intelligence/rationality is rightness/justice.)[17]

This being the case, it is perfectly correct to substitute the word *uugi* (intelligence, reason) for the word *kihooto* (rightness, justice) in all the above examples (both epistemological and moral) or in any other context. This is possible thanks to the notion of reason/intelligence which is always implied in the word *kihooto.* In other words, for the Gikuyu people what is right is *ipso facto* reasonable.

Following what has been argued in this paper, one can safely assert that the morality taught and practised by the Gikuyu people--which is mostly expressed in their proverbs-- qualifies as an ethics on the basis of its metalinguistic aspects and for being founded on reason.

The University of Nairobi, Nairobi, Kenya

NOTES

1. G. Barra, *1,000 Gikuyu Proverbs*, With translations and English

Equivalents. (London: Macmillan and the East African Literature Bureau, 1960), No. 847. (The literal English translations are mine in this and subsequent proverbs.)

2. Ngumbu Njururi, *Gikuyu Proverbs* (London: Macmillan and Co. Ltd, 1969), No. 475. Here, too, the literal translations are mine.

3. Barra, *1,000 Gikuyu Proverbs*, No. 336. (I am using only the last part of the proverb.)

4. In T.G. Benson, ed., *Gikuyu-English Dictionary* (Oxford: University Press, 1964), p. 203.

5. Ngumbu, *Gikuyu Proverbs,* No. 394.

6. Barra, No. 74.

7. Barra, No. 75.

8. Ngumbu. No. 192.

9. Benson, *Kikuyu-English Dictionary,* p. 227.

10. Benson, p. 285.

11. Benson, p. 180.

12. Barra, No. 313.

13. Barra, No.475.

14. Barra. No. 359 and 357.

15. Ngumbu, No. 220.

16. Barra, No. 267.

17. Barra, No. 885.

CHAPTER IV

CULTURAL PLURALISM AND DEVELOPMENT

THE ETHNIC SITUATION OF GUATEMALAN YOUTH

ANTONIO GALLO and *LUISA MOLINA**

The study of this theme should take account of three dimensions, of which only the first is developed below:

1. ethnic group boundaries as a problem of identity;
2. differences between groups and ethnic hegemony: the case of Guatemalan youth; and
3. a philosophical epistemological explanation of the intra- and inter-group communication required for vital and harmonious development.

This study begins from the observation by G. McLean above that culture "is more bridge than barrier." The present chapter deals with the fundamental concepts involved in a concrete situation such as the Guatemalan ethnic complex. There, two or three different ethnic groups continually interact in daily life. They experience great difficulty overcoming ethnic discrimination and struggle for self-realization and evolution, both as individuals and as communities.

In this, the first concept to be discussed is that of identity in its twin aspects: personal and group. The second concept is that of group as an analytic tool. Perhaps the "ethnic group" is the more perfect and complex realization of a human group. Drawing upon and supporting ethnic identity and, consequently, personal identity, it enables one to develop both as a person and as a citizen. Difficulties arise, however, when in beginning to work with a group we find that this concept does not correspond to reality and we must construct some analytic tool to deal with this.

The third concept is the "relation" between the individual as a person and the group. This relation gives the individual an opportunity to appropriate both the meaning and symbols of the group's identity, to integrate the group identity with his or her own, and to understand (or practically accept) the barrier that separates one group from another in a negative or antithetic relation.

Here, culture and ethnicity are entangled only indirectly. Sometimes the same culture contains two different ethnic groups. Hence, we could not speak of the French and the Italian groups as two different cultures in Switzerland; it is the same culture with two different groups. Similarly in Spain there are not two different cultures in Catalonia and in Castile, though these are two ethnic groups. Hence, we will not deal with the concept of culture.

Frequently, in such important cultural objects as language, traditions and social structures differences can be an excuse for ethnic resistance or opposition. However, the origin of this discontent is not the culture itself, but something more hidden, such as economic needs, psychological attitudes or some internal patterns of the group structure. In other words, it is the living beings in the community who create the antagonism. In Guatemala in order to communicate with each other, many ethnic groups with basically the same culture, such as Quiches-Ixiles, Kekchis-Pocomchies and Mames-Canjobales, use a Spanish language which they can hardly speak. Though this seems impractical from the point of view of the group, it is a way of being more fully themselves. Here culture is considered only as an "expression" of the identity of a particular group.

Ethnicity is a difficult term. Many studies, articles and reviews are published at the anthropological or ethnological level about ethnicity, new ethnicity, ethnology, ethnic groups and the human context. We are analyzing the subject from a slightly higher level or in a more speculative sense. Ethnicity itself is the context through which the identity of the group expresses itself. We take it, not at an empirical level (as does science), but as a set of practical principles or, if one prefers, as a pattern of endeavor that characterizes the group. Of course, as an immediate correlate of identity, a parallel might be established between ethnicity and group identity, as between the personality and the "Ego" of the same person. Ethnicity can easily be observed in the interrelations between persons from different ethnic groups as they express themselves through their respective cultures as functions of the group's identity. Generally, in everyday life, groups try to impose their own culture upon other groups.

A second dimension of the present theme is the real case of Indians (Mayans) who are monolingual in a bilingual situation. The reality of the ethnic groups in Guatemala makes this fairly universal. People must accept the imposition of the dominant Spanish cultural group, Spanish language and its style of life which, along with its related symbols and way of thinking, they do not perceive as their own. In contrast, ethnic groups possess a vast culture, their own symbols, customs and special way of thinking. The objective impact of the two cultures and their inter-relations should be analyzed from the point of view of the superior and the inferior as the person develops from childhood into a citizen and is incorporated into his community. The interchange is unequal, and operates at multiple levels of human concerns: family, community, village and region, natural and human environment, education, economy, intellectual and spiritual world. An understanding of the concrete path of one's development among men and nature in space and time is needed in order to understand which mechanism or strategy a specific individual adopts in order to survive in adverse circumstances. This will make it possible to introduce the concept of dialogue, interchange and harmonious development as remedies to the traditional struggle and oppression.

The third dimension of the present theme is in the epistemological field and focuses upon the metaphysical problem, but without abandoning one's special phenomenological insight. Why is a person so intimately involved in a particular culture, custom, tradition or set of human relations? Why is it so difficult for one to overcome the culture created by the group and by oneself?

By going beyond the individual, toward an understanding of the general foundational values on which the unity of mankind is based, one can reach the source of the being of the person himself, both as a unity and as openness. There may be a demiurgic function between two extremes: on the one hand, a closed unity with holiness, plenitude, perfection and power; and, on the other hand, an openness with poverty, possibility in its negative-positive meaning, implementation, finitude and need for meaning. This dialectical contradiction of a human person as an "I," an "Ego" and "myself" is found in the immediate relation of one person to another: in the discovery of others who are not really objects, but "subjects" like myself or other "Egos" for themselves. This contact with, or advancement to, the "other" as a subject--a living, thinking and willing principle of decisions--is not abstract or universal. It is simply my immediate and singular action as this particular "Ego"; it is I and my acts of knowledge in my unique and centralized world and with my own space-time situation.

In this basic interchange, where each person plays the role of both subject and object, we can discover the real material and spiritual dimensions of experience. Consequently, it will be possible to discover the real problems of good or bad interpersonal understanding, the proper means of self-expression in contrast to alienation, and the roots of a static or dynamic attitude toward the development and life style of the person. In this sense the community, and more properly the ethnic group which has the potential of satisfying the essential needs of all those who live in the context of its culture, provides an epistemological basis for all the dimensions of human nature: its historical conditions, concerns and values.

GROUP BOUNDARIES AS A PROBLEM OF ENCOUNTER BETWEEN IDENTITIES

The chapters by Profs. Asike, Baltazar and Kromkowski note a characteristic of the last decade which has spread throughout the world. This is the growing consciousness of national and ethnic identity and the danger of ethnic struggles and divisions which threaten the unity of many states and have many political consequences. The strengthened consciousness of ethnic distinctiveness makes even more difficult encounter and interrelation between different races, nations, regions or groups in everyday interchange on cultural or political issues.

Conflicts increase when antagonisms are established in the narrow limits of a region or a small country. This is the case of Guatemala, a nation with some eighteen different languages which divide the territory into a similar number of cultural and ethnic groups. This emphasizes the problem of ethnic inequality and of human oppression which (as its history is dialectically interpreted by Severo Martinez) has existed since the Spanish conquest and occupation four centuries ago.[1]

The different degrees of modernization between the indigenous and at times conflicting peoples is well expressed by the anthropologist, Ricardo Falla,[2] as "different forms of being Mayans." In each case we meet the same problem: a small group of people with a very distinctive culture who struggle to develop their cultural elements in response to their vital need to define their collective personality and history. Pope John Paul in his allocution in Canada paraphrased the Apocalypse: "Yes, you are from almost all tribes, languages, people and nations."[3]

This problem is found also in Europe. France, traditionally a model of modern national integration and identity, is one of the states experiencing this issue. Immigrants from all over Europe, groups from Morroco, Algeria, the Middle East and Corsica, confront this old and unresolved problem, as do people in Britain, Alsace and the Basques. Other European nations such as Italy, Yugoslavia, Belgium, Spain and Switzerland are even more ethnically divided. In Germany the Greek, Italian, Spanish and Portuguese workers still conserve their national identity. Sweden and Norway, traditionally isolated from such conflicts, have recently received large quotas of immigrants from the Central and Eastern Mediterranean region. To the many peoples from its old colonies, such as India, New Zealand, Australia and others, England has now added Sicilians, Vietnamese and Africans.

The same phenomenon can be found in many other countries of Africa, South America and Asia. Regions which were rather pacific in the past are now experiencing the sudden birth of racial barriers and linguistic and cultural competition by citizens who feel within their legal rights in defending and perpetuating their historical and ethnic status.

Moreover, immigrants of the most recent generations, instead of seeking to assimilate into the host population, now claim with growing force their right to profess and develop their culture, language and social organizations. In these circumstances the humanitarian ideals of being the same, of sharing and communicating are becoming strongly utopic and improbable.

To give but one example, the Bishop of LataCuga (Ecuador) in November 1984 wrote a note about the Quechuas population expressing concern that though they constitute one third of the peasant population, they hold (in any clearly legal sense) only 5% of all the goods of the nation. But the Bishop added that he did not consider this to be the greatest evil, for the most important good of which they have been deprived is education. They have lost any "true" education, because the very little they are receiving is given in a language they do not understand and in a completely foreign cultural context. To be an Indian has become--not so much in theory but in practice--synonymous with "inferiority."

Identity

The main concept inherent in this problematic situation is that of ethnic group identity. We shall approach this only descriptively, without pretending to analyze it as an object. We shall build the concept gradually as we grow closer to its subject. The very reality of the human person is the "Ego" considered in its concrete existential situation: I am myself, all myself. This "Ego" is consciousness; but it is also a concrete real existence here and now. Upon this one builds all the spacial and temporal relations, and upon these all the other dimensions. "I" am the subject, and my identity includes my history, all my spacial relations and all the objects I appropriate.

From another point of view, my situation (Ortega y Gasset),[4] my being (*das Sein*) (Heidegger),[5] or my phenomenological experience (Husserl)[6] includes my identity as the foundation both of my unity and continuity and of my differentiation from all that is not purely myself. My experience, actions and acts of willing and thinking all surround me as other beings or objects; they are part of me, but at the same time distinct from myself.[7]

This experienced consistency and continuity of my identity with its multiple dimensions cannot be separated mentally or psychologically from my identity itself. Nor does it make sense to separate them, because identity without external, cultural, social, aesthetic or moral determinations does not exist. This, it would appear to me, is the nucleus of the whole problem: my identity is myself "with-the-whole" of my existential environment; I cannot separate them. Yet I can understand the differences and the reciprocal polarity of the two terms: "my-ego" and "my-identity." Identity is the established relation, the living being, with its consciousness of the present, its historical properties and all the things I have more or less intimately appropriated.

The inability to define identity probably is due to its unicity, which is not an abstract or conceptual unicity, but a reality that is not distant from the world. The common contextual world is there around me as a limit or possibility (K. Jaspers),[8] or as an horizon which I ought to interpret (G.H. Gadamer).[9] One's identity is being one-with-others. This reflects the presence of non-intellectual things inside one's intelligence, and of the non-emotional things within one's emotions. This unity could not be disrupted without affecting the "Ego" itself, for this world is concretely and immediately my own; it identifies me.

This study does not deal with the word "personality," which here is taken more in a "psychological" than an epistemological sense. Nor does it deal with the word "person" which must be considered at a deeper, more essential or metaphysical level: here the "person" is seen as deeper than identity. Nor, finally, does this study deal with the word "culture," which must be referred in general to the model rather than to the individual style of endeavour. In this sense, it is more external and directed toward the world.

Identity continually deals with the external world as well as with my essence as a man. Perhaps at this deeper level, identity and person could be taken as one. In reality they are one, but identity cannot be elevated to the abstract and universal, whereas the term person can. On the other hand, the person cannot be in contact with material or individual things without the mediation of identity which makes these things mine.

The identity of a person is that of a being really existing as this particular person and as a member of a community, and in the process of becoming a man and assuming responsibility in the world. One is neither an anonymous nor a generic object; rather one supports and gives shape and color to all the characteristics of one's subjectivity. One's identity is one's own not in the semantic sense, but in the sense of "*lebens welt.*" In this living sense, identity involves one's culture with all its social, economic, historic and psychological factors.

My identity is built upon these cultural determinations; it needs them in order to be a continuous, coherent and well developed human being. Hence, one's culture is the natural context for the existence of one's identity: the cultural group, more than the culture itself, is one's natural environment. Through this particular environment the individual must communicate, learn, evolve and achieve his fulfillment--even extending to that of the group itself and the culture. This makes it necessary to extend the analysis of identity to the group itself.

But first we must conclude from the above that people have but one identity. An individual could not change his identity, just as he could not cease to be himself. He could, of course, extend the terms of his identity to such higher and deeper levels as learning a new language and obtaining new skills and techniques in order to have broader knowledge, etc. This is not properly a change, but the extension of one's identity to include new dimensions without losing one's personal or group identity.

Sometimes one can cast off some of the former elements of one's personal identity if these are not very integrated in one's personality or are less important. But generally to lose part of one's identity is to lose part of one's self. We cannot talk about a shifting-identity, but only about a shift between one and another incompatible objects should we prefer something new, want to develop other dimensions of our personality or wish to expand our concerns to new fields. But this is not to shift the identity of the person or of the group.

This, I believe, is the key to understanding this phenomenon. We can lose very important facets of our identity, but in that case we are alienated and leave the ethnic group. Such ethnic alienation affects the group only indirectly; directly it affects the individual, and to lose all the elements of one's identity would be to become mad. In any case, to lose some elements of our identity is a bad wound when we accept it freely; it is aggression when it is imposed.

All persons must change some things during their lives. When a child becomes an adult he/she must change many customs and ways of thinking; this is a natural evolution, just as he must change his teeth, the curls of his hair, etc. But one does not change identity: one remains oneself for one's entire life. Indeed, to have to renounce some elements of one's particular identity generates great trauma, as when someone discovers that his parents are not his natural mother and father. In general, damage is inflicted upon one's identity by limiting or depriving a person with regard to some important element. Forced changes of customs, tradition, language or social structure are undoubtedly acts of coercion against individuals and groups.

We assume that the reason for this is the very close connection between identity and the person as the basis and center of human rights. Here the subject of rights is not only the individual person, but the collectivity, which in our supposition is the ethnic group. Hence, the sense of personal identity leads to the problem of group identity. What is a group?

Ethnic Groups

We approach the group in the same phenomenological manner used on the concept of identity above. The group exists, with its distinctive style of life, language, special style and color of clothing, ecological environment, products, and social structure. The many examples of real ethnic groups are easy to identify and to distinguish. One does not need to know where they are from, but only to see them; one does not know how they were formed or when, but only accepts them. They are there, and they are many. But note: this concept fits not only Indians, Africans, Basques, or people from Tyrol; it is a quite general phenomenon. People constitute groups and are seen to live in them when they fulfill all the characteristics which anthropologists attribute to true ethnic groups.

One issue is empirical and must be resolved empirically, namely, when does an ethnic group exist? For the answer we depend upon anthropologists and ethnologists. Ania Petersons[10] provides a good summary of the different approaches to interpreting the existence of groups; many more recent studies deal with this concept and modify it.

Philosophers, however, consider the concept itself. First, it must be separated from the traditional concept of class. This is generally understood as an horizontal stratification on the basis of one's personal income and is statistically and economically clear. But in reality men generally live not "in" a class but in a group, which may not coincide exactly with a class. The group concept is opposed to the vertical one; it is pluridimensional or total and covers man as a whole in his material, emotional and spiritual dimensions. One intersects with people of many different classes. Further, class is characterized by mobility; but even though one can easily trespass the level of his or her class, one cannot do so with regard to the group. Of course, some times a class (read, "high class") could consider itself and function as a group, but this is not generally the case. Ordinarily, a person has a group and lives with artists, politicians, intellectuals, etc. This takes in other people, workers, authorities, etc., with whom one identifies: to be in a group is to identify with its members.

In these examples it is clear that it is not the limits or the contrast to other groups which cause the cohesion of a group. We develop our personality in a real human context, which is the complete realization of our life. This is Barth's concept of group, and it has two principal advantages. One is that it is phenomenological and allows for an analysis of the concrete situation as the form in which one identifies oneself within the group. This is not merely a question of membership. As Ania Peterson points out, Barth[11] attends to boundaries because his approach is experimental; but he goes deeply into the fundamental reasons which support human endeavour in this particular situation. The second advantage is that his analysis can be complemented with new elements found in other circumstances.

At the present time, special emphasis is placed upon the ecological element and linguistic structures. The views of Spicer,[12] based upon a theory of opposition between groups, seem inadequate in that they seek an explanation based upon a negative concept. Opposition is only the "other's view"; it cannot produce anything without the reaction or positive interpretation of the group which is living, reacting and constructing its life. Since in this process the human group generates a culture, the concept and issue of group becomes that of the ethnic group.

Perhaps we could agree with the view of De Vos[13] that consistency of behavior enables "others to place an individual or a group in some given social category." But it is not only the consistency of behavior which generates identity. This is based upon the group itself with all its components; its divergent as well as its common behavior, its limits and trends, all are elements or cultural objects which support the identity of the group.

The new concept of ethnic-group arises from two factors: the human group and identity. Without identification of its members there would not be a group. This type of identity differs from personal identity. Behavior, technology, spiritual values and language are common or similar. But in addition to these objective elements there is sense of unity and of solidity which strongly binds individuals to the group. This is a community of values, customs, traditions, thought, social relations, scale of values, sensibility, historical heritage, and environmental interrelation; all these support what we call "group-identity." When all these elements come together there is "ethnic-identity."

In real life, however, this ethnic identity does not exist; it is a collective concept. In reality there exists only the personal identity of the members of the ethnic group. How can one explain that what does not exist is the strongest tie between men, more consistent and lasting than any other? The answer must be that the human person and the human group are in some form the same thing. There exists a bipolar reality, a natural or essential continuity which from the person or individual makes the group, and from the group makes the person: this is a co-constitution. The group has and develops a particular culture; the members of the group are active members of this construct. The group is a "whole" of persons, and nothing else, while persons are necessarily a group and have a group-identity. This statement can be proved only by experience, and may be only a phenomenon of our times.

An ethnic group possesses a special wholeness and is able to satisfy all human needs in the multiple circumstances of life: birth, wedding, death, social status and work. It enables the individual to respond personally with direct communication and emotional sensitivity. The ethnic group can perdure across centuries through changes in culture, states and political regions, as for example, with Israel, the Russian nationalities, and ancient pre-Columbian groups in Latin America. Though their culture may not be the same after four centuries, they retain their actual identity with a consciousness of continuity and spiritual unity with the past. The historical is not the most important aspect of this identification, but only one of many. Instead, consciousness of the value of their self, of their world vision and of their human relations is the true core of the significance and transcendence of their identity.

This is the case of the Basques in Spain, the Scots in Britain, the Bretons in France, and of Ulster in Ireland. Perhaps "ethnicity" is the highest expression of the human community precisely because its roots are not geographical, historical or economic, but anthropological in the philosophical sense, that is, gnoseological and metaphysical.

Ethnicity is not only a consciousness; indeed sometimes it is not conscious, for people can ignore the foundation of their special uniqueness in choosing the elements of their distinctive identification. However, the objectivity of this differential character can be verified experimentally with respect to external cultural elements and to some extent as regards such deeper components as psychological attitudes, aesthetic taste, spiritual predilections and the interpretation of one's world.

Does this second perspective restrict the broader concept of the mobile and evolutionary structure of the "self"? Ethnicity is not material because it is so close to the person itself and to conscience, yet it is not a spiritual thing either. It emerges from the dialogue between the "ego" and one's proximate situation, between the personality of individuals and collective needs. In ethnic identity, the group plays the role of a collective personality in response to the individual's and people's demands, as well as to pressure from surrounding forces.

Relation Between the Person and the Group

Now we must focus upon the third concept identified above, namely, the "relation" between the individual and the group. Without more clarity on this it will be impossible to answer any fundamental questions about the development and modernization of groups. Besides it will provide greater insight into the relation between personal and individual being: the individual with his unique and incomparable specificity, the group surrounded by the real world with its temporal changes and the interplay with other men and other groups.

The linguistic form for stating this relation is the pronoun "we." "We" are thinking, "we" have this tradition, "we" are . . . etc. "We" embraces the group and me: the group and I are thinking . . . we have the same customs, opinions, communications, means, etc. There are three poles in this relation: the cultural object, the collective-subject and the individual-subject. There is an identification between me and the group; this is the first level of identity. But on the other hand, the group does not really exist; it is nothing more than a collection of the individuals which compose it. It is a very special form of identity, different from 2=2 where there are two identical objects: two and two. In the situation of identity there is no "equivalence" as there is in $(5+4) = (6+3)$, which is a proportion with four objects. In the case of ethnicity there is one-object and one-subject (with three relations). In reality there is a third object-subject: "the others," for the others do exist.

A. I am declaring my openness to the others, my "human-transcendence" to the other men. My life is intimately mingled with the others in a unity that is true, unique and an absolutely distinct type of identity. I am myself, but the others of the group are also myself. This could be true only if ethnicity could satisfy all that concerns human life. The others are a set of people with whom my own existence is auto-extended and shaped. This is what we call ethnic identity. It is extended to everyone of those who form a limited group. They live in this specific place and time, with a specific economy and culture. I am among them in all that; I know them more than does anyone else in this world, just as they understand me more than anyone else.

This is a true relation of identity, but not in a static sense; it is dynamic. I go to the people, and they come to me in a process of identification that is a generative relation. My self-gift to others generates a group identity and the response of the community creates my own identity. Again it is a case of co-building, possible only because the others are also subjects or human persons. This is possible only in a very limited group, for the ethnic group is an expression of human limitation.

At this point one could ask: Can this argument be extended to all men? Surely it can, but very abstractly and not in a practical form. The huge world of men is very distant, quite different, very anonymous and constituted of a large quantity of cultural objects which do not mean anything to me.

B. This last factor leads us to the second of the three relations, namely, that between me and the culture. We must envisage the linkage between man and all the cultural objects with which the community is dealing. I cannot speak about culture because from inside the group there is no limit to the culture, no definition, but only a specific set of cultural objects that the community, with its individuals, have built or adopted from other groups or received from the past.

Generally, anthropologists agree that a culture is the product of a group, but this is not very exact. The "culture is a group," or better, a group is a specific "culture." We will see this later as the third relation. The culture "is" the group in the sense that the culture is another abstract concept which we do not want to adopt, for we are dealing with the set of cultural objects which a group has produced. A member of the community knows those objects whether material such as houses, weavings and pottery, or social objects such as language, education and technologies.

When people say "we," usually it is not a generic word stating a plurality, but an accurate utterance of identity. "We the Cackchiqueles" or "We the Mames" expresses this along with the geographical, ecological, biological and social connotations which support the mysterious reality of the group and its culture. Cultural objects, such as language and customs, are always related to the statements of identity, with its ambivalent and ambiguous relation to the elements which distinguish the group. Two analogous concepts refer to the cultural objects: personal identity related to the individual experience and ethnic identity related to group experience. In both cases, the basic support of the relations is the person; it is a cultural thing.

The similarity is very close. In both relations, it seems that the subject can choose between assuming a cultural object or substituting it for another if the circumstances and the overall good demands it. The relation of identity in this second kind of identification is not so important as in the first (as changing the style of clothes as contemporary fashion presses forward). Theoretically, all cultural elements could be substituted, but that is not the case in reality. Persons and groups develop their behavior very slowly. Cultural objects can be incorporated more or less into the consciousness of one's identity and consequently generate or weaken resistance to their removal. Individuals of the group can play an extremely important function in introducing new cultural objects without their being refused as contrary to its identity. This second relation could be the path to peaceful introduction of cultural elements from different cultures.

C. The third relation is the trend that induces the group to choose this particular cultural element in place of another. The poles of the relation are the group, on the one hand, and the set of cultural objects, on the other. The group identifies itself with these cultural elements, not as a receiver, but as a creator. This is one's particular culture because one's group has built it and is still building today. As we noted before, this is a co-building by both the individual and the collectivity. Why do two different ethnic groups choose different ecological niches: the one farming and the other cattle raising? If the highest criteria were economic the response to the environment would have to be the same. Of many recent studies in this field we shall cite only a few: S.M. Michael,[14] Pedro Ramet,[15] Noam Chomski,[16] Donna Birdwell-Pheasant,[17] M. Gaborieu,[18] Joyce N. Chinen,[19].

Anthropologists, ethnologists and sociologists usually study the way people take their decisions, without considering why they took them. Mechanisms of decision-making are internal to the group and without any apparent reason. If we do not agree with Pavlov's theory of mechanical or biological reflexes at this point we must open some space for human creativity.

The third relation of ethnic identity, between the group and the culture, directs our attention to the production of culture. The group performs a demiurgic function amid individuals in the world. Everyone knows the uncertainty and fears we suffer in facing the world. The group, with its previous experience mediates the understanding of the world and protects against its dangers. That is the first pattern of mediation: between the person and the natural world. We must deal with it and we need the surrounding group in order to be able to do so.

The second relation of mediation between the group and the world is to make sense of it. Man is searching for meaning and every signification needs a symbol. The second demiurgical function of the relation of group to culture is that of symbolization: the group gives the world the power to signify. The production of culture is the production of symbols, as the group allows us to understand the world through a chain of symbols in symbolic understanding. The creation of culture is the creation of symbols which provide particular "interpretations" of the world.

But the group is nothing more than this particular "set of persons"; consequently the group is the "demiurge" of creation. It brings out old meanings and fixes new ones. The demiurgic function of the culture creates a structure of symbols whose significance is common to the members of the ethnic community. Of course, the products of civilization are quite useful and productive, such as houses, work instruments, language, music; they fulfill the needs of ordinary existence. But they are symbolic also and create the meaning of the whole universe. This meaning, as it is created by the members of the group, is generally unknown to the other groups, just as others' cultures do not have their complete significance for our group.

Generally, cultural objects obtained from a different group may have a practical function and can be useful, but they lack the semantic implication of our cultural objects. That, I feel, is the root of many misunderstandings of the group. We want to give them a set of cultural objects (read "developments"), but the group does not want to accept them because they are not significant to the group. This is the social-cost of so-called "change": is it worth it? To them it is not. One would not substitute an object that lacks meaning to him for one that has meaning. One would not integrate his life into something devoid of semantic implication, when one is able to create something with more significance.

Language is an external thing, universal, generic and open to all people; in contrast the meta-language of the internal meaning for the group is esoteric, collective, local, exclusive and suitable to this community. The language of things does not develop ties between people and make the material and natural worlds human; the human world is a spiritual one built by persons through rational cultural products.

The group brings to the individual the opportunity to appropriate his or her own surroundings and to create a new world. One person alone cannot create a culture, but this can be done by a group. This esoteric communication establishes a constant and common support for individual life in the context of the community and separates this portion of society--one's physical, emotional and spiritual world--from other groups and peoples. As with every other language, communication within the group has two directions, from the group to the person and from the person to the group. This dialogue may be broken by a particular individual who does not agree in some fundamental issue with the community and leaves it to go to a bigger world.

The understanding of the world through the culture is the means for man to appropriate or interpret his world and destiny. Things known and verified become part of man himself and constitute the truth of the world. Man is a being open to the world, but his main way of reaching the world is through his intellect and emotions, that is, his culture. Consequently all cultural objects are integrated in the creation of the world. Indeed, the bridge by which a man goes to the world, as well as the structure of his world, is his culture.

The pattern of a group and consequently the difference between two ethnic groups is not only economic, social or technical, but semantic; it is a difference of worlds. The struggle generated at the frontier between two groups is usually not a desire for conquest or a dispute about a piece of land for material advantage, but a struggle for significance and meaning. The acts and behavior, the values and laws of a strange group are meaningless; their symbols are semantically poor and devoid of relation to another world. The group can sometimes adopt a new cultural object in order to survive or have material benefits, but their meaning is lost. For generally it belongs to the meta-language of the other group and is out of the way, inaccessible, uneasy and meaningless.

Alienation from the Group

A citizen can leave the group and become involved in the vast world outside with a different scale of values, a different language and different technical knowledge. He thus alienates himself from his group. The alienated individual will not be able to be incorporated into the other group for precisely the same reason, namely, he does not understand the secret rules of the game of the new group, its unique meta-language. He will be forever condemned to suffer permanent marginalization.

Of course, he can learn to use one of the conventional languages of general or international culture at an inter-group level. He can live and produce at a superficial level; he can develop some practical but superficial substitute for an identity without the ability to grasp the deeper intensive meaning of the world or have real communication and share human partnership and concerns.

This person has lost his identity in his group, yet not his personal identity; the group alienates him, but he is not personally alienated. But at some level, however, he has suffered a decrease in his personality, losing contact with his community's identity and his integration into that world--which for him is the only real world. He can never substitue for this private and intimate dimension, even if it will be compensated for and covered by his broader, more general cultural improvement.

Abstractly and in principle the two cultural dimensions are absolutely compatible and could co-exist in the same man, so that the subject retains his former involvement with his group. In this case we would speak about higher and lower levels of identity or, more exactly, of different trends or paths. But to the man who loses the group's cultural view and its symbolic construction and appropriation of the world, the second situation is not enough. He needs a new group, but none will accept him. As anthropologists state, with few specific exceptions one cannot be integrated into a different ethnic or quasi-ethnic group. One of the conditions of sharing the identity of such a group is to be born into it.

This is our last insight in this matter and it leads us to the problem of the growth of the new generation of a group. To be born in-group means to turn into an adult in terms of that group. The process of rapid transformation of the new born is a process of identification of the person with the external world, the human world and the meaning which the group and the cultural symbols give to it. What happens when a young man faces the external world (in our case, the strange and dominating Spanish culture) and tries to interpret it? Education as an ethnological process of evolution for the person by which the culture transmits a language and economic technical skills is present in all societies; it cannot be distinguished from the process by which society survives and transforms itself.

The ethnic group has an education without schools and with no books, but it has other institutions which express and communicate local tradition and thought in a complete and formal fashion; it is a living education. To cite but one example, we can repeat the words of a young Maya theorician, Manuel Salazar Tetzaguic:[20] "I am plunged into the Cosmos. What benefit does this produce? I am a part of nature: animals are my brothers; I live with them. I look for ways to work in nature: to cultivate the maize, to build a house, to cut timber. All around there is a spirit; every man has a Nahual." The ethnic identity through its vision of the Cosmos sets the person and the group in a universe with a cosmic attitude reflecting his conception, with a literary tradition and oral communication, with hopes and fears, and with faith in the energies of nature: earth, mountains, woods, or peculiar ritual sites. In ethnic education traditional patterns are made manifest in linguistic formulae which are assimilated as components of one's identity.

Ethnic Education

For the young man, the fundamental structure given by ethnic education becomes his mental structure. During this period, a child develops the mental instruments to communicate with his fellows and neighbors, to organize his thoughts logically and to find the path to expression and creativity.

When the young man encounters Spanish culture at the elementary school, and with it a set of symbols which are meaningless from the point of view of his community, he experiences frustration and internal stress. He can learn the words mechanically and shape his behavior to the rules imposed by teachers, but he will never assimilate the spiritual content and the semantic values of the dominant culture.

The official intention to substitute Spanish as the national culture and to suppress one's ethnic worldview is not merely aggression; it is a real destruction of the biological, psychological and intellectual development the group begun and promoted by the new generation. At this point of our analysis we can understand why this is so, for the analysis has clarified some complex mechanism of the group's structure and of the ethnic identity.

Reflections

From this starting point we can draw some initial conclusions:

1. The ethnic group is not an accidental or secondary structure of human society because it concerns very intimate dimensions of the person.

2. Ethnicity is not a romantic idea to exhalt some particular human minority or the lore of some culture; it is a difficult and universal issue.

3. Ethnic identity is an expression of the fundamental right of the individual person and the human community to be free and creative.

4. Ethnic identity is an intellectual and gnoseological being, which is not primarily economic or political, but cultural.

5. We must recognize the existence of ethnicity and of ethnic identity instead of trying to change a people's culture.

6. We must develop these cultures and make clear the semantic values of the world they create.

7. We must deal with cultural pluralism to find an understanding between different ethnic groups.

8. Cultural pluralism is not a problem, but a fact.

9. Cultural pluralism is not opposed to unity because it merely brings out problems of understanding and of personal evolution; an official culture makes no sense.

10. The complex ethnic and personal identities have many levels, trends and areas of concern which overflow the limits of the group and imply intercultural bonds.

11. The promotion of people must not merely take place in a local culture which it disregards, but from that group's culture.

12. We must cooperate with persons in the local culture to develop the project of growth from within the community or region.

13. Development cannot be understood as the imposition of technical or commercial patterns, but as human understanding and adaptation and as the creation of meaning.

14. We must overcome the confusion between "differences" and "inequalities." Differences are free and creative; inequalities are unjust and oppressive. We must eliminate the inequalities and respect the differences.

Here, we would repeat the suggestion of the Mexican anthropologist Bonfil Batalla,[20] "We have restricted human values to the economic ones." We have assimilated the external elements of the culture and made people interiorize an inferiority complex about their culture. The human group is the source of cultural expression: all must begin from the group and their form of life.

Universidad Rafael Landivar
Guatemala, Guatemala

NOTES

*See Discussion IV.

1. Severo, Martinez: *La patria del Criollo* (Guatemala: Univ. de San Carlos, 1978).

2. Riccardo Falla, *El Quiche Rebelde* (Guatemala: Univ. de San Carlos, 1980).

3. Pope John Paul II, *Osservatore Romano* (Sept. 17, 1984).

4. Ortega Y Gasset, "Commentaire au Banquet de Platon," *Revue Philosophique*, 157 (1967), 145-64.

5. Martin Heidegger, *Nietzsche: Nihilism* (New York: Harper and Row, 1982).

6. Edmund Husserl, *Formal and Transcendental Logic* (The Hague: Nijhoff, 1969).

7. M. Carrither, S. Collins and S. Lukes (eds.), *The Category of Person* (Cambridge: Cambridge Univ. Press, 1986); Mary Douglas (ed.), *Food in the Social Order* (New York: Russell Sage Foundation, 1984).

8. Karl Jaspers, *Philosophy* (Chicago: Chicago Univ. Press, 1969), Vol. IV.

9. Paul Ricoeur, *The Conflict of Interpretations* (Albany: SUNY Press, 1982).

10. Ania Royce Peterson, *Ethnic Identity: Strategies of Diversities* (Bloomington: Indiana University Press, 1982).

11. Karl Jaspers, *Philosophy* (Chicago: Chicago Univ. Press, 1969), Vol. IV.

12. Edward Spicer, "Persistent Identity Systems," *Science*, 174 (1971), 795-800.

13. Peterson, *Ethnic Identity*.

14. S.M. Michael, "The Politization of the Ganaati Festival," *Social Compass*, 33 (1986).

15. Pedro Ramet, *Nationalism and Federalism in Yugoslavia, 1963-1983* (Bloomington: Indiana Univ. Press, 1984).

16. Noam Chomski, *Turning the Tide* (Boston: South End Press, 1986); "Middle East Terrorism and the American Ideological Lyte," in *Race and Class*, 28 (New York: Institute of Race Relations, 1986).

17. Pheasant Donna Birdwell, "Domestic Process in the Transition from Labor-flow to Cash-flow Enterprise in Belize," *Urban Anthropology*, 4 (1985).

18. M. Gaborieau, "Hierarchie sociale et mouvement de réforme," *Social Compass*, 33 (Belgium, 1986).

19. Joyce Chinen, "Working Wives and the Socio-economic Status of Ethnic Groups," *Humbolt Journal of Social Relations*, 12 (1984), 11.

20. José Manuel Salazar Tezaguic, "Los valores de la cultura Maya," in Dominican Seminar, May 23, 1986, Guatemala.

21. Guillermo Bonfill-Batalla, First National Congress on Cultures (Guatemala, Dec. 11-13, 1986), mnscr.

CHAPTER V

THE DEVELOPMENT OF

ETHNIC CONSCIOUSNESS

IN THE UNITED STATES

NEW DIRECTIONS IN RESEARCH AND POLICY

*JOHN KROMKOWSKI**

The development of ethnic consciousness in the United States during the 1960s raises interesting questions about cultural change in modern societies. Immigration and internal processes of cultural formation have shaped ethnic variety in the United States. In the 1960s analysis of ethnic phenomena erupted in many academic disciplines and has remained a recurring topic of social concern. Social interpretations of ethnicity and their attendant influence on cultural formation constitute philosophic problematics because they frequently influence popular political consciousness. Social interpretations are on-going features and processes of the American reality and regime. In some measure social interpretation and cultural formation contribute to the unexpected emergence of ethnic consciousness. But the emergence of ethnic consciousness significantly depends on insight into cultural change. Not the least of these findings are the power and passion of ethnic phenomena. These findings underscore the ontic importance and persistent relevance of ethnicity. An especially interesting dimension of ethnicity in pluralistic societies can be observed in community-based institutions in contemporary societies that are experiencing rapid change. Analysis at the community level of human interaction reveals the need for bonds of social solidarity. Such discoveries promote new pathways for thought which may inspire action that yields social justice at the intersection of cultures.

SOCIAL INTERPRETATION AND CULTURAL FORMATION

Two decades ago one could read confident political, social and economic forecasts about modern development. Progress through modernization would improve, if not transform, the limited expectations and achievements of traditional cultures. Industrialization, technological change, secularization, urbanization and efficient bureaucracies in the public and private sectors were the exalted engines of modern development. Rational, democratic institutional change would direct human consciousness and behavior.[1] Modernity would replace the "parochial localism" of tradition and ethnicity. Whereas ethnic consciousness and ethnic behavior were derived from traditional associations based in peasant experiences and rural communities, the modern project would enable humanity to establish new relationships with nature and among persons. Modernity would displace the foundations of traditional relationships with nature and within society which had been based upon rurality, status, craft, kinship, religious faith and practice.[2]

A few decades of rapid economic and political experiments and their consequences provoked critiques which, at first, were dismissed as symptoms of romantic nostalgia. Yet, persistent social and environmental trauma, debt and debilitation, as well as instances of utter social-cultural collapse and subsequent fundamentalist revolutions and ethno-religious revivals raised stronger doubts about the direction and expectations of modern development.[3] Today naive trust in modernity and romantic recoveries of tradition have given way to serious multi-disciplined inquiries into the dynamics and the essential characteristics of relations between modern and traditional cultures. Attendant questions about the development of ethnic consciousness, social interpretation and the cultural formation of multi-ethnic modern regimes are related to the search for new directions in theory and policy.[4]

Events such as the emergence and development of ethnic consciousness and social interpretations that included consciousness of ethnicity are signs of this theoretical problematic and practical reassessment. Cultural cooperation and cultural conflict brought on by modernization have become particularly interesting in multi-ethnic societies. In the United States such processes of cultural formation have oscillated between national, regional and local approaches to diversity and unity.[5] Similarly, the ethnic cultural legacies of the founders and of the immigrants and their respective descendants have induced mainstream patterns of behavior and consciousness varying from isolation and exclusion to imitation and absorption.[6]

In some fashion the prevailing mechanism of cultural formation of all regimes and the foundational articulations of culture not only influence behavior but shape, if not create, the interpretations of socio-cultural realities which legitimate a regime. Regimes are sustained by the transmission of cultural legacies through various processes. Regimes maintain a social reality and provide members with the experience of cultural continuity. Yet, from time to time regimes are required to address challenges brought on by change in the size, composition, location and economic activity of the population. Other factors induce change such as the waning of cultural credibility and such utterly contingent factors as a disaster, a discovery, a heroic practice, the retheoretization of a problematic, or an unexpected and amazing event. Such experiences in the 1960's, accompanying the discovery and practice of ethnic activities, proclaimed the need for the retheoretization of ethnic phenomena and provoked passionate, social, political and economic action.[7] Consciousness of ethnic variety constitutes a powerful source of change. Its salience induced an unexpected dimension into the analysis, explanation and interpretation of cultural formation in the United States.

Periods of economic and political change and the attendant reformulation of the foundational sources of order are especially interesting
because of their consequences for persons and societies. Such moments of
profound change offer a rare opportunity to observe crucial phases of
social and cultural development. Yet, such dramatic episodes of cultural
change and new relations between cultures require underscoring the
perduring significance of the moral disposition of hope for the human
condition and the importance of many disciplines to the search for wisdom and understanding in the face of baffling diversity and awesome
surprises. Few circumstances and events of cultural and paradigmatic
shift as well as changes in social formation are more demanding of such
dispositions and virtues than those in which one's personal and group
identity is challenged. To be engaged in the lived experience of such a
process is to be invited forcefully to reexamine one's personal identity as
well as the dense and differentiated symbols that constitute the social,
political and cultural relationships that are shared with others.

At the experiental level, social change and the development of
ethnic consciousness in the United States are related to the massive migration to cities.[8] As a migrant receiving regime until the 1920s, the
problematic of cultural change was an ongoing drama in the United
States. However, an especially interesting series of convergent changes
occurred during the decades that led to the 1960s. The precursors of the
major cultural reconfiguration of the 1960s were the massive and auto-
mated thrust of modernization that transformed economic production.
Modernization also included a resettlement of the economic order and
the empowerment of a managerial regime. Driven by complimentary
political, cultural and economic interests after World War II, this regime
expanded. Its fiscal and economic productivity accommodated large
segments of society. The postwar cultural accord and the economic and
political agreement to pursue production and consumption in metropoli-
tan settlements linked by highways yielded the stability of the 1950s that
fueled the dreams of the 1960s.

The unexpected development of ethnic consciousness began to
percolate in this context. Ethnicity erupted in the 1960s prior to the reform of immigration laws and the influx of new immigrant populations.
Thus, the emergence of ethnicity in the United States was not forecast
by either economic analysis or academic explanations. Consequently, the
unanticipated salience and efficacy of ethnicity provoked the reexamination of the processes and components of cultural formation and development.

In broadest outline, this study examines the development of ethnic
consciousness. It weighs the evidence for the emergence of ethnicity,
explains the nature of contemporary ethnicity, and assesses the development of ethnic consciousness and the consciousness of ethnicity as an
aspect of the contemporary America. These findings reveal characteristics of cultural formation that influence the entire regime. Contemporary
cultural development and the fresh interpretation of social reality sug-

gested by the persistence of diversity and the discovery of ethnicity reveals human and cultural needs and opportunities that have been eclipsed by less complicated paradigms for analyses and approaches to the constitution of human settlement, production and consumption. The findings suggest the relevance and perhaps naturalness of community-based ethnic institutions. These sources of social solidarity and the agenda of leaders of neighborhood-based organizations in a multi-ethnic society cast new light on the importance of local level experiences and their normative claims, as well as upon their political relationship to social-cultural research and the economic and social policies derived therefrom in large-scale modern regimes.

ETHNIC CONSCIOUSNESS

Its Initiation

Oscar Handlin was among the formative academic interpreters of the cultural dynamics during the post World War II era. His vision did not shape contemporaneous decisions, but it stimulated the emergence and discussion of ethnicity in America. Handlin described the initial project of his 1951 Pulitzer Prize study, *The Uprooted*: "Once I thought to write a history of the immigrants in America. Then I discovered that the immigrants were American history."[9] Handlin's thesis was attractive to post World War II students, many of whom were the children of the uprooted. Written from the heights of Boston and Harvard, this work constituted a curiously inclusive yet eminent and timely challenge to the prevailing "non-immigrant" and mainstream interpretation of cultural formation for the American reality. His argument for the ongoing process of immigration proposed a worldview which could displace the ideal of an expected assimilation of all into the host culture. Handlin's evidence supported the claim that the stability, primacy, integrity and special prerogatives of America were not simply static nor solely foundational. He expressed a credible critique of the monocultural image of America. By the mid-1950s assimilation was no longer entirely credible. The notion that the American reality was more than a black-white racial dilemma resonated among the children of the uprooted. Anyone who thought about the issue could not ignore the cultural terms and its imperative--the recognition of persistent diversity.

In restrospect it seems clear that an epoch of historical consciousness was ending. The urban crises of the 1960s exposed the scandal of the monocultural mythology and the bankruptcy of racialist approaches. The United States reaped the legacy of searing social divisions that had been resolved unsatisfactorily after the Civil War. The economic well-being temporarily achieved by the practices of recruiting and then excluding European peasants, rather than incorporating African-Americans and indigenous peoples into the political economy, social anatomy, and common citizenship could not be sustained. Racialist mythologies were no longer viable substitutes for the social formation needed to assure consensus and the legitimacy of the regime. Modernization intensified the need for appropriate cultural formation and *a fortiori* accelerated the search for remedies and therapies for the disparities and discontinuities that had been ignored and neglected.

In 1963 Moynihan and Glazer's *Beyond the Melting Pot*[10] extended Handlin's critique by delineating the political importance of ethnic consciousness. Moreover, this analysis legitimated the persistence of ethnicity and certified the reality of multiethnic variety in America. Their celebration of "the valued variants of a common humanity" shifted the dominant and prevailing language of political analysis, social formation and self-interpretation which had shaped the American consciousness since before the large scale immigration to American cities. The American foundational culture which inspired the social imagination for over seven decades began to give way to the social reality and a new mythology. However, Moynihan and Glazer's normative exhortation 'to value diversity,' expressed in the sociological jargon of the day, would require a thoughtful and profound reexamination of the rationale and the mechanisms of cultural formation. The language of social interpretation, and in some respects the social reality, had changed profoundly. The search for public policy and cultural practice shook the very foundations of the regime.

A new phase of the process of defining policy and culture began with the events of Selma (1965); its legacy was embodied in the Kerner Commission Report (1968). As the civil order floundered, new analytics for public policy and cultural formation proliferated. On the existential level events included: migration to and from the urban neighborhoods of older industrial cities, popular cultural ferment and political violence focused on foreign and domestic policy. On the interpretative level re-theoretization included: the renaming of populations, proliferation of radical and critical methodologies, and frequent and divisive critique of institutions. Practice and theory swirled throughout the country. Nonetheless, the discovery of ethnicity born of necessity by this 'nation of immigrants' produced a crisis of growth that reveal primordial realities which transcended the content and context of traditional divisions of the American people--white, black, native-born, rural, urban as well as economic and ideological notions of class. By the beginning of the next decade, to become an ethnic, as we shall see, was a way of becoming American. In some respects, the popular recovery of citizenship in a managerial state, which presumed the end of ideology and that political action was not only an illusion, became suddenly and amazingly possible at the local level in community-based institutions--the social invention which created the social entity known as ethnicity.

Its Development

In the early 1970s Rudy Vecoli initiated and chronicled telling changes in historical interpretation and cultural consciousness among descendants of immigrants. His articles "European Americans: From

Immigrants to Ethnics" and "Ethnicity: A Neglected Dimension of American History"[11] announced the new consciousness of ethnicity. Vecoli's historical works along with the sociological findings of Andrew Greeley and William McCready, the romantic manifestos of Michael Novak, as well as the pragmatic cajoling and advocacy of Msgr. Geno C. Baroni and Irving M. Levine, sponsored in part by the Ford and/or Rockefeller Foundations, produced a new language of social thought that included the ethnic factor. These efforts generated a new élan in the discussion of urban and cultural policy. Today, almost three decades into the process, the emergence of ethnicity, ethnic consciousness and changes in ethnic mix brought on by the latest wave of immigration are reshaping the social imagination of the United States. It can be argued that American culture for the decades to come will be shaped by its capacity to discover and articulate meaning in, from and through this new peoplehood. An ongoing feature of this dynamic will be discovered at the neighborhood level. The multi-ethnic cultures that are emerging at the intersection of the new immigration and the new consciousness of ethnicity that emerged in the 1970s is slowly making its way into the process of cultural formation.

The claim that ethnicity and consciousness of ethnicity in the United States of America did not exist prior to the 1960s could be supported by the paucity of references to the topic in scholarly analysis and popular publications. In 1973 Richard Kolm's *Bibliography of Ethnicity and Ethnic Groups*[12] was a pioneering, comprehensive effort of only 451 entries. Moreover, a case can be made for the claim that prior to the 1960s the words "ethnic" and "ethnicity" were used exclusively by ethnographers and ethnologists to analyze phenomena and peoples at anthropological sites--'exotic', non-modern, traditional societies.

Yet, by the mid 1980s the magnitude and frequency of references to topics related to ethnicity in various academic disciplines concerned with the analysis of America (as well as by the mass media and in popular usage) had stunningly increased. Scholarly literature and popular articles on the ethnic factor in psychological adjustments, family life, patterns of behavior and community structures abound. Consciousness of ethnicity had shifted from the margin to the mainstream of contemporary America. Evidence of this growth can be documented in various ways. In 1985, using the Library of Congress, the National Center for Urban Ethnic Affairs (NCUEA) compiled a bibliography of over 14,000 items related to contemporary American immigrant-ethnic groups. Its content analysis of newspapers and magazines revealed steady increases in references to things ethnic. Patterns of ethnic-group political affinity in campaigns persisted at the local level. Moreover, the ethnic factor extended to new techniques of electoral polling and data analysis. Ethnicity became a regular feature of the political culture thirty years after mainstream political power had declared its demise.

Far from declining, ethnic awareness was fostered in various ways. The publication in 1976 of Miller's *Comprehensive Bibliography for the*

Study of American Minorities[13] allows us to measure the scale of "ethnic studies" literature and the inclusion of ethnicity in elementary and secondary textbooks. This two-volume work contains 29,300 entries. The United States Department of Education funded courses and teacher materials on ethnic studies, including black studies amd bilingual-bicultural education. Concerns about national origin, ethnic discrimination and strategies for assuring remedies related to equal protection and due processes that were denied because of ethnicity became ever-present in the legal culture. Official governmental acknowledgement of ethnicity emerged into the public 'information industry' when the 1980 U.S. Census asked the question: "What is this person's ancestry"? Thus, the self-identification of ethnicity of persons, e.g., Polish-American, German-American, Chinese-American, Irish-American, African-American and Mexican-American entered the data-bases in contemporary America. Such entries enabled the development of ethnic niche markets in the private sector as well as electoral and policy constituencies for public enterprises.

The ancillary sources about ethnicity in The Gale Reference Series expanded its 1976 *Guide to Ethnic Information*[14] from one to two volumes in 1983. A typical entry for an American Ethnic group indicates the scope and range of ethnicity. Data categories include addresses, telephone numbers and names for the following sources: Embassies, United Nations Missions, Information Officers, Tourist and Travel Offices, Fraternal Organizations, Professional Organizations, Public Affairs Organizations, Cultural and Educational Organizations, Foundations, Charitable Mutual Aids, Religious Organizations, Research Centers and Special Institutions, U.S. Government Programs (esp. the U.S. Library of Congress' Special Subject Collections), Museums, Special Collections, Newspapers and Newsletters, Magazines, Radio and Television Programs, Banks and Trade Organizations, Festivals, Fairs, Celebrations, Airline Offices, Ship Lines, Bookdealers and Publishers. The typical entry includes a bibliography of materials published in English by foreign governments for distribution in the United States and a list of books and audio-visual material about ethnic people in America produced and published in the United States. Consciousness of ethnicity, generated and sustained through information, seems then to be thriving in the United States.

A *U.S. News & World Report* article, "Why Ethnic Press is Alive and Growing" (Oct. 29, 1984), explored the vitality of contemporary ethnic newspapers, providing a glimpse into the contemporary ethnic phenomena. The articles claim that ethnic papers are established to preserve the traditions and networks of older ethnic groups or to serve as an organizing and communications link between newer immigrants. One thing is clear: the readership of ethnic papers is both diverse and growing. The *News* article indicates that "Scores of them, many printed in foreign languages, serve about 8 million subscribers nationwide and have an estimated readership of six times that number." NCUEA's analysis of the format and scope of these newspapers reveals that they are as diverse as the various audiences they serve. Some are very political in nature, while others focus much more on the humanities. Some have a national or even international scope, while others focus their attention on city-wide or neighborhood-wide concerns. Other characteristics such as size, frequency and circulation methods vary considerably from paper to paper. The following profiles of publications illustrate their scope and types: Political, Ethnic Cultural, Ethno-Neighborhood, Fraternal, Multi-Ethnic, and New Immigrant.

- *The Ukrainian Weekly*, published since 1933 by the Ukrainian National Association, carries articles ranging in scope from the coverage of local events to commentary on national and international policy questions. Many of its articles are political in nature and focus almost exclusively on events which relate to the Ukrainian community.

- *Polish American Voice* is published monthly in Buffalo, N.Y. Its articles focus on various areas including politics, the humanities, leisure entertainment and local events. Although its readership extends well beyond the greater Buffalo area, its advertising indicates that the local Polish community is of primary importance to its publishers.

- *The Slavic Village Voice* is a free tabloid distributed twice monthly to Cleveland's near southeast side communities. Although a few of its articles focus on topics of national or international scope, most center heavily on what is happening in the local community. Because of this neighborhood orientation, many of the articles are multiethnic in character or not ethnic at all.

- *The Polish Falcon*, much like *The Ukrainian Weekly*, is an ethnic newspaper distributed as the official publication of a national fraternal organization, The Polish Falcons of America. The articles, which focus almost exclusively on the interests of the Polish community, range from politics to athletics, to human interest stories, to events. Much of the material contained in this paper relates specifically to the present organization.

- *Northwest Ethnic News*, affiliated with the Ethnic Heritage Council of the Pacific Northwest, is very multi-ethnic in character. Distributed primarily in Seattle, this paper's articles focus mainly on the cultures and traditions of the wide range of ethnic groups in the area. In addition to a variety of articles, it publishes a monthly calendar of events.

One characteristic seems common to these and other ethnic newspapers: they are flourishing because they address needs and interests in areas not covered by the mass media. *US News* quotes James Tinney of Howard University, "There'll be a place for these papers as long as there is a majority press that doesn't fully cover the needs of ethnic people, and that is likely to be a long time."

Another assessment appeared in the *Northwest Ethnic News*. Mayor Charles Royer of Seattle expressed the sentiments common among ethnic citizens:

> We are now a destination for people from every corner of the world, people who come hoping to find new opportunity, new freedom, or just safety for their children. Languages never heard on our streets are now common there. Vietnamese farmers and Hmong textile designers now share the stalls at the Pike Place Market with Italians, Filipinos, Irish, Germans and Swedes who have been there for generations. The blend of all these voices in the morning air is something as old as the market, as new as the ink in the morning paper. There is always something missing in that morning paper. It tells us a lot about this moment in time, but precious little about how we came to be here. It reveals much about the troubles the world's people are enduring, but nothing of the priceless lessons some part of humanity may already have learned that might show the way out of the trouble.

The lessons that Mayor Royer points to are the essence of the multi-ethnic cultural reality of the United States. The need to preserve and to explore such meanings is what brought ethnic papers into being. Yet a deeper phenomenological probe into the reality of ethnicity indicates additional dimensions of the development of ethnic consciousness running parallel to the aforementioned evidence of ethnicity.

Its Causes

Ample evidence from a variety of sources for the emergence of ethnicity in America suggests that a few currents strongly influenced this shift in cultural development. Such influences include: Post World War II attention to the barbarity of regimes which violated ethnic groups' rights, the subsequent arrival of new immigrants, and the reform of immigration policy in the United States. The political climate and economic attraction of a strong, growing and mobile country-economy fostered the hope for cosmopolitan cultural development in the liberal and progressive imagination. Moreover, the national communications systems energized awareness and participation in the Civil Rights movement, which exposed the lack of equal protection and due process and cultural-ethnic equality in the rural South and in the entrenched ethnic political machines of the urban North. The ethnicization of television reporting and situation comedies brought ethnic variety into the living rooms of mainstream households. The mass processes of cultural formation reported the epochal change, and this reportage shaped the common fund of shared images and metaphors. By the mid-70s it was clear that the American reality was far from homogenized.

The assimilationist and segregationist models of cultural formation and social interpretation were obviously inappropriate to the American reality and its existential variety. However, meaningful, credible and realistic cultural formation required more than alternative modes of ethnic analysis and creative methods of multi-ethnic articulation. The social reality would not be molded into the prevailing explanations. Thus consciousness of the emergence and the persistence of ethnicity emerged as a feature of the American reality. This phenomenon provoked practical scholarly and popular ambivalence and ambiguity. Such dissonance could be expected during a period of intense social and paradigmatic change. The multi-ethnic mass culture, the homogenized mass existence, the enclave cultures and proponents of change, both the modern and traditional, interacted and clashed. The experiences of ethnic consciousness that persisted and perdured at the neighborhood level of lived experience and the growing and easily measured national phenomena of cultural diversity and consciousness of ethnicity should not be simply equated. The ethnic consciousness of persons that constitute ethnic groups in America warrants the consciousness of ethnicity. But consciousness of ethnicity may be fruitfully viewed as an interpretive category--an aspect of the neo-analytics employed for theoretic and perhaps ideological discovery--used in social inquiry and for cultural interpretation. These distinctions and differentiations of experiences and dimensions of the American social reality had been eclipsed in most earlier American cultural formation and the standard modes of cultural-social analysis. Research that shaped the cultural policy of the regime and determined processes of cultural formation were confronted and confounded by the salience of ethnicity on each of these levels. Moreover, intensity and magnitude of both phenomena varied for context and time.

On the experiential level, ethnicity and ethnic group differences varied, they did not vanish. The persistence of various cultures in the American regime required forms of analysis and explanation that acknowledged the theoretic and practical aspects of ethnic phenomena and the locus of such phenomena. The theoretic search for understanding ethnicity must be derived from careful observation of persons and their institutional practices because ethnicity in many respects is a contextual phenomenon. Thus, realism that is true-to-context ought to drive inquiry into the essential features of ethnicity. Among the variety of contexts available, the analysis of local experiences are especially meaningful. The practical and verifiable consequences of local contexts and the politics of a specific time and place coincide with the ground and processes of essentially ethnological findings. An inquiry of this sort addresses the reality of inter-ethnic and intra-ethnic concord and conflict among and between ethnic populations, and finally the relationship of a locality to the larger mechanisms of social, economic and political order. Overwhelming evidence from a variety of regimes and periods of history confirms that ethnic differences are a passionate arena of personal conflict and group mobilization. Ethnicity has the capacity to generate the intensity of hatred required to wage protracted violence and destruction. Thus, peaceful resolution of such conflict is profoundly important. However, ethnicity appears to be an exceedingly complex political factor because of its permeability into social, religious, cultural, economic and political as well as private and personal realms. Thus multi-factored issues which in their own right are fraught with conflict and contention, as well as uncertainty, and indeterminacy, are usually exacerbated and made even more complex by ethnic factors and spirited rhetoric which imputes, implies, invokes and evokes ethnic passion.

On both the theoretic and practical levels ethnicity poses basic questions about the ordering center of community life and *a fortiori* about the personal identity and group praxis that are shaped and constituted by such social, cultural, economic and political relationships that become charged with ethnically powerful incantations and exhortations.

DIMENSIONS AND PRINCIPLES OF ETHNIC STUDIES

Prior to elaborating other implications of the discovery of ethnicity and consciousness of ethnicity as a political force in American culture, our understanding of ethnic phenomena can be sharpened by an examination of various elements that are included in the study of ethnicity. The emergence of ethnicity in the academic, scientific literature is confirmed by the following:

G. Carter Bentley's *Ethnic and Nationality: A Bibliographic Guide*[15] includes 308 annotated and 2029 unannotated items published through 1979. This scholarly collection of only English language materials includes: 1) ethnic studies on the basis of its nonanalytic nature, 2) materials of the sort found in Miller's *Bibliography*, i.e., biographies, autobiographies, ethnic literature, dance, drama, folklore, individual or group ethnographies, 3) studies aimed at legislative or administrative questions which evaluate public policies and tend to be valuable sources of data. Bentley arrays the scientific materials in Table I. This reference key indicates the range and scope of the ethnic factor in the sciences of person and society.

Another body of humanistic and historical inquiry into American ethnicity was produced under the direction of the editors of the *Harvard Encyclopedia of American Ethnic Groups*. They recommended the checklist found in Table II which served as an outline of elements for the history of the 116 ethnic groups included in the collection. An introductory essay includes another catalogue of elements of ethnicity. These criteria, found in Table III, may be regarded as essential aspects of American ethnicity. The combination of essential characteristics and the historical checklist are the components of the "history of peoples" and constitutive of 'The American ethnique.'

The Harvard collection of ethnic historical narratives implies a shared historical experience and cultural identity. Such historical narratives facilitate the shaping of a form of consciousness based in the 'historio-folkloric' ethnic criteria and social, economic, political and demographic categories that are deemed relevant. However, the stunning absence of *the neighborhood* as a characteristic of ethnicity among the criteria and categories undermines the veracity of the entire analysis. Nonetheless, in terms of the consciousness of ethnicity, the publication of the encyclopedia as a scholarly and prestigious synthesis of group histories is an important milestone in the process of incorporating ethnicity into cultural formation. The 116 ethnic group narratives suggest a new meaning and order to American cultural development. Inasmuch as such historical statements become shared objects communicated within and about these histories and their cultural production, they generate and constitute a coherent body of new answers to primordial questions of identity and of affiliations on the part of the American population. Personal identity as well as the imputed record of participation in the group process of becoming an American may be elucidated and legitimized by the Harvard canon of historical scholarship. Such histories, along with the thematic essays listed in Table IV, fashion a quasi-national unified, yet pluralistic, interpretation of cultural formation and development in the United States.

The ideologies of cultural isolation and assimilation are transcended in the historiographic synthesis developed by the contributors and editors of the *Harvard Encyclopedia of Ethnic Groups in America*.[16] Thus in the *HEAEG* and in the scholarly works compiled in G. Carter Bentley's bibliography one finds a new canon and substantial evidence for the emergence of ethnicity as an accepted and acceptable category of social analysis, interpretation and the humanistic imagination.

Some caution is required in using the historical and assumed archtypical characteristics of ethnic images, especially in the selective use of historical material and the importation of meaning and direction to the past. Though historical imagination has severe limitations, it has been appropriated as an important source and rhetorical aspect of the civil ideologies of modern states. In this regard, Pokrovskii's words on historiographical truth-value: "history is politics projected into the past,"[17] are worth recalling. If, however, politics is understood as a science of order based upon ontology and ethics, as well as upon 'the historicality' of a phenomenological process of reality, Pokrovskii's pithy critique becomes a statement of the complexity, rather than a reproach, of historical and experiential grounding. At bottom political order and cultural formation are too important to be left to the historical or creative imagination of imputed ethnic archetypes and presumed models of group development which ignore the existential ground of ethnic experiences developed at the level of neighborhood settlement. Similar caveats must be voiced about the constraints and limits of the truth-value of the "modern social sciences" and their application to ethnicity.

An admirable summary by Bentley warrants special attention.

The governing concepts in most ethnicity studies are incapable of systematically informing inquiry. Such studies take refuge in the forms of scientific research, reflecting even a fetish of technique in which methods of data collection and analysis are placed before the questions they are supposed to answer. Detailed expositions of hypotheses, variables, and data are brought to bear on such essentially trivial questions as "demographic correlates of race relations and the methodology of racial attitude scales" (van den Berghe, 280, p. 6).

Unfortunately technical sophistication can say nothing about the explanatory value or meaning of research results (see Williams, 296, p. 134; Mills 1960, pp. 60-86). Research topics defined mainly to fit the latest software are likely to be neither informative nor interesting. For all their technical sophistication they lack a sufficient theoretical context to give their results meaning and importance. In his review of sociological studies of ethnicity, Williams (296, p. 126) bemoaned the lack of a theoretical base. "The several hundred books and articles reviewed for this chapter contain an appalling number of *ad hoc* variables and indicators." All this leaves the literature on ethnicity in a theoretical quagmire. Each new increment makes it a larger aggregate of disconnected bits of information.

Exclusive adherence to a "scientific" research model inhibits the more flexible and speculative thinking that might eventually lead to integrative theory. Schermerhorn (244, p. 253) makes this point satirically by raising "the frightening thought that the Ph.D. dissertation may have subtly become the paradigm for research design in our generation." Focus on method at the expense of substance also allows social scientists to preserve their 'cloak of neutrality,' a mask for political cowardice. As Andreski (1972, p. 116) puts it, "Excessive preoccupation with methodology provides an alibi for timorous quietism."

Not all the fault lies with students of ethnicity however, for the phenomena themselves are dauntingly complex:

We must note carefully the complex referents that are variously attached to the concepts 'racial' and 'ethnic.' In their psychological aspects, ethnic relations are characterized by variations in salience, clarity, importance, hostility or positive affect, ambivalence, commitment, identification. In the cultural system, ethnicity may involve language, religious beliefs and practices, institutional norms and values, expressive styles, food preferences, and so on. Ethnic collectivities vary in size, interconnectedness, definiteness and strength of boundaries, relationships with allies and enemies, internal interdependence, degree and kind of social control of members (Williams, 296, p. 125).

Each of these is itself conceptually complex and subject to ambiguous interpretation. The obstacles that must be overcome in developing adequate theories of ethnicity are considerable, even if they have been exacerbated by ideological intrusions and a restrictive research model.[18]

Thus, the emergence of ethnic consciousness in the 1960s and the artifices of ethnic analysis and group archetype and history introduce new representative and interpretative texts into and about ethnicity and the cultural formation of American reality. Ethnic peoples and their cultures become constitutive of American history in the sense suggested decades earlier by Oscar Handlin, a contributing editor of the *Encyclopedia* and fittingly the author of the article on the Yankee as an ethnic group.

This is not to say that the *Encyclopedia* and social analysis of ethnicity are shameless promoters of ideological positions. Not only is ethnicity dauntingly complex, but this is compounded by ethnicity being a moving target that is clearly recorded best at the local level. What seems evident at the national level, however, is that since the 1960s the mainstream processes of cultural formation and interpretation have attempted to pose alternatives to earlier monocultural rationales. Neither Israel Zangwell's vision of the Great American Melting Pot nor Horace Kallen's vision of the legitimacy of pluralistic, democratic cultural enclaves of ethnic groups in America any longer command the adherence, nor do they provoke consent or debate.[19] The social imagination which created the salience of Kallen's and Zangwell's visions no longer resonates in social experiences or social analysis. Consequently, credible formulations must reach beyond simplistic hope for either assimilation or segregation. The contemporary problematic includes concerns regarding the foundational status of the ethnic group and its self-interpretation and histories. This process invokes thousands of local essays, research projects and popular searches for cultural meaning and ethnic identity--for roots within a modern culture. Such activities are symptomatic of a reconfiguration of consciousness in the great modern state. Large scale social, economic, and governmental systems have induced such searches for meaning in memories and in common-sense local experiences. Moreover, in addition to production and consumption, persons and societies need civil theologies--cultural artifices which yield primordial mythic and religious intimations of meaningful order. Answers to such questions of identity and cultural cohesion are preciously important and desperately sought. The maintenance and enhancement of social order and cultural vitality are at stake. The urgency of a search for such sources turns our attention to the ordering experience of ethnicity at the community-based level.

An approach to the development of ethnic consciousness which is essentially rooted in the experiences of local communities as they struggle to understand ethnicity and resolve ethnic conflict was developed by Philip Rosen in a book produced in conjunction the field experience of the National Center for Urban Ethnic Affairs,[20] *The Neglected Dimension: Ethnicity in American Life.* It includes three useful evaluative instruments which measure three distinct aspects of ethnicity that are measured at the immediate level of community: identity, social distance, and ethnic-related public issues.

(a) *Who Am I* measures one's sense of identity assessing historical origin, ancestry and the depth of ethnic affinity (Table V).

(b) *How Do I Feel About Others* measures one's acceptance of ethnicity and the wider contexts of inter-ethnic relations that exist in a multi-ethnic society (Table VI).

(c) Table VII provides an array of opinions as well as open-ended responses which circumscribe the universe of ethnic salience in public life. The questionnaire scales opinions about the following topics: ethnic neighborhoods, foreign sounding names, friendship groups, marriage, voting, political opportunities and other-nation loyalties.

The inadequacy of analysis and interpretation of ethnicity in America that produced national generalizations and frequently reduced ethnic-racial conflict to zero sum contests provoked the sort of measurements and therapy developed by Rosen. Work and findings derived from this scale of inquiry led in turn to other levels of the search for the clarification of ethnicity and ethnic consciousness. Though the historical and theoretical literature on ethnicity is abundant and varied, its social, analytical and historical grounding usually does not extend to the horizon suggested by the lived experience of ethnicity. Consequently, Rosen's book and NCUEA's field experience with hundreds of neighborhoods filled a methodological gap which enables, and yet generalizes, an approach to the experience and shared human consciousness that is formed at the local neighborhood and community level. Thus, under the aspect of localism, ethnicity becomes a discoverable and discernible, yet pluriform, manifestation of human consciousness. Thus, for Rosen and NCUEA ethnicities are a form of small-scale consciousness articulated at the intersection of the private world of the family and the small-scale public world of the neighborhood. Attention to community-based ethnic awareness and neighborhood institutions is a necessary step toward the retheoritization and reconstitution of the bonds of social solidarity. The relation between these experiences and the larger scale corporate and public order suggest the following theses and findings.

THE NEED AND OPPORTUNITY OF COMMUNITY-BASED INSTITUTIONS

Czeslaw Milosz, in his Nobel Award lecture argues that, for all of their weaknesses and supposedly closed character, the structures of society that bring people together at the human face-to-face level remain the most lasting and effective guarantee of personhood and civil well-being. Milosz points toward the enormity of the loss that must be overcome if these little worlds of learning, meaning and social solidarity are destroyed:

> Perhaps our most precious gift . . . is respect and gratitude for certain things which protect us from internal disintegration and from yielding to tyranny.
>
> Precisely for that reason, some ways of life, some institutions become a target for the fury of evil forces--above all, the bonds between people that exist organically, as if by themselves, sustained by family, religion, neighborhood, common heritage.
>
> In other words, in many countries traditional bonds of *civitas* have been subject to a gradual erosion and their inhabitants become disinherited without realizing it.[21]

Thus, in many respects ethnicity is an antidote and immunology for moral collapse. It includes but extends beyond the poor, powerless and ignored ethnic and excluded racial groups. There are many signs of unfulfilled promises and profound disintegration of the generous and open spirit which made these promises of liberty and justice a stunning irony for various ethnic populations. Yet the experience of ethnicity generally resounds hopefulness about the promised dignity, liberty and justice for all. Thus it can be argued that ethnicity is a thrust to rebuild community on an understanding of its complexity, its pluralism, and the capacity of small-scale community-based institutions to create a pathway to justice. If community is not trampled by governmental and corporate penetration, the engines of evil fury to which Milosz calls our attention, a new blossoming of justice may yet emerge.

During the 1970s, new migrants began to change the face of America. In the New York-New Jersey region for instance in areas such as Brooklyn, Jersey City, the Bronx, Elizabeth, Nassau County and Paterson, entire neighborhoods have changed or are changing their ethnic composition. In some cases, ethnic neighborhoods which had stabilized or begun to decline have gone through a resurgence as immigration from their countries of origin has increased. Manhattan's Chinatown and Brooklyn's Polish Greenpoint are examples of communities which have expanded beyond their original boundaries because of a large infusion of new immigrants.

There are, however, conflicts between the new immigrants and the ethnic communities into which they have moved. Understanding the contemporary immigrant as well as the ethnic experience is an essential element of neighborhood initiatives designed to include *new-Americans* in the creation of personal identities and economic, political and cultural harmony. The one million aliens who registered in 1980 in New York-New Jersey came from 164 countries and dependencies. Although such diversity is not as great in Chicago, Washington and Miami, there appears to be more diversity in these cities even than during previous migrations. In the Northeast and Midwest, the influence of political repression and economic depression in Europe caused an increase in immigrants from such European countries as Albania, USSR, Poland and Italy. Population change is very dramatic in Miami, which since the 1960s has become essentially an immigrant city. Quotas for the sending areas were revised upward by the United States in 1965. A good example of the resultant diversity is that Catholic mass is celebrated in 25 different languages in the New York-New Jersey area, including Albanian, Creole, Korean, Maltese, Slovak, Polish and Italian.

So, it is clear that the new immigration is not a single, undifferentiated process. It has many streams and its impacts on politics, society and economy are varied in the extreme. What Frank Thistlehwaite wrote of the pre-World War I migration is equally true of the present one.

> Seen through a magnifying glass, this undifferentiated mass surface breaks down into a honey comb of innumerable particular cells, districts, villages, towns each with an individual reaction or lack of it to the pull of migration. This is not simply a question of Scottish Highlanders emigrating in a body of Upper Canada, Rhinelanders to Wisconsin, Swedes to Montana, Northern Italians to France and Argentina, Southern Italians to the United States, though these elementary distinctions are important. We only come to secret sources of the movement if we work at a finer tolerance. We must talk, not of Wales, but of Portmadoc or Swansea, not of North or South Italy but of Venetia Giulia, Friuli, Basilicata and Calabria, not of Greece of even the Peloponnese, but of Tripolis, Sparta and Megalopolis, not of Lancashire but of Darwin or Blackburn, not of Norway but of Kristiana and North Bergenhus. . . . Only when we examine . . . districts and townships, and trace the fortunes of their native sons, do we begin to understand the true anatomy of migration.[22]

Scholars of the old immigration have learned also that this need for "a finer tolerance" is as necessary for the study of the pattern of settlement in the U.S. as it is for the study of the emigration pattern in Europe. In the final analysis, the immigrants did not settle in Pennsylvania or even in the anthracite fields, but in small coal towns and tiny patches. They did not move to Detroit, Chicago or New York, *but to particular neighborhoods*, to certain parishes and even to individual streets. It is only at the neighborhood level that one finds a complete picture of the great immigration that transformed and continues to recreate America.

Research in this field must attend to the following:

- The nature and demographic structure of the incoming groups, and the size of the influx;

- The degree of similarity and/or difference of the religions, cultures and races between the receiving neighborhood groups and the immigrants;

- The earlier history of the area and the neighborhood groups and of their status and position in the city;

- The institutional strength and level of organization of entering and receiving groups;

- The social, political and economic environment of the urban setting in which the neighborhood and its institutions are imbedded; and

- The previous relationship between resident groups.

In some cases the introduction of a new group or groups into a neighborhood changes the relationships of established groups. Residents in the receiving area relate to each other and to changing impacts on each other in different ways. In certain areas the dynamic of a neighborhood or parish for older and newer residents is determined to a significant degree, and at times primarily, by the relationship of two or more new immigrant groups to each other. Finally, the character of group leadership appears to set the tone for intergroup relations.

Many of these 'old immigrant--new immigrant' neighborhoods need mechanisms which limit the strain of conflict and succession. Others need to build their capacity to shape the social, economic and political revitalization of a neighborhood. All offer the possibility of observing first hand and at close range cases of "ethnization" of immigrant groups against the background of our knowledge of the variety of ways this process of acculturation took place among earlier immigrants. Knowledge of self-help approaches and comparison of the ways in which immigrants become an American ethnic group begins to explain the achievement that neighborhoods have accomplished. Such activities include:

- The development of local institutions and their relationship and importance to neighborhood and city.

- The incorporation of popular American culture and norms into more traditional world views and vice versa.

- The creation of community in a dramatically new country and among people who would often have been strangers to each other in the land of origin.

Factoring such findings and information into inquiries is essential to an intelligent assessment of the current realities of urban life and to the future of the city and its neighborhoods. The research and policy agenda for the 90s ought to assess and address those features of corporate and governmental policy which have deleterious effects on the capacity of persons and groups to sustain the social and cultural infrastructure of threatened neighborhoods. The spatial dimensions of social reality at its smallest public level is increasingly relevant as a unit of analysis. For example, The Social Science Research Council argues this case and derives its warrant from disaggregated data. In *The Nature of Poverty in the United States*, Gephart and Pearson report that poverty:

> is found less among elderly and people living in non-urban areas and more among children living with one parent--in households headed principally by young women. Poverty has also become increasingly concentrated in urban America, in neighborhoods where a small core of the disadvantaged face the prospect of remaining impoverished, unable to participate meaningfully in the broader social and economic life of the country. . . . Although a portrait of the urban underclass is not yet complete, one of its most salient dimensions is spatial; the location of poverty in the United States has shifted dramatically during the last 25 years. Poverty--although still pronounced in America's rural areas--is an increasingly urban phenomenon. And within urban areas, poverty is increasingly concentrated in areas in which substantial proportions of the population are also poor.[23]

In addition to the problems of clustered poverty, the modern multi-ethnic regime needs to develop competency in the social and cultural experience of persons and groups at the level of their local ethnic affinity. In 1984 a Task Force of urban ethnic group leaders assessed and addressed the development of a range of concerns with which most of them had been involved since the early 1960s. Among the findings of the group was the conspicuous neglect and ignorance regarding neighborhoods and the localness of ethnicity. The Task Force proposed an interpretive guide and policy recommendations which capsulized the development of ethnic localism in the United States. The Task Force was keenly aware of, but not combative, about inter-ethnic competition. It was critical, but not defensive about, the persistent fear of ethnicity fostered by the dynamics of large scale institutions of governance and production as well as by the habits of mono-cultural modernity deposited in mainstream American culture. The Task Force report includes four topics: Ethnicity, Defamation, Neighborhood and the Elderly. Their clarifications and proposals are by far the clearest and most comprehensive summary of the development of local ethnic consciousness in contemporary America. Its definitions and descriptions of the issues and its specific recommendations bear reporting in their entirety.[24]

Specific Areas

Ethnicity. Ethnic identity in the United States is a modern identity. It was created in the new immigrant communities to replace older local and status identities and to bind together in cities people who would have been strangers to each other in the old country. Ethnicity in the U.S. became a constantly changing complex of class and occupational identifications, of ties to regions of origin, of local parochial or civic loyalties, or American national identity and religious affiliations existing in dynamic tension one with another. The saliency of each, alone or in combination, for a group or individual, changed with time, place and circumstances. Each generation created anew its ethnicity. Thus, on the one hand, the "new ethnicity" of the sixties and seventies was an attempt to redefine ethnic identity with a new pride by educated, middle-class and professional people who represented the younger generations of American ethnic groups. On the other hand, it was an attempt by people still living in the older neighborhoods to make their ethnicity a defensive, public identity in a time of turmoil, when it appeared that public benefits were being dispensed on the basis of group identities. The two trends merged to create a complex and often misunderstood phenomenon. The legacy of that period, however, was a growing appreciation of multi-cultural pluralism as well as of the need for, and value of, coalitions between ethnic groups to affect public policies.

To perpetuate our multi-cultural heritage, we must address such tasks as:

- Language preservation
- Ethnic studies
- Education for a pluralistic society
- Documentation of ethnic history and society

To promote understanding of ethnic groups among themselves and in society, we must address such tasks as:

- Inter-ethnic networking and communication
- Research, publication and dissemination of studies
- Positive representation in the media

Defamation. Although significant strides were made in combating discrimination and defamation against Americans of various ethnic groups, much still remains to be done. Unflattering and often distorted stereotypes of ethnic Americans continue to appear in the media. In the national and local media, ethnic Americans still remain substantially under-represented in many areas. The effort to inform our fellow countrymen and women as well as our children of the history and culture of ethnic groups through programs of school and public education has suffered a serious setback with the ending of the Ethnic Heritage Program and the cutbacks in funding for the arts and humanities. Many of the institutions and foundations that were in the forefront of the struggle to create a genuine multi-cultural pluralism, to promote better understanding between various groups of Americans and to end discrimination have adopted other agendas for the 1980s.

To secure rights and justice for all, we must address such tasks as:

- Fairness and equal treatment under the law
- Compilation of full and accurate data on the ethnic composition,
- The appointment of public officials who are representative of, and sensitive to, America's ethnic diversity.

Neighborhood. "Neighborhood" became part of the public dialogue in the sixties. It became one way of speaking about ethnicity and about the value and ties of geographically defined face-to-face local urban communities which were under attack by urban planners and highway builders. While neighborhoods are not always communities, they do represent clusters of local public and private institutions around which people structure their daily lives and in which they realize their communal and ethnic identities. The churches, the political subdivisions, the commercial strips, the schools and libraries, clubs, bars and settlement houses all represent the network of institutions which tie a neighborhood together and allow its various peoples to carry on political participation and private communities. It is at the neighborhood level that ethnic coalitions are created in the actual struggle for common goals. This is the seedbed and proving ground of multi-cultural pluralism. A humane and civil urban life is impossible without neighborhoods. Thus, federal, state and local public policies which maintain neighborhoods and promote their revitalization are necessary if the city is to survive and if ethnicity is to remain a creative and positive force in politics.

Elderly. One of the major concerns of most urban ethnic groups is their elderly. Whether left behind in the changing old neighborhood or transplanted to senior citizen high-rises or the suburbs, the ethnic elderly often find it difficult to maintain the kind of dignified life they had envisaged for themselves in their old age. Living among people who do not share or always value the language and culture in which they have grown up, deprived of services and care because of linguistic and cultural barriers, isolated by fear for personal safety and economic circumstances, many ethnic elderly feel lonely and alienated. We need to discuss and promote programs to reintegrate the elderly into church, neighborhood and community, to provide support, information and service in the vernacular they use and in a way that takes account of their culture and sensitivities. The ethnic elderly, like all our senior citizens, represent an important human resource for our society which we misuse at the peril of damaging the social fabric. They represent an earlier chapter of the story from which our children must draw the materials and strength to build a future.

To assure people's well being in all facets of their lives in their families, neighborhoods and communities we must address such tasks as:

- Strengthening family life
- Care for the elderly
- Neighborhood revitalization

- Development of ethnic sensitivity in social and health
  services
- Promotion of vigorous and sustained economic growth.

The proponents of this approach and agenda perceive it as extending liberty and justice to all. It can appeal to all because of the importance of family institutions for all groups as the bond and core institution of neighborhood and community. The churches are equally important and should perhaps become the vehicle for bringing people together. The Black church has long been the major integrating institution of urban working-class Black communities and the source of their moral strength in the battle against racism. The Hispanic and ethnic working-class in turn, largely Catholic but with some Orthodox members, also built its communities around its churches, which still provide the moral and social universe for the majority of their members. This moral universe ought to be linked to the larger mechanism of order. This can be achieved only through the recovery of political power.

THE RECOVERY OF CITIZENSHIP

It is axiomatic that people will accede to even unpleasant policies if they played some role in shaping them. Therefore, once trust and communication are developed among persons at the local level a political recovery would begin with research and policy forums to develop grassroots accommodations and consensus regarding the allocation of resources. Such forums need not be meetings in which "victims" accuse their "oppressor" or "oppressors," nor is there much to be gained from, wittingly and unwittingly, enemies forcefully informing each other of their transgressions and expected repentence. The purpose of such forums is the recovery of local level citizenship in which Americans work as equals on common problems enlightened and guided by the moral and social precepts that they all find most compelling. Such other local organizations as labor unions and neighborhood and fraternal associations also must be involved in these forums.

It is out of hundreds of these local meetings that understanding and bonds can be developed between individuals and groups and that possible solutions can be transmitted to government, private social agencies and employers. Neighborhood grassroots work should inform official and quasi-official decisions and give them legitimacy, rather than vice versa. Out of these local efforts the new language of social integration and justice will be born by drawing on the best and most generous traditions of persons and local institutions.

It is also through these local forums that people who only a short time before have undergone the trauma of migration from European villages, Asian villages, South, Central, Caribbean America, as well as internal migrants can share their experiences and institutions with the new immigrants. Various ties can ease the integration of the newcomers and develop structural ways of dealing with the inevitable conflicts of culture and competition for work and living space.

The Task Force report and policy recommendations propose a politics of ethnic consciousness which would lay to rest ethnic divisiveness. The neighborhood ethnic agenda is a plan for a non-exclusionary recovery of public well-being. Its interests include: promoting heritage, combating discrimination, preserving neighborhoods and assisting the elderly--an agenda as American as spaghetti, kielbasa and the neighborhood store.

CONCLUSION

The practice of liberty and justice for all always has been easier to say than to do. In so far as public disparities can be credibly attributed to some ethnic factor, the potential for the exploitation of ethnic fear and hatred will continue. Nevertheless, the persistence of ethnicity as a shared consciousness offers meaningful answers to the search for identity and belonging. Given the pluriformity of peoples, nations and tongues that constitutes the human ecumene, the search for understanding these various articulations of local consciousness must include common, different and equivalent symbolizations for the experience of participation in the American cosmion and its legacy of liberty and justice for all. These variously shaped and shared forms of local human consciousness intersect with modern political, cultural and economic institutions whose focus is not local--the state, the communications system, and the corporation. It is at this intersection of the ethnic with the modern consciousness that the premier questions of the American regime and its ability to resolve conflict and equitably distribute resources will be posed and finally answered.

In the sixties and seventies, ethnicity--that is, the consciousness of group identity--established its legitimacy. On one level, to be ethnic meant to stress differences in language, culture and religion. However, closer examination of the ethnic experience of Americans revealed that ethnicity was also a powerful integrative force in American society. Ethnicity brought people together and laid the basis for community. Ethnic traditions impled moral and social models for a united, yet culturally pluralistic, America. Out of the pluralistic experience of each group many persons learned to appreciate a common harmony. In the last two decades to be an ethnic became above all a way of being an American.

America is just beginning to acknowledge that neglecting social, cultural and economic exchanges at the neighborhood level has taken an enormous toll on people and their community institutions. The urban burden is aggravated further by large-scale corporate and government policies which foster social and economic tendencies that isolate and insulate persons. The urban immigrant and ethnic experience poses challenges to suburban and upwardly mobile populations. The underevaluation of urban life and the demeaning of the working-class and of the family-centered focus of persons who live in urban neighborhoods point to the loss of *civitas*. In sum, well-being is not correlated with economic status and social mobility.

To be sure economic well-being is stabilizing, but difficult economic times will require solidarity and cohesion. Such times demand specific and relevant approaches and remedies derived from the lived experience of persons at the local level. Preachment about rights, racism, brotherhood and the American dream are insufficient; in some contexts they simply fuel tensions and exacerbate conflict. The discussion of intergroup relations too often has been sketched in broad national strokes or sensationalized in times of crisis. Such discussion fosters misunderstanding because it often leaves people angry, guilty and fearful. The mainstream American hope for economic mobility and legal remedies to assure equal protection and equal outcomes are similarly faulted and unachievable. Neither the record of corporate practices nor the mechanisms of legal protection seem entirely adequate in a segmented and stratified multi-ethnic society. Policy planners for corporations and government, as well as well-meaning universalists and even romantic protagonists of ethnic folk festivals have fostered caricatures of the American experience. Folkloric ethnic fantasies and rational corporate calculus are disengaged from the lived experiences and exchanges of neighborhood life.

A new pathway to cultural and economic justice is emerging from the experiences of urban ethnic life at the neighborhood level. This struggle for justice has moved beyond the rhetoric of blaming enemies, making slogans and praising victims. The recovery of cultural legacies and the discovery of social and economic inventions at the neighborhood level are forces which are shaping new pieces of the American reality. Understanding the dynamics which drive this process and applying these findings to various processes of social formation and to various forms of policy may enable the American regime to fulfill its promise to all who settled here. New directions in research and policy limned in this paper can help to find ways of linking the need for bonds of solidarity at the local level with the imperatives of social justice that are revealed at the intersection of ethnic consciousness and the larger scale political, economic and social institutions of a modern regime.

The Catholic University of America
Washington, D.C.

TABLE I*

1. *General Coverage*
   a. Collection or anthology
   b. General textbook
2. *Data orientation*
   a. Bibliography
   b. Primary data
   c. Secondary data
   d. Sample survey
   e. Survey of literature
   f. Other or none
3. *Scale of study*
   a. Community study
   b. National study
   c. Interethnic comparison
   d. Cross-national comparison
   e. Other or none
4. *Academic field*
   a. Anthropology
   b. Economics
   c. Geography
   d. History
   e. Linguistics
   f. Political science
   g. Social psychology
   h. Sociology
   i. Other or unknown
5. *Theoretical orientation*
   a. Assimilation
   b. Conflict or intergroup competition
   c. Ecological
   d. Identity
   e. Nationalism
   f. Pluralism
   g. Prejudice
   h. Situational
   i. Stratification
   j. Internal colonialism
   k. Other or unknown
6. *Demography*
   a. Population data
   b. Spatial distribution
   c. Urban/rural distribution
7. *Migration*
   a. Emigration
   b. Immigration
   c. Internal migration
   d. Urbanization
8. *Economics*
   a. Income
   b. Occupations
   c. Socio-economic development
   d. Market processes
9. *Stratification*
   a. Caste
   b. Class
   c. Intergroup ranking
   d. Intragroup ranking
   e. Social mobility
10. *Politics*
    a. National or local authority structure
    b. Intergroup competition or conflict
    c. Subordination domination
    d. Political movements
    e. Political parties and elections
    f. Leadership
    g. Police or military
11. *Beliefs, attitudes and ideology*
    a. Ethnocentrism and intergroup attitudes
    b. World view or ideology
    c. Stereotyping
    d. Ideological bases of government policies
12. *Ethnic identity*
    a. Ancestry or origin
    b. Consciousness of identity
    c. Culture or customs
    d. Communal sentiment
    e. Language
    f. Race
    g. Religion
    h. Tribe
    i. Common values or ethos

13. *Education*
    a. Educational levels
    b. Values associated with
       education
14. *Family and kinship*
    a. Family structure or
       composition
    b. Extended kin networks
    c. Marriage
15. *Voluntary associations*
16. *Communication*
    a. Language
    b. Media
17. *Religion*

*Stephan Thernstrom, ed., *The Harvard Encyclopedia of Ethnic Groups in America* (Cambridge, MA: Harvard Univ. Press, 1980)

TABLE II*

CHECKLIST/OUTLINE FOR GROUP ENTRIES 7/16/76

(This outline is designed to be suggestive but not prescriptive. It is assumed that each contributor will organize the data available to him or her in the way that works best. Furthermore, these questions and categories are not equally applicable or significant for all groups, but when they do apply they are meant to have both historical and contemporary relevance. Finally, this is a long list but it does not exhaust all possibilities or viewpoints.)

Origins:
- from where does group originate? nation-state? state of mind? region? ancient state? present province? new state? awakened nation? are group members exiles or refugees? national community? a people among peoples? a linguistic group? a remnant?
- what languages has (does) the group spoken, written?
- what is the racial composition of group? religious affiliations? majority or minority faith at point of origin?

Migration:
- who migrated? why? how many? where? when? who stayed behind? what were the circumstances of the migration? how was it organized? what policies at point of origin affected migration? at point of arrival?

Arrival:
- when did group first arrive? how? in one or several waves? over a short or long time? did immigrants come alone, one by one, in small groups, or in a stream?
- how did group take shape? was it forcibly incorporated by conquest or slavery? were immigrants voluntary or involuntary? exiles or refugees?
- what kind of society did group enter? colonial? frontier? rural and agricultural? urban? industrial?
- has group been continually or sporadically refreshed by new arrivals? what governs reinforcement? distance? transportation? borders? government policy? changes in place of origin? has there been return migration? re-immigration?

Settlement:
- where did group settle? what was pattern of distribution? rural/-urban? scattered/concentrated? dispersed/segregated?
- what was pattern of geographical mobility? toward dispersion or segregation? from country to city? from city to city?
- what was ecology of settlement? relations among home, work-place, community?

Economic Life:
- what was entry employment? was there specialization in economic activity? among first and subsequent generations?

- what is the characteristic pattern of enterprise? service? entrepreneurial? special resources? characteristic organization of business? relationship to unions? civil service?
- what is economic base of community?

Social Structure:
- relations between class and ethnic group? stratification within ethnic group? how did it develop? parallel or incongruous with system of larger society? has it changed? what have been patterns and sources of social mobility?

Social Organization:
- what have been patterns of association? voluntary associations? parochial schools? religious activities and institutions?
- what have been patterns of informal organization? are neighborhood and territory important dimensions of community? are these characteristics social and visiting patterns?
- who are group leaders? how have they emerged or been chosen? for what reasons? from the center or periphery of group? what is their relationship to larger society?

Family and Kinship:
- what is characteristic family form? what is importance of kinship ties? what are marriage patterns? intermarriage? with whom? why?
- how is transition from generation to generation organized? formal institutions? informal *rites de passage*?

Behavior and Personal/Individual Characteristics:
- are there data on literacy, level of education, mental health, physical health, alcoholism, divorce, childbearing, leisure-time preferences, consumerism?

Culture:
- has group maintained its language? orally? in written form? everyday or ceremonial use? how has it been maintained and by whom?
- what are characteristic forms of expression? literary tradition? folklore? folk customs? music? dance? costume? gastronomy? art?
- are there or have there been journals, newspapers, theatres, radio programs, TV?
- does folk tradition survive? where? in what forms?
- are group writings, etc., directed to group alone or to general public?
- ethnic specialists and intellectuals? who have they been? how have they emerged? how have they maintained themselves?

Religion:
- what is the religious identity of the group? shaped in USA or continuous with place of origin?

- what are the characteristic patterns of belief or unbelief? has religion been consonant or dissonant with ethnic identity? does religion divide or unify?
- what features of religious practice have been important? high or low participation? generational differences? periodic revivals?
- what have been the characteristic forms of religious organization?

Education:
- how has group been educated, formally and informally, over the generations? significant changes? parochial vs. public education?
- what relations among culture, education, and religion?

Politics:
- when did group enter local and national political life?
- what political organizations are characteristic?
- what coalitions have taken shape? on what base?
- what patterns of participation and behavior have evolved?
- what motivates participation? ideology? interest?

Intergroup Relations:
- what contacts has group had with the Anglo-Americans and other ethnic groups? what accommodation has been reached with the larger society? acculturation? assimilation? minority status? separation?
- what conflict/consensus marks interaction between specific group and American society? what experience of racism, prejudice and discrimination?

Group Maintenance:
- what resources have been utilized to maintain the boundaries of community? what informal agencies and what formal institutions?
- what role is played by kinship and marriage patterns? what role is played by educational and religious institutions? by peer pressure?
- what role have relations with the homeland played?

Individual Ethnic Commitment:
- what are the individual roots of commitment? has there been a change over time? a change with age or with the generations? is it persistent or intermittent? steady or subject to fashion?

Bibliography:
- please list no more than ten important works--works that will be available to the encyclopedia reader in paperback or in a moderate-sized public or college library. Do not list highly specialized, highly technical, or difficult to obtain works.

*Thernstrom, ed., *The Harvard Encyclopedia of Ethnic Groups in America.*

TABLE III *

Ethnicity is an immensely complex phenomenon. All the groups treated here are characterized by some of the following features, although in combinations that vary considerably:

1. common geographic origin;
2. migratory status;
3. race;
4. language or dialect;
5. religious faith or faiths;
6. ties that transcend kinship, neighborhood and community boundaries;
7. shared traditions, values and symbols;
8. literature, folklore and music;
9. food preferences;
10. settlement and employment patterns;
11. special interests in regard to politics in the homeland and in the United States;
12. institutions that specifically serve and maintain the group;
13. an internal sense of distinctiveness;
14. an external perception of distinctiveness.

*Thernstrom, ed., *The Harvard Encyclopedia of Ethnic Groups in America*

TABLE IV *

THEMATIC ESSAYS

American Identity and Americanization--Philip Gleason
American Indians, Federal Policy Toward--Edward H. Spicer
Assimilation and Pluralism--Harold J. Abramson
Concepts of Ethnicity--William Petersen
Education--Michael Olneck and Marvin Lazerson
Family Patterns--Tamara K. Hareven and John Modell
Folklore--Roger D. Abrahams
Health Beliefs and Practices--Noel J. Chrisman and Arthur Kleinman
Immigration: Economic and Social Characteristics--Richard A. East
Immigration: History of U.S. Policy--William S. Bernard
Immigration: Settlement Patterns and Spatial Distribution--David Ward
Intermarriage--David M. Heer
Labor--David Brody
Language: Issues and Legislation--Abigail M. Thermstrom
Language Maintenance--Joshua A. Fishman
Leadership--John Higham
Literature and Ethnicity--Werner Sollors
Loyalties: Dual and Divided--Mona Harrington
Methods of Estimating the Size of Groups--Charles A. Price
Naturalization and Citizenship--Reed Ueda
Pluralism: A Humanistic Perspective--Michael Novak
Pluralism: A Political Perspective--Michael Walzer
Politics--Edward R. Kantowicz
Prejudice--Thomas F. Pettigrew
Prejudice and Discrimination, History of--George M. Fredrickson and
    Dale T. Knobel
Prejudice and Discrimination, Policy Against--Nathan Glazer and Reed
    Ueda
Religion--Harold J. Abramson
Resources and Research Centers--Edward Kasinec
Survey Research--James D. Wright, Peter H. Rossi and Thomas F. Jura-
    vich

*Thernstrom, ed., *The Harvard Encyclopedia of Ethnic Groups in America*

TABLE V*

(With the help of your parents and an exploration of your own feelings answer the questions below. Try to answer as many as you can as honestly as you can since class discussion will be based on the answers. The information will give the class an idea of the diverse backgrounds in our room and provide ideas that will be employed later. You may choose to eliminate some questions for personal reasons.)

1. Who was the first member of your family to immigrate to America? (Yourself, parent(s), grandparent(s), great grandparent(s), or earlier ancestor). Specify which member.
2. Tell country(s) from which you or your parents, grandparents, or ancestors came. Specify who came from where.
3. Does anyone in your family still speak the language of a country of origin (the country from which they came) or a language of folk living in a foreign land? Specify who speaks what language.
4. Do you or any of your relatives keep in touch with relations or friends in country(s) of origin or some other foreign country?
5. With which religion (sect or denomination) do you identify?
6. How strongly do you identify with this religion? (Very strongly, moderately, in name only).
7. Of which national origins group do you feel a part? (Afro-American, Irish-American, Polish-American, British-American, etc., mixed, no particular group).
8. Place the following terms of identity in the circles according to which category is closer to yourself:
   American
   national origin (English, Irish, German, Puerto Rican, etc.)
   religion (Protestant, Catholic, Jewish, etc.)
   race (white, black, Mongoloid [Asiatic], other)

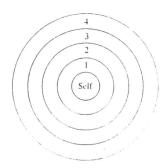

9. What interest do you have in the history and culture of your national origins group? (Great interest, moderate interest, a little interest, no interest).

little, none).

*Philip Rosen, *The Neglected Dimension: Ethnicity in American Life* (Notre Dame: Notre Dame University Press, 1980).

TABLE VI*

HOW DO I FEEL ABOUT OTHERS?
A SOCIAL-DISTANCE SCALE

A social-distance scale measures how close we feel toward others and how much we accept them. In our acceptance and rejection of others we define ourselves. This scale is anonymous; do not sign your name; merely provide the requested information concerning yourself on the first group of lines below. Please give your first feeling reactions in every case. Mark each group even though you have had no contact with the group. Check as many of the six columns as your feelings dictate.

race	religion		national origin group			sex
American ethnic group	Would marry	Would date	Have as close friend	Have as next-door neighbor	Have speaking acquaintance with	Have in same school
Arab						
Armenian						
Catholic						
Chinese						
Czech						
English						
French						
German						
Greek						

Indian						
Irish						
Italian						
Japanese						
Jewish						
Mexican						
Norwegian						
blacks						
Polish						
Protestant						
Puerto Rican						
others (as suggested)						

*Philip Rosen, *The Neglected Dimension: Ethnicity in American Life* (Notre Dame: Notre Dame University Press, 1980).

Table VII*

1. *Ethnic Neighborhoods*

_____ A. Neighborhoods should be integrated with people of all different backgrounds to promote good intergroup relations and break down artificial divisions in American society.

_____ B. Neighborhood preference is a matter of personal choice; clustering into neighborhoods by members of the same ethnic group is acceptable so long as there are no secret agreements to keep out members of other ethnic groups.

_____ C. People are better off living in neighborhoods with their own kind; they feel comfortable and avoid interethnic conflict.

_____ D. Other:

2. *"Foreign-Sounding" Names*

_____ A. A person with such a name should change it to an American-sounding one; he or she is living in America now.

_____ B. Names are a means of identity; a person should not feel embarrassed if he or she keeps or changes his name.

_____ C. A person should have pride in his or her name, for it is inherited as a birthright. If people have trouble in pronouncing or spelling the name, the person should take care to explain it to them.

_____ D. Other:

3. *Friendship Groups*

_____ A. Choosing friends on the basis of similar ethnic background threatens good group relations and divides our country. People should seek interethnic associations.

_____ B. An individual should feel free, without a sense of guilt, to choose friends within his own ethnic group, or seek multiethnic contacts, or even change his ethnic identification if he desires.

_____ C. People are better off, more comfortable, and safer when they stay within the bounds of their own ethnic group. They should seek friends from their own kind.

_____ D. Other:

4. *Joining a Fraternity or Sorority*

_____ A. Fraternities and sororities should be multiethnic so that the membership can learn to get along with all kinds of people.

_____ B. Fraternities and sororities which do not have as their goal the preservation of religious or nationality values should be made open to all; those that are ethnically sponsored may place ethnic criteria for membership.

_____ C. People should feel free to set up criteria in their social organizations any way they choose; this includes ethnic criteria.

_____ D. Other:

5. *Interethnic Marriage*

_____ A. Interethnic marriages are a good way to break down barriers between people and bring about a united America.

_____ B. Interethnic marriages are a private affair between the couple involved, a matter of free choice if ethnic references mean little to them.

_____ C. People are better off marrying within their own ethnic group; there are enough potentially good mates within one's own group.

_____ D. Other:

6. *Voting for an Ethnic Candidate*

_____ A. One should vote for the best candidate and not consider at all the candidate's ethnic background.

_____ B. A voter who votes for a candidate from the same ethnic group as himself may be making sense if the candidate is qualified and takes a position that would serve the best interests of the voter and the group to which he belongs.

_____ C. A voter should prefer a candidate from his own ethnic group since it is more likely that a candidate once in office would look after the interests of the ethnic group.

_____ D. Other:

7. *Ethnic Considerations for Appointments to Public Office (Judges, etc.)*

_____ A. The choice of a person for a public office should rest solely on merit. Ethnic considerations are irrelevant.

_____ B. Ethnic considerations do make sense when a large ethnic population resides in a voting area, yet has no representation on important governmental bodies.

_____ C. An ethnic group should have the exact proportion of representatives in governmental bodies as its numbers in the voting population would indicate.

_____ D. Other:

8. *Other-nation Loyalties: Concern for Peoples Outside the United States*

_____ A. Concern with brethren overseas is narrow. One should be concerned with all people, how they are treated and whether they are suffering, not only with those with whom there are historic nationality ties.

_____ B. Concern for overseas brethren seems natural, but the makers of foreign policy have to be guided by the self-interests of the nation, not the concerns of one group.

_____ C. Americans who have historic ties to brethren overseas are the people who naturally will show the most concern. Exerting pressure on government officials is a democratic right of all Americans, and a democratic government which professes concern over the desires of its citizens must modify its foreign policy accordingly.

_____ D. Other:

*Philip Rosen, *The Neglected Dimension: Ethnicity in American Life* (Notre Dame: Notre Dame University Press, 1980).

NOTES

*See Discussion V.

1. The ideas of progress can be traced to a variety of sources. See J.B. Bury, *The Idea of Progress* (New York: Dover Books, 1955). From the Enlightenment philosophies onward European Positivism and Socialism merge in this vision of development. For earlier origins see Eric Voegelin, *The New Science of Politics* (Chicago: University of Chicago Press, 1952) and Norman Cohn, *The Pursuit of the Millennium* (New York: Harper & Row, 1961). The American political and economic as well as the anthropological-sociological treatment of cultural modernization is a massive literature, but exemplars of various positions and the history of issues related to the intellectual clarification of this problematic can be found in the following: Dwight B. Heath and Richard N. Adams, eds., *Contemporary Cultures and Societies in Latin America* (New York: Random House, 1965); Bert Hosolitz, ed., *The Progress of Underdeveloped Areas* (Chicago: University of Chicago Press, 1952); Lucien W. Pye and Sidney Verba, eds., *Political Culture and Political Development* (Princeton: Princeton University Press, 1965); Robert L. Heilbroner, *The Great Ascent: The Struggle for Economic Development in Our Time* (New York: Harper and Row, 1963); Albert Hirschman, *The Strategy of Economic Development* (New Haven: Yale University Press, 1958); David E. Apter, *The Politics of Modernization* (Chicago: University of Chicago Press, 1965); A.F.K. Organski, *The Stages of Political Development* (New York: Knopf, 1965). K.H. Silvert, ed., *Expectant Peoples: Nationalism and Development* (New York: Random House, 1963); MIT Study Group, "United States Foreign Policy: Economic, Social and Political Change in Underdeveloped Countries and Its Implications for United States Policy" (1960) in Claude E. Welch, ed., *Political Modernization: A Reader in Comparative Political Change* (Belmont, CA: Wadsworth Publishing, Inc. 1969); Karl W. Deutsch and William J. Folz, eds., *Nation-Building* (New York: Atherton, 1963); Robert Redfield, *Peasant Society and Culture: An Anthropological Approach to Civilization* (Chicago: University of Chicago Press, 1956); C.E. Black, *The Dynamics of Modernization* (New York: Harper & Row, 1966); L.I. Rudolph and S.H. Rudolph, *The Modernity of Tradition: Political Development in India* (Chicago: University of Chicago Press, 1967); Rupert Emerson, *From Empirie to Nation* (Cambridge: Harvard University Press, 1960); Hugh Seton-Watson, *Nations and States: An Inquiry into the Origins of Nations and the Politics of Nationalism* (Boulder: Westview Press, 1977); and Joseph A. Amato, *Guilt and Gratitude: A Study of the Origins of Contemporary Conscience* (Westport: Greenwood Press, 1982).

2. See Robert Packenham, *Liberal America and the Third World* (Princeton: Princeton University Press, 1973); S.W. Eisenstadt and A. Schachar, *Society, Culture and Urbanization* (Newbury Park: Sage, 1987); S. Eisenstadt, *Tradition, Change and Modernity* (New York: John Wiley, 1973).

3. See Shaul Bakhash, *The Reign of the Ayatollahs* (New York: Basic Books, 1984); Farrokh Moshire, *The State and Social Revolution in Iran* (New York: Peter Lang, 1985).

4. See John H. Hallowell, ed., *Development for What?* (Durham: Duke University Press, 1964); Fred Riggs, ed., *Frontiers of Development Administration* (Durham: Duke University Press, 1969); Ralph Braibanti, ed. *Political and Administrative Development* (Durham: Duke University Press, 1969). See two short histories of this problematic written nearly two decades apart: Ralph Braibanti, "External Inducement of Political-Administrative Development: An Institutional Strategy," in *Political and Administrative Development*; James P. O'Leary "Toward an Intellectual History of Development: Notes on Contemporary Reserch," *Teaching Political Science*, 15 (1987); Ernest R. May, *"Lessons" of the Past: The Use and Misuses of History in American Foreign Policy* (New York: Oxford University Press, 1973).

5. See Irving Louis Horowitz, *Three Worlds of Development* (New York: Oxford University Press, 1966); Nathan Glazer and Daniel Patrick Moynihan, eds. *Ethnicity: Theory and Experience* (Cambridge: Harvard University Press, 1975); Daniel E. Weinberg, *Ethnicity: A Conceptual Approach* (Cleveland: Cleveland State University, CEHS, 1976); Clifford Geertz, ed., *Old Societies and New States* (New York: Free Press, 1963); Wendell Bell and Walter E. Freeman, eds., *Ethnicity and Nation-Building* (Beverly Hills: Sage, 1974); Lawrence H. Fuchs, *American Ethnic Politics* (New York: Harper & Row, 1968); Otto Feinstein, ed., *Ethnic Groups in the City* (Lexington, MA: Heath Lexington Books, 1971); Michael Parenti, "Ethnic Politics and the Persistence of Ethnic Identification" *American Political Science Review* 6 (1967), 717-726; Raymond Wolfinger, "The Development and Persistence of Ethnic Voting," *American Political Science Review, 59* (1965), 896-908; Thomas J. Pavlak, "Social Class, Ethnicity and Racial Prejudice," *Public Opinion Quarterly*, 37 (1973), 225-231; Edward O. Laumann, *Bonds of Pluralism: The Form and Substance of Urban Social Networks* (New York: Wiley, 1973); Donald E. Pienkos, "Foreign Affairs Perceptions of Ethnic Politics," *Ethnicity, 3* (1974), 19-33.

6. See thematic essays in Stephan Thernstrom, ed., *The Harvard Encyclopedia of Ethnic Groups in America* (Cambridge: The Belknap Press of Harvard University Press, 1980), esp. Philip Gleason, "American Identity and Americanization"; Milton Gordon, *Assimilation in American Life* (New York: Oxford University Press, 1964); Rolf Dahrendorf, *Class and Class Conflict in Industrial Society* (Stanford: Stanford University Press, 1959); Melford Spiro, "The Acculturation of American Ethnic Groups" *American Anthropologist, 59* (1955), 1242-1256; Joel Williamson, *A Rage for Order: Black-White Relations in the American South Since Emancipation* (New York: Oxford University Press, 1986); Arthur Mann, *The One and the Many: Reflections on the American Identity* (Chicago: University of Chicago Press, 1979), esp. his discussion of the works and intellectual development of Israel Zangwill and Horace Kallen.

7. See Andrew M. Greeley, *Ethnicity in the United States: A Preliminary Reconnaissance* (New York: Wiley, 1974).

8. Edith Abbott, *The Tenements of Chicago 1908-1935* (Chicago: University of Chicago Press, 1936); Thomas Lee Philpott, *The Slum and the Ghetto: Neighborhood Deterioration and Middle Class Reform 1880-1930* (New York: Oxford University Press, 1978); Edward R. Kantowicz, *Polish-American Politics in Chicago 1888-1940* (Chicago: University of Chicago Press, 1975); Thomas Kessner, *The Golden Door: Italian and Jewish Immigrant Mobility in New York City 1810-1915* (New York: Oxford University Press, 1977); Michael H. Ebner and Eugene M. Tobin, eds., *The Age of Urban Reform: New Perspectives on the Progressive Era* (Port Washington, NY: Kennikat Press, 1977); John K. Buenker, *Urban Liberalism and Progressive Reform* (New York: Charles Scribner's Sons, 1973); Stanley Lieberson, *A Piece of the Pie: Black and White Immigrants Since 1880* (Berkeley: University of California Press, 1980). Frank Thistelwaite, "Migration from Europe Overseas in the Nineteenth and Twentieth Centuries"; John Higham, "Origins of Immigration Restructuring 1882-1897: A Social Analysis"; Samuel P. Hays, "The Politics of Reform in Municipal Government in the Progressive Era" in Stanley N. Katz and Stanley I. Kulter, *New Perspectives on the American Past: 1877-Present* (Boston: Little, Brown, 1972).

9. Oscar Handlin, *The Uprooted* (Boston, MA: Little, Brown and Co., 1951), p. 3.

10. Nathan Glazer and Daniel P. Moynihan, *Beyond the Melting Pot* (Cambridge, MA: MIT Press, 1964).

11. Rudolf J. Vecoli, "Ethnicity: A Neglected Dimension of American History," in *The State of American History* (Chicago: Quadrangle Books, 1970); "European Americans: From Immigrants to Ethnics" *International Migration Review*, 6 (1972), 403-434.

12. Richard Kolm, *Bibliography of Ethnicity and Ethnic Groups* (Washington: NIMH, 1973).

13. Wayne Charles Miller, *et al.*, *A Comprehensive Bibliography for The Study of American Minorities* (New York: New York University Press, 1976).

14. Paul Wasserman and Alice E. Kennington, *Ethnic Information Sources of the U* (Detroit: Gale Research Company, 1976 and 1983).

15. G. Carter Bentley, *Ethnicity and Nationality: A Bibliographic Guide* (Seattle: University of Washington Press, 1981).

16. *Harvard Encyclopedia of Ethnic Groups in America* (HEAEG).

17. Anatole G. Mazour, *Modern Russian Historiography* (Berkeley: University of California Press, 1938), p. 85.

18. Bentley, *loc. cit*; Pierce L. Van Den Berghe, *Race and Racism: A Comparative Perspective* (New York: John Wiley, 1978); Robin Williams, "Race and Ethnic Relations," *Annual Review of Sociology*, 1 (19-75); Robert A. Schermerhorn, *Comparative Ethnic Relations* (New York: Random House, 1970); Stanislav Andreske, *Social Science as Sorcery* (London: Deutsch, 1972).

19. For an excellent treatment of Zangwell and Kallen, see Arthur Mann, *The One and the Many: Reflections on the American Identity* (Chicago: University of Chicago Press, 1979).

20. Philip Rosen, *The Neglected Dimension: Ethnicity in American Life* (Notre Dame: Univ. of Notre Dame Press, 1980).

21. Czeslaw Milosz, *Nobel Lectures* (New York: Farrar Straus Giroux, 1980).

22. Frank Thistlehwaite, *loc. cit.*

23. Martha A. Gephart and Robert W. Pearson, "Contemporary Research on the Urban Underclass," *Social Science Research Council Items*, 42 (nos. 1/2, 1988).

24. *National Ethnic Leadership Conference, Task Force Report* (Washington, D.C.: NCUEA, 1984).

CHAPTER VI

THE NATURE OF CULTURE

AND HUMAN NATURE

T. I. OIZERMAN

DEFINITIONS OF CULTURE

There are a great many definitions of culture. Is this good or bad? If we refer to the multiplicity of content-relevant definitions of culture it is good, for even the mutually exclusive definitions of culture record and reflect the richness of the content and form of this uniquely human phenomenon.

Spinoza said, "Omnis determinatio est negatio." From the point of view of dialectics, a definition is more than mere rejection of other definitions of the object in question; it is also rejection through restriction of the lop-sidedness of its own content. Consequently, the scientific analysis of culture transcends the restrictions of each separate definition and establishes connections between them all in order to obtain, thereby, a more profound and concrete understanding of the subject.

Culture is studied by a number of scientific disciplines: archaeology, history, ethnography, anthropology, art-criticism, sociology and philosophy. The archaeologist, for instance, studies the instruments and household utensils of the late Stone Age in order to draw conclusions regarding the culture of the people who lived at that time--what they could make, and to what degree their practical know-how, skills and traits of character (such as persistence) were developed at the time. These "savages" were capable of roughing and polishing a piece of granite, which was then drilled (without benefit of tools, of course) in such a way as to fashion an axe. This fact alone decisively points to the unique historic value of late Stone Age culture. It goes without saying that modern man would find it beyond his power to manufacture a stone axe using the implements of our distant ancestors. Even though the superiority of modern technological culture over its preceding forms is unquestionable, it is equally clear that we have yet to rise above the practical skills of "the savage," exhibited, as it were, in his respective sphere of production-related activity. Moreover, in some respects we are even inferior to people who lived in the late Stone Age.

This consideration has no bearing upon the argument that cultures of different historical eras cannot be compared. Scholars who advocate this not infrequently consider cultural progress to be an empty notion: from their point of view, it is at least incorrect to speak of a greater or lesser development of a people's culture. This author adheres to another viewpoint, crediting cultural progress with the important role of a major parameter of world history. To be sure, progress often implies not only gains but losses, and the attainment of a higher level of social development at times entails negative phenomena previously unknown. But it should be borne in mind that cultural progress includes also the ability to deal with negative phenomena which originated in the past.

The ethnographer sees the main content of culture in the way of life, customs, traditions and beliefs of a given people in a given epoch. The anthropologist who studies a "primitive" race of cannibals is apt to include cannibalism in the sphere of culture. Citing similar phenomena which are inconsistent with modern culture, British anthropologist B. Malinowski concludes that such cultural *realia*, which are alien to us, nevertheless are "essential relatives of universal and fundamental elements of human culture." In his view these include above all ways for satisfying physiological needs of the individual under specific historical conditions at the corresponding level of social development, and so on.[1]

The historian who studies, for instance, events in the past centuries immediately preceding the formation of modern society is bound to single out such elements of culture as the development of schools and higher education, technical creativity, aesthetic needs and tastes, sports, music, various games, hobbies, a growing interest in the lifestyle of other nations, abundance of newspapers, books, etc. In this case, the historian's approach coincides with our everyday concept of the "cultured man," who is opposed to the "uncultured". Here, the term "culture" implies only that which is worthy of emulation and appropriation: what characterizes man as a rational being capable of developing and wisely applying his powers.

The above cited examples indicate that two major types can be singled out from the multiplicity of definitions of culture: on the one hand, descriptive definitions, and on the other, normative definitions. For example, one definition of the concept "culture" on the basis of the etymology of the term holds that "culture is everything created by man as opposed to that created by nature." An example of the other, normative, type of definition holds that culture "is the sum total of a society's achievements in the domain of enlightenment, art, science and other spheres of spiritual life; the ability to use accumulated knowledge and practical experience to subjugate elemental forces, to expand production, and to solve pressing problems of social development." Both these definitions appear one-sided and, consequently, inadequate. The first disregards the normative aspects of culture which are essential or, at any rate, obligatory within the framework imposed by each historically defined culture. The latter definition, on the other hand, excludes the cultural elements that cannot be characterized as achievements or values to be preserved and multiplied.

We cannot consider everything created by man to be culture, despite the fact that cannibalism and other phenomena alien to humanness were elements of historically defined cultures. The concrete historical approach to cannibalism does not attempt to justify the phenomenon, but merely to explain its existence by the material conditions in prehistoric tribes and the mystic beliefs they engendered. Nor does the monstrous vandalism of the Nazis--Hitler's camps with gas chambers specifically designed for the extermination of millions of people, etc.--have anything to do with culture. Hence, the definition of culture as that which is made by man makes it in principle impossible to draw the line either between levels of cultural development, or between culture and the monstrous depravities that contemporary international law calls "crimes against humanity."

The inadequate nature of definitions of culture as mere achievements of science, technology, art, etc., is that it eliminates the negative sides to culture which inevitably are created by the specific historical conditions that underlie social progress. Slavery in antiquity is a graphic illustration. Yet, without slavery, the great achievements of ancient sciences, philosophy and art would have been hardly, if at all, possible. The reduction of culture to man's achievements is also unjustified in that this approach sheds no light whatsoever on the historically passing, fleeting nature of these achievements, or at least the majority of them. For many thousands of years the stone axe, a major achievement of the late Stone Age culture, has been merely a monument of culture, not a real functional elements of culture. The same is true for numerous other objects, implements, traditions and institutions which have lost their significance in the last hundred years of human history.

There also exist, however, permanent *cultural values,* notably in the domain of art. But, since they account for an insignificant part of the cultural legacy, these values cannot be regarded as the main content of culture or as a starting point for a study of its essence.

Recognition of the need for both the descriptive and the normative definition of culture thus leads us to the need for an *historical evaluation* of cultural phenomena. That which constituted a great cultural achievement of one historical epoch ceases to be a cultural phenomenon in another epoch, due both to social progress and the evolution of living conditions, social consciousness and customs. It would be naive therefore to picture cultural continuity as the mere accumulation and multiplication of all the cultural achievements known to history. Elements of culture which belong to various historical epochs are frequently incompatible, which is why the appearance of a new cultural phenomenon becomes possible only after certain elements in the preceding culture, or even the entire network of its institutions, disappear--either dying out by themselves or having been eradicated violently.

In their account of bourgeois revolutions Marx and Engels noted:

> The bourgeoisie, wherever it has got the upper hand, has put an end to all feudal, patriarchal, idyllic relations. . . . It has drowned the most heavenly ecstasies of religious fervor, of chivalrous enthusiasm, of philistine sentimentalism, in the icy water of egotistical calculation. It has resolved personal worth into exchange value, and in the place of the number-

less indefeasible chartered freedoms, has set up that single, unconscionable freedom--Free Trade.[2]

Not stopping at the description of the destruction wreaked by the bourgeoisie, Marx and Engels go on to describe the creative side of its activities:

> The bourgeoisie, during its rule of scarce one hundred years, has created more massive and more colossal productive forces than have all preceding generations together. Subjection of Nature's forces to man, machinery, application of chemistry to industry and agriculture, steam navigation, railways, electric telegraphs, clearing of whole continents for cultivation, canalization of rivers, whole populations conjured out of the ground--what earlier century had even a presentiment that such productive forces slumbered in the lap of social labor?[3]

The multiplicity of historical forms of culture and their constituent elements, the multiplicity of cultures that exist in a single historical epoch, contradictions between cultures and contradictions inherent to each individual culture are all valid reasons which explain the lack of consensus on either the definition of culture, or the characteristics of its development. Today, many "culturologists" insist that "culture" does not exist, only "cultures." From this point of view, the term "culture" reflects the erroneous judgment of those who are misled by the seeming commonness of cultures which does not exist in reality. Cultures of the past and the co-existing cultures of various peoples today are so different as to make it all but impossible to combine them into a single entity even in thought.

The paradoxical nature of this concept resides in that it simultaneously claims absolute distinction for the cultures of various epochs and peoples, and continues to rely on the term "culture," thereby admitting that there does exist a degree of uniformity between phenomena which, according to this concept, have nothing at all in common. Essentially, it is a nominalistic interpretation of the concept "culture" akin to the views of L. Wittgenstein who said that games are alike only in that they are games, i.e., that there is not one common feature or quality characteristic of the entire multiplicity of games.

Nominalism is a subjectivist concept; yet the study of culture demands the investigation of its objective content. The fact that this content is multiple in form and contradictory, together with the existence of numerous cultures which often really are incompatible, is not at all surprising. Far from that, such contradictory multiformity is historically inevitable, since culture is humanity itself in the entire scope of its historical characteristics, which are unavoidably personified and expressed through the self. The problem lies in the study of multiple links between cultures, and in the attempt to answer the question: Is there a common basis for this multiplicity of cultures? Is there a unity (a contradictory unity, of course) of different cultures? Is a common human culture, or at least certain vital common human cultural norms, possible? Besides being of great theoretical importance, such a statement of the problem has a direct bearing upon the ultimate survival of humanity.

In order to answer or at least to properly formulate all these questions, it is necessary, in the author's opinion, to begin, *ab ovo*. Since culture is a specifically human activity-- indeed, the objective and institutional expression of humanity--the statement of the problem hinges upon the understanding of what makes a human being to be human. To be sure, there exist conflicting views on this matter, too. The point of view proposed here is one of materialism's central postulates in the study of history.

HUMAN NATURE AND LABOR

When human nature is discussed, the term "nature" is presumed to have the same meaning as when it was first used in ancient philosophy. Thus, in his *De rerum naturae*, Titus Lucretius Carus associated the nature of things with permanent elements, or atoms as they were called by Leukippus and Democritus, and later by Epicurus. Medieval philosophy used the term "human nature" to denote man's allegedly unchanging essence--that without which man cannot be man. From the point of view of scholastic "realism," human nature resides in man's human-ness, just as does a horse's in its horse-ness. Alteration of such human-ness would mean, according to this concept, transformation into non-human-ness, for if changes do occur in man or in other things they never influence the essence.[4]

Modern philosophy rejected Scholastic reasoning, but nevertheless maintained the postulate of man's unchanging nature, which was interpreted as a set of main qualities that make *homo sapiens* different from other living creatures. Since man's anthropological characteristics have remained the same throughout the history of humanity, this assumption was widely interpreted as the statement of an empirically established fact. Even the dialectically-minded Hegel, who worked on a theory of development, unfortunately failed to rise above this dogma.

A radically novel approach to human nature became possible only with the Marxist theory of the determining role of material production in the development of society and of the human individual. Naturally, the impossibility of human existence without material production was recognized by scholars before Marx. Yet the distance is great indeed between necessity as *a condition sine qua non* of human existence and the materialist understanding of history. Marxism views social production as both the production of things necessary for sustaining life and the production of social relations, of man as a social being or member of society.

Nor did Marx restrict himself to the economic aspect of the theory of labor and production. He also elaborated a philosophico-sociological doctrine pertaining to man's labor-oriented, active essence, whose historic development led to anthropogenesis and the subsequent evolution of humanity as a whole. In his economico-philosophical manuscripts, written in Paris in 1844, Marx called world history "the creation of man by human labor."[5]

Labor is man's subjective activity; yet, as a system of relations and interaction between people, as the use of historically determined implements of production, and as the ratio of live labor to accumulated, objectivized labor, labor forms the content of the *objective*, determining foundation of society--material production. Hence, social production is a subjective-objective process, the unity of purposefully organized human endeavor and the objective conditions for such endeavors, laid down by preceding generations and as such independent of each given generation.

This interpretation of labor and production define more than the biblical explanation, according to which Adam and Eve were doomed to a life of labor in punishment of the original sin. The concept of labor prevalent in the bourgeois society is not that far from the beliefs of Christianity in that it, too, accepts the inevitable necessity for labor for those who have no other means of sustenance. It should be pointed out that this erroneous view does reflect, and at the same time absolutize, the real state of things in a society where the means of production do not belong to the working people. Naturally, Marx repeatedly pointed this out, explaining it with the antagonistic character of production relations under capitalism and the social class formations that preceded it.

The concept of productive relations, i.e., the social relations of production, is a major category in the materialist approach to history. This concept was beyond Adam Smith and David Ricardo (even if they did elaborate the concept "productive forces"), for they did not investigate production from the *historical* point of view--that is, they did not analyze its qualitatively different historical forms. These celebrated economists viewed slavery and feudal extra-economic coercion, not as historically determined (and passing) social forms of the development of productive forces, but rather as irrational, economically unjustifiable, arbitrary legal creations. Until Marx, it could not be proved that slavery and feudal serfdom had been historically inevitable, necessary and, at a given level of development of production forces, progressive. In the course of such development they emerged as the social relations of production corresponding to the aforementioned level. Capitalist social relations of production are likewise necessary and, at a higher level of development of productive forces, progressive. However, they too must give way, since the development of productive forces under the conditions of bourgeois society generates the need to substitute production relations based on private property by public ownership of the means of production.

The fact that the main content of Marxist economic theory and historical investigations is the analysis of antagonistic (above all, capitalist) production relations shows that Marx could not have been further from a romantic assessments of labor. In his Paris manuscripts of 1844, he praises Hegel's true vision of labor as an essential characteristic of man, but at the same time criticizes the idealist genius for his failure to see the *negative side* of labor, i.e., its historical definiteness which is determined by antagonistic productive relations. In the same work, Marx articulates the concept of *alienated labor*, i.e., labor that oppresses and enslaves man, becoming a hated form of activity for the working man."[6] This entails a loss or alienation of the human essence, which "is objectivized in an inhuman way."[7]

Despite this striking contradiction--man's enslavement by his own essence, the anguish of labor and the suffering of the creators of social wealth--labor or social production form the decisive basis for social progress as a whole in all spheres of human activity, no matter how far they might be from production. Furthermore, despite the antagonistic character of productive relations, their development and that of the forces of production ultimately is tantamount to the development of man with his various talents. It is, after all, man or people who work who are the main productive force. Yet, it is equally clear that the development of man's talents is warped by the domination or exploitation of man by man. It is this approach to labor and production, which, together with the comprehension of contradictions in their development, offers the key to understanding culture with its grandeur and negative characteristics.

Karl Marx equates labor with the change of external nature by man, a process that ultimately influences human nature *per se*. Here, we are dealing with man's social nature, not only because man's biological formation had been complete in the prehistoric age, but mainly because man is a social being. The social aspect is a specific characteristic of the human essence. The meaning of the famous Marxist thesis is as follows: human essence is not some abstraction characterizing a separate individual, but the entire sum total of social relations. Consequently the alteration and development of social relations (in accord with the development of the productive forces of humanity) is the alteration and development of the human essence.

Development of production is, according to Marx, "the esoteric revelation of man's essential powers."[8] The essential powers of man--his developing talents, knowledge, needs, skills and know-how--make it possible for man to interact with other men in the process of production and to master the elements, to govern himself, and to fashion various forms of personal contact, social institutes and organizations, creating both material and spiritual values. "In labor," wrote Marx, "all the natural, spiritual and social variety of individual activity is manifested."[9]

OBJECTIVES

Man and Animal

Marx anticipates the objection that some animal species are also social creatures, and that for this reason man's social nature does not signify his *differentia specifica*. True, biologists call bees, ants and some other animal species "social animals," and the author has no intention of contesting their terminology. But terms are not important--content is. The bond between individual animals of a social species has no essential influence on the animal's main characteristics as an individual. Each biological organism is formed mainly prior to birth. Many centuries of observations of the life of bees, ants, beavers and other social animals have failed to detect any essential change in the characteristics of individual members, of their communities or of their way of life.

The human community and its members offer a radically different picture. No particular effort is required to perceive the difference of European society of the last quarter of the 20th century from that of the beginning of the century, let alone from 19th century Europe. Man's social essence is not restricted to simple existence in a society of similar individuals. Furthermore, it should be pointed out that man is not born a man; he becomes one in, and due to, society. Human language, the capacity for which is "programmed" biologically, becomes the language of the human individual only as a result of contact with other men. If a child is not taught to walk he will keep moving about on all fours, despite all the biological preconditions for erectness he might have.

In the animal world, there is only biological, genetically programmed transmission. This means that any experience that an individual animal may have accumulated during its life span cannot be transmitted to its descendants. The reason is that the experience and knowledge acquired by the individual animal are not objectivized, at least not in a form which would make it possible to accumulate, multiply and pass on to the next generation the achievements of individuals. In human society there exists what may be called *social inheritance*, i.e., multiplication of objectivized knowledge, experience and skills. This enables each successive generation to assimilate the knowledge and experience of past generations.

Social history testifies to the ever-progressing difference between human individuals. This means that man's social essence is, to borrow dialectical phraseology, not an abstract, but a concrete identity, which contains an internal difference that is as significant as the identity itself. It can be said even that the greater the identity, the greater the difference. Engels said that relations between man and woman represent unity of identity and difference, with the identity becoming significant due only to the difference, and the difference to the identity. Paradoxical as it may sound at first, identity is also non-identity. This shows that T. Adorno's claim that the identity and the non-identity are mutually exclusive opposites is deeply erroneous.

Applying the concept of concrete identity to the problem of human nature and essence, it becomes possible to determine the singularity, individuality and subjectivity of the human being to be an expression of the objectively existing difference between human individuals, which difference is as substantial as the identity. Yet, the concept of subjectivity is free of subjectivist overtones. "Man," wrote Marx, "emerges as an individual only due to the historic process."[10] This means that individuality, without which of course there can be neither subjectivity nor human essence, is the product of social historical development, the division of labor, the ever-growing multiformity of forms of contact, the production of novel needs, knowledge, and so on. Without division of labor, Marx and Engels pointed out, the appearance of geniuses would be impossible. Specialization and the deliberate restriction of the sphere of activities it entails is the necessary precondition for the development not only of production, but of science and the arts, as well.

Another feasible objection boils down to the statement that animals, like people, are apt to change their habitat. There is hardly any need to examine this thesis. Animals change the environment by adapting to it, whereas humanity adapts the environment to its historically developing needs. Animals influence the environment sporadically and unconsciously, while social production, which is the main way people change nature, is consciously organized activity whose scale has been growing throughout the existence of civilization. Humanity is today the main geological factor, while the changes wrought by animals can hardly be considered irreversible.

Finally, the animal that changes its micro-environment does not change its essence, which is governed only by its *differentia specifica*. The changes that animals do introduce into the world around them are conditioned by their specific characteristics, which have remained the same for thousands of years. As for human nature, it is not restricted to the specific characteristics of *homo sapiens*, i.e., the biological features of the species. Biologically, man belongs to the primates; but man's difference from the orangutan is far greater than the orangutan's difference from animals that belong to other orders. This difference, of course, lies not in the biological, but in the social domain, characterizing man in a specific way.

Man's difference from the anthropoids is growing greater in the course of history. This is possible due to the fact that the historical development of humanity transcends man's species-imposed limitations to acquire a multiformity of lifestyle and activity which is completely alien to animals. "An animal," wrote Marx,

> forms objects only in accordance with the standard and the need of the species to which it belongs, whilst man knows how to produce in accordance with the standards of every species, and knows how to apply everywhere the inherent standard to the object. Man therefore also forms objects in

accordance with the laws of beauty.[11]

This makes the animal a one-dimensional being, whereas man is a multi-dimensional and, in that sense, a "supernatural" or social being.

Existentialism, Personalism and Philosophical Anthropology

Some scholars in view of the dramatic changes in the life of men, their modes of activity, their needs and so on admit that human life has spawned phenomena which are totally uncharacteristic of animals and which until recently have been absent from human history as well. Yet, they interpret these radical changes as completely irrelevant to human nature, which allegedly is unchangeable. This approach to the problem reduces the concept of human nature to an abstraction, whose content is made up of emotional characteristics of man as a feeling and suffering being conscious of mortality. But the concrete nature of emotional characteristics does not make the concept of man concrete, for it leaves out the fact that even these most general characteristics of the human being are modified by history and filled with new content, i.e., changed. Moreover, contemplation of man as a mere individual isolates him from society and eliminates his social and personal qualities. Yet, it is social life that forms the content of man's personal life; his individual characteristics stem also from social life. "Man is the world of man, the state, the society," wrote Marx.

Doubtless, advocates of existentialism, personalism or philosophical anthropology will disagree with what they see as too generalized an interpretation of human essence. Representatives of these philosophical branches are characterized by a tendency for clear-cut contrasts between the individual and the social, the subjective and the objective. Yet, concrete historical, sociological, anthropological and ethnographical investigations prove the presence of the social in the individual, and of the objective in the subjective. Only recognition of the unity of the individual and the social, the subjective and the objective allows one to comprehend the phenomenon which is man with the unique distinction of human individuality. It is for this reason that it is impossible to agree with J. Ortega y Gasset when he writes: "Society or the collective is not something human."[12]

This approach to the problem absolutizes the phenomenon of alienation and ignores the obvious fact that alienation of the individual is a social phenomenon. This is why there are and can be no grounds for denying the *social* nature of man which forms the only framework that can explain the infinite plurality of human individualities. No protest against the alienation of human essence can form the basis for the following statement made by the above-mentioned scholar: "Human life is always the life of each individual man, it is individual or personal, life. . . . In the proper and original sense, only that is human which I make of myself with consciousness of my own goal."[13] This statement, which appears only to establish the fact, in reality is subjectivist--an individualist interpretation of the direct given-ness of human existence.

Recognition of the change and development of society and humanity together with a negation of the change of human nature and essence: this is the awkward situation which describes philosophical anthropology today. Its proponents are well aware of the need to harmonize these two opposite characteristics of mankind and of man. The most widespread attempt to solve this problem while preserving the thesis of the permanence of human nature is associated with the anthropological concept of scientific and technological progress as the only possible compensation for man's natural (specific) inferiority. Indeed, the development of man as a being that cognizes and changes nature would be impossible without certain biological preconditions. This conclusion appears all the more accurate since animals, too, are capable of cognition and instinctive forms of labor appropriate to their specific characteristics.

However, philosophical anthropology is not content with the recognition of these facts. It goes considerably further and attempts to form the grounds for a purely speculative thesis: all the achievements of science, technology and art are realized due to a genetic program of the human species. This concept can be called "culturological preformism." It is comparable to the preformist theory of the famous Swiss biologist, A. Haller, who tried to prove that the people who lived in the past and will live in the future pre-existed in embryonic form in the ovaries of our common mother, Eve.

As a matter of fact, the reduction of all human achievements, past and present, to the mere realization of a genetic program is one of the versions of the concept of the permanence of human nature. It is not difficult to see that culturological preformism completely ignores the socio-economic conditions of the development of man and of mankind, since these conditions cannot be included in the genetic program. Crediting man with an inherent ability for infinite development of cognition, technology and art (and admitting that this makes man radically different from animals), culturological preformism ignores, in addition, that such ability is incompatible with the specific limitations of every living being. This theory rejects man's specific characteristics which transcend biological restrictions imposed by the species of *homo sapiens*, and thereby precludes the possibility of supplying the phenomenon of culture with a scientific explanation.

CULTURE AS A SECOND NATURE: THE OBJECTIVATION OF HUMAN ACTIVITY

The key to the nature of culture lies rather in the above line of reasoning in support of the thesis that the entire history of humanity is tantamount to the alteration and development of the nature and essence of man. Man creates a "second nature" by objectivizing his activities. This term implies, on the one hand, a man-modified environment, and on the other, man himself who commands mankind's prior achievements and uses them to discover the previously unknown, to create while continuing to develop his active essence. Marx has the following to say about this process: "Only through an objectively unfolded richness of man's essential being is the richness of objective human sensibility (a musical ear, an eye for beauty of form, in short, senses capable of human gratification, senses affirming themselves as essential powers of man) either cultivated or brought into being."[14]

Culture is man's greatest difference from animals. This difference is not biological, of course, but social, constantly developing and acquiring increasing multiformity corresponding to the multiformity of conditions of existence of various peoples, their histories, development and social reforms. Culture is nothing but the ever-changing and developing human nature in the entire multiplicity of the objectivizations of human activity. This definition is, of course, far from complete, for it does not include the normative aspect of culture and thereby the historical process which is responsible for the negation of certain elements of the preceding cultures, cultural selection and amelioration of culture. This definition is a starting point on the path of dialectical synthesis of various definitions of culture, the only synthesis capable of producing a concrete definition of the concept "culture."

The multiformity of past and present cultures of various peoples is not the only qualitative multiformity. There exists also the qualitative multiformity of various types of culture. The culture of labor, production, organization and management is one. The culture of thought, language, oral speech is another. The culture of spare time, physical culture and aesthetic taste is yet another. For all the disparity of these cultural types of activity with their corresponding objective realia, they form a single entity as forms of the existence and development of human nature (and, consequently, of society--the plurality of all forms of interaction between human individuals). It should always be borne in mind, of course, that human activity is objectivized not only in material objects, but spiritually, as well, since man's education, professional skills and talents, works of art and science, for all their material "tangibility," are objectivizations of social consciousness and knowledge. The same is true for spiritual needs as cultural phenomena: they are necessarily objectivized, all the while remaining spiritual rather than material needs.

We speak of the culture of production, the culture of management, the culture of personal contact and of moral culture, thereby introducing a normative aspect into the characteristics of production, management, personal contacts, etc. This is an extremely important demarcation line within the essential identity of culture and production, an identity which includes a difference which at times outgrows into negation. This concerns cultural values as an aspect of culture which is formed and changed in the course of historical development. If, for example, we take the history of agriculture, it at once becomes apparent that agrarian culture changed in history and that the agricultural methods that had been prevalent not only are obsolete, but have ceased to be essential elements of agriculture. Analysis of the history of industry affords an even better view of the historically changing character of the culture of production, i.e., the fact that cultural development includes the rejection of obsolete forms and their substitution by newer and more rational ones. This is confirmed by the process of rationalization and intensification of production which is constantly going on. Therefore, material production per se, i.e., without reference to certain historically formed standards of rational realization of this process, is not rightfully a cultural phenomenon; it becomes one only in the quality of a certain level of the culture of production, technological culture, the culture of organization and management, and so on.

The product resulting from a process of production cannot be considered, in itself, an object of culture, either: it becomes one as a means for the development of human nature or the formation of the self, with its talents, knowledge, tastes, etc. The product of labor is a phenomenon of culture only insofar as it constitutes the objectivized expression of an historically defined culture of production. The means of production directly serve production, and indirectly the development of the person who masters them, in which light they are objects of culture. Food products in themselves are not objects of culture, whereas the method for their preparation and consumption is a phenomenon of culture. "For the starving man, it is not the human form of food that exists, but its abstract existence as food. It could just as well be there in its crudest form, and it would be impossible to say wherein this feeding activity differs from that of animals."[15]

However, human consumption of food, which is variedly distorted in a society where masses of people live in poverty, is, despite this distortion, a specifically human, cultural process, which reflects the antagonistic character of the class structure of the society in question.

Historical analysis of culture, i.e., the analysis of its development, recognizes the negation of obsolete elements of past culture. It thereby singles out those cultural elements which not only are accepted in the course of subsequent development, but preserve, as it were, their permanent cultural value, not infrequently representing unattainable samples of creative culture. Above all, this concerns outstanding artistic masterpieces which objectivize an outlook that can never be reborn for the simple reason that the conditions under which these masterpieces were created have been dismantled in the process of subsequent development. Marx pointed out that the charm which attracts us to Ancient Greek art is not in opposition with the undeveloped social stage which spawned it. On the contrary, it is its result and has a direct bearing on the immature social conditions under which it had emerged, could only have emerged, and would never recur.[16]

It should be pointed out that not only in the art, but in the material production of the past, for example, the culture of artisanship, there have been elements which could have enriched the subsequent cultural process had these "professional secrets" not been irretrievably lost.

Among the multiple objectivizations of human activity, which are forms of development of the social nature of man, it appears necessary above all to single out those objects and means of culture whose *only purpose* resides in the satisfaction of people's spiritual needs. Since social progress historically forms the need for cognition, aesthetic needs and the desire for physical perfection, then books, works of art, musical instruments, sports games, gymnastics, etc., are the *direct* being of culture. This acts not only as a means for the resolution of social tasks, but as an activity for its own sake, i.e., the goal of this activity is the human individual who engages in this activity. This fact is reflected in everyday life: primary importance usually is attached to the spiritual image of the person in question, to education, needs and interests, and to the ability for sound appraisal of the circumstances of life in an intelligent manner which first and foremost is exhibited in personal contact and in one's attitude to other people. Though it is impossible to overestimate these characteristics of culture, it would be erroneous to limit the concept of culture only to these characteristics. Culture concerns both the individual and society as a whole, material production, politics, ideology, and so on.

This makes culture tantamount to historically developing human nature with its multiformity of spiritual and material objectivizations and the plurality of all social relations that form the human essence. The anthropological unity of humanity is the first historical precondition for its historically developing contradictory unity. Indeed, the notion "history of mankind" does not coincide with the notion "world history," which implies neutralization of the disparity of peoples via economic and other bonds. Strictly speaking, world history is made only in the course of capitalist development. However, antagonistic contradictions, which characterize the capitalist system, cannot but manifest themselves in relations between people and their cultures. The development of nations and national cultures manifests, according to Lenin, two opposite tendencies. One is a centrifugal tendencies, expressed, first, in the self-determination of nations (the positive side) and, second, in bourgeois nationalism (the negative side). The other is the constantly progressing tendency for rapprochement among peoples, the objective basis for which is the internationalization of production, consolidation of workers in their struggle against capitalist dictatorship and liberation of colonial peoples from the imperialist yoke. This second tendency is becoming prevalent, for deep in the capitalist system the economic preconditions are taking root which eventually will open the way for a new, socialist culture which will be international in content.

Social progress is the way to common human culture, which is formed in the process of comprehensive peaceful contacts among nations. Local civilization theories advocate the thesis of the incomparability of cultures, mainly citing ancient civilizations which existed long before the appearance of world history as one of the major factors of cultural progress. In fact, one of the essential features of culture, a feature which characterizes the longevity and level of development of a culture for this or that people, is its ability to assimilate the cultural achievements of other peoples. This was accurately observed by Charles de Montesquieu in his *Considerations on the Causes of the Greatness of the Romans and Their Decline.* He writes that "the Romans became masters of the world mainly due to the fact that in their never-ending wars against all nations, they invariably gave up their customs when they noticed that these could be changed for the better."[17] For instance, they gave up their sword when they learned of the Spanish sword. Victors, they nevertheless learned from the vanquished nations. Montesquieu was driven to write about antiquity by more than a simple interest in the distant past,[18] for his work bears a marked anti-feudal character. Speaking about the ability of Romans to assimilate the cultural achievements of other peoples, he laid bare the vices of feudal culture, namely, its poor orientation to the achievements of other nations.

The wealth of each people can be assessed according to numerous parameters. Yet in our day and age the revolution in science and technology, while multiplying social wealth, simultaneously spawns ecological dysfunctions which, independently of the nuclear threat, lead to the disintegration of the natural environment. It is becoming totally clear that the greatest expression of social wealth resides in cultural achievements, and in the ability of a culture to deal with its negative sides. Marx had the brilliance to foresee this historical situation in his characterization of wealth without reference to its bourgeois, commodity form. Marx wrote:

> Casting aside the limited bourgeois form, what is wealth if not universality of needs, capabilities, means of consumption, productive forces, etc., of individuals attained by *universal exchange*? What is wealth if not the absolute detection of creative talent, without any preconditions save for preceding historical development, which makes a goal in itself of this integrity of development, i.e., the development of all human powers per se without reference to any *pre-set* scale chart"?[19]

CONCLUSION

The Marxist description of the most important, i.e., cultural, wealth of humanity is more than a mere statement of a fact which seemingly is obscured by capitalist relations of production and exchange. It also opens a great vista which is vital for putting an end to hunger, squalor, alienation and, of course, for ridding mankind of the looming nuclear holocaust. For this reason cultural cooperation between peoples and mutually beneficial cultural exchange are vital factors of peace on earth. It is time to realize (from the entire course of world history) that the differences between the currently existing cultures are, essentially, differences within the fundamental unity of all peoples that make up humanity. To blow these differences out of all proportion, to present them as unsurpassable barriers that divide mankind, is to claim that past isolation of peoples and their cultures is an eternal law, an absolute norm. Yet, today, rapprochement between cultures of different peoples is a law which fully corresponds to the socio-economic changes and scientific breakthroughs we are witnessing. Global problems, the common human character of which is beyond doubt, are a formidable illustration of the unity of the major cultural needs and of the tasks of the world's peoples. It is equally important to close the gap in the economic, scientific, technical and cultural spheres of relations between countries and regions. This is a major goal on the way towards fraternal unity of nations.

Naturally, there are numerous obstacles on this historical progression towards a common human culture (which does not preclude the cultural individuality of each people as the product of many centuries of the history of that people). However--and this must be realized first of all--most of these obstacles lie outside the sphere of culture, namely, in the economy and in politics. Millions are dying of hunger in Africa and Asia every year: the geography of hunger copies economic geography. This is the real context of the hundreds of billions of dollars that are wasted on the arms race each year! Yet these sums, which are spent mainly on the production of weapons of mass annihilation, could be used to prevent the destruction of humanity's natural environment.

Over 60 years ago, Lenin said that culture must teach us to fight for peace among nations, to overcome the negative consequences of modern civilization and to promote the fraternity of different cultures which, despite all, are united by their human essence.

There is no other way.

USSR Academy of Sciences
Moscow, USSR

NOTES

1. B. Malinowski, *Scientific Theory of Culture and Other Essays* (Chapel Hill: The University of North Carolina Press, 1944), p. 39. The example of cannibalism should not be regarded as something alien in principle. Even in his day, J.-J. Rousseau understood the ambivalence of culture. The modern epoch convincingly illustrates the opposition of good and evil in cultural development. Speaking at the 17th World Congress of Philosophy, E. Levinas characterized culture as the rational being of man, but admitted its inherent "radical evil" which found its horrible embodiment in Hitler's death camps. The opposition of humaneness and inhumanity within the cultural framework is by no means casual. According to E. Levinas, this is the "barbarity of being, and stems from the very beginning within the being, and is fraught with estrangement that takes root in the transcendence and estrangement of other men. Such estrangement is greater than any spatial remoteness" (E. Levinas, "Determination philosophique de l'idée de culture," *Actes du XVIIᵉ congrés de philosophie* [Montreal, 1966], pp. 81-82). Disagreeing with E.

Levinas's abstract concept of the sources of cultural ambivalence, I attach the highest importance to the comprehension of the substantial content of this contradiction and its socio-economic roots.

2. Karl Marx and Frederick Engels, *Manifesto of the Communist Party*, in *Collected Works* (Moscow: Progress Publ., 1976), p. 486.

3. *Ibid.*, p. 489.

4. Such reasoning is not uncommon among modern philosophers. For example, C. Giacon insists that "in man, there is an essence, which is such and such and would cease to be human essence, man, were it different. What this essence is from the ontological point of view is a matter for future investigation; here, suffice it to conclude that it is that which makes man man, rather than dog or God," *Proceedings of the XVth World Congress of Philosophy* (Sofia, 1974), III, 63.

5. Karl Marx, *Economic and Philosophic Manuscripts of 1844* (New York: International Publishers, 1964), p. 100.

6. *Ibid.*, chapter on "Estranged Labor."

7. *Ibid.*, chapter: "Critique of Hegelian Dialectics."

8. *Ibid.*, Vol. III, p. 303.

9. *Ibid.*, p. 236.

10. Karl Marx and Frederick Engels, *Works*, vol. XLVI, part I, p. 485 (in Russian). Cf. also K. Marx, *Grundrisse der Kritik der politischen Okonomie* (Berlin: Dietz-Verlag, 1972).

11. Karl Marx, *Economic and Philosophic Manuscripts*, p. 113-114.

12. J. Ortega y Gasset, *El hombre y la gente* (Madrid: 1957), p. 27.

13. J. Ortega y Gasset, *op. cit.*, p. 23.

14. Karl Marx, *Economic and Philosophic Manuscripts*, p. 96.

15. *Ibid.*

16. Karl Marx and Frederick Engels, *Works*, XII, p. 737 (in Russian).

17. Charles de Montesquieu, *Considerations on the Causes of the Greatness of the Romans and Their Decline* (New York: Free Press, 1965).

18. Charles de Montesquieu. *Selected Works* (in Russian) (Moscow, 1955), p. 49. Speaking of the fall of the Roman Empire, Montesquieu notes: "Rome was not a city of tradesmen; it had hardly any artisans. Plunder was the sole source of wealth left for its citizens" (*ibidem*, p. 51). The very wars that increased Rome's wealth ultimately became the reason for internal strife, deterioration of military might and the fall in the struggle with "barbarian" peoples.

19. Karl Marx and Frederick Engels, *Works*, XLVI, part 1, p. 476 (in Russian). Cf. also K. Marx, *Grundrisse der Kritik.*

PART II

CULTURES IN

CHANGE AND CONFLICT

CHAPTER VII

SOCIAL HARMONY

AND PERSONAL FULFILLMENT

AN ANALYSIS OF TRADITIONAL

CHINESE CULTURE*

CHEN NA

> The Dao that can be trodden
> is not the enduring and unchanging Dao.
>
> *The Dao De Jing*

Like the Dao, the culture that can be told is not the genuine culture. This is especially the case of Chinese culture, which has a continuous history of approximately 2,500 years if counted from the time of Confucius. The present paper, then, will attempt only a highly limited view and a brief analysis of the Chinese culture as a whole. Even so, I must stress the incompleteness of this work as the topic calls for a book rather than a paper.

Harmony is much more appreciated in our world today than ever before as the people of the world move literally to form a global village and intercultural contacts become more frequent and unavoidable. Further, due to the development of sophisticated skill in killing, any conflict between cultures might lead to catastrophes, if not to the annihilation of humanity. Our task here is to search for possibilities for mutual understanding between cultures and for the realization of the harmonious coexistence of different cultures.

Harmony has been one of the most important concepts in the Chinese tradition, both philosophically and socially. A Western scholar who visited China in 1920--when, the Chinese tradition had long been in a low state, but, I believe, was also engaged in the long process of rebuilding--was deeply impressed by the Chinese manner of harmonious life.

> The Chinese have discovered, and have practiced for many centuries, a way of life which, if it could be adopted by all the world, would make all the world happy. We Europeans have not. Our way of life demands strife, exploitation, restless change, discontent and destruction. Efficiency directed to destruction can only end in annihilation, and it is to this consummation that our civilization is tending, if it cannot learn some of that wisdom for which it despises the East.[1]

How the Chinese traditional concept of harmony should be understood, how it was realized in traditional Chinese society, and what it means to a person as a member of society in the present are questions to be discussed in this paper.

NATURE, SOCIETY AND MAN

To begin, we must look at the view of nature in Chinese philosophy, since to trace the origin of social harmony in the Chinese tradition one must know the Chinese view of nature to which the Chinese view of society is closely related. *The Dao De Jin* says:

> The Dao produced One; One produced Two; Two produced Three; Three produced All things.[2]

Here, the "Dao" refers to the absolute being which is a non-existence and cannot be named. "One" is an existent being which is nature in its unified or chaotic status; "Two" refers to *Yin* and *Yang*, which are two opposite cosmic forces that complement each other; "Three" is *Yin* and *Yang* plus *He Qi*, which is the harmonious atmosphere with *Yin* and *Yang* well balanced; then, all things are produced.[3]

We must pay special attention to "Dao" and "One." "Dao" is often translated literally as "Way," which means the principle or law. When "One" is produced from *Dao*, it signifies, on the one hand, the unified status of nature before all specific things are created, and, on the other hand, that there is one fundamental principle or natural law (*Dao* or Way) embodied in nature as a whole and in everything else within nature including man himself and human society.

Also it should be noticed that all things are produced with *He Qi*, that is, in a harmonious atmosphere; nature as a whole, therefore, is an harmonious being. The forces of *Yin* and *Yang* within nature are at once opposite and complementary, and thus make nature move by an inner dynamic. The way by which nature moves is *Dao*. There are times when nature moves away from its right Way because one of the forces has become too strong or too weak. But Chinese philosophy believes that "the movement of the Dao by contraries proceeds,"[4] that is, when things reach their extremes it is time for them to turn around, so that in time harmony will be regained and nature will keep to its right way.

Human society, as part of nature, also moves by its *Dao*, which is represented by the way according to which social harmony is reached. Man himself, as both a natural and a social being, must behave according to *Dao*, which is represented by ethical, moral and social codes, including law and all kinds of customs. In the Chinese tradition these are generally termed "Li" (which literally means etiquette or courtesy, but also means ritual) and "Gui Ju" (literally, compasses and square). They keep harmony among people, in society, and with nature as a whole.

At the time of the Western Han Dynasty (206 B.C.-24 A.D.), philosopher Dong Zhongshu (179-104 B.C.) summed up the ancient Chinese philosophy and developed his theory of "Tian Ren Ganyin." "Tian" literally means sky or heaven, but in Chinese philosophy it usually represents the absolute being of nature; "Ren" here means man; and "Ganyin" means interaction. Therefore, Dong's theory is a theory of "interaction between man and nature," which is part of a very complicated theoretical system that can be used to explain all things in the world by referring to *Yin* and *Yang*, and to the five fundamental elements in nature: metal, wood, water, fire and earth.

The basic idea goes like this: Man is a creature of *Tian* and represents *Tian's* will; *Tian* moves along *Tian's Dao*, and Man moves along Man's *Dao* which is a copy of *Tian's Dao*; both of these are constant, as Dong Zhongshu says, "the fundamental principle of (Man's) *Dao* comes from *Tian*, and *Tian* shall not change, nor shall *Dao*".[5] There are even exchanges of feelings between Man and *Tian*, such that, if Man goes against *Dao (Tian)* he will be punished. People might take *Tian* here for the punishing God in *The Old Testament*, but that is not the idea, at least it is not the key idea.

The essence of Dong's theory is to justify *Dao*. By relating *Dao* to the absolute being of *Tian*, Man's *Dao*--the Way of Man or of Human Society--is made absolute. Just as *Tian* (nature) moves harmoniously with its inner rhythm and law (*Tian's Dao*), represented by its regular changes of seasons and weather, so does human society move with social rules and principles (Man's *Dao*). Accordingly every man must keep to certain principles as a member of society. As the movement of *Tian* cannot be changed the way in which society and man move shall not change. Hence, the rule of the sovereign, the order of society, and the blood and social relation between people are all absolute. This theory became tremendously influential in Chinese history, for all Chinese feudal rulers adopted Dong's theory to justify their rule and to keep social order and harmony.

Dong's theory was further developed by the Li Xue School of the Song Dynasty (960 A.D.-1279 A.D.). Some of the philosophers of the Li Xue School so emphasized the absoluteness of the set social order based upon human relations that the order itself was taken as the fundamental principle of the whole world, and the social harmony based upon the order was made absolute and eternal.[6] This theory of the Li Xue School dominated Chinese society ideologically in the last eight hundred years of its feudal period.

DAO OF SOCIETY AND SOCIAL HARMONY

Dao of society consists of two aspects: a structure of social hierarchy and "Li"--sets of rules and principles to keep the hierarchy in order and society in harmony.

The social hierarchy was structured, of course, with the Emperor at the very top and his subjects below. Unlike some other cultures with social hierarchy which is built on a system with castes and the outcasts ranked in a hierarchical order,[7] the Chinese social hierarchy is based on bureaucratic and blood-line systems. As early as the Chin Dynasty (221-207 B.C.), China was a unified country under one central government, with a unified monetary system, a unified system of length, capacity and weight, a unified highway design and a unified written language. All these guaranteed political, economic and cultural unity. The whole country was divided into many counties (the system was later developed by more levels of provinces and regions) and was governed by administrative officials sent by the central government, that is, the court headed by the Emperor. From the level of county up to the central government all the administrative departments with their officials formed a well-organized hierarchy.

Below the level of county was that of village. One county could have dozens or more villages. Each village was often one clan, or consisted of members of two or more clans. Sometimes, one big clan consisted of several villages. The clan head and some other persons, usually with higher positions in the blood line and of fairly old age, were in charge of clan and village affairs. One clan originated from one ancestor, that is, all members of one clan bore the same family name. Quite often, villages were named after the family name, e.g., Wang Village, Big Wang Village, Small Wang Village, etc. Villages consisted of the basic social cells, families, within which there was a small hierarchy arranged according to positions in the blood line, sex and age.

This was the general framework of traditional Chinese society. Especially noteworthy are two points: one is that, compared with Christian or Islamic societies, the whole framework was basically secular. It is true that the Chinese worship "Tian," but *Tian* was considered as an absolute being mainly to justify the absoluteness of the secular order or of the *Dao* in this world. Besides, people did not expect an everlasting life through *Tian*; there is no such concept as redemption and salvation in the Christian sense in the original Chinese tradition.[8] Although Chinese people did resort to gods in their daily life, that was for practical secular purposes; thus Chinese gods were more like the Greek than the Christian.[9] Another indication of the prevalence of the secular was that the family was the center of everyone's life while the social structure was an enlarged copy of an extended family. The whole framework assumed the characteristics of a large secular family. In Chinese, "public" is "gong" which is often understood as "gong jia"--a "public family"; "country" or "state" is "guo jia," which means "state family"; and the official in charge of county affairs is otherwise called "fumu guan," which literally means "parents official."

To keep this big "social family" in order, there was "Man's Dao" (the Way of Human Society), which corresponded to and was justified by "Tian's Dao" (Way of Nature). The fundamental principle of "Man's Dao" is, in time, developed into "Three Gang and Five Chang" (*Sang Gang Wu Chang*)--"Gang" literally meaning the headrope of a fishing net or the key link; "Chang" refers to something normal and invariable. Here "Three Gang and Five Chang" stand for three cardinal guides and five constant virtues.[10] "Five Chang" are the principles for self-cultivation and individual behavior, which will be discussed later. "Three Gang"--the three cardinal guides--are "ruler guides subjects, father guides son and husband guides wife."[11]

The three cardinal guides are explained by Dong Zhongshu in light of his theory of *Yin* and *Yang*. According to Dong, "Tian's destiny prefers *Yang* rather than *Yin*" (*Tian shu you Yang bu you Yin*), that is, *Tian* always places *Yang* in the dominant position and *Yin* in a subsidiary position.[12] Therefore, Dong says:

> The doctrines of ruler and subject, father and son, and husband and wife are all from the *Dao* of *Yin* and *Yang*. Ruler stands for *Yang*, while subject for *Yin*; father stands for *Yang* while son for *Yin*; and husband stands for *Yang* while wife for *Yin*.[13]

The relation between each related couple, however, is not absolutely uni-directional. The *Dao* of Three *Gang*, while undoubtedly dominant over the other, is understood in a reciprocal and dynamic way: while the subject should be loyal to the ruler, the ruler should respect the subject; while the son should be filial, the father should be loving; while the wife should be obedient, the husband must be harmonious.[14]

With these principles settled, the general framework of this secular society is set in order. While the Three *Gang* are the headrope of the network, there are many sub-ropes and basic strings to make the whole network. These are the detailed principles for individuals to observe in and out of the family.

FAMILY AND CLAN

Within a traditional Chinese family, there is a similar hierarchical system on a smaller scale. The family hierarchical order is arranged on the basis of natural relations: every man owes his life to his parents, so he should be filial and obedient to his parent. As parents have their parents in turn, so the old aged are highly respected and the ancestors are worshiped.[15] In addition, according to the theory of *Yin* and *Yang*, the male *(Yang)* is superior to the female (*Yin*), so the family hierarchy is arranged in the same manner according to age and sex. This, of course, can be understood also according to the nature of a patriarchal society. In order to maintain the family order, among family members we have "Li" (etiquette or courtesy) and "Jia Gui" (family principles), both identified with Man's *Dao*. The patriarch has an absolute position in the family; in return, he is responsible for the family's order, fame, prosperity and happiness.

Every member in the family learns from a very young age to figure out his own position in the hierarchy. He or she learns (and also is taught, of course) to be respectful and obedient to those in higher positions and to be friendly and considerate to those in lower positions. In daily life, the various relations between different roles in the family are kept according to "Li," and any breach of "Li" might invite a lesson or punishment according to "Jia Gui" (family principles). This depends upon how strict the "Jia Gui" is in a given family: usually the more decent the family the more strict will be the "Jia Gui," but the basic hierarchical relation is universal. An analysis of the terms for family members in Chinese language will help to give some idea of this.

The Chinese language has created a whole set of terms to distinguish different memberships in the family. There is not the equivalent single word of "parent" in Chinese, but either "father" (*fu*) or "mother" (*mu*); there is not the word "brother," but either "elder brother" (*ge* or *xiong*) or "younger brother" (*di*); there is not the word "sister," but either "elder sister" (*jie* or *zi*) or "younger sister" (*mei*). If you want to express the meaning of "parents", "brother(s)," or "sister(s)," you have to put the two words together to form a compound. Therefore, we have the compound words of "xiongdi" (brother or brothers), "jiemei" (sister or sisters), and "fumu" (father and mother). Unlike Westerners, who usually introduce or mention another family member of their own generation as a "brother" or "sister," the Chinese, especially in the old days, almost always do so with the specification of "elder brother" or "younger brother," or "elder sister" or "younger sister"; in a family with many children, one has to say "eldest, or first elder brother," "second elder brother," or "second younger brother," etc., according to the precise relation.

The order and relation are important and subtle. These words are not merely titles or appellations, but symbols with considerable specific cultural connotations of respect, obedience, responsibility, authority, etc. Especially in the case of father and mother, there is no such word or compound word as "parent" to stand for either father or mother. ("Qin" for father or mother, or father and mother, is used in some situations, but this is a very loose word that can be used for any close blood relation. One never says "my qin" in making an introduction.) Father is father, mother is mother; how can they be confused? Husband guides wife; this is the absolute principle.

On the basis of honoring shared ancestors, the clan system is organized and developed in essence as an extended family. The traditional Chinese family is extended to such a degree that people within "Jiu Zhu" (nine generations, that is, one's own plus four generations earlier and four generations later) are considered of the same family.[16] In one area, people with the same family name are usually of the same clan, because the Chinese (of the Han people that form more than 90% of the Chinese population) have been an agricultural people with fairly fixed location for about ten thousand years.[17] They have formed a tradition of remaining in the same area, according to the Chinese proverb: keep to your old land and be serious about moving (*an tu zhong qian*). Some can trace their family to as many as 36 generations in the same village. Because of this extreme lack of mobility, clans are developed very highly.

> Over a whole area all people may be exclusively of one clan and, in addition, families living in far-away cities are their

clan fellows. In populous areas like Kwangtung all the clan members unite in keeping up great clan-halls and on stated days they venerate as many as a thousand ancestral tablets of dead clan members stemming from a common forebear. [18]

Within a large extended family or clan a correspondent hierarchy is built according to generation, age, sex, etc. Similarly, there are un- imaginably over-elaborate formalities ('*Li*') and clan laws (*Zhu Fa*) to keep the clan in order and in harmony. By these, relations are main- tained and responsibilities and obligations are assumed.

An average Westerner would be totally at a loss to determine his station among literally dozens or hundreds of relatives, or among thou- sands of clan members. But every Chinese has a name consisting of two parts: "Xing" (family name) and "Ming" (given name). In contrast to the Western practice, the Chinese place their family name before the name given by the family, usually by parents, grandparents (more often by the father than by the mother) or close relatives. The family name shows one's relation to a certain family or a clan.

The given name, of either one or two characters, usually shows one's generation. (Of course, the given name usually has its own meaning for the character(s) chosen--the Chinese are great players of words.) There are two ways: one is to chose the same character as one of the two characters of each given name for all members of the same generation, the other is to choose one character-component as a part of one character of each given name. In *The Dream of the Red Chamber,* the first gener- ation of two members are named Jia Yan (賈　演) and Jia Yuan (賈　源); here Jia (賈) is the family name, while Yan (演) and Yuan (源) are given names both with a three-drop-of-water compon- ent (氵) in the characters. Each of the families has a son, and with two other cousins they form the second generation. Their names are Jia Dai- hua (賈代化), Jia Dai-shan (賈代善), Jia Dai-ru (賈代儒) and Jia Dai-xiu (賈代修). In each name there is a character "Dai" (代); so this generation is called the "Dai" generation of the Jia Family. Later genera- tions will have their special characters or character-components. All this is decided by the clan and every clan member can easily spot his own station in the clan and make clear the relation between himself and a relative.

In English, as well as in some other Western languages, there are but a few words to name our relatives, such as uncle, aunt, cousin, etc. In Chinese, there are many more equivalents with specific meanings to distinguish the explicit relationship between relatives. In Chinese for "uncle" there are "bo" (father's elder brother), "shu" (father's younger brother), and "jiu" (mother's brother, younger or elder). The word "cous- in" often gives difficulty in translating from English into Chinese, for in Chinese there is no exact equivalent word for "cousin," though there are many more specific words: "tangxiong" or "tangge" (elder male cousin from a paternal uncle's family), "tangdi" (younger male cousin from a uncle's family), "tangmei" (younger female cousin from a paternal uncle's family), "biaoxiong" or "biaoge" (elder male cousin from a paternal aunt's or both maternal uncle's or aunt's families). There are still more distinctions: from a paternal aunt's family or a maternal uncle's family, the cousin relation is "gubiao"; from a maternal aunt's family, the cousin relation is "yibiao," etc. When people meet, especially for the first time, they always take some time to make clear all these relationships.

Language is the window of culture. All these terms are not simply words but are significant cultural codes. It is true that the Chinese language, compared with Western languages, tends to be vague and implicit, but regarding family relationships it is much more explicit and distinctive. This reflects the importance of the family relationship in the Chinese culture and the development of the hierarchical structure in the Chinese family. People always pay more attention to what they consider important, and this, in turn, is reflected in language. It is common knowledge that in the comparatively underdeveloped language of the Eskimoes there are more than forty words to describe ice and snow in their different states because they live in a world of ice and snow all the year round and through all their generations. Similarly, in English, as a language of Christian culture, there are dozens of words for God in different specific senses.

An organized hierarchy means unity, conditioned harmony, responsibilities and obligations. A family clan, if big enough, owns its lands, property and temple. It keeps track of dispersed members and publishes elaborate geneologies from time to time. The fame of the family and clan is important. Any success on the part of an individual is considered not only as their own glory, but also that of their family, clan and ancestors. (This is somewhat similar to the Christian tradition in which people speak of all glory being owed to God.) In a culture with a tradition of scholar-administrators, the greatest glory (the Right *Dao*) is to pass the official examinations of different levels and take governmental positions. For this, the whole family would support the schooling of the son or sons as far as they can afford; the clan also raises funds to pay for the education of any promising son of the clan. All clan members are supposed to help each other, especially when there are conflicts with people from the outside. The clan has the duty to take care of all its members in difficulty or with social problems.[19]

Hierarchy also means authority. Any breach of the family principles or clan rules would be punished, those who are being punished are supposed to receive the punishment obediently.

> The clan rules are basically instructions. They depend on moral persuasion. . . . The punitive provision in some of the clan rules--oral censure, ritual discipline, cash fines, corporal punishment, denial of clan privileges, expulsion from the clan group, and legal indictment--are paradoxically less punitive than protective. They are designed to warn the offen-

der to see to it that there will be no need for the law to pun-
ish him except as a last resort.[20]

Severe punishment, however, did exist in some districts and was imposed
particularly upon "unfilial" sons and "undecent" daughters; it could be as
grave as death. In *The Mind of China*, we have a 19th century Chinese
picture of the members of a family drowning an "unfilial" son in a
well.[21] A patriarch who fails to discipline his children is considered a
great failure and may bring disgrace upon the whole family. If the family fails to execute the family discipline in a timely and proper manner,
the clan has the right to exercise its authority according to the clan rules
because the unfilial and the undecent are considered to have defamed the
clan as a whole. In some remote rural areas, as late as in the 1930's, girls
who had "undecent" love affairs were drowned in ponds by the clan authorities.[22] Though cruel, this is also "just," because all these hierarchical
and non-hierarchical principles represent *Dao*, and *Dao* is justified with
Tian, the absolute. Any cruel thing is possible and can be done with
righteous indignation and spiritual satisfaction so far as the action is
justified by the absolute.

The Chinese are famous for their strong family ties, unlike their
Christian tradition, in which people commit themselves to a great extent
to the religious community and to the service of God. It differs also from
some other cultural traditions in which the real sense of life is not in this
world, but in the world-to come, so that people do not care so much
about family life and social relations in this world. In the orthodox Confucian tradition, however, the real sense of life is in this world, which is
part of *Tian* (Nature) and mirrors the absolute principles of *Tian*. People
commit themselves totally to their family, their family clan, their state
and to life in this world. As there are hierarchical structures of different
levels in the family, the clan, and society as a whole, from the cradle to
the grave one is constantly fixed at a certain hierarchical spot. Like
strings in a network fixed to different knots, all kinds of relational duties, responsibilities and obligations bind one.

Suppose everyone keeps to his spot and all hierarchies are in perfect order, how harmonious the whole society would be! But how would
personal fulfillment be realized in this harmonious society?

PERSONAL FULFILLMENT

All people expect to live a meaningful life. People in different
cultures live a meaningful life in different ways. For a Chinese Confucian,** a meaningful life is fulfilled mainly in three aspects: self-cultivation, family life and social career.

The ideal Confucian government is one of fiduciary relationships[23]
which require every member of the society to be loyal to his proper
position so as to maintain an harmonious structure. Although people do
resort to severe punishment, the Chinese generally believe in "the doctrine of the mean,"[24] that is, not to go to the extremes. As they believe

also in the original goodness of human nature,[25] they resort more to human conscience than to law and punishment.

I believe this can be understood also on the basis of the Chinese philosophical tradition which emphasizes more the inner factors than those coming from outside and leading to change. Therefore, the movement of the universe is caused by its inner contradictory forces of *Yin* and *Yang*, which are at once opposing and compensatory, rather than by an outside prime mover. Also, according to traditional Chinese medicine, one contracts a disease mainly because one has lost his inner balance; the doctor's task is to help him to readjust this inner balance.

The Chinese tradition stresses the importance of moral education and self-cultivation. The Confucian classic *The Great Learning (Da Xue)* points out:

> From the Son of Heaven down to the mass of the people, all must consider the cultivation of the person the root of everything besides.[26]

Here, the Son of Heaven refers to the Emperor. All in the hierarchy, from the very top down to the bottom, must take self-cultivation as their fundamental life-long task. This, of course, is an important means for reaching the goal of harmony. Yet, the means, emphasized too much, may itself become the end, and this is the case of Chinese self-cultivation. It is so important that if a man has done nothing else in his life but make himself an acknowledged well-cultivated man he is considered a great success and is highly respected. On the other hand, if a man has succeeded notably in politics or academics, but failed to be (morally and ethically) cultivated, to a considerable extent he will be considered not to have been worthwhile.

A well-cultivated man is "Jun Zi," while a perfect "Jun Zi," such as Confucius, is "Sheng Ren" (the translation as "Saint" or "Sage" is not exact). The opposite of "Jun Zi" is "Xiao Ren" (literally "petty man," often translated "mean man" or "inferior man"). The fundamental principle of *Jun Zi* is the doctrine of the Mean, as Confucius says:

> *Junzi* embodies the course of the Mean; *Xiaoren* acts contrary to the course of the Mean. *Junzi*'s embodying the course of the Mean is because he is a superior man, and so always maintains the Mean, *Xiaoren*'s acting contrary to the course of the Mean is because he is a mean man and has no caution.[27]

So, to cultivate oneself one has to be very cautious and try to keep precisely to the course of the Mean, because "to go beyond is as wrong as to fall short."[28]

Generally speaking, the basic task of self-cultivation is to practice the "Three Gang and Five Chang," for they are the fundamental principles of the Chinese Confucian society. While the "Three Gang" are set relations that keep the social hierarchy in order, the "Five Chang" are "five constant virtues" as basic ethical and moral codes for personal culti-vation. These are "ren," "yi," "li," "zhi" and "xin," sometimes translated as: benevolence, righteousness, propriety, wisdom and fidelity.[29] Of course, the original meaning is much more rich. Taking "ren" as an example, its principle meaning is charity. Confucius says, in answering his disciple Fan Chi's question about its meaning, that "ren" is to "love all men."[30] But "ren" is understood also in many other ways, even in the same chap-ter of "Zi Lu" in *The Analects of Confucius*. In one place:

> Fan Chi asked about 'ren.' Confucius said: 'It is, in retire-ment, to be sedately gracious; in the management of busi-ness, to be reverently attentive; in dealing with people, to be strictly sincere. Though a single man go among rude, uncul-tivated tribes, these qualities may not be neglected.'[31]

In another place:

> Confucius says: "The firm, the enduring, the simple, and the modest are near to 'ren'.[32]

The main means of self-cultivation is self-examination, as des-cribed by Zen Shen, one of Confucius's principle disciples:

> I daily examine myself on three points (or for three times):--whether, in transacting business for others, I may have been not faithful;--whether, in dealing with friends, I may have been not sincere;--whether I may have not mas-tered and practiced the instructions of my teacher.[33]

In the long years of the development of Confucianism, there have appeared many specific books for people in different positions to learn to behave and examine themselves, such as *The Classic of Filial Piety (Xiao Jing), The Classic of Daughters (Lu Er Jing), The Principles for Brothers (Zi Di Gui)*, etc. Even in *Three-Character-Line Book (San Zin Jing)*, first published in Song Dynasty (960-1279 A.D.) and since then a primer for literacy for all the children in China until the early 20th cen-tury, the ideas of "Three Gang and Five Chang" and other basic moral and ethical ideas are all embodied and written in short (three characters to a line) and easy-to-memorize sentences.

Undeniably, many of the elements in the traditional Chinese moral and ethical codes are acceptable or may be acclaimed in most, if not all, other cultures. The tradition of self cultivation did contribute immensely to social harmony and stability in Chinese history and thus helped win China the fame of the "country of *Jun Zi*" (*Jun Zi Zhi Guo*). But all these codes are created on the basis of the Chinese cultural situation. Many of them have gone too far along the road of seeking perfection in long years of development. The direct result of the emphasis on moral education and self-cultivation is that a great majority of the Chinese are gradually shaped to fit the life positions laid out ahead of them when they are born. Some Chinese do take self-cultivation as a life-long task, and high moral standards as a life pursuit. Unfortunately, many of them become very pedantic and tend to cling to outworn rules and ideas; they are rarely creative or original.

According to the Confucian tradition, "filial piety is the first of all virtues"[34] and Mencius said, "there are three things which are unfilial, and to have no prosperity is the greatest of them."[35] Family life, therefore, is the most important aspect of personal fulfillment. In this one's self-cultivation is put into practice and one has his first experience of a social career. In Confucian theory society or state is only the family written in capital letters.

Family life has two layers of meanings: life before marriage and life after marriage. Before marriage, one is disciplined by the cardinal guide: father guides son. Then, his personal fulfillment is to play the role of a son, who is supposed to obey and be filial to his parents, grandparents and great grandparents, and to be on good terms with other members of the family according to the nature of the relation and the consequent duties and obligations. In a large extended family it is not easy always to keep harmony, which is reached through set rules and principles. Though this is not without personal feelings and affections, so much has been taught as required that it prevents the feelings and affections from being naturally developed and expressed.

Marriages are generally arranged by parents--quite often, with the help of relatives and matchmakers. After marriage, a son remains such, is guided by the father and has the full duties of a son; meanwhile he assumes the duty of husband as guide of his wife. In time he will be at once son, husband and father, which means he will be heavily burdened with all kinds of relations together with duties, obligations and responsibilities. He is now in the center of a network with strings from all directions fixed upon him. Much of his energy is spent in balancing all these relations, since, although he is in the center, he is not at the position of the head-rope. Actually, from the time one is born he is placed at a certain spot in the network. The process of his personal fulfillment is to move from one spot to the other, each stereotyped according to the structure of the hierarchy, which is a dictatorship of patriarchs. A newly married couple is at a transitionary spot.

> If they moved away from the ancestral home, or if they outlived the senior members of their family, they would become family heads in their own right, and, wherever they were, their children would serve them respectfully as they had once served their own parents. Life was likely the same to anyone, even a woman, who survived it long enough. Having paid the price of obedience, the survivor could relax into the comfortable dictatorship of Chinese patriarchs.[36]

Because of the unrelenting emphasis upon filial piety and the absoluteness of order, the process of personal fulfillment is rarely to express and realize one's individual personality, but to suppress it in order to maintain harmonious relation with others and to play well one's stereotyped role. "Instead they must learn to separate their feelings from their actions, suppressing the former and controlling the latter by strict rules of etiquette."[37] This partly explains why and how, as some researchers have observed, a Chinese person seems to move from childhood to manhood without the necessary transitionary period to adulthood that is psychologically expected.[38]

For a Chinese, one's social career, as part of one's personal fulfillment, has two dimensions: the micro and the macro. In the traditional Chinese agricultural society, it is not uncommon for a person to live his whole life within a small rural area. Even during the Cultural Revolution (1966-1976), people going to the countryside found there some old people who had never visited the nearest town. Their social career, then, would mean life only within their neighborhood or nearby villages, and usually in their own clan which, with some differences, is literally an enlarged family hierarchy. There, all one has to do is to figure out his position and play his role well. This is a social career in micro dimension.

A social career in macro dimension meant taking local and national examinations and becoming a scholar-official in the various levels of government. According to Confucianism, self-cultivation, family regulation and state government are closely related.

> Their knowledge being complete, their thoughts were sincere. Their thoughts being sincere, their hearts were then rectified. Their hearts being rectified, their persons were cultivated. Their persons being cultivated, their families were regulated. Their families being regulated, their states were rightly governed. Their states being rightly governed, the whole kingdom was made tranquil and happy.[39]

John K. Fairbank once referred to these words as a series of illogical deductions,[40] but culturally speaking they are quite logical. That is why they are among the very first lines in the key passage of "Great Learning," the first of *The Four Books*, the most important Confucian classics,[41] and have been taken for granted as axiomatic for all those who took examinations for official positions for more than one thousand years. These words reflect the Confucian way of "self-cultivation, family regulation, and state government. They also express the Confucian idea that all those who are able should serve the state, according to the saying: "Take the fate of 'under the Heaven' as one's own responsibility" (*Yi Tian xia wei ji ren*).

The Chinese examination system began in the Tang Dynasty (618-907 A.D.). Since then the main road leading to official positions and power, and consequent privileged treatment, was through official examinations. This system helped to further develop the Confucian tradition of book learning.

To prepare for the examination, one had to go to school and thereby enter the relation between pupil and teacher.[42] It is reasonable for the by enter the relation between pupil and teacher.[42] It is reasonable for the pupils and the teacher to respect each other. In a hierarchical society, however, the general tendency is to make all relations hierarchical and the teacher-pupil relation is no exception. In the Confucian tradition, *Tian* (sky or heaven), *Di* (the earth), *Jun* (the emperor), *Qin* (parents), and *Shi* (teachers) are arranged in a series to which everyone must show absolute respect. Hence, any disobedience to one's teacher is considered as being against *Dao*. This goes along with the traditional teaching method, which requires pupils to memorize mechanically what the teacher presents without necessarily understanding it. It is also cohesive with a social demand for absolutely obedient citizens.

To pass the examinations and join the ranks of officials meant entering into another network whose general headrope was in the hand of the Emperor.

> China was a status-oriented society in which social relationships tended to be structured vertically; all social relationships, that is, tended to be between individuals who acted as either a superior or a subordinate in the relationship.[43]

This was particularly true for one who took up an official career. It was the officials' duty to report the situation of the people and to satisfy their demand, but often they fail to do so because authoritative power comes from above and officials often are busy trying to satisfy their immediate superior. As the whole country represents the will of The One at the top, the wisdom of the emperor is the crux. Unfortunately, most emperors in history, especially those who succeded to the throne by inheritance rather than by their proper efforts, proved not to be so wise. Therefore, in most cases, the government was not creative, but only kept the country in an ideal--orderly and harmonious--state. The main task of the individual official was to play a set role, rather than to express himself and to realize his own original ideas.

Because of the overdeveloped network of blood and personal relations, one's official career affected all who were related to him. As the saying goes: "if one gets the *Dao*, his dog and cock will follow him to Heaven"; on the other hand, if one looses his *Dao*, his dog and cock will suffer with him. According to traditional law a felonious criminal might suffer the severe punishment of having his whole family beheaded. Plotting to murder the emperor was punished by the beheading of all members of the felon's extended family within nine generations (*mi men jiu zhu*); in some cases, even their friends and teachers were punished in some manner. This is the result of the relation-network tradition which, in turn, it reinforces. As a matter of course nepotism prevails in such a culture, which makes it difficult for those who take office to fulfill themselves or express their own personality.

Even those who rise very high in the hierarchy find it difficult to act authentically. In some sense, the higher one's rank the more difficult it is to play the role. Thus, the prime minister had a most difficult posito accompany a tiger." The task of a minister was more to understand and put into practice the will of the autocratic emperor than to express himself or to work for the interests of the state and people. It follows as a rule in Chinese history that officials with strong personality and originality rarely had good ends.

CONCLUSION

Any culture as an organized community must have certain beliefs, organization and principles to maintain the order and harmony required for its very existence. Members of the culture, while enjoying the order and harmony, must pay for it at the personal costs of limitation of individual freedom. A well developed culture, while maintaining its order and harmony and developing as a whole, should allow all its members to develop themselves as individuals to the degree possible.

In certain cultures in history, because of an overdevelopment of their organization and principles, and an overemphasis on harmony and the interest of the whole--either the small whole of the family or the big whole of the state--the development of individuals has been reduced to an extremely low degree. In some aspects, it would not be an exaggeration to say that the very existence of the individuals was twisted and deformed. A typical case is the traditional Chinese culture in which the term "individualism" has always been very negative and has been used pejoratively in the sense of the Chinese expression: Give the dog a bad name and hang it. One who lives in this culture does enjoy the experience of stability and security. Especially for one born there and never having a sense of individuality or privacy, life may be admirably peaceful and harmonious, as described by the Western observer cited at the beginning of this paper. But when one goes more deeply into this culture and examines it from the viewpoint of the individual, one forms a different opinion.

> A Confucian family good in its own terms was able to give both physical and psychological security. A member of such a great family-organism would not be abandoned to himself. He knew who he was and what he had to do, and he had little of the solitary European's need to find himself in Promethean acts. It was comforting, then, to belong to a Confucian family, but very tiring. You were always having to check your natural aggressiveness. In the worse cases, it was like always being on the verge of a headache, your courtesy masking your anger. The Chinese needed a way to rest from the strain and to restore the contact between their outer, courteous faces and their inner, immediate selves.[44]

The tradition of Daoism does provide the Chinese with a way to do this. Different from Confucianism which advocates an absolute social order and encourages people to enter into society and accept its rules, Daoism is interested, not in society and social competition, but in the

Dao of nature. A generally passive attitude towards social life is taken in the Daoist tradition; self-cultivation is a preparation, not for a social career, but for identification with nature. For those who suffer setbacks or totally fail in their social career, Daoism is a constant spiritual port of refuge, where they can either adjust and gather strength or find enduring tranquility. The slogan for those who are struggling in their official career is: if I succeed in my official career I will benefit all people under Heaven; if I fail in it I will be a well-cultivated man myself (*Da ze jian ji Tian xia; Jiong ze du shan qi sheng*). For more than two thousand years these two contradictory traditions, Confucianism and Daoism, both based on the absoluteness of nature, have gone side by side without essential conflict. They compensate for each other and form the Chinese culture as an organic whole.[45]

Although it is an important component of Chinese culture, Daoism is not the orthodox center of society. Anyone who lives as a member of Chinese society is a product of Confucianism. Those who are called Daoists cannot escape the brand of Confucianism, any more than one could escape socialization while being a member of society. The process of socialization in traditional Chinese society means, to a great extent, to shape oneself into certain stereotypical roles. This is much like the traditional Chinese "art" of foot-binding. The standard foot, the most "haocan" (good-looking), it is said, is of about three or four inches long. Girls must begin at a very young age to compress their feet to meet the standard. The bigger the potential size of their feet, the more they suffered. Likewise, in the process of one's socialization, the stronger one's personality, the more one will be tortured and twisted.[46]

As Confucianism stresses family relations and harmony, the rules and principles (also called "Gui-ju") used to shape its social members tend to give the impression of being moral and humane, with a generally familial atmosphere. Therefore, when one is thus being shaped by the "Guiju,", uncomfortable as one is, one will not be able even to find a way to complain.

Research by modern psychologists and anthropologists show that culture is the dominant factor in the formation of personality. Except in the case

> of a few small societies whose members have a homogeneous heredity, where the influence of physiological factors in determining the psychological potentialities of the majority of these members cannot be ruled out, culture must be considered the dominant factor in establishing the basic personality types for various societies and also in establishing the series of status personalities which are characteristic for each society.[47]

It has been proved also that child training has significant meaning in the formation of an adult, which is both conditioned by, and helps explain the reasons for, the given cultural configurations.[48]

Child training, under the influence of an integrated and integrating cultural ego, systematically narrows the number of these potentialities (of trait configurations based on the organism and the organization in time and space of its basic needs) by creating hypertrophies and atrophies the integration of which is the cultural trait configuration characterizing all members of the group. It does so by utilizing that basic polarity of human childhood which makes child care and child training necessary, namely, initial helplessness and prolonged dependence, on the one hand, and insatiable desire for independence, mastery, and investigation, on the other.[49]

That is, child training shapes a child culturally and limits the possibilities of the development of one's personality, thus further limiting the cultural trait configuration. We cannot rule out the possibility that a child with a strong personality may be limited and shaped to some extent during his childhood, but that when he reaches the age of independence his personality may sprout, blossom and grow into its destined future. Even this possibility, however, is generally ruled out in traditional Chinese culture, where there have developed all kinds of "Gui-ju" and a universal network, not only to limit and shape a child, but also strictly to limit and shape any member at every stage of his life. The "Gui-ju" and network are so harmoniously worked out that they reflect the law of nature (*Tian Dao*) and, like the four seasons of the year, operate with absolute inevitability. It is natural, then, that any "irregularity" within the network should be nipped then and there or in the bud.

On the whole, harmony has long been a predominant tendency in traditional Chinese culture. As a result, it has formed a tradition that highly values the harmony of society as a whole and, at the same time, developed an organic social structure that maintains the absoluteness of social harmony. As we search for a harmonious future for our world today this tradition of China is certainly a very good source for reference. Meanwhile we must see the other side of this tradition, which has been emphasized in the present paper, that is, that the absolutized harmony of society as a whole is reached, to a great extent, at the cost of the fulfillment of individuals as unique and creative beings.

Peking University
Beijing, People's Republic of China

NOTES

*"Tradition" in this paper refers to the tradition before 1911, when the last Chinese feudal dynasty was overthrown. It is understood that all

things discussed in this paper, except those with specific denotation, are within this time limit.

** Here, we refer mainly to the male. As shown in the "Three Gang," the female is at the very bottom in the society. Limited by an even more strict "Female Dao," females are much more unfortunate and need special study.

1. Bertrand Russell, *The Problem of China* (New York: Century, 1922), p. 12. One thing which should be taken into consideration is that Russell made the observation not long after the First World War when the Western world, and Europe in particular, was confused ideologically.

2. Lao Zi, *The Dao De Jing*, Chapter 42. The translation is taken from *The Sacred Books of China; The Texts of Taoism*, translated by James Legge (Oxford: At the Clarendon Press, 1891). I have adapted the old translation of "The Tao Teh King" into "The Dao De Jing" according to the new spelling system for translating Chinese into English.

3. For the explanation of "Dao" and "One" see *The Sacred Books of China*, pp. 85-86; also see *History of Chinese Philosophy*, Volume I, compiled by The Department of Philosophy, Peking University (Beijing: Zhonghua Shuju, 1980), p. 96.

4. *The Dao De Jing*, Chapter 40, James Legge translation.

5. "Biography of Dong Zhongshu," *History of Han Dynasty (Han Shu)*.

6. *History of Chinese Philosophy*, Volume II, pp. 66-67.

7. India and Japan are examples. For Japan see Ruth Benedict, *The Chrysanthemum and Sword, Patterns of Japanese Culture* (Boston: Houghton Mifflin, 1946), pp. 57-58.

8. By the "original Chinese tradition," I refer to the tradition before the introduction of Buddhism into China during the Eastern Han Dynasty (25-220 A.D.). See also note 45.

9. See Justus Doolittle, *Social Life of the Chinese* (New York: Harper, 1876); also, Lewis Hodous, *Folkways in China* (London: Arthur Probsthain, 1929).

10. The translation of "Three Cardinal Guides and Five Constant Virtues" is taken from *A Chinese-English Dictionary* compiled by the editorial board of CED, English Department, Beijing Foreign Languages Institute (Beijing: Commercial Printing House, 1986), p. 585.

11. *Ibid.*

12. *History of Chinese Philosophy*, Volume I, p. 204.

13. Dong Zhongshu, *Fundamental Meaning (Ji Yi)*; the quotation is taken from *History of Chinese Philosophy*, Volume I, p. 208.

14. This is the basic understanding of "Three Gang" that can be found even in *San Zi Jing* (a traditional primer for children's literacy). See *San Zi Jing* (Changsha, Hunan Province: Yuela Shushe, 1986).

15. In the Chinese tradition, ancestors are respected and honored; in return, the ancestors are believed to help by protecting their descendants.

16. See *San Zi Jing*.

17. See Liu Ruilong, "Adjust Our Attitude toward Chinese Agricultural Heritage," *Archaeology of Agriculture* (No. I, 1981).

18. Ruth Benedict, *The Chrysanthemum and the Sword*, pp. 40-50.

19. See Hui-Chen Wang Liu, "An Analysis of Chinese Clan Rules: Confucian Theories in Action," in *Confucianism and Chinese Civilization*, ed. by Arthur F. Wright (New York: Atheneum, 1965).

20. Arthur F. Wright, ed., *Confucianism and Chinese Civilization*, p. 17.

21. Ben Ami Scharfstein, ed., *The Mind of China* (New York: Basic Books, 1974).

22. Deng Kaifan's talk about his hometown, Beijing, 1986.

23. Confucian political idea is best represented by Mencius' doctrine of "Ren Zhen" (benevolent government), which is based upon the inseparability of morality and politics, and "the correlation between the self-cultivation of the ruler and the governability of the people." See Frederic Wakeman, Jr., "In Search of National Character."

24. *The Doctrine of the Mean* is one of the "Four Books," which were among the basic books for taking official examinations leading to an official position; the other three books were *The Confucian Analects, The Works of Mencius* and *The Great Learning*.

25. There are different views of human nature in the Chinese tradition, but belief in the goodness of human nature has been central to the Confucian School. The very first two lines of *San Zi Jing* read: in the beginning of man, human nature is good.

26. *Great Learning*, English translation from *The Four Books* with notes by James Legge (no publisher and no date).

27. *"Zhong Ni," The Doctrine of the Mean (Zhong Yong)*. The English translation is by James Legge with my revision.

28. *"Xianjin," Confucian Analects*, James Legge's translation.

29. *A Chinese-English Dictionary*, p. 585.

30. *"Yan Yuan," Confucian Analects*, James Legge's translation.

31. *"Zi Lu," Confucian Analects*, James Legge's translation with my revision.

32. *Ibid.*

33. *"Xue Er," ibid.*

34. *The Classic of Filial Pie*ty *(Xiao Jing)*.

35. *The Works of Mencius*, Book Four, J. Legge's translation.

36. Ben Ami Scharfstein, ed., *The Mind of China*, p. 6.

37. Lucian W. Pye, *Asian Power and Politics: The Cultural Dimensions of Authority* (Cambridge, Mass.: Belknap, 1985), p. 186.

38. Sun Lung-kee, *The Deep Structure of Chinese Culture* (Hong Kong: Jixian She, 1983). See Chapter Three, espec. section 3.

39. *Great Learning (Da Xue)*, James Legge's translation.

40. John K. Fairbank, *The United States and China* (Cambridge, Mass.: Harvard University Press, 1971), pp. 68-69.

41. In some editions *Confucian Analects* is put as the first of *The Four Books*.

42. About traditional Chinese school, see Ben Ami Scharfstein, "Rulers and Sons: The Villager at School," in *The Mind of China*; see also, Lu Sun, *From Herds Garden to Three-Taste Reading House.*

43. Lloyd E. Eastman, *The Abortive Revolution: China under Nationalist Rule, 1927-1937* (Cambridge, Mass.: Harvard Univ. Press, 1974), p. 288.

44. Ben Ami Scharfstein, ed., *The Mind of China*, pp. 25-26.

45. In this paper I purposely avoid the discussion of Buddhism. This imported religion in time became an important component of Chinese culture, but so far as personal fulfillment is concerned Buddhism, much like Daoism, functions as an alternative resort or compensation for Confucianism.

46. Justus Doolittle, Vol. II, pp. 198-199.

47. Ralph Linton, *The Cultural Background of Personality* (New York: Appleton-Century, 1945), pp. 145-146. The passage in this paper is quoted from Francis L. K. Hsu, *Under the Ancestors' Shadow* (New York: Columbia Univ. Press, 1948), p. 257.

48. Frederic Wakeman, Jr., *In Search of National Character*, p. 14.

49. Erik Erikson, *Observation on the Yurok: Childhood and World Image* (Berkeley: Univ. of California Press, 1943), p. 292.

CHAPTER VIII

LANGUAGE AND NATIONAL UNITY

THE PHILIPPINE EXPERIENCE

EULALIO BALTAZAR

This study will consider the relation of language to the quest for Philippine national unity. The Philippines belongs geographically to South-East Asia, which is divided into the mainland: China, Thailand, Cambodia, Burma and Vietnam, on the one hand, and, on the other, the Malay world comprising the crescent of islands from Sumatra, Java, Celebes and the Philippines, Borneo and New Guinea. There are deep differences in culture and religion between the mainland and Malay. The former is a world of Buddhist priests and kings; the latter a world of mosques and sultans--except for the Philippines which is uniquely Christian and Catholic due to the Spanish conquest and colonization of the islands.

The Philippines is composed of over seven thousand islands, populated by many ethnic groups each with its own culture. Filipino native cultures have been deeply influenced by Chinese culture due to the Chinese migrations as early as the 10th century, by Hindu culture by way of the Malay peninsula and Java (700-500 A.D.), by Islam which reached the southern Philippines in the 15th century, by Spanish culture (1521-1898), and most recently, by American culture (1898-1946).

The Philippine native languages of which there are about 75 linguistic groups are branches of the Malay-Polynesian stock. Three of these are major languages: Ilocano in the north, Tagalog in the central region, and Visayan (Ilongo and Cebuano) in the south.

PROBLEM OF NATIONAL UNITY

The problem of achieving national unity is a difficult one which implies two basic tasks. The first is the need to modernize and create a viable economy, for the fragile democracy recently established will not last if the hopes and aspirations of the poor are not met. Many of the rural poor have gone over to the National People's Army, a communist rebel group, because past governments failed to address their grievances. Demonstrating farmers pressuring the government to move quickly on land reform have been shot upon by the military with several deaths. Military factors have staged abortive coups to protest the soft treatment of communism by the government. Solution of this unrest requires modernization and a more fair and equitable distribution of wealth.

The second task is the need to achieve cultural identity. The recently ratified and promulgated Constitution states that "the State shall foster the preservation, enrichment, and dynamic evolution of a Filipino national culture based on the principle of unity in diversity in a climate of free artistic and intellectual expression."[1] Because of the many ethnic cultures which have been profoundly influenced by Chinese, Indian, Islamic, Spanish and American cultures, this is easier said than done.

While it is true that there is no such thing as a pure culture and every culture is "mongrel or an amalgam of cultural borrowings," Filipino anthropoligist Francisco Claver adds that "neither does this mean there is no such thing as cultural identity."[2] But how is one to define this cultural identity? Considering the diversity and multiplicity of native cultures and subcultures is it possible to arrive at some universal traits, some common patterns of thinking and behavior that we can call the national character and culture? The typical Filipino would consider his pattern of thinking and behavior Asian, yet he is perceived by his South-East Asian neighbors as more American than Asian. The typical Filipino has a predilection for things American: for American-made goods, for American free-enterprise, American-type democracy and modernity. Considering these ambivalences, the Philippines is a nation in search of its cultural personality.

In the process of modernization and the search for cultural identity some native cultural values could be lost or eroded. But one cannot choose not to modernize or to insulate one's culture from others. As Bishop Claver advises:

> Culture is a *now* event, a present process, continually evolving, but at the same time rooted in its antecedents. The direction it may take at any given moment will not therefore be completely haphazard but will be dictated to a great extent by those same antecedents interacting with whatever influences are impinging on the culture from the 'outside'.[3]

In the process of modernization and inculturation, language plays an important role. To this question we will now turn.

LANGUAGE: OFFICIAL STATEMENT AND ACTUAL PRACTICE

The recently ratified Philippine Constitution contains official statements concerning language in its relation to national unity. In section 6 of article XIV it states:

> The national language of the Philippines is Filipino. As it evolves, it shall be further developed and enriched on the basis of existing and other languages.

> Subject to provisions of law and as the Congress deems appropriate, the Government shall take steps to initiate and sustain the use of Filipino as a medium of official communication and as language of instruction in the educational system.[4]

Note that by the term "Filipino" applied to the national language is meant the Tagalog language, which, however, is spoken mainly in central Luzon. In northern Luzon, Ilocano is mainly spoken, along with other native languages such as Pampamgeno, Pangalatot, Igorot, etc. In the Bicol region in southern Luzon, Bicolano is spoken. In the Visayas and Mindanao, Ilongo, Cebuano and Moro languages mainly are spoken. Furthermore, there are many Filipinos who are more at ease speaking English, Spanish and Arabic than the native languages. In view of these facts, making Tagalog the national language and the medium of instruction has met with some resistance. Taking cognizance of these facts, the Constitution adds:

> For purposes of communication and instruction, the official language of the Philippines are Filipino and, until otherwise provided by law, English.

> The regional languages are the auxiliary official languages in the regions and shall serve as auxiliary media of instruction therein. Spanish and Arabic shall be promoted on a voluntary and optional basis.[5]

Note the special role and privilege that English is given in comparison to Spanish and the other regional languages. It is almost on a par with Tagalog in importance for it is made, not only an official language along with Tagalog, but also the medium of instruction. That Tagalog was chosen as the national language is not based on its popularity for more Filipinos speak Cebuano than Tagalog and perhaps an equal number of Filipinos speak Ilocano as speak Tagalog. The reason is that it is the language spoken in the most influential region of the Philippines, namely, central Luzon.

> English is more widely spoken in the Philippines than is Tagalog.

> Because of the many Philippine dialects used in many parts of the islands (even as much progress has already been made in the nationwide use of Filipino as the national language) it is a common phenomenon to find communities of Filipinos coming from different regions (as in convents, schools, dormitories, offices, conferences, etc.) using English because it is the only language they can communicate in efficiently and profitably.[6]

In Manila, the capital of the Philippines, the more than ten daily newspapers and weekly magazines are all printed in English. On TV and radio, news commentators and reporters speak mainly English. However, in TV discussions and debates on national issues and in everyday conversations at home and in business a mixture of Tagalog which natives call "Taglish" is spoken. For example, a speaker would utter a sentence in Tagalog, then he would continue in English. Or, in one and the same sentence, a phrase would be expressed in English and the next phrase in Tagalog, or he would use a phrase consisting of both Tagalog and English words. For those fluent in Spanish--many Filipinos of the older generation--Taglish is interspersed with Spanish.

Summing up the language situation in the Philippines, we believe that both Tagalog and English will be the dominant languages in the years to come. Tagalog will be dominant because it is imposed by the government as the national language and the medium of instruction at least at the elementary and high school levels. English will continue to be dominant because parents want their children to learn English as a means for obtaining good jobs and economic success. This brings us to the role of English in the modernization process.

ENGLISH AND MODERNIZATION

National unity as we noted earlier is closely tied to modernization, as this depends on the application of western science and technology in order to achieve economic development. Entry to western science and technology for the Philippines is through knowledge of English. Therefore, the government sees that English is taught in the schools where it is also the medium of instruction.

While it is the means to the acquisition of knowledge of western science and technology, English is also the means of contact with western culture: and this experience of modernization has resulted in "the collapse of values and of spiritual refuge."[7] It is possible, therefore, that impersonal institutions and relationships necessary to the success of modernization may supplant the interpersonal values of kinship, close family ties and poetic and mystic solidarity with nature of the Filipino psyche. The banning of English as some misguided Filipino nationalists have suggested is not the way to counteract these negative effects of modernization. Some balance between modernization and tradition must be achieved.

ENGLISH AND PHILIPPINE CULTURE

As a result of contact with western culture, Philippine culture has been Americanized, because of which some Filipino intellectuals fear that the uniqueness of the native cultures could be lost. Francisco Claver does not think so.

> In borrowing traits, artifacts, values, patterns of behavior, norms, world views, etc., people make them their own by making them over to fit their own cultural image, ethos, etc.
>
> Countless examples can be cited to illustrate this phenomenon, from the borrowing of material items (jeeps, guns, coca-cola, etc.) to the acceptance of non-material ones (democracy, Moonism, Catholicism, etc.). In every instance of borrowing, the recipients give the borrowed item something distinctively their own.[8]

Jaime Bulatao welcomes the interaction between western culture

(American and Spanish) and eastern Filipino culture as liberating the Filipino from ethnocentrism.

> My culture is second nature to me. In fact unless I become culturally aware, I shall mistake my culture for "natural law" and shall demand that others obey this natural law. Without experience of another culture, cultural awareness cannot come. Like the fish in the water who is not aware that he lives in 'water' (note the apostrophes, the sign of reflective awareness), so also the man who has lived all his life in an Italian village cannot become aware of 'culture.'
> Awareness of culture loosens some of the power that culture has over the mind. Pluralism on the other hand gives birth to another culture. In fact so dynamically changing can a culture be that one has to be ever alert lest while condemning the blindness of the people in one culture one runs the danger of being blind within one's own.[9]

Further studies have to be done in order to assess both the positive and negative aspects of the Philippine cultural meeting of east and west.

Let us now consider how English as a second language directly impacts on the perception, thinking and world view of the English-speaking Filipino. On the relation between language and culture in general, Jaime Bulatao notes the following:

> Language, of course, has much to do with culture and may rightly be called the main vehicle of culture. Not only is culture stored in and transmitted through language, but one's world view itself is formed by one's language because the "gestalt" of the language forms the mind that thinks in it. The language that refers to outsiders as "foreign devils" is bound to transmit a peculiar view of the outside world.[10]

This Whorfian viewpoint may have some truth in it, but the question is how deep does language affect the psyche and cultural personality? As this question needs ongoing study, any discussion of the question is highly speculative, but let me report the speculation of some Filipino intellectuals on the matter.

Josefina Constantino, a Filipina writer, former newspaper columnist, notes that among all Asians "the Filipino is the most unique in the use of the English language" which has played a role in shaping the Filipino perception of reality.[11] For the ordinary unschooled Filipino, she says, the world view is non-dualistic: there is "no dichotomy between object and subject: it is an integrative view."[12] She then contrasts this nondualistic perception to that of Filipinos who have learned to think in English:

> But the Filipino who has learned to think in English is more liable to think dualistically. Trained in handling abstractions

and concepts, he unconsciously interiorizes the dualism of subject and object which analytical thinking makes necessary.[13]

She does not, however, see English as necessarily having a negative impact on the Filipino psyche.

> Yet a Filipino who is mature intellectually and emotionally, or one whose interior life (of truths and values) has remained integrated, in the process of growth and accretion of gifts of mind and characters, operates successfully in both the concretizing and conceptualizing planes of perception and expression. This is true, however, of all men of this category no matter what nationality.[14]

Leonardo Mercado also notes that both the Visayan and Tagalog languages are 'subjective' languages similar to the "Hebrew language which is also a concrete language"[15]; in contrast the English language is 'objective'.[16] He agrees with the observation of the Japanese linguist-scholar Nakamura that "westerners are inclined to comprehend an object of observation as an objective matter . . ." because "the accusative by definition has an objective sense and cannot express a subjective sense" - whereas "Visayan and Tagalog are not accusative languages."[17]

Manuel Yap, a Filipino biblical linguist, notes also that while the westerner looks objectively at quality, the Filipino, by contrast, looks at it subjectively as part of himself, the viewer. "The westerner dualistically splits object and subject, but the Filipino synthetically views them together."[18]

While a synthetic and subjective view of reality has its merits in promoting mysticism and religiosity and preserving the poetic sensibility of the Filipino, it also has its shortcomings. Constantino assesses Filipino culture as follows.

> On the whole, it can be summarizingly said that Filipino culture has not given supreme value to the life of the mind. It is this pervasive lack of a robust intellectual excitement and lack of sustained scholarship that render the cultural milieu tepid, dull, and uninspiring.[19]

The verdict of Filipino intellectuals, it would seem, is that the use of English as a second language has more positive values for both national unity and cultural identity than negative ones, if at all.

CONCLUSION

The Philippine cultural experience is one of tension. In the Filipino psyche there is an ongoing process of diffusion, acculturation and interiorization of various cultures, native and foreign. He is at once Filipino, Spanish, American, Chinese, etc. Whether he can integrate all these and attain a unified cultural identity, only time will tell.

The hope for national unity and cultural identity is complicated by language. If language affects the way we relate to the world, then English which is objective and the native language which is subjective produce an ambivalence and tension in one's perception, cognition and behavior. Can contrasting language structures be integrated?

I believe with Chomsky that there are deeper structures common to all languages which affect both the psyche's unconscious and symbol making dimension and its conscious, conceptual and logical part. It is possible, therefore, for the psyche to be integrated at this deeper level where all languages are rooted.

Awareness of, and facility in, several languages such as most Filipinos possess is not necessarily an obstacle to national unity and cultural identity. True national unity according to Teilhard de Chardin is one subordinated to world unity and citizenship. One must be a citizen of the world first before one is a citizen of a nation. Facility in several languages allows one to be aware of other cultures besides one's own and interact with them, to integrate them within one's own psyche and thus attain a measure of world consciousness. To be at once Asian, American, Spanish, etc., is an antidote to ethnocentrism and ultranationalism which are antievolutionary.

University of the District of Columbia
Washington, D.C.

NOTES

1. *The Constitution of the Republic of the Philippines* (1986), Art. XIV, Sec. 14.

2. See his article, "Some Notes on Inculturation," in *Inculturation, Faith and Christian Life* (Loyola Papers No. 6; Manila: Ateneo University, 1976), p. 27.

3. *Ibid.*, p. 28.

4. *The Constitution*, Art. XIV, sec. 6.

5. *Ibid.*, Art. XIV, sec. 7.

6. Josefina Constantino, (ed.), *Asian Religious Sensibility and Carmelite Spirituality* (Quezon City: Carmelite Monastery, Gilmore, 1976-77), p. 228.

7. Guy Hunter, *South-East Asia--Race, Culture, and Nation* (New York: Oxford University Press, 1966), p. 165.

8. *Op. cit.*, p. 27.

9. See his article, "Inculturating Christianity in East Asia," in *Inculturation, Faith and Christian Life*, p. 6.

10. *Ibid.*, p. 5.

11. *Op. cit.*, p. 230

12. *Ibid.*, p. 229.

13. *Ibid.*

14. *Ibid.*

15. *Ibid.*
16. *Ibid.*
17. *Ibid.*, p. 230.
18. *Ibid.*
19. *Ibid.*, p. 808.

CHAPTER IX

NATIONAL UNITY AND ETHNIC IDENTITY

THE RUSSIAN EXPERIENCE

PRISCILLA R. ROOSEVELT

INTRODUCTION

Multi-ethnic states are today a global phenomenon. Only fourteen states have no sizeable minority group, and of these fourteen, half have an irredentist population beyond their borders constituting an extraneous challenge to national unity.[1] At the beginning of the 20th century, there existed two quite different visions of the future for such states: democrats and nationalists insisted that every people, no matter how small, deserves political and cultural autonomy, while socialists and communists looked forward to a nationless world community. From the perspective of 1987 it appears that the Wilsonian vision of the "self determination of peoples," however idealistic in principle, in practice amounts to a sentence of political impotence for most nationalities when national boundaries are redrawn to reflect ethnic boundaries as, for instance, after World War I in Eastern Europe. Not only is this often a politically undesirable goal, in many cases it is unfeasible, particularly for states where minorities are geographically dispersed. In view of these harsh realities, it is somewhat surprising that recent research shows an increasing tendency among many minorities to identify themselves ethnically first and nationally second, and to wish or demand to restructure their lives in accordance with this rediscovered sense of ethnicity. For the multinational state this amounts to a renewed challenge which has made the issue of meeting the cultural demands of national minorities without sacrificing political integrity a pressing one for states such as Canada, Belgium, the USSR, and Nigeria. In the academic community it has caused a rift between those who are optimistic about the chances of survival for such states and others who find cause for pessimism in the new trends.[2]

The Russian state, because of its long history of varying strategies for coping with the threat posed to national unity by demands from its indigenous ethnic minorities, provides a laboratory for assessing the efficacy of particular approaches to conflict resolution between cultures. Having said this, I must immediately qualify it by noting the ways in which the Soviet Union is atypical of today's multi-ethnic state. First, it stands alone in sheer numbers of ethnic minorities: close to one hundred distinct groups exist today, speaking around 140 distinct languages or dialects. Of these, 14 are sufficiently large to have their own Union Republic within the Soviet Federation; and 22 minorities number one million or more. Second, the fact that the modern Soviet state was formed by a process of Great Russian colonization and conquest of surrounding territories means that most minorities in the USSR have a territorial base from which to advance their claims, whether cultural, political or economic.

This paper will examine both the intentions of the Russian and Soviet governments towards minorities, and the results of their efforts, through the microcosm of language policy, particularly with regard to education. Most students of ethnicity agree that language is a key aspect of ethnic identification and hence of vital importance to the survival of indigenous nationalities within a multinational state. Yet, it is also agreed that such states cannot function effectively without some *lingua franca.* Hence, there is a built-in tension between the linguistic priorities of the national government and the perceived needs of its minorities. Historically, the multinational state has usually relied on the language spoken by the majority of its citizens, or, in a few cases, has used an extraneous language to provide a common language of political discourse between national or ethnic groups within the state. In the Russian/Soviet case, Russian has consistently been the language of the central government, though over the years varying rationales have been advanced for this policy. My main questions will be: how did the historical development of the Russian state influence its approach to minority groups? What premises have shaped the language policies of the national government? Can some policies be judged to have reduced, and others to have heightened, ethnic tensions? What is the present situation, and what does it portend in terms of cultural conflict and political stability for the USSR? Is language still a key element of ethnic identification? Does the present trend towards minority bilingualism and/or linguistic assimilation mean that ethnic identification and tensions are waning, or is the USSR, as some claim, an ethnic time-bomb waiting to explode?[3]

LANGUAGE POLICIES UNDER THE TSARS

Muscovy, the nucleus of the future Russian empire, began as a small and ethnically homogeneous state of Great Russians located in the center of the vast Eurasian plain. Culturally separated from Europe and Byzantium during the Mongol period (1240-1480), Muscovy developed a culture which was unique and isolated. As the "Third Rome," heir to the true faith (Russian Orthodoxy), Moscow felt a certain sense of superiority towards the outside world with which it had virtually no contact. Muscovy was bounded on the north by Swedish and Baltic German possessions, to the west and southwest by Lithuania-Poland (both culturally more advanced areas), and on the southeast and east by steppe lands inhabited by nomadic Asiatic tribes. In the 16th century its rulers began the process of exploration and conquest which eventually would put most of the Eurasian plain under Russian control. The first sizeable minority was acquired in the 17th century. At that time a Cossack revolt against Poland brought part of the Ukraine, including Kiev, capital of the first Russian state (862-1240), back into Russian hands. Although the Russians could and did claim an historic right to these lands, politically they had been under Polish-Lithuanian rule for four centuries, their population spoke a different language, and during this time both their culture and religion, less isolated from outside influences, had developed along different lines. The confrontation between Ukrainian ways and those of Moscow precipitated a schism in the church which was the first blow to Muscovite culture.

In the 18th century Muscovite complacency was irrevocably shattered by Peter the Great's insistence that Russia modernize technologically and culturally along western lines. From this time on the Russian upper classes increasingly experienced an identity crisis. Peter had forcibly changed their style of dress, the organization of the church, and even their language: by the end of the century many nobles spoke French rather than Russian. Russia continued its westward expansion, gaining the Germanic Baltic coast (modern Estonia, Latvia, and Lithuania) from Sweden, and a large portion of Poland via partition. In the late 18th and early 19th centuries the Kingdom of Georgia, menaced both by Persia and the Ottomans, first became a protectorate of Russia by treaty, and then was incorporated in 1801. Victorious campaigns against Persia and the Turks yielded the rest of Transcaucasia and Bessarabia. During the Napoleonic Wars Alexander I acquired Finland from Sweden, and by the Congress of Vienna the "Congress Kingdom" of Poland. Both of these areas had special status within the Russian Empire: Finland was administered as a Grand Duchy, and until the revolt of 1830 Poland had a constitution and a Diet, or Parliament.

The 19th century also witnessed the completion of the Russian drive to the Pacific coast, begun in the 16th century with the conquest of Kazan, Astrakhan and the Mongols east of the Ural. By the end of the century all of Central Asia and Siberia, populated mainly by nomadic tribes, had been brought into the Empire. Thus in 1917, the borders of the Russian empire, with the exception of Finland and western Poland, were almost exactly what they are today, encompassing a vast number of different nationalities and ethnic groups, some of which boasted older, more western cultures threatening to Russian self-esteem, while others could be viewed, from a colonial perspective, as in need of civilizing.

In contrast to today's Politburo, the rulers of Imperial Russia had no hesitation in proclaiming the Russian language the official state language, the "cement" of the Empire. With the exceptions of Poland and Finland, all official business was conducted in Russian by the Russian administrative apparatus set up in newly-acquired territories. The language of culture was another matter. The Russians themselves had no satisfactory literary language until the early 19th century, and until then, no attempt was made to introduce a general system of secular education. Schooling was largely in the hands of local churches: in Russia proper, the Orthodox clergy, but in Poland, Catholics, in the Ukraine, Uniate priests, in the Kingdom of Georgia, the Georgian Catholic church, and so on. As early as the mid-18th century the Russian autocracy manifested its intention to dispose of any potentially threatening local culture: with expansion southward into the Ukraine came an attempt to russify Ukrainian church rituals, and 866 Ukrainian church schools were closed between 1740 and 1800. But until the mid-19th century when romantic nationalism swept across Europe, provoking among both historic and non-historic ethnic groups an inquiry into their roots and destiny, the Russian rulers of this vast polyglot empire were relatively untroubled by demands from their minorities. Important exceptions were the Poles, whose memories of statehood remained vivid after the partitions; the Ukrainians, whose ethnic consciousness, preserved in their language and religion, received further stimulus through a cultural revival in the early part of the century; and the Jews.

Though early Russian policies towards these three groups did not amount to russification on ideological grounds, they reveal a consistent tendency to view linguistic demands from minorities as tantamount to a political challenge to autocracy. Whenever this threat actually materialized, the tsarist regime either attempted to assimilate the unruly element or, if necessary, to annihilate the native culture. Yet tsarist policy was, on the whole, pragmatic for much of the 19th century. After the partitions of Poland, for example, the Poles were initially allowed, if not encouraged, to retain their own educational system (which far surpassed in scope and quality the fledgling Russian school system), with Russian being taught as a second language. In the reign of Nicholas I (1825-1855) the autocracy acquired a russophile slogan, "Orthodoxy, Autocracy, and Nationality," yet Nicholas respected Poland's special status for the first five years of his rule. After the rebellion of 1830, however, several universities and scores of lycees and gymnasiums were summarily closed; in the Ukraine the secret Pan-Slav organization, The Society of Cyrill and Methodius, was disbanded and Taras Shevchenko, the great Ukrainian poet, arrested and exiled in 1847.

The Jews, clustered mainly in these two problem areas, presented the different challenge of an ethnic group without a real territorial base which steadfastly resisted efforts by the autocracy to encourage assimilation and the use of Russian rather than Yiddish. In 1804 Alexander I had granted Jews the right of attending all local schools and universities, but the vast majority continued to receive instruction in Yiddish from private teachers. In 1835 Nicholas decreed that Jews be allowed to open their own schools, but this produced only four private Jewish schools with Russian as the language of instruction. This prompted the Minister of Education, Sergei Uvarov, to create special state schools for Jews. Eventually these schools, all located within the pale of settlement, did produce a sizable number of Jews who spoke Russian, but did nothing else to encourage Jewish assimilation (which, in fact, was discouraged by laws restricting their settling outside the pale, buying farm land, or entering certain occupations.)

Elsewhere in the empire, national minorities until the early 20th century either lacked the ethnic consciousness necessary to precipitate confrontation, or were satisfied with their status within the empire. From the reign of Peter the Great the Baltic German nobility had assimilated rapidly; they played an active role in the upper administrative echelons of the empire and ruled the Latvian and Estonian native populations at home. The Duchy of Finland, whose elite was culturally Swedish, enjoyed more self-government under the Russians than it had under the Swedes, and a Finnish nationalist cultural movement began only at mid-century. In both these areas, Russian was taught as a second language with no local resistance. To the south, the Georgians, though proud of their history and culture, which antedated that of Russia, remained grateful for Russian protection against the continued threat of Persia. The same was true of the Armenians, the Turkoman tribes of the Caspian, who preferred the Russians to the Persians, and the Kirghiz, who submitted to Russia between 1863-67 in return for protection against the Uzbek Khiva.

Walker Connors has identified four levels of governmental response to a challenge from a national minority: the granting of group autonomy either political, cultural, or both; and efforts towards assimilation, towards expulsion, and towards genocide.[4] While, unlike the Soviet regime, the Russian autocracy never turned to expulsion or genocide as means of controlling its minorities, from the 1860s to 1917 its policies became increasingly repressive, both in response to an increased Russian national chauvinism in court circles and because of a growing assertiveness on the part of the national minorities. In 1863, after the second Polish rebellion, Polish schools were russified. Perhaps because for centuries the Poles had looked down on Russians as culturally inferior, in general even liberal Russians had little sympathy for Polish separatist demands, including the right to use their own language. (One Russian conservative, speaking at the turn of the century, went so far as to declare, "It is shameful to think of the possibility of allowing the Polish language to be used even as an auxiliary language.")[5] Two minority languages, Ukrainian and Belorussian, which were linguistically closest to Russian, were targeted for linguistic assimilation. By Imperial edict Ukrainian was proclaimed merely a Russian dialect, and Ukrainian books which were "religious and educational, and books generally intended for elementary reading by the people" were banned.[6] The persistence of Ukrainian 'societies' led to a further decree in 1876 "wholly confining Ukrainian publications to historical documents, forbidding Ukrainian theatrical or musical performances."[7]

From the 1880s on, under Alexander III and Nicholas II, the Russian government adopted an even more aggressive policy of russification, with the ultimate aim of producing homogeneity throughout the empire through a process of forced assimilation to Great Russian cultural norms. This meant an end to religious toleration, and the transformation of all local schools into copies of their Russian counterparts. Paradoxically, in some areas these policies, by weakening a native elite, allowed a new surge of ethnic sentiment to arise from below. This was the case in the

Baltic, where the German elite was overpowered by an emerging Latvian and Estonian cultural and economic revival, and in Poland, where the Lithuanian minority began rediscovering its past. In the Grand Duchy of Finland, Finnish nationalists began contesting the authority of the Swedish-speaking elite; general resentment of Russia became particularly strong after 1899, when Nicholas II abrogated Finland's constitution and autonomy. With the new insistence on Russian Orthodoxy as the official religion, religious persecution increased. Like Great Russian prejudice against the Catholic Poles, intolerance towards Jews was widespread in 19th-century Russia, and this period was notorious for increasingly frequent and savage pogroms, prompting many Russian Jews to join revolutionary parties.

In the eastern part of the empire the situation was somewhat different. The Russian conquerors perceived little in the way of a threat from the illiterate Muslim natives, and in any case, thought more highly of Islam than of Judaism or non- Orthodox Christianity. In the 1860s the first governor-general of Central Asia had adopted a policy of benign neglect towards the Muslim faith, hoping that it would die a natural death, and had established a few native-language schools to promote literacy. The majority of children, however, continued to go to religious schools. From 1880 to World War I the Russian governors expanded the system of schools for the natives, hoping to use the local languages to teach Muslim children Russian culture, but they were an exception to the general rule throughout the empire of Russian as the language of instruction in state schools.

The low level of literacy outside European Russia in the late Imperial period may well have been due to the lack of native language schools. According to the 1897 census, the literacy rate for Poland was 41%, for European Russia 30%, for Siberia and the Caucasus 16%, and for Central Asia a mere 6%. Yet such was the tsarist regime's fear of non-Russian nationalism that any proposal for native language schools for the minority nationalities was not only rejected, but its authors frequently persecuted.[8] The intentions of the government were plain to all. As V. I. Charnolussky declared in 1909, "The higher the cultural level of a nation to be 'russified,' the more relentlessly was the native language driven out of the official schools assigned to this task."[9] He singled out treatment of the Ukrainians and Belorussians as particularly severe. Perhaps hoping to sway the Ministry of Education, the Union of Secondary School Teachers in 1914 pointed out how counterproductive this policy had turned out to be: "The school has taken upon itself to become the tool of russification and has aroused deep hatred of the Russian language and Russian culture in outlying areas; instead of serving as the arena for autocratic propaganda it has bred dissidents."[10] That same year the All-Russian Congress on Public Education called both for sweeping reforms in schools for minorities and for measures designed to improve the training and enhance the status of teachers in native language schools; no such reforms were implemented until after the Bolshevik revolution.[11]

There can be little doubt that the russification policies of the late Imperial period amounted to a tacit acknowledgment by the central government of its inability to combat the centripetal nationalist forces at work in the early 20th century, and that these policies in fact increased rather than diminished nationalist sentiment. Yet despite the hostility aroused by russification, the only ethnic groups prior to the revolution which desired complete separation from Russia were the Poles, Lithuanians, and Finns; others, notably the Ukrainians and Georgians, anticipated autonomous status within a federal system rather than full political autonomy. With the above exceptions, national minority demands on the Russian autocracy up to its demise tended to be cultural, not political. This was, in most instances, a reflection of the fact that a group identity had been forged comparatively recently through rediscovery of native culture; many groups, the Estonians and Latvians as well as Central Asian or Siberian minorities, had no history of political autonomy to which they could refer. Such minorities could have been satisfied by a commitment on the part of the regime to respect native language, culture and religion; the fact that the last two tsars responded in precisely the opposite way contributed much to the revolutionary cause.

THE SOVIET PERIOD:
LANGUAGE POLICY FROM LENIN TO GORBACHEV

Communism, at least in theory, offered the chance to heal the two cultural rifts of the past, both of which had contributed to the revolution: the divide between a Europeanized elite and tradition-minded peasantry; and the rift between Russians and other ethnic groups. The Bolsheviks came to power well aware of the errors of their Tsarist predecessors in their dealings with minority nationalities, and of their opportunity to make a fresh start which would gain them the allegiance of these minorities. Hence the Soviet period has been marked by some radical departures from Tsarist policies towards minority languages and culture. Imperial policy took the superiority of Russian and the necessity of minority assimilation as its point of departure, though from one reign to another, depending on circumstances, the zeal with which this goal was pursued varied. Soviet policy, by contrast, has been dualistic: it "seeks to promote the culture of backward nationalities and, at the same time, to push many national cultures toward a merger with the Great Russian," thus continuing the earlier policy.[12]

Communist theory had predicted that class interests would override nationalist concerns whenever the two came into conflict. To some extent this theory was validated by the events of 1917 in Russia: much of the Georgian, Finnish, Baltic, and, to a lesser extent, Polish and Ukrainian nobility had sided with the autocracy against their revolutionary co-nationalists, and along with the autocracy had gone down to defeat. It followed that in the classless state national conflicts would not exist, nor would one nationality dominate others. The "new Soviet man" would have a proletarian consciousness: language would be merely a tool for him, not a powerful means of identifying himself as different from his comrades.

Well aware of the widespread antipathy to Great Russian chauvinism, Lenin had encouraged restive nationalist sentiment before the revolution as a method of further weakening the autocracy. After taking power, he acceded to a federal structure for the new Soviet state which gave limited political autonomy to the largest nationalities. With regard to the culture of all nationalities, no matter how small, Lenin encouraged diversity. Though Stalin is responsible for the formulation, it was Lenin who initiated the policy that within the USSR, culture should be "national in form, socialist in content."

The main issue during the Soviet period has been whether or not the common Soviet culture necessitates a common language. Although some scholars consider Lenin's tolerance of native languages mainly the product of necessity, others feel that he genuinely considered language a neutral medium. For this reason, he proclaimed that all languages which could be used to broadcast the new ideas of socialism were equally valuable. As early as 1918, partially as a means of drawing dissatisfied minorities to their side during the civil war, the Bolsheviks started publishing books and periodicals in non-Russian languages, and in 1921 began the task of creating alphabets (chiefly Latin rather than Cyrillic) for languages which had no written form.[13] In the 1920s the new policy of *korenizatsiia,* or 'becoming rooted' in one's native culture, encouraged the use of a large number of non-Russian languages in education, local government, publications and cultural organizations.

From this time until the early 1930s the Russian language was treated as merely one of the languages spoken in the USSR. Lenin insisted that it should never become an official language nor a compulsory school subject for non-Russians. The Cyrillic alphabet was even criticized as "the alphabet of autocratic oppression, of missionary propaganda, of Great Russian chauvinism," the Latin alphabet praised, and the eventual triumph of a universal proletarian world language (possibly Russian, but also possibly English, or Esperanto) predicted by Bolshevik linguists and Lenin himself.[14] Within the USSR, Russians who lived in non-Russian areas were expected to master the native language, not the reverse. In all areas of the Soviet Union native languages were to be the chief medium of instruction, no matter how few the speakers of a given tongue, with the object of producing indigenous Communists by the thousands as quickly as possible.

As an ironic byproduct of this tolerant policy, not only was a sense of ethnic identity bolstered in the larger minorities of the USSR in the 20s, in some instances where it had previously been absent it was created by the elevation of a dialect to full language status, or by the research of cultural anthropologists into the origins, history and folklore of previously unidentified groups. By the end of the 1920s, most non-Russians were going to school through the first four-year, primary level, and they were being educated in their native languages according to a standard-ized curriculum. This curriculum, moreover, emphasized the study of native culture rather than the Russian heritage; as a result, within a decade there emerged a native intelligentsia in most areas of the USSR.

Stalin's "Third Revolution," which began in 1928, did not bring an immediate reversal of Lenin's language policy, even though Stalin (per-haps because he himself was an assimilated Georgian) was in general an ardent opponent of nationalist tendencies. In 1922 he had proposed (to no avail) that the new constitution downgrade the union republics to the status of autonomous republics, and Lenin, as is well known, expressed great displeasure at Stalin's harsh treatment, as Commissar of Nationali-ties, of his fellow Georgians.[15] Yet like Lenin, Stalin seems at least ini-tially to have viewed language as neutral. From 1924, the year Lenin died, to 1934 the number of languages used for Soviet textbooks rose from 25 to 104.[16] In each republic minorities were taught in their mother tongues. Thus, for example, in Uzbekistan there were primary schools operating in 17 languages, and in Dagestan in 20.[17]

Yet paradoxically, Stalin was also primarily responsible for the shift back to a stress on the importance of the Russian language and the glories of the Russian tradition. Eventually his hostility to localism took forms which surpassed in ruthlessness the russifying efforts of the tsars. By the mid-30s, partially because some native leaders had started de-manding political as well as cultural autonomy, Stalin began a drive to eradicate entirely any signs of local "chauvinism." In the late 30s, purges of local communist leaders effectively decimated the new native intelli-gentsia Lenin's reforms had created, and new laws presaged a return to Tsarist russification practices. In 1938 the Russian language was made a mandatory part of the curriculum for all Soviet students, and Russian began to be restored to its special status. In the Ukraine, for instance, it was decreed that Russian, as a language "superior" to Ukrainian, was to become a compulsory subject in the Ukrainian school system, and U-krainian writers were urged to abandon nationalist subjects and their native language in favor of Russian themes and the Russian tongue.[18]

A recent study has concluded that Stalin's policies towards the Ukraine in the 1930s were aimed at genocide.[19] If so, the Ukraine was not unique. During World War II Stalin's mass deportation of suspect minorities such as the Crimean Tartars and Volga Germans from their homelands to Central Asia or Siberia was tantamount to a death sentence. After the war, Stalin's famous toast to the Russians as the "greatest" of Soviet peoples was coupled with an increasingly virulent anti-Jewish campaign. By 1938 all Jewish schools in the USSR had been closed; by 1948 there were no publications in Yiddish nor Jewish publishing houses; and in 1952, prior to the famous Doctors' plot, around thirty Jewish writers were summarily shot, a prelude to the planned deportation of all Jews from central Russia which only Stalin's death averted.[20]

During Khrushchev's era certain trends under Stalin intensified, creating the first theoretical shift from Lenin's insistence on linguistic parity in the USSR. Stalin had glorified the Russian people and their accomplishments, and proclaimed their language to be "the language of socialism."[21] But he had not challenged the principle that every Soviet child should be educated in its mother tongue (except for the Jews who, as we have seen, have always occupied an exceptional position). As late as 1958 a volume commemorating the fortieth anniversary of native language schools was issued, the authors urging an increase in their role.[22] In that same year, however, Khrushchev initiated a series of educational reform laws which so altered the status of native languages in education as to challenge the old formula, 'national in form, socialist in content.' Though the preamble to these laws reiterated the Leninist principle that native language constitutes the language of instruction in Soviet schools, the new laws actually made the language of instruction a voluntary matter to be decided upon by the "free choice" of the people. While the new laws could be interpreted as even more liberal than the old, more cynical observers saw them as the beginning of a new russification policy, since the local authorities in practice often "chose" for the people.[23] The New Party Program, introduced at the 22d Party Congress in 1962, deviated from its predecessors by specifically praising Russian as "the language of inter-nationality, communication, and cooperation of all peoples of the USSR," and by reaffirming every citizen's freedom to choose his preferred language of instruction rather than his former right to an education in his native language. Russian was now clearly assigned a preeminent role in the hastening of the fusion of nationalities into a single communist society which, Khrushchev predicted, would occur as early as 1980.

The Russian language retained this role under Brezhnev, whose linguists openly proclaimed the superiority of Russian and created new theories to back this point of view.[24] Language was no longer neutral: Russian, as the language of Lenin, was now proclaimed to "carry within itself the ideology" of communism.[25] Secondly, it was invested with the "international function of developing the national cultures themselves, and thus becomes a component part of their culture," the more so since, it was argued, many nationalities now found their own languages insufficient for their own scientific and technical needs.[26] Thirdly, Russian was seen as the vehicle par excellence which "cements the unity and the monolithic nature of Soviet society."[27]

The new note of specifically Russian nationalism in the 70s was a reaction against Khrushchev's insistence on *slianie*, or the merging of cultures, rather than *sblizhenie*--a drawing together. But it also has amounted to a reassertion of the superiority of Russian language and culture, including Russian Orthodoxy, which for minority nationalities is perilously reminiscent of tsarist chauvinism. Along with more frequent public references to the "great Russian people" has come an upsurge in official anti-Semitism disguised as anti-Zionism. The "third emigration" of the late 70s, heralded in the West as the mark of a "liberalized" policy, could also be viewed as a resort to expulsion as a means of dealing with

Russia's historically most unwelcome minority. Why the shift? One explanation might be that, as Dr. Kromkowski pointed out, ethnic consciousness tends to come in waves, intensifying when the meaning of life becomes more tenuous. The stagnation under Brezhnev made the old ideological slogans of the Communist party appear meaningless for many; the result among Great Russians has been a turn to nationalist or religious identification, a dangerous trend for any multinational state.

Language policies in the national schools have continued to reflect both this new Russian nationalism and a desire to promote bilingualism. Particularly after the May, 1979 Tashkent Conference on the teaching of Russian to non-Russians, the teaching of Russian has steadily risen: the number of classroom hours devoted to it per week have increased, the age at which children are exposed to Russian has dropped in some areas to the preschool level, and many organized extracurricular programs are devoted to promoting love of the Russian language and all things Russian. These measures are apparently intended to promote bilingualism, a desirable goal from the point of view of the central government for several reasons, among them the necessity of more labour mobility, a common scientific language, and an efficient army (in which Russians constitute the majority of officers, and other nationalities the rank-and-file). The results of these measures, along with the new freedom to choose the language of instruction, have been a dramatic change in the languages of instruction in non-Russian areas, and an increase in the number of non-Russian Soviet citizens who can speak Russian fluently. While efforts to promote Russian as the state language for union republics have been strenuously resisted (in the Georgian case, through rioting), many parents truly seem to prefer that their children be educated in Russian, the language one needs to get ahead in the Soviet Union, and enrollment in non-Russian schools has declined.[28] Thus in the USSR, there seem to be a few areas in which the central government's promotion of Russian as a *lingua franca* and minority interests converge.

Forty-five nationalities still have schools where their language is the primary language of instruction, and education through secondary school in the Union Republics is conducted in the native language. But in the Russian Union Republic (RSFSR) native-language schools for non-Russians gradually have been eliminated, and it appears to be a general law that where a particular group has no political status it loses the right to education in the native language, which then becomes restricted to private, family use. Does this mean that the USSR is gradually moving towards bilingualism, that ethnic identification is receding and assimilation growing among the minority groups of the USSR? Statistics from the 1979 census certainly indicate a rise in bilingualism, particularly in Central Asia. But the only groups to show signs of linguistic assimilation are urban male Ukrainians and Belorussians (for whom the switch to Russian is relatively easy) residing in the Russian Republic; whether or not this has been accompanied by psychological assimilation is unclear.[29] What is clear is that the rise in the numbers of non-Russians declaring Russian as their native or second language means that more can and will compete with Russians for jobs and resources. As this type of conflict rises, it tends to heighten, not diffuse, national identification among minorities. Russian-speaking Belorussians present one clear instance of this somewhat paradoxical result of linguistic assimilation.

Among dispersed major groups, and smaller groups which have been absorbed into larger nationalities, particularly in the Northwest, Siberia and the Far East, one finds a decline both in use of the native language and use of Russian as a second language.[30] Yurii Bromley, head of the Institute of Ethnography of the USSR Academy of Sciences, points to the decline in the number of ethnic groups from the 1925 census when 194 appeared, to the 1970 census which listed 104.[31] The 1979 census puts the number at 92, or less than half of 1925. Obviously, then, some *slianie* is taking place, but it seems to be doing so only among marginal ethnic groups. One must remember that of these 92, (72 when combined) account for only 3% of the population of the Soviet Union.

All of these statistics suggest that perhaps language is the wrong measure to use in making judgments about the level of ethnic conflict in the Soviet Union today. Central Asian support of bilingualism may be viewed not as a desire to assimilate but rather as a method of speeding up modernization in their republics: bilingualism, one scholar asserts, along with the Central Asian demographic explosion, will be "one more asset in maximizing the importance of Muslims within the Union."[32]

CONCLUSION

The balance sheet at this time presents a mixed picture of little predictive value, particularly given the scope of Gorbachev's reform initiatives. On the one hand, the Russian experience seems to validate a pessimistic view of the possibility of managing ethnonationalism within the existing political structure of the USSR. Where bilingualism or linguistic assimilation has advanced, it has not necessarily done so at the expense of previous ethnic identification; on the contrary, as has been noted, since a good command of Russian is necessary for political and economic advancement in the USSR, bilingualism might be merely the prelude to a renewed demand by the stronger Union Republics for a more equitable distribution of resources and political power. In some recent instances, increased contact between cultures (in the army, or when groups of Central Asian workers have been transported to job sites in European Russia) has led to more, not less, ethnic friction. Likewise, the central government's attempts to promote bilingualism through quotas for minority groups in institutions of higher education has bred hostility and increased Great Russian nationalism. The majority of Russians appear understandably apprehensive about any policy which advances Soviet minorities at their expense. Yet Gorbarhev's new initiative to do away with affirmative action in education seems sure to engender hostility among previously favored minorities. In the Russian case, ethnic identification has fed on both adversity and concessions; it shows no sign of diminishing, and current linguistic changes may in the end strengthen rather than weaken the aspirations and power of the national minorities in the USSR. Will a larger share of power for minorities result in the political fragmentation of the Soviet Union? Scholars like A. Bennigsen say it will point in particular to the demographic changes likely to occur by the end of this century in the USSR. Russians themselves speak of the "yellowing" of the USSR: the birth rate among Moslems is 3 to 5 times as great as that for Great Russians. By the end of the century, the indigenous populations of the Central Asian republics, for decades outnumbered by Russian immigrants, will for the first time constitute a majority at home. Within the USSR as a whole, if present trends continue, Great Russians, now 51.5% of the population, will have lost their majority. Some scholars see an inevitable dissolution of the Soviet empire once these changes have occurred. Yet others point to more hopeful signals that Russian chauvinism is waning, and that the central government will, perforce, bow to some of the demands of its minorities in the interests of preserving the union. Though Russians still occupy the vast majority of top political positions, some Central Asians have recently risen to the top. The handing-over of management and investment decisions to the collective farm has produced some multi-million ruble collectives in Central Asia.

There are also hopeful signs that some minority cultures are coming into their own. One of the most popular writers in the USSR today, Chingiz Aitmatov, hails from Kirghizia. Significantly, his renowned novel, *The Day Lasts More Than a Hundred Years*, pits the history, values, and customs of neighboring Kazakhstan against the achievements of Soviet science in this instance, space exploration. This book could not have been so highly publicized nor have such resonance for Soviet citizens were not some accommodation taking place between the Russian center and a stronger Central Asia. Equally significant is the fact that the rioters of December, 1986 in Alma-Ata, angered by the replacement of the corrupt Kazakh Party leader, Kunaev, by a Russian import, demanded not that Kunaev's successor be an ethnic Kazakh, but that he be a native of the Kazakh Republic. This would seem to indicate that regional identification today is more important than such more traditional flags as race, religion, or language. If so, the key issue for the Gorbachev era will be the equitable sharing of power and resources among the republics of the Soviet Union, and the main arena of struggle will be economic and political competition between national elites. In a sense, the Russian leaders of the Soviet Union have been the victims of their own success: educational gains among minorities have been spectacular in the last 25 years, particularly for the most disadvantaged groups.

According to official polls, when asked to name their "fatherland" (*rodina*) the overwhelming majority of non-Russians now identify themselves first as Soviet citizens, not as members of an ethnic minority. Yet their attachment to the republic in which they live, regardless of their own ethnic background, has also intensified during this period.[33] Thus,

Paul Goble argues, a dramatic change has occurred in the "primary source of national identity and nationalism" in the Soviet Union. This, he feels, renders the ongoing debate among Western scholars about the significance of persistent folk traditions and of popular resistance to Sovietization "not so much wrong, as sterile." The old approach focuses on what is going on at the grass-roots level, not what is happening among national elites, who are the element most likely to press claims against the central administration.[34] We need to use a new conceptual frame: rather than continuing to view the Soviet Union as an empire faced with problems of keeping down restless natives, and looking chiefly at issues such as language and loyalty, Goble argues, we should be analyzing the new and different kind of national identity which has emerged among the "most mobilized and sovietized" national elites.

I find the evidence that the Soviet nationalities problem has changed qualitatively, not quantitatively, compelling. It means that Gorbachev is confronting problems both different and more difficult than those of either his tsarist or Soviet predecessors. Recently he has shown greater sensitivity to nationalist feeling, but in so doing he has risked alienating his Great Russian constituency. On the other hand, the type of economic satrapies which Brezhnev allowed to develop in the Union Republics work against the economic efficiency Gorbachev is dedicated to promoting. Ultimately, the difficulty of revamping the Soviet economy in such a way as to satisfy both the Great Russians and those minority elites which had free rein under Brezhnev may prove Gorbachev's greatest challenge.

As recent demonstrations in the Baltic Republics, the Ukraine, Georgia and Armenia have shown, demands for native language use continue to be placed on the minority agenda. Like the nationalities problem as a whole, they too have changed qualitatively. They are no longer an end in themselves, but rather a symbol of the greater political and economic autonomy which reform-minded elites in the USSR's minority republics are seeking. Satisfying this new agenda will prove far more difficult than acquiescing to cultural demands alone.

The Catholic University of America
Washington, D.C.

NOTES

1. Walker Connors, "The Politics of Ethno-Nationalism," *Journal of International Affairs*, 27 (1973), 1.

2. For general discussions, see the article cited above, which takes the pessimistic view, and Milton Esman, "The Management of Communal Conflict" (Paper presented at the American Academy of Arts and Sciences Conference on Ethnic Problems in the Contemporary World, October 26-28, 1972), which presents the case for optimism.

3. Among those who see the USSR disintegrating from ethnic

pressures are Alexandre Bennigsen and Lermercier-Quelquejay (*Islam in the Soviet Union*) and Helène Carrère d'Encausse (*L'Empire Eclaté*); research on ethnic identification by some younger scholars such as Barbara Anderson and Brian Silver tends to challenge this view.

4. Connors, "Politics," p. 16.

5. Jaan Pennar, Ivan I. Bakalo, and George Bereday, *Modernization and Diversity in Soviet Education* (New York, 1971), p. 24.

6. For a concise discussion of the reasons for the secret instructions of the Russian Minister of Internal Affairs P. A. Valuev of June 20, 1863 (0. S.) which effectively halted the efforts of 1856-62 to promote literacy among Ukrainian peasants (a movement previously hailed by Russian intellectuals and given limited financial support by the Russian government), see Basil Dmytryshyn's introduction to Fedir Savchenko, *The Suppression of the Ukrainian Activities in 1876* (Harvard Series in Ukrainian Studies, Vol. 1415, 1970; reprint of the Kiev, 1930 edition, Munich), xv-xxix.

7. Robert Conquest, *Harvest of Sorrow* (Oxford: Oxford Univ. Press, 1986), p. 29.

8. Pennar et al., *Modernization*, p. 163.

9. *Ibid*., p. 24.

10. *Ibid*., p. 23.

11. *Ibid*., p. 13.

12. Zvi Gitelman, "The Jews," *Problems of Communism* (Sept.-Oct., 1967), p. 95.

13. Some 52 new and 16 revised alphabets were created in the 20s. See V. A. Avrorin, *Problemy izucheniia funktsional'noi storony iazyka* (Leningrad, 1975), p. 4.

14. Cited by Isabelle Kreindler in her focus article, "The Changing Status of Russian in the Soviet Union," *International Journal of the Sociology of Language* (33, 1982), p. 8. This entire issue of IJSL is devoted to the question of Soviet policy towards national languages.

15. Roman Szporluk, "Nationalities and the Russian Problem in the USSR: An Historical Outline," *Journal of International Affairs*, 27 (19-73), p. 26.

16. F. F. Sovetkin and N. V. Taldin, eds., *Natsional'nye Shkoly RSFSR za 40 let* (Moscow: 1948), p. 11.

17. Kreindler, "Changing Status," p. 10; A. K. Azizian, *Leninskaia natsional'naia politika v razvitii i deistvii* (Moscow, 1972), pp. 245-256.

18. Yaroslav Bilinsky, "The Rulers and the Ruled," *Problems of Communism* (Sept.-October, 1967), pp. 16-26. Special issue on nationalities and nationalism in the USSR.

19. See Conquest, *Harvest of Sorrow*.

20. Gitelman, "Jews," p. 97.

21. V. V. Vinogradov, *Velikii russkii iazyk* (Moscow, 1945), p. 5.

22. Sovetkin and Taldin, eds., *Natsional'nye shkoly*.

23. Avrorin, *Problemy*, p. 264.

24. See Kreindler, "Changing Status," pp. 17-21.

184 National Unity and Ethnic Identity: The Russian Experience

25. *Russkii iazyk v natsional'noi shkole* (no. 4, 1977), p. 9.

26. V. C. Barmichev, *V Edinom Soiuze* (Minsk, 1972), p. 204; cited by Kreindler, p. 19.

27. Iu. D. Desheriev, *Razvitie obshchestvennykh funktsii literaturnykh iazkov* (Moscow, 1976), p. 7.

28. Brian Silver, "The Status of National Minority Languages in Soviet Education," *Soviet Studies*, 26 (1974), p. 29.

29. See the conclusions of Brian Silver, "The Impact of Urbanization and Geographical Dispersion on the Linguistic Russification of the Soviet Nationalities," *Demography*, 11 (1974).

30. Teresa Rakowska-Harmstone, "A Political Perspective," *International Journal of the Sociology of Language* (no. 33, 1982), p. 105.

31. Yu. V. Bromley, *Soviet Ethnography: Main Trends (Problems of the Contemporary World*, no. 42; Moscow, 1977), pp. 151-152.

32. Rakowska-Harmstone, "Political Perspective," p. 110.

33. *Sotsial'no-kul'urnyi Oblik Sovetskikh Natsii* (Moscow, 1986), p. 243.

34. See Paul A. Goble, "Running against the Republics: Gorbachev and the Soviet Nationality Problem," unpublished paper delivered at the Wilson Center Seminar on Soviet Nationalities, Washington, D.C., February 24, 1987.

CHAPTER X

THE ROYAL COMMENTARIES

OF THE INCAS

ROBERTO HOZVEN

The *Royal Commentaries* of Inca Garcilaso de la Vega is a symptomatic mediation--not always successful, and at times even tragic--between Spanish and Inca cultures.* This interaction generally has been considered by critics more as evidence of cultural integration than of a clash of culture.[1] The signs of the tension in Inca Garcilaso's conflictive movement back and forth between the two cultures can be detected by describing the conditions of their interaction. This constitutes a two-way street, in that each cultural perspective appears against the other and therefore is not only itself but also a reflection and an illumination of the other. Inca Garcilaso interprets the Incan world to the Spaniards in Hispanic terms, while also translating Hispanic culture to his deprived compatriots.

Inca Garcilaso was one of the first Spanish American writers to suffer the alienating effects of "having a footing in two worlds simultaneously," which is to say that he undertook responsibility for coping with the problems raised for the Quechuas by the assault from Spanish civilization.[2] He took charge and tried to describe the mental dislocations inherent in a cultural transposition that is mediated by languages in an unbalanced power relation, namely, that between the interpreting Spanish and the interpreted Quechua. In this interrelationship Inca Garcilaso de la Vega makes note of the cultural horizons which Hispanic discourse cannot reflect. This is why from the opening pages Inca Garcilaso de la Vega describes his work as a "rectification of follies," and as "comments for stopping the errors and the madness." He has an acute consciousness of the specific semiosis of each language, and is able to diagnose the reason for the Spaniard's error as a case of cultural blindness which his language cannot perceive:

> Although the difference between this meaning of 'mourn' [*huaca*, when pronounced gutturally] and the others ['idol', when *huaca* has a palatal articulation] is so great . . . the Spaniards, however diligent (as they ought to be), take not the slightest notice of this pronunciation or others in the native language, because they do not exist in Spanish.[3]

The dislocations and misunderstandings of communication between the two interlocutors (Spaniard and Inca) become most visible in their dialogic confrontation which unveils the intersubjective reactions adopted by the Incas in their desire to be recognized by the Spaniards:

(a) in anticipation of Hispanic repudiation, censoring themselves in their expression of certain themes:

> The Indians . . . did not dare to state the true meaning of these [religious] things with their proper meaning, in view of the fact that the Spanish Christians abominated them all as being of the devil, nor did the Spaniards ask information about them in simple terms, but they affirmed them to be diabolical as they had imagined before inquiring.[4]

(b) identifying with some of the conquistador's symbols that seem best to reflect the Spaniards:

> That they should say that the god was three in one and one in three is a new invention of the Indians, made after hearing of the Trinity and of the unity of our Lord God. . . . All this is invented by the Indians with the object of gaining some benefit from the resemblance.[5]

(c) assuming the subject-object role, mirroring the wishes of their interlocutors:

> On account of these public confessions . . . the Spanish historians have sought to assert that the Peruvian Indians confessed in secret, as we Christians do. . . . This, however, is a false account which the Indians have given to flatter the Spaniards and ingratiate themselves with them, replying to the questions they are asked according to what they think is the wish of the questioner, and not in conformity with the truth.[6]

That is, impelled by the wish to be recognized, the Incas subject the recognition of their desires to the desire of the addressee. When in some tight juridical spot they want to reverse the situation, they come up against censorship:

> The judge took the oath. . . . The *curaca* replied, but seeing that they asked nothing about the victims, who had been the aggressors in the dispute, he asked to be allowed to say all he knew about it, for his understanding was that if he told one side and was silent about the other it was equivalent to lying, and he had not told the whole truth as he had promised. And though the judge told him it was enough that he should answer what he was asked.[7]

(d) assuming their cultural transposition to the point of absurdity, for example, unlearning what had been learned:

> When the tutor abandoned them, they returned to their primary school until a new tutor arrived, who taught them on different principles from the old and if they remembered

anything of what they had learnt before, told them to forget it because it was all wrong.[8]

(e) living communication as a generalized chaos:

> Worst of all, each side had only a very defective and incomplete knowledge of the other's language as a basis for asking and answering questions. . . . Very often either party understood the opposite of what was said; otherwise something similar but not the exact meaning, and it was only rarely that the true sense was conveyed.[9]

As for the Spaniard, what are his intersubjective reactions regarding the Inca? This can be deduced through an examination of a lexical dis-heteronomy perceptible in the fraternal paradigm of Quechua. The Inca Garcilaso de la Vega declares:

> They have four different words to name brothers and sisters. Brother calls brother *huauque*, "brother." Sister calls sister *nana*, "sister." If the brother said *nana* of his sister, it would imply he was a girl, and if the sister said *huauque* of her brother, it would imply she was a boy. Brother calls sister *pana*, which also means "sister." Sister calls brother *tora*, which means "brother." But one brother cannot call another *tora* though it means "brother," because it would imply he was a girl, and one sister cannot call another *pana*, though it means "sister," since it would imply she was a boy. There are therefore two words with the same gender and meaning, one appropriate for men and the other for women, and they cannot be interchanged without the implications I have mentioned.[10]

The difference is not merely numerical (four nouns in Quechua, two in Spanish); the difference lies in the specific mode in which each speaker conceives himself as a subject within the enunciative circuit prescribed by the structure of his language. Where Spanish gives a name according to the sexual reality of the person addressed, Quechua duplicates that distinction with consideration of the sex of the speaker himherself as he/she considers him/herself from the sex of the other. Where the Spaniard produces a message whose interpretive self-recognition (that is, recognition from the addressee) is un-noted in the code of his language,[11] the Quechua produces one from the double, significant intention that defines all enunciative processes.[12]

When talking with the Spaniard within the Spanish enunciation, the Quechua seems to embody the servile role in the eyes of the Spaniard as well as in his own eyes. The Spaniard, on the other hand, plays the dominant role in their dialogue, both in content and in acknowledging the Quechua. The Quechua figures in the Hispanic enunciation as a blind spot, an opaque mirror which in the light of the Spanish language does not reflect a distinct image of the Quechua for the Spaniard. In view of this lack of awareness with respect to the Quechua, the Spaniard was unable to conceive and enrich himself as an heterogeneous subject, not identical or reducible only to his own culture, but able to enrich it by opening himself to structures and patterns not conceivable within the Spanish language.

In a way the Spaniard made himself worthy of the disdain the Inca Garcilaso de la Vega expresses for the cannibals of the pre-Incan era: "and they all devour flesh very rapidly, without cooking it or roasting it thoroughly or even chewing it. They swallow it in mouthfuls so that the wretched victim sees himself eaten alive by others and buried in their bellies."[13] The shock of the image is more syntactic than semantic: it comes from the reflexive conjugation of two verbs that are "inconceivable" under that modality in Spanish. The syntactic and symbolic criticism of the Spanish blindness carried out in this dazzling and shocking image could well be aimed at shocking the Spaniard from his blindness. It is also allegoric of the way the Quechua saw himself, endured and projected himself within the point of view of the anthropophagic Hispanic enunciation. Homologous to that "wretched victim," the Inca, the privileged speaker in the reflexive (i.e., he speaks and sees himself and expresses himself by means of the presence of the other), also saw and endured his cultural uniqueness being "eaten" alive by the culturalcentrism of an enunciation blind to any singularities which it did not possess. Thus, the Inca in his discourse is forced to forge his identity in the blind spot of Hispanic recognition. He comes about like the orphaned, wandering accidents within the symbolic misunderstanding that forged the name of the country *Perú* as: the synthesis of two misunderstandings that result in a large corruption.

> Having cajoled him to help him overcome his fear at the sight of their beards and unaccustomed clothes, the Spaniards asked him by signs and words what land it was and what it was called. The Indian understood that they were asking him something . . . but he did not understand what they were asking, so he told them what he thought they wanted to know. . . . He quickly replied by giving his own name, saying, *Beru*, and adding another, *pelu* [river]. He meant: 'If you are asking my name, I'm called *Beru*, and if you're asking where I was, I was in the river'.[14]

This nominal corruption setting the origin of a country in a blind spot, in its historical abandonment along with its inhabitants, is described three centuries later in the Mexican figure of Octavio Paz's *Ninguno*: "No one is the emptiness in our look, the pause of our conversation, the reticence of our silence . . . the ever absent, the hollow that we never fill. It is omission . . . but always present.**[15]

Apart from the Spanish and the Inca voices, however, the *Royal Commentaries* also unfolds a third voice inscribed within the strained system of interchanges or mediation which constitute the text.[16] This third voice is a dissident one, and we will hear it as long as we pay close attention to the parapraxes of the text. An example is an acknowledged slip which is retroactively repudiated by the Inca Garcilaso de la Vega-- his fear of the Inquisition:

> All this [concerning the knowledge the Incas had about the immortality of the soul and the universal resurrection] I wrote in the history of Florida, taking from its place in obedience to the venerable fathers of the Holy Society of Jesus, . . . who instructed me to do so. I have now taken it thence, though late, because of certain tyrannical acts, and restore it to its place, so that so important a stone may not be lacking in the edifice.[17]

This is to say that in one of his previous works (i.e., *La Florida del Inca*) Inca Garcilaso de la Vega assumed the same alienated attitude toward the search for Spanish recognition that he will later criticize in his Royal Commentaries. The error is realized and stated together with tacit consent: "I do not know how or by what tradition the Incas may have received the resurrection of the body as an article of faith, nor is it for a soldier like me to investigate it; nor do I think that it can be established for certain until the Most High God be pleased to reveal it. I can only truthfully say that they did believe it" (*loc. cit*). If in the first paragraph Inca Garcilaso de la Vega states his critical awareness of a past error, in the second he repeats it in the present, since "it is not for a soldier to investigate it" and he will be unable to settle the matter "until the Most High God be pleased to reveal it." In other words, Inca Garcilaso de la Vega still does not believe what he knows is truth; he believes without believing or the belief coexists with disbelief. This is a denial and makes evident the dislocation between the belief of the Inca Garcilaso de la Vega's consciousness (in the vanguard of those in his time)[18] and the scenario of his writing. In this way, the *Royal Commentaries* bears witness to ideology (by reproducing it), even while separating itself from ideology and becoming a criticism in action of its own presuppositions.

Another major dissonance in the *Royal Commentaries* is provoked by the dialogue between citations taken alternatively from Quechuan or Hispanic contexts. Let us briefly recapitulate: The Incan present, corrupted by the Spanish, is framed as an equivocation whose historical rectification will be proportionate to the degree of recognition of the error. It is this recognition that leads the Inca Garcilaso de la Vega through his writing and because of that he accumulates his comments in order "to put a stop to the corruption." But, to do so, he must not only rectify semantic fields that are defectively translated or simply unknown (such as of *huaca*); also and more fundamentally he must reconstitute the tri-dimensional verbal body of a word by means of a sentence or another form of extended discourse that could evoke in the text the infinitely varied aspects of the global Quechuan world. As the Quechuan language is the double of the Quechuan world, he attempts to reach its limits by restituting the emotive reaction of an Indian woman to the appeal of the various tonal inflections of a flute: "One might say that he [the lover] talked with his flute."[19] The language pervades music itself. For the Conquest, the Quechuan cosmological fable about the origin of storms has to be reactivated through the combined power of the three major languages intervening in the conquered world: Quechuan, Latin and Spanish.[20]

The function of the numerous Hispanic citations is to confirm and alienate vis-a-vis the restitutive function of the Quechuan citations: to embody the Inca's culture by means of words which evoke and restore what is gone or disappearing. The Spanish citations confirm[21] since their explicit function is to accredit the real, effective and truthful character of what is maintained in the Quechuan language: "whose authority (referring to Father Joseph de Acosta) along with that of the Spanish historians I employ against those who speak evilly, (hence) there is no need to make up stories in support of my fatherland or kinsmen."[22] Paradoxically, however, the Quechuan cultural adequacy, maintained by the Hispanic citations, will also imply its alienation and inadequacy as a cultural discourse since the authorization comes from a superimposed culture. It is impossible "to validate" the categorization of experience made by one culture from the perspective of another. There is no such thing as an exact correspondence between cultures. That is to say, the validity of Hispanic accreditation works only within the framework of its own semiosis. The validation of the Quechuan citations by Hispanic ones reveals a lack of awareness of the semiotic singularity of the former by the latter--or so Inca Garcilaso de la Vega seems to conclude.

This difficult process of synonymy crystallizes in the narrative as Inca Garcilaso de la Vega artfully manipulates not only the Hispanic citations, but also his audience and even his own writing. Inca Garcilaso de la Vega treats citations as explosive material: he introduces them under the mode of the one who bears witness--very far from the exalted mode he uses to associate himself with the Quechuan citations--and he always takes them from renowned intellectual or social authorities, never from questionable ones. There is no mention, for example, of Bartolome de las Casas, who would have endorsed many of the Inca Garcilaso de la Vega's criticism of the Spanish cultural blindness. Regarding his audience, Inca Garcilaso de la Vega addresses the Spaniard tangentially through the interposed persona of the historiographic knowledge of the epoch. The Spaniard is corrected, censured and catechized indirectly, obliquely, as if the Inca Garcilaso de la Vega would not dare to appeal to him directly. In reality the Spaniard's behavior appears as the photographic negative of the positive portrayal of the Quechem behavior conveyed through the Spanish historiographic citations, like the unmentioned contrast of copied excellence.[23] Just as the Quechuan figures within the Spanish enunciation as its blind spot, as its *Ninguno*, the *Royal Commentaries* in turn, in accordance with the exemplary ends of history (the omission of infamy, but the perpetuation of grandeur), responds to the Spaniard by bringing him face-to-face with the results of his destruction. Inca Garcilaso makes him confront the negative present with the magnificent past culture of the Inca kingdom--alleged and attested as such by the Spanish historians themselves--magnificence which the Spaniard does not see in his present Quechuan interlocutor. Consequently, the *Royal Commentaries* responds to the Spaniard's enunciative blindness by inscribing the Spaniards into the text as an unmentionable shadow of the past.

With respect to his own writing, the interaction of the citations subject the Inca Garcilaso de la Vega to true semiotic stress: how could he transpose a culture while conserving its semiotic autochthony? How could he enable it to be recognized in its specificity by interlocutors who cannot know that specificity in their own cultural discourse? The only possible answer is to *poetize* or, rather, to construct a discourse which splits and denounces in its own writing the interweaving of consciousness correlative to the conflictive superimposition of cultures. It was that conflict which constituted him as a bastard, a half-breed, an Indian among Spaniards, a Spaniard among Indians, an interpreter in danger of becoming estranged from both worlds and subject to suffer a kind of spiritual schism of his own soul, an anguished intellectual in search of protectors, an indignant witness, but also a cautious commentator of follies.

As a result, I would enumerate the following dissonant consciences which appear in their respective interlocutive codifications:

1. A codification of the native culture in the Spanish accounts. The interpretation of the Incan world to the Spaniards in Hispanic terms. This is the "colonialist" consciousness that expresses the ideology of those "who are looking toward Spain as the center of their happiness."**[24] This consciousness rules the general meaning of the *Royal Commentaries*, especially at its historiographic, ideological and narrative levels. It is expressed in the "Foreword" when the Inca Garcilaso de la Vega corrects his countrymen "with his index finger from Spain."**[25]

2. A recodification of the Spanish accounts by the native culture. This is the consciousness that glosses, corrects and rectifies the follies through the knowledge supplied by the "urban-maternal" metaphor: "as a native Indian from those parts --what the Spanish historians, as strangers, have told in brief because they did not know the language properly and could not suck in with their mother's milk, as I did, these fables and facts."[26] It is the polite consciousness whose criteria of circumspection, balance and "harmonizing philosophy" have been so greatly appreciated by the critics.

3. A codification of the native culture by the standards of the native culture. This is a critical consciousness which is based upon knowledge supplied by oral tradition and the Incan cosmogony, and which contrasts timidly, by insinuation, the past perfection and good

government of the Incan administration to present chaos and disorder introduced by the Conquest.

4. The parapractic transpositions between the two cultures diagnosed previously as "lapsus" and the contradictory relation between the citations. This is the consciousness of restlessness which toward the end of the second part of the *Royal Commentaries* is interpreted as "tragedy." Critics have alluded to it in various ways: "the deflected Indian sentiment," "the baroque soul," "the divided sensibility," the "tormented and depressed spirit," etc.

5. A codification of the Ideals of the narrator which are expressed under the name of Inca Garcilaso de la Vega in the *Royal Commentaries*, that is, the ideals of narcissistic omnipotence formed by the subject in his relations with the authorities and by whose identification he will structure, by reflection, his relations with the other, with himself and with the surrounding world. The terms used by Avalle-Arce who suggests the problem (*op. cit.*, p. 10) are: "the defense mechanisms," "the systems of identification" that would situate Inca Garcilaso de la Vega into the *Royal Commentaries* in relation to the Spaniard, the Creole, and the Indian. The identifications become more and more specific as Inca Garcilaso de la Vega is placed by his text in a position either of Ego ideal, which means that he undertakes the "ideals" of his father, of the Fathers of the Holy Company, of the Spanish Providentialism, etc., or of ideal Ego which means that he leans more on the maternal lineages and its symbols (mother's milk, the city-mirror, etc.), on the rescue of Quechuan cultural greatness or on the "uniformismo" of man.

The description of the relations of strength between the two ideals--first within the name itself,[27] and then its crystallization in various narrative figures in the *Royal Commentaries*--would be the itinerary by which we would continue the development of the problematic of our cultural Hispanic-American identity. This is the question we are trying to develop, like a ventriloquist setting up the *Royal Commentaries* as another protagonist of our burning contemporaneousness, rather than merely as the monumental but long dead witness portrayed by a former classic-centrist critical approach.

The University of California
Riverside, California

NOTES

*The main subject of this article, conflictive relations between cultures, is a long time concern of the author. In a previous article ("Aproximaciones semiológicas a la literatura hispanoamericana," *Eutopías* 1, vol. 3 [1985], 77-112), it was first undertaken and studied as "European Interpreting Discourse vs Latin American Interpreted Praxis." Subsequently, this concern brought about a book manuscript dealing with the experi-

ence of writing the Latin American exile into the land of North American Multiculturalism (*Cara a cara: semiótica de un encuentro*).
**These three translations only are by the author.

1. Although both readings are possible, as Julio Ortega points out: "El Peru de Garcilaso tiene dos rostros, dos destinos, que el sutilmente confronta: el país utópico de la armonía social lograda por el buen gobierno de los Incas, y el país actual de los españoles donde la historia se ha vuelto errática. Por un lado, hay una experiencia arquetipíca, . . . por el otro, . . . el vértigo de los hechos. . . . en su recuento del incario confluyen la voluntad utopista y la crítica histórica" (*La cultura peruana* [Mexico: F.C.E., 1978], p. 10). In Ortega's terms, on this occasion, I would rather emphasize the sense of "erratismo de la historia" and "el vértigo de los hechos" than "la experiencia arquetípica" or "la voluntad utopista." Do that "erratismo" and that "vértigo" somehow reach us in the task of our own critical investigation?

2. Description which fits well in what Arnold J. Toynbee calls "intelligentsia" in his "Foreword" to the *Royal Commentaries of the Incas*. All citations will refer to this edition: Trans. and introd. by Harold V. Livermore, foreword by A.J. Toynbee (Austin/London: University of Texas Press, 1966), XII-XIII. Citations will be by numbers of Book, chapter, and page.

3. *Ibid.*, 2, 5. 79.

4. *Ibid.*, 2, 2, 71-72.

5. *Ibid.*, 2, 5, 80.

6. *Ibid.*, 2, 13, 97.

7. *Ibid.*, 2, 4, 75.

8. *Ibid.*, 2, 28, 133.

9. *Ibid.*, 2, 6, 81-82. Also in Book 1, 5: "They [the Spaniards] found some men, who, on being asked the name of a large village nearby, said, '*Tectetan, tectetan,*' meaning 'I don't understand you.' The Spaniards thought it was the name of the place, and corrupting the word, always called it *Yucatan*, a name that will never cease to be used." In conclusion "the first words uttered by the Indians, when they were spoken to and asked names of the land, were applied to them, since the true meaning of the words was not understood, and it was imagined that the Indians were answering the questions correctly just as if they and the Spaniards spoke the same tongue" (pp. 18-19).

10. *Ibid.*, 4, 2, 211.

11. In the Inca Garcilaso de la Vega's discourse, but not in that of Alonso de Ercilla: "Cosas diré harto notables . . . Raras industrias, términos loables . . . *Que más los españoles engrandecen; / Pues no es el vencedor más estimado / De aquello en que el vencido es reputado*" [my emphasis]. *Araucana* (Paris: Baudry, 1840), First Canto, Second Octave, Lines 1, 5-8.

12. As Antoine Culioli stated: "Toute énoncé suppose un acte dissymétrique d'*énonciation*, 'production' et 'reconnaissance interpretative.' Ramener l'énonciation à la seule production et l'énonciateur au

locuteur, c'est, en fin de compte, ne pas comprendre que l'énoncé *n'a pas de sense* sans une double intention de signification chez les énonciateurs respectifs. Ces derniers *sont à la fois* emetteur et recepteur, non point seulement en succession, mais au moment même de l'énonciation." "Sur quelques contradictions en linguistique," *Communications*, 20 (1973), 86, note 3.

13. *Royal Commentaries*, 1, 11, 34.

14. *Ibid.*, 1, 4, 18.

15. See *El laberinto de la soledad* (México: F.C.E., 1967), pp. 40-41.

16. Tense relations crossing at various levels: narratively it is the junction of the "discourse of memorable lives and facts" with the "account of usages"; thematically it is the dialogue of the functions of the "general tongue" (which are to civilize, evangelize, symbolize, rectify, etc.) with those of the city-omphalos (Cuzco, whose function is to be a reduced model of the Incan Empire: the dazing reduction of an empire to a city-mirror. The city-mirror is reduced to the dimensions of a book, the book to the dimensions of a rectifier of error and corruption). Ideologically, it is the conflictive dialogue between Spanish Providentialism (a utopian future baffled by its aberrant present) and the past Incan utopianism (set up in an archetypic and leading past). Analogically, it is the rectification of the blind knowledge of Hispanic power by the power of knowledge praised in the Quechuan language. In terms of writing, finally, it is the "tragedy" of a subject exceeded by his writing (*Royal Commentaries*) which reveals to himself the extent of his alienation through unfolding that of the others.

17. *Ibid.*, 2, 7, 85.

18. For example, when he postulates the fundamental psychological uniformity of man (the uniformism of sixteenth-century deism) plus the proposition of a rationalist individualism, this means, theologically, the belief in the rationalist universalism that transcends the frame of the providentialist concept of history, as it was justified by the Spanish Church-State in its Catholic-Imperialist expansion. But--as J.B. Avalle-Arce states in his illuminating "Introduction"--this ideological boldness of the Inca Garcilaso de la Vega coexists antithetically with "el gran tema del Providencialismo como sentido primordial de la Historia"; from which he concludes that "en esa misma antitesis se puede hallar una nueva y complementaria explicacion de la desasosegada actitud del Inca." See *El Inca Garcilaso en sus Comentarios* (Madrid: Ed. Gredos, 1964), pp. 9-33.

19. "Late one night a Spaniard came upon an Indian girl he knew in Cuzco and asked her to return to his lodging, but she said: Let me go my way, sir. The flute you hear from that hill calls me with such tender passion that I must go toward it. Leave me, for heaven's sake, for I cannot but go where love draws me, and I shall be his wife and he my husband." *Royal Commentaries*, 2, 26, 125.

20. *Ibid.*, 2, 27, 128.

21. "But first I must substantiate what I have said with accounts of the same matters from the Spanish historians." (*Ibid.*, 2, 9, 89). And the rubric of the next chapter which declares: "The author compares what he has said with statements of the Spanish historians." (*Ibid.*, 2, 10, 90). Inca Garcilaso de la Vega authorizes his discourse both with, and through, the Spanish discourse in the same way as the Inca recognized that his project was under the Spanish eye.

22, *Ibid.*, 5, 6, 252.

23. Against whom does all the praise taken from Blas Varela work? For example, on "just war": "Since their earliest kings, . . . they never waged war unless moved by causes that seemed to them sufficient, such as the need that barbarians should be reduced to a human and civilized existence. . . . Before they went to war, they used to warn their enemies one, two, or three times." On good government: "The rest of the mild administration of the Inca kings, which was superior to that of any other kings or peoples of the New World." On taxes: "The burden of the tributes imposed by the kings was so light that what we are about to say may well appear to the reader to have been written in jest." *Ibid.*, 5, 12, 264-66.

24. According to the suggestive expression utilized by Cabildo of Caracas in a letter to the King (April 14, 1776), cited by Angel Rosemblat, *La población indígena y el mestizaje en America,* Vol. 2 (Buenos Aires: Edit. Nova, 1954), pp. 183-184, note 2.

25. The translation given by Harold Livermore does not convey the sharpness of the original: "For my part, it is sufficient that I point out for them from Spain the principles of their language, so that they may maintain its purity. . . ." *Royal Commentaries*, p. 6.

26. *Ibid.*, 2, 10, 93.

27. The name by which we know him (Inca Garcilasco de la Vega) is the last in a long chain of onomastic experiments that stretch from his establishment in Montilla, Spain (in 1561), to the publication of the *Royal Commentaries* (in 1609): Captain Garcilaso de la Vega, Captain Suarez de Figueroa, Garcilaso de la Vega Inca, Garcilaso Inca de la Vega and, at last, Inca Garcilaso de la Vega. Remaining to be studied is the symbolic "marriage" of the father's name with the eponym of the mother in the structuration of his last two major works: *The Royal Commentaries* and its second part, *Historia general del Perú.*

CHAPTER XI

CULTURAL IDENTITY

AND MODERNITY IN AFRICA

A CASE FOR A NEW PHILOSOPHY

JOSEPH I. ASIKE

INTRODUCTION

The introductory pages of Engel's short book, *Feuerbach and the End of German Philosophy*,[1] provides an interesting testimony of the impact of *The Essence of Christianity* upon his and Karl Marx's generation of German intellectuals. Engel's testimony not only throws light on a significant moment in the development of the ideological system to which he made such an important contribution, but also in broader terms illustrates the correlation between the political and social conditions of an historical period and the movement of ideas of which it is a reflection. In the particular instance of mid-nineteenth century Germany and with specific reference to the development of Marxism as a system of thought, Engel's testimony points to the realization among young German intellectuals of the lack of a real correspondence between the idealism of established German philosophy--in particular its Hegelian brand--and the socio-economic transformations that were then taking place. Feuerbach was thus an important stage in the reaction against Hegel, of which Marx's dialectical materialism was to be, in one particular direction, a culmination.

The lesson one might derive from the above is best demonstrated in Chinua Achebe's two best novels: *Things Fall Apart* and *Arrow of God*. Achebe believes that the task of a writer is to lead his people out of the mistakes of the past and on to new paths and new directions for the future.

We would like to suggest in this paper a comparable approach in Africa in the realm of thought. This approach surely would have implications for the way in which Africans perceive themselves and their position in the contemporary world, for the way in which they conceive not only their historical being, but their possibilities within the historical process as it unfolds in these times. The change we have in mind involves an overhaul of the assumptions and tenets that have gone into the formation of what is now the African "Weltanschauung," and which have found an articulation in the prevailing intellectual reaction to the colonial experience. Gradually there is beginning to be a redefinition and an emergence of what one might call a new African world-view and problematic. This redefinition appears to be related to the changed realities of the contemporary African situation in the post-colonial era. The new perception of African problems which is gradually unfolding is affecting, as a consequence, the mental processes implied in the emergence and evolution of the nationalist consciousness.[2]

THE PROBLEM OF IDENTITY

When one considers the broad movement and the major preoccupation of contemporary African thought, it appears clear that the central problem is that of identity and that the central theme of reflection has been that of the self-definition of Africans. The search for identity in Africa, according to Uchendu, is comprised of four sometimes conflicting alternatives:

(i) The need to create a united Africa compelled a search for continental identity, which became an instrument for decolonization and a weapon for post-independence international diplomacy.

(ii) A uniting "black" racial identity, motivated by social pride, makes it meaningful to speak of these Africas: Arab Africa, Black Africa and white minority Africa.

(iii) There is the search for national identity.

(iv) There is the demand for ethnic identity within the multi-ethnic state systems.[3]

Whatever might be its immediate purpose, the search for identity in Africa has always faced a dilemma in its choice of which symbols should project continental, racial, national or ethnic identity.[4] The notion that modern European scholars have engaged in the search for the 'self' is a critical common-place, but this offers no guarantee that it is true. In fact it could be argued that sincerity was no longer the problem for the European because he had lost his obsession with the attempt to bring what is--that is, one's self--and what one appears to be--one's role--into some kind of accommodation. This raises the issue of authenticity, the concern to transcend what one seems to be by what one really is, beyond sincerity and hypocrisy. Authenticity is a flight from what society, state, culture and history have tried to make man.

For Africa, this authenticity is a curiosity. Though trained in systems dominated by European culture, the African's concern is not with the discovery of a self that is the object of an inner voyage of discovery. The African's problem--though not, of course, his subject--is his public role, not his private self. If the European intellectual, though comfortable inside his culture and tradition, has an image of himself as an outsider, the African intellectual is an uncomfortable outsider, seeking to develop his culture in the directions that will give him a role. The relation of the African to his history is a web of delicate ambiguities. If he has learned to despise it or tries to ignore it, and there are of course many witnesses to the difficulty of this decolonization of the mind, he has still to learn how to assimilate and transcend it. Though the European may feel that the problem of who he is can be his private problem, the African asks always not 'who am I' but 'who are we'--his problem is not his own, but his people's.

The fact that we are social beings raises the problem of authenticity, for in the end it is others who, according to Sartre, conceal ourselves from ourselves. The problem of who I am is raised by the facts of what I appear to be. It is essential to the mythology of authenticity that this fact should be obscured by its existential prophets. What I really appear to be is fundamentally how I appear to others, and only derivatively how I appear to myself.

Yet, and this is the crux of the matter, for the European these 'others' who define the problem are his people, and he feels he knows who his people are, what their worth is. For the African, the answer is more complicated--he is an ethnic man, Ibo, Ashanti, Yoruba, Housa, Bantu, Dogon, etc., or he is a Marxist, feudalist or capitalist, or perhaps still, he is a Muslim, Christian. But does this yet mean anything; for the African is a black man, and what is the worth of the black man? Regardless of how many skeptics and observers look at the situation, there is a growing consciousness that the African will one day overthrow his unlivable existence with the whole force of his oppressed personality. He will try either to become different or to reconquer all the dimensions which colonization tore away from him. Of these, the latter seems more appealing for it could be a prelude to a positive movement, the regaining of self-control.

THE CREATION OF A NEW PHILOSOPHY

The demolition of an existing social order and the establishment of a new one are in an important sense a matter of style, of doing culture. Every style of culture is in turn related to the religious question of how people view the ultimate meaning of their life and society. The question concerning the religio-cultural impulses behind the evolution of western societies is easier to pose than to answer. A famous thesis proposed by Weber in this regard states that the spirit of capitalism was shaped especially by Calvinism. In Weber's famous essay, *The Protestant Ethic and the Spirit of Capitalism*,[5] he argues that capitalism can be characterized, in terms of ideal types, as a societal system in which accumulation of capital is central; therefore it is constantly imperative to save. This system presupposes a spirit of industry, which considers labor, production, and accumulation of capital to be meaningful even when they do not lead directly to a commensurate increase in possibilities of consumption. Thus, on the one hand, rational labor acquires an ethical significance apart from the possibilities of consumption which it creates, while, on the other hand, saving and investing become independent virtues in the knowledge that every human being will later have to give an account of his possessions before God. Weber's argument, therefore, rests on the premise that men can achieve a heavenly blessing here on earth: human labor on earth is a 'call' as good as any other spiritual call.

The question is, what spiritual barriers characteristic of medieval European society had to be removed before that society, through the industrial revolution of the 18th and 19th centuries, could become the vanguard of western culture? Only by finding an answer to this question can one hope to expose more clearly the deepest spiritual impulses underlying the rise of modern European society. For it seems very likely that the forces which ultimately made possible the easing of these barriers are the same as those which in part evoked as well the spirit and reality of modern society.

The first barrier which had to be removed was the one of church and heaven. The vertical orientation of life had to be transformed into a horizontal one. This transformation was the accomplishment of both the renaissance and reformation which inadvertently were fixed by Cartesianism. Consequently, the culture that emerged can be described as that in which the legal order, the prevailing public morality and the organization of socio-economic life grant unobstructed play to the forces of economic growth and technological development. In such a social structure, a vertical direction of life loses its significance, and instead a horizontal orientation dominates. Development and expansion are directed to earthly possibilities.

The analogy becomes clear, namely, that a comparable horizontal orientation of the African cosmological vision definitely would engender a new image of man in Africa in which, to quote Peter Gay, "man is free, the master of his fortune, not chained to his place in a universal hierarchy but capable of all things."[6] In other words, the earth becomes man's domain as the platform and instrument with which he can realize himself in the arts, in science, in commerce as well as in his contacts with *others*, including people of other cultures. Man directs his attention to this world in order to come to a better understanding of it and consequently of himself.

This has not been the case in Africa, however; nor has there been any conscious signs of it. African society is structured cyclically. Everything is ordered and related in such a manner as to ascend, descend and disperse, from the realm of nature to that which alone ultimately can provide meaning to earthly existence--the spiritual realm. Tempel's *Bantu Philosophy* provides an excellent reading on this which he summarizes thus: "the world of forces is held like a spider's web of which no single thread can be caused to vibrate without shaking the whole network."[7] In such a worldview, the dialectical contradiction between the opposites: matter and mind, inside and outside, theory and practice, etc., is reduced by making the one pole continuous with the other. Thus, one finds a synthesis of the dialectical moments by making them continuous or abolishing them in a holistic ontology. This apparent Hegelianism is relatively logical and interrelates such purely intellectual categories as subject and object, quality and quantity, limitation and infirmity, and so forth. The thinker comes to understand the way in which his own determinate thought processes, and indeed the very forms of the problems from which he sets forth, limit the results of his thinking.

Dialectical thought is in its very structure self-consciousness and may be described as an attempt to think about a given object on one level, and as we do so to observe our own thought processes. In other words, it reckons the position of the observer within the experiment itself.

In more recent times, this holistic view of African culture is being challenged by many radical Marxists. Their thesis is premised on the fact that the self-consciousness aimed at is the awareness of the individual's position in society and in history itself, and of the limits imposed on this awareness by the individual's class position. In short, it is awareness of the ideological and situational nature of all thought and of the initial invention of the problems themselves.

To avoid entering into the polemics of Marxism and its prescriptions, it should be noted that insofar as Marxism is a critical rather than a systematic philosophy it is not a coherent position in itself, but rather a 'correction' of other positions. It is a rectification in a dialectical fashion of some pre-existing phenomenon, rather than a positive doctrine of a positivistic variety existing in its own rights. This is to say that the Marxist model cannot be applied in the African situation until we grasp that which it is directed *against*, that which it is directed to *correct*. Marx came to critical self-consciousness through a critique of the varied intellectual traditions and attitudes of his time. None of his works can therefore be understood unless within the ambit of the opposites to which Marx implicitly or explicitly makes reference. For instance, against the young Hegelian associates and their leader Bruno Bauer, Marx adduces the argument for materialism. Marx defends the principles of activity and reciprocity which were central to Hegel's dialectic against the passive materialism of Feuerbach. Against absolute idealism and its fatalistic thesis, Marx asserts that man makes his own history.

It could be argued then that the dialectical strategy of Marx grows more profound whenever the ideology of the dominant classes takes on a religious or spiritualistic form, whenever religion becomes the principal weapon in the struggle against change and social revolution. This is the conviction of the so-called Marxists in Africa, a conviction which fails to understand the radical difference between the cultural settings of Marx's Europe and present-day Africa. In other words, a distinction has to be made between the idealism of Hegel in all its forms, on one hand, and, on the other hand, the unitary (holistic) world of the African.

For Hegel through the dialectical process the absolute comes to realize itself as ultimate, but for the African the verticality one finds in Hegel is resolved by a cyclic view. Nothing realizes itself as ultimate because the synthesis of the dialectical moments is continuous in a cyclical manner. Thus, while Marxist materialism makes sense against the background of Hegel's pantheism, it becomes spurious to apply the same to the African context. Our rejection of Marxism in Africa stems from this analysis.

A possible solution to the dilemma does not lie in Marxism, nor do we recommend straddling Western and African cultures because a society that does so is rarely well seated. What is needed at this point is a reexamination of the question of the *basic relationship* of the African to other cultures.

DEFENSIBLE ALIENATION

In considering the question of the basic relationship to the cultures and achievements of other peoples one might begin by insisting on the priority of some fundamental reciprocity between men preceding any later, historical form of antagonism and conflict. The structure of that fundamental reciprocity is difficult to determine, though the intention behind the concept is somewhat clearer. For the idea of initial reciprocity is intended to undermine the purely economic doctrine of the manner in which particular, historically determinate models of human relationships result from the modes of economic production at a particular period. Human relationships thus would seem to be mere instinctual or biological reactions and adjustments to different types of material surroundings. This, in fact, takes reification at face value, so that human relationships are seen not only as thing-like, but actually as inert objects subject to geographical and external influences. Human relationship is a concept laced with alienation. In *Critique de la raison dialectique*, Sartre notes that "there cannot be alienation unless there was first something to alienate, some prior form of human relationship to serve as the object of distortion."[8] We never are all alone with each other. Every confrontation takes place against the background of what a little hastily is called human society, or at least against the background of swarms of other human relationships. In this light, the notion of the couple and the resistance to the idea of the 'third', Sartre's very pertinent aphorism here is a way of making room around ourselves, trying as it were to persuade ourselves that our world is filled with empty spaces, and that there is no such thing as genuine solitude or privacy. Since the couple cannot really be a unity, unification must be mediated by a third party, by an outside observer or witness. The crucial role thus played by the 'third' confirms the priority of the triadic over the dyad relationship.

The historical heritage which Africa shares with the western world is mediated through ancient Egypt as the third party. The primary objective of Cheikh Anta Diop's sociology, which we find highly important in this regard, is to demonstrate the negro origin of ancient Egyptian civilization, and thereby to refute the general assumption that the black race has produced no great civilization. As Immanuel Wallerstein in his work *Africa: The Politics of Independence* points out, "Other scholars, such as W.E.B. Dubois, had earlier presented the argument that ancient Egyptians were negroes."[9] Diop's works demonstrate the continuity between ancient Egyptian civilization and the contemporary cultures of black Africa. It is not our intention to review the whole of Diop's thesis here, but it is not without interest to trace the main lines of his thought to gain some understanding of his position. Diop's thesis is, in fact, the intervention of an African in a debate that long had been going on in the West about the racial origin of ancient Egyptians. Diop's motivation stems from his dissatisfaction with the point of view of those scholars who against all objective evidence deliberately classified ancient Egyptians among the white race. Diop attributes this point of view to the effect of racial prejudice against the black race resulting, as Akiola Irele puts it, "in a falsification of Abiola history."[10] Diop's examination of ancient Egyptian institutions and thought from a range of special fields provides him with a cultural argument for postulating an essential affinity of the forms of social organization and the cosmology of the ancient Egyptians with those that appear to him to characterize the traditional African world.

Two clear moments seem to evolve from Diop's thinking. Firstly, there is an effort to establish a historical and cultural connection between ancient Egypt and black Africa in such a way as to promote contemporary African consciousness. Secondly, there is the will to place the African continent and the black race firmly within the movement of universal history in which Diop's thesis provides a foundation for the idea that human life is in its very structure collective rather than individualistic. This has the inherent value of encouraging ways in which the isolated culture of Africa can overcome its weakness. Human beings can be united either in their search for cultural and intellectual evolution or by historical evolution or by the historical heritage they share. There is need to abandon the self-consciousness that goes with cultural nationalism, and to transcend this position to an entirely new ground.

CONCLUSION

The key problem for Africa now is not necessarily between the dominant ideologies of the contemporary world, between idealism and materialism, between neo-colonialization and pan-Africanism, nor even between Christianity and Islamism, but the much more deeply philosophic issue of the consensus concerning the framework within which dialogue may take place. Despite the differences of ultimate outlooks, this must enable leaders and citizens to build a culture that increases the quality of life, a society where the people's deepest intuitions about life and destiny are not only tolerated but respected and cultivated. There is need for a new cosmological vision in Africa, a new spirit of adventure fired by a modern imagination, a new way of thinking that will enable us to transform our present state of alienation from a passive condition we confusedly endure into an active, collective existential project. We need to take control of our objective alienation by assuming it and endowing it with positive significance. This implies a conscious and willed dynamic movement out of the 'self' to a purposive drive for new horizons of experience.

The strands of argument we have so far elaborated, when taken together, answer to a common objective: to lay to rest the issue of African identity and to chart a new direction for African thought more appropriate to the changed historical situation of the continent. This thesis finds an expression in Frantz Fanon's, *Les Dames de la Terre*, which argues that culture does not refer to a pre-determined model offered by the past, but lies in the future as a perpetual creation, as a continuing effect of a vast, ever-unfolding existential project. In a word, culture is not a *state* but a *becoming*.[11]

The "Greek miracle" which marked the birth of a new cosmological vision in Europe was the result of human interrelationships. Given the contention that ancient Egypt was of black racial stock, it stands to reason that Africa may lay a claim to the evolution of Western civilization, as well as having in that civilization a considerable stake as the instrument for the necessary transformation of the African world. It is in our best interest to make good that claim and to adopt strategies that make our stake in that civilization pay handsome dividends. The black peril could one day (as the Japanese have proved in their own case) become the black paradigm. We cannot achieve this if we continue an illusory and endless search for identity, the unfortunate outcome of our colonial experience, which is only intensified by all forms of cultural nationalism.

University of Port Harcourt   *Visiting Prof., Howard Univ.*
    Port Harcourt, Nigeria   *Washington, D.C.*

NOTES

1. Friedrick Engels, *Feuerbach and the End of German Philosophy* (New York: International Publishers, 1941; Marxist Library, Works of Marxism-Lenism), Vol. 15.

2. Cf. Abiola Irele, *African Cultural and Intellectual Leaders and the Development of the New African Nations* (Ibadan, Nigeria: University of Ibadan Press, 1982), p. 154.

3. Victor Uchendu, "The Dilemma of Ethnicity and Polity Primacy in Black Africa," in *Ethnic Identity Cultural Continuities and Change*, edited by George de Vos and Lola Romanucci-Ross (Palo Alto, CA: Mayfield Publishing Company, 1975), p. 269.

4. *Ibid.*, p. 269.

5. Max Weber, *The Protestant Ethic and the Spirit of Capitalism*, tr. by Talcott Parsons with a foreword by R.H. Tawney (London: Unwin Univ. Books, 1930, 1967).

6. P. Gay, *The Enlightenment: An Interpretation*, 2 vols. (New York: Alfred A. Knopf, 1967-1969), vol. I: *The Rise of Modern Paganism* (1967), p. 266.

7. P. Tempels, *Bantu Philosophy* (Paris: Présence Africaine, 1959), p. 61.

8. J.-P. Sartre, *Critique de la Raison Dialectique* (Paris: Gallimard, 1960), vol. I, p. 241.

9. Immanuel Wallerstein, *Africa: The Politics of Independence* (New York: Vintage Books, 1961), pp. 129-130; see also Chiekh Anta Diop, *The African Origin of Civilization: Myth or Reality*, ed. and trans.

by Mercer Cook (Westport, CT: Lawerence Hill and Company, 1974).

10. Abiola Irele, *op. cit.*, p. 154.

11. F. Fanon, *Les Dames de la Terre* (Paris: Masepero, 1961).

CHAPTER XII

CONSENSUS IN AFRICAN

INTEREST-GROUP CONFLICT

DEMOCRATIZATION AND SOCIALIZATION OF LABOR

ATOMATE EPAS-NGAN (ARMAND)

It may appear surprising to speak of democracy and socialism where the issue is one of conflict between cultures within a given society. But one cannot ignore that "culture" implies "humanism," which in turn presupposes "persons" or "individuals" related to others to become together a "family," a "community," a "people." To speak of the culture of a people refers in turn to their various forms of life, of which the political is one. To this extent democracy, as a political system appropriate for a "body politic" aspiring to be a sovereign unit, has much to do with the culture of a people--all the people.

INTRODUCTION

Forms of thought differ among human beings. Of the great philosophers, for example, Plato thought differently from Aristotle, and Hegel differently from Kant. But as groups Whites do not think differently from Blacks, either about politics or about anything else.

If this contention is accepted, then the transfer of political ideas and blueprints, including that of democracy, from one continent to another and from one country to another becomes, not only normal, but sometimes desirable. The Ricardo formula for optimal mutual benefit in this "trade", however, remains to be discovered.

Europe has learned the hard way that conflict among organized interests, lobbying of pressure groups and bargaining for sometimes untidy compromises are not a corruption of democracy and a public scandal, but necessary ingredients of a democratic political system. As soon as a government *totally* prohibits interest groups from consolidating themselves and bargaining freely that political system ceases to be a democracy.

In the case of Africa, group interests are often perceived in tribal terms, and ethnically based (traditional) political systems tend to act as interest groups exercising pressure on the "national" system. The trouble is not that ethnic pressure groups exist: this is a natural thing whenever individuals experience social security and solidarity on an ethnic level. The difficult lies in the fact that other interests are not organized adequately and that every small group wields disproportionate power.

Perhaps for this reason the most important set of political ideologies imported into Africa from overseas during the 1960s and early 1970s was *Socialism*. It came as a controversial bundle of very different kinds of socialism, not all varieties of which arrived in Africa at the same moment or in all the countries of Africa. Some writers draw a sharp distinction between a type of moderate "African" or Populist Socialism presumably derived from Western Europe's Social Democracy, and "Scientific" Socialism of Afro-Marxism or Afro-Communism or Marxism-Leninism derived from the Soviet Union's state ideology. It seems necessary, however, to stress the continuity between these concepts.

Socialism of all persuasions became popular in Africa because it promised some form of economic independence, the lack of which was bitterly felt immediately after the hoisting of so many new flags. The particular brand of Socialism chosen by an African leader depended more on his personal "state of mind," his decision on how fast his people should "run" and his loss of illusion about previous experiments, than upon a fundamental choice between Western democracy and the Soviet political system.

The concern of this study is to demonstrate how in the last twenty years socialist ideology has undergone a considerable evolution away from such humanistic "African socialism" and toward orthodox Marxism-Leninism.

It will be shown that this ideological evolution was not the only change taking place among the African socialist countries. Their policies, in fact their politics, also underwent a metamorphosis over the years. States which started out in the early or mid-1960s with remarkably similar ideological approaches ended the 1970s with quite different political and economic systems.

This is relevant because it highlights the difficulties of socialist transformation on the African continent and points to some of the critical factors affecting the outcome. There is no reason to believe that Marxist-Leninist countries will be immune to these difficulties. While we believe that the different ideological choices may be extremely important, that is only one among a number of factors determining the end result.

Special attention will be focused upon four African countries which consider themselves socialist: Zambia, Tanzania, Guinea and Algeria. This choice is not arbitrary; these four countries are the longest surviving experiments in socialism anywhere in Africa and have some of the oldest regimes under the same leaders. Because of this continuity, they are particularly good case studies of what non-Marxist socialism has meant in practice.

This chapter does not present an expository analysis of the problems of democracy in Africa, but it is hoped that the analysis of socialist ideology in its evolution away from humanistic African socialism and toward orthodox Marxism-Leninism may throw light on how the concept and value of democracy has been discovered on the continent.

The study is divided into five sections. The first section focuses on the "pre-colonial" period characterized by what shall be called the "return to the sources." Section two approaches the "transitional" period marked by a fundamental shift in socialist ideology. The third section bears on the "post-independence" period dominated by an intensification of class struggle. Section four looks at the "present-day" period, while the last section revolves around the implications of socialist planning on the achievement of democracy.

PRE-COLONIAL PERIOD: "RETURN TO THE SOURCES"

In the early 1960s the prevalent notion was that socialism was an economic and social system already deeply rooted in the ways of traditional Africa; all Africans had to do was to "return to the sources," that is, to their old habits of community-oriented work and thinking.

The predominant argument in favor of this "return to the sources" was that, for most socialist African leaders, African society before the coming of colonialism was basically classless and communal because there was no private ownership of land and the community was more important than the individual. As a result, since there were no classes or exploiting and exploited groups within the confines of the tribe, there was no real intra-tribal conflict. African tribal society was quite literally one big harmonious family in which all members contributed to the general welfare and in turn were taken care of by the community in case of need. In effect, prior to the arrival of the European colonial powers there existed an African welfare state based on the principle of communalism.

To support the argument Julius Nyerere of Tanzania points out that socialism was the original state of the African man. This "natural" African tribal man--so goes the expression--lived in basic harmony with his brother. Thereupon, Nyerere writes: "The foundation, and the objective of African socialism is the extended family."[1] For him, socialism simply means "familyhood," the English equivalent of *Ujamaa* in Swahili.

It follows that this society was free of social conflict and that the idea of "class" or "caste" came with European colonizers.[2] Therefore, the task of an African socialist leader was to restore African society to its pristine classless self. This could be done by ending private ownership of land and other means of production and reestablishing the communal approach to all human activities.

L.S. Senghor of Senegal sought to give the doctrine a stronger cultural base by rooting it in a whole African philosophy he termed "*Négritude*." He considered the "Negro-African, humanistic" mode of looking at and experiencing reality to be distinctly different from the Marxist European "materialistic" outlook. Traditional African society was 'classless' and 'community-based' and the main task for contemporary African socialist leaders was bringing (traditional African) political and economic democracy back to life[3] and reestablishing a '*société communautaire*'.[4] Senghor termed this ideology "African socialism." Kenneth Kaunda of Zambia named it "humanism" or "African democratic socialism," with particular attention to the individual person and to the need for his good behavior in a Christian sense in order for socialism to blossom.[5]

Sékou Touré of Guinea, speaking of the "national democratic revolution" of his country, explains that it was based on the "communocratic" character of African society. He concludes that colonial rule had not essentially altered this characteristic.[6]

The reason for this view of African socialism was twofold. The first was the search for "African self-assertiveness," that is, to use Kwame Nkrumah's words, the need to "create (our) own African personality and identity." Thus, he writes, the African personality had become "a strong driving force within the African Revolution."[7]

In the pre-colonial African period, this quest for "African-ness" was accompanied by the quasi general rejection of the idea that there is only "one socialism" based on the principles of Marxism-Leninism to which the Africans had nothing to add. Thereupon, Nyerere states: "I think that this idea that there is one 'pure socialism' is an insult to human intelligence."[8] "In my view, he continues, socialism is a vague concept which can have as many different meanings and variations as there are people who advocate it."[9] Sékou Touré argues along the same lines when he speaks of "the African path" toward socialism. He warns that "trying to 'Westernize or Easternize' Africa leads to denying the African personality."[10]

To embody this African self-affirmation, Senghor erected a whole African philosophy of "Négritude," based on "Negro-Berber humanism." Kaunda brought out a political ideology he called "African humanism." Kwame Nkrumah of Ghana termed this "Pan-Africanism," that is, an ideology and strategy for African unity aimed at breaking the West's political, economic, and cultural hold over the continent and obtaining the complete independence of Africa from all forms of foreign domination.

For our case study, two implications of Pan-Africanism in the 1960's are very important:

- the creation of the "Organization of African Unity" (OAU) in 1963 and subsequently an African bloc in United Nations; and

- the rise or birth of the "Nonaligned Movement" in order to mobilize Third World nations against the hegemony of either the East or West and to combat the extension of the Soviet-American cold war outside Europe. To use Nkrumah's words, the nonaligned movement is both "a protest and a revolt against the state of affairs in international relations caused by the division of the world into opposing blocs of East and West."[11] In the same way, Sékou Touré calls Africans to use the nonaligned movement to assert their own united force in order to oblige both blocs to work for the liberation of Africa.

Therefore, both Pan-Africanism, on the one hand, and nonalignment as a Third World bloc standing up to both East and West, on the other hand, could be considered to this extent to be the natural foreign policy components of African socialism as an authentic African ideology.

The second reason for the view of African socialism as a return to African sources was the consolidation of the mosaic of tribal groupings making single national units by inculcating a sense of nationalism to replace narrow tribalism. The "mass" party was the main means for a-chieving this sense of national solidarity with its enormous emphasis upon the notion of unity and communality of interest among all segments of African peoples.

Explaining to the *World Marxist Review* why Guinea had early on sought to include "all the inhabitants of the country" in the "*Parti Démo-cratique de Guinée*," one of its Political Bureau members remarks: "It was the party that created the state and the nation by uniting the conglomer-ate of tribes into a single Guinean people."[12]

In the same way, a leader of Zanzibar's Afro-Shirazi Party justified that country's mass party to the *Review* in these terms: "We don't think that in our conditions a vanguard party is an indispensable guarantee of effective politics. . . . To bring about revolutionary changes, the masses building socialism must be able to participate directly in politics. We don't believe this opportunity should be a privilege of the few."[13]

Kenneth Kaunda went to great lengths in his doctrine of humanism to stress the notion that the new nation, like the old tribe, was a "mutual-aid society" in which everyone should participate for the overall good of the community. "This means," he writes, "that there must be fundamental agreement upon the goals and all must act together."[14]

As might be expected, this attitude implies a free will or "voluntar-ism." To the point, Nyerere writes: "Socialism cannot be imposed upon people; they can be guided; they can be lead. But ultimately they must be involved."[15] In addition to this, he explained in 1967 that the task of the government "is not to try and force people into communal activity in Ujamaa villages but to explain, encourage, and participate."[16] For his part, Sékou Touré stresses that "the Guinean revolution is founded on voluntary adherence of the people and not on any coercion exerted on the people by a minority."[17]

Altogether, it is quite tenable to explain the stress on the classless nature of traditional African society and its communal values as part of the post-independence view of national identity and national solidarity.

TRANSITIONAL PERIOD

Almost fifteen years later, the idea of the "return to the sources" had become totally discredited and most socialist African leaders, in reaction to the notion of various kinds of socialism, were asserting that there was, and is, only one "true" socialism, namely, that set forth in the writings of Marx and Lenin and implemented first as a coherent overall system in the Soviet Union.

The question here is: Why and how this dramatic change in socialist ideology came about?

The reasons why include both the particularities of the problems en-countered by the "transitional" socialists in their efforts to implement socialism in their respective countries and the weakness of the "mass" party which, incorporating everybody and anybody, failed to serve either as a secure base of power or as an effective instrument for mobilizing the population.

As to how the change took place, early on Kwame Nkrumah, among the most articulate representatives of transitional socialists, made it clear that he aimed to establish a socialist society in Ghana, even while shunning use of the term Marxism-Leninism to describe his ideology throughout his time in power. Instead, he named Ghanaian socialism "Nkrumahism" and developed his own philosophy of "Consciencism" blending Islamic and Euro-Christian traditions with "the cluster of humanistic principles which underlie the traditional African society."[18] Therefore, he created a party program founded on the basis of socialist production and distribution and termed it: "Programme for Work and Happiness."[19] Consequently, it appears that Nkrumah was far less concerned about refining his views on socialism than about devising and promoting a strategy for Pan-Africanism and a Union of African states led by Ghana and himself.

After its collapse, Nkrumah began to castigate the whole notion of "African socialism" as being fundamentally "meaningless and irrelevant."[20] "African socialism," he wrote, "appears to be more closely associated with anthropology than with political economy." Uncertainties concerning the meaning and specific policies of African socialism, he continued, "have led some of us to abandon the term because it fails to express its original meaning and because it tends to obscure our fundamental socialist commitment."[21] According to Nkrumah, it is an easy simplification to conceive the traditional African society as either classless or naturally humanistic. "Such a conception," he writes,

> makes a fetish of the communal African society. But an idyllic African classless society (in which there were no rich and poor) enjoying a drugged serenity is certainly a facile simplification; there is no historical or even anthropological evidence for any such a society. I am afraid the realities of African society were somewhat more sordid.[22]

To support his thought, Nkrumah argued that although there was "a certain communalism" in many African societies and these were imbued with a kind of humanism, they existed a long time ago and were not "coterminus" with contemporary African ones. A return to the communalistic society of ancient Africa might be a "charming thought," he said, but it offered no real solution because "we are faced with contemporary problems which have arisen from political subjugation, economic exploitation, educational and social backwardness, increases in population, familiarity with the methods and products of industrialization (and) modern agricultural techniques."[23] A return to an idealized notion of traditional African society, he concludes, was "quite unexampled in the evolution of societies."[24]

As Nkrumah took direct issue with the view that traditional African society was either classless or imbued with a natural spirit of humanism, he also had the same attitude toward the voluntary approach in socialism. He argues that "socialism is not spontaneous; it does not arise by itself. There is only one way of achieving socialism: by devising policies aimed at general socialist goals", that is, based on the universal laws of scientific socialism and adapted to the "specific circumstances of a particular state at a definite historical period."[25]

What is very important for our case study is the radical changes of Nkrumah's views on the nature of class conflict in Africa. Redirecting his attention inward to the state of African society, he remarks that "a fierce class struggle has been raging in Africa. The evidence is all around us, he says. In essence, it is, as in the rest of the world, a struggle between the oppressors and the oppressed."[26]

The change in Nkrumah's thinking marked his reaction to the African socialist argument (that of Nyerere, Kaunda and Senghor) that the communalism and egalitarianism of traditional African society still prevailed just below the surface of the present-day one. He states that the fallacy of this argument was exposed immediately after independence "when class cleavages which had been temporarily submerged in the struggle to win political freedom reappeared, often with increased intensity, particularly in those states where the newly independent government embarked on socialist policies."[27]

To demonstrate and illustrate the truth of class struggle in African society, Nkrumah went on to list and analyze the various classes he saw emerging within African society. The results of this investigation in terms of social exegesis was published under the title *Class Struggle in Africa*. This theoretical elaboration illustrates the deep and radical change in his thinking while reflecting on a very concrete problem with which he had grappled while in office. This problem had been formulated as follows: how to make a revolution with a mass party incorporating representatives of all groups, including those opposed to socialism, that is, a mass organization bringing together in the nationalist struggle all social groups irrespective of their tribal origin or economic standing; in a word, a mass party which does "not support imperialism, colonialism, tribalism and radicalism."[28]

After remarking with great regret that "for twelve years, twelve long years (1949-1960), no conscious, consistent effort had been made to provide party members with the requisite education in the party's ideology of socialism,"[29] Nkrumah tackled this delicate political task by trying to create a small corp of "vanguard activists" to lead and educate the rest of the membership. Thus was born the National African Socialist Students' Organization (NASSO). The role of this small wing of Nkrumah's Convention People's Party (CPP) was both to act as the "custodian" of the party's ideology and to provide the "torchbearers" of Nkrumahism, serving as the "bark" of the "mighty tree" which "cements the physical and organizational unity of the CCP."[30]

Nkrumah was also "transitional" in his changing attitude toward the notion of nonalignment and of the relations between the African socialist and communist states. In an article written in 1968 for the *Labor Monthly*, he categorically states that "there is no middle road between capitalism and socialism." Therefore, he divided the world into two great conflicting blocs of "revolutionary" and "counter-revolutionary" peoples.[31] He went to great lengths to say that nonalignment was an "anachronism." What he wanted was an outright alliance between the African socialist countries and the communist ones to wage war in common against "the capitalist world with its extensions of imperialism, colonialism and neocolonialism."[32] Nkrumah liked to repeat that the African socialist revolution "is an integral part of the world socialist revolution," and of the "world revolutionary process."[33]

This realignment of the African socialist regimes with the communist bloc would become later a clearly stated policy objective of the Afro-communists.

Besides Nkrumah, Sékou Touré is another transitional figure. His thinking reveals some of the same changes. He started as a typical African socialist stressing the "communocratic" nature of African society. He strenuously denied the relevance of class or class conflict to the Guinean revolution and stressed the overwhelming importance of national solidarity as embodied in his *Parti Démocratique de Guinée*, a mass party of practically the entire adult population. Later, he declared class conflict a "universal reality"[34] and produced a tortuous exegesis of the Koran, citing the most famous first verse, the "Fatiha," to prove that even Islam "proclaims the class struggle."[35]

As Nkrumah, he also called at one point for the formation of a vanguard party and set up an ideological school to train party cadres. Eventually he backtracked, however, reviving the notion of a mass party of "all the people in the country without distinction of religion and philosophy," whose main purpose was to distill a "collective conscience" at the village, regional and national levels.[36]

The culmination of his ideological peregrinations was the concept of the "party-state" first enunciated in the late 1960s and subsequently embodied in the local institution known as the *Pouvoir Révolutionaire Local*. Speaking to a visiting Common Market delegation in 1976, he proudly proclaimed that "very soon we are going to pass historically to the phase of the party-state. Nowhere in the world has anyone reached this stage. It is an original enterprise."[37] In practice, he explains elsewhere, "this means merging the organs of the party and the state into single organs of revolutionary power, delegating to them political and administrative functions and gradually extending the responsibility of local authorities."[38].

By and large, such a concept of party and state in a socialist country can be considered only heretical from a Marxist point of view.

Like Nkrumah, Sékou Touré rejected the original concept of Pan-Africanism as a "parochial identity" and particularly its identification with Senghor's ideal of *Négritude* which he castigated as "the most harmful, the most alienating form" of Pan-Africanism.[39] For Touré, "the racists of Southern Africa and the poets of *Négritude* all drink from the same fountain of racial prejudice and serve the same cause--the cause of imperialism, exploitation of man by man, and obscurantism." Senghor's philosophy of Negro-Africanism, he continues, "is fatal to Pan-Africanism and should therefore be destroyed and its offshoots made to parch in the burning sun of Africa."[40] He proposed instead a new definition for what he called "revolutionary Pan-Africanism" in which Africans would identify themselves "not by the color of our skin . . . but in terms of our goals."[41]

Much as Ghana under Nkrumah and Guinea under Touré, the Algerian brand under Ahmed Ben Bella must be mentioned here as an example of transitional socialism trying to integrate Marxist and African elements. Like Nkrumah, Ben Bella rejected the notion that African society was classless and strove to transform the wartime *Front de Libération National* (FLN) from a coalition of nationalist but ideologically diverse groups into a vanguard party with a quasi-Marxist ideology. Like Touré, he reiterated that Islam and Marxism were not necessarily in conflict and that Algeria thus was not foregoing its Arab and African personality by turning to socialism.[42]

After the collapse of Ben Bella, his successor Houari Boumédiène took issue with the Marxist-Leninist notion of "one socialism." According to him, Marxism was simply too dogmatic and did not take into account the specific conditions of Africa. His regime's main ideological document, the "National Charter" of 1976, mentions that there was no "single, obligatory model" which a Third World country had to follow to qualify as socialist; every nation must derive its own "national socialism" from its specific experience.[43] Furthermore, the same document states that "socialist ideology requires a permanent theoretical refinement which is continuously enriched through contact with experience."[44] From the preceding lines, it is apparent that Boumédiène was concerned above all with the creation of a "stable and efficient state."[45]

POST-INDEPENDENCE PERIOD:
INTENSIFICATION OF CLASS STRUGGLE

What do the Marxist-Leninists believe--in theory at least? It can be said simply and succinctly that first of all they hold unanimously that there is no "African," or "Asian" or "Latin-American" socialism distinct from Marxism-Leninism, which is the only "true" socialism.

To support the argument, Samora Machel of Mozambique, describing emphatically his country as the Africa's "first Afrocommunist," declares:

> Frelimo identifies with Marxism-Leninism . . . as a science of the workers . . . as a fundamental instrument for the analysis of society . . . as the greatest instrument for understanding class struggle. The divergences are secondary. The great thing about Marxism is that, it being a science, it can adapt to all conditions. There is no African Marxism, Asian Mar-

xism, European Marxism. There is only one Marxism.[46]

In the same way, Lucio Lara, the leader of the *Movimento Popular de Liberataçâo de Angola* (MPLA), castigating what he called "these original species of socialism," states:

> clearly for the MPLA there has always been only one expression of socialism, known precisely as scientific socialism. Experience has shown that all that rhetoric (about African socialism) has not led to concrete steps showing a true socialist option . . . The colonial presence, the presence of neo-colonialism, is obviously in all of them. Their capitalist orientation is clear. . . . These "socialisms" are basically disguises for one or another form of colonial exploitation."[47]

For his part, Somalia's military leader Mohamed Siad Barre, explaining earlier Somalia's option for socialism, writes: "Our socialism cannot be called Somali socialism, African socialism, or Islamic socialism. . . . Our socialism is scientific socialism founded by the great Marx and Engels."[48]

What is important for our case study is the class and/or conflict aspect of the African Marxist theory of revolution. The central tenet of this theory is that society can only be understood in terms of class analysis and with the acceptance of class conflict as the moving force. Contrary to the African socialist leaders who desperately needed to present their peoples with a "reconciliation" rather than a "conflict" model of the new national society, all the Marxist-Leninist leaders talk of their political problems and of their countries' history in class terms. They refer constantly to the "petty bourgeoisie," the "working class," the "national bourgeoisie" and the "peasantry" as the basic social units of their societies. They see the post-independence period as marked by inevitable bitter conflict among these classes, or even, as the *Frente de Libertaçâo de Mocambique* (FRELIMO) asserts, the "intensification of the class struggle."[49]

The most crucial aspect of this struggle is the role of the petty bourgeoisie in which tend to be lumped together civil servants, traders, small businessmen, university graduates, intellectuals, middle-ranking military officers, and school dropouts. This petty bourgeoisie class is at the same time glorified and vilified. But in spite of this ambivalence it is acknowledged that theoretically the initial leadership and impetus for the liberation struggle came from its ranks.[50]

Therefore, in the field of concrete action, experience revealed that, in some countries, the petty bourgeoisie tended to go astray. In the case of Angolan MPLA, Lucio Lara asserted that "it has very strong propensities toward opportunism and personal ambitions" and "lacks the kind of maturity which makes for consistency in the analysis of problems."[51] Similarly, individuals and groups opposing Frelimo in Mozambique were regularly condemned as "reactionary petty bourgeois" who have lost their way and must be dealt with ruthlessly.

Along the same lines, the first leader of the nationalist guerilla struggle in Guinea-Bissau, Amilcar Cabral, argues, like Franz Fanon, that the petty bourgeoisie must "be capable of committing suicide as a class in order to be reborn as revolutionary workers."[52]

Thereupon, Lucio Lara, in agreement with his peer Marxist-Leninists, concludes that the working class must be strengthened in order to "neutralize" progressively the petty bourgeois elements.[53] How is this possible? Stressing the need for a broad coalition of all progressives for bringing the working class to power, Frelimo explains the process in the following lines:

> The Mozambican proletariat, the peasants, particularly those in co-operatives, revolutionary intellectuals, artisans, workers in general, are in the process of gaining a clear awareness of their situation and their historic destiny. They are gradually organizing themselves, under the leadership of the working class, to mould society in accordance with the interests of the Mozambican proletariat.[54]

What is significant for our case study is the fact that the step in the revolutionary process just after independence can be considered as a struggle to create the correct political, social, and economic conditions "for the development of the dictatorship of the Proletariat." This stage is variously referred to as "people's democracy" or "national democratic revolution."

What is meant by "people's democracy"? In its efforts to define this expression and thus the reality that it represents, Frelimo states that "people's democracy is the historical phase in which the laboring masses, under the leadership of the working class, strengthen their Power, establish the dictatorship of the Proletariat and put into effect the Power of the majority in all spheres of social life."[55]

The important lesson we can learn from the preceding lines is that no real revolution can take place without the working class being in control, that is to say, the working class plays an important role in the national liberation struggle. In a discussion of this issue with the South African Communist Party organ, *The African Communist*, Lucio Lara remarked that "it has always been and still is the working class which gains true political consciousness in the struggle and which grasps the process of the revolution and of the transition to socialism with the required degree of reliability and consistency."[56]

To the point, the African Marxist-Leninists differ from the earlier African socialists. The first difference resides in the fact that the former stress the working class as the social basis of the revolution, and thus of the party, while the latter focus upon a broad coalition. In insisting on the role of the working class, the African Marxist-Leninists are ready with a good Marxist explanation for why the worker is so important to the process of building socialism, even in African countries where the vast majority of the population is peasant and the workers constitute but a small minority of relatively privileged people. They argue that it is only the worker who does not own any means of production and "lives by the collective property" of the state. It is the working class alone that can teach the peasants and other groups "the collective spirit, the spirit of organization and the spirit of collective property."[57]

To justify their preference toward the working class, at the expenses of the petty bourgeoisie, African Marxist-Leninists are agreed in acknowledging that progressive petty bourgeois, civil servants, intellectuals, nurses, and teachers are too influenced by the ideas, customs and tastes of the bourgeoisie to be entrusted with the leadership of the revolution. According to Frelimo's explanation, these elements have first "to wage internal combat within themselves," absorb the values of the working class and acquire a new mental outlook "whereby they renounce the bourgeoisie and identify themselves with the working class."[58]

Consequently, there is complete agreement among African Marxist-Leninists that the revolution must be led by a small vanguard party whose social base is the working class and whose ideology is Marxism-Leninism. Since they see society as essentially wracked by irreconcilable class conflict, there is no question of a mass party incorporating either the entire adult population as in Guinea, or the revolutionaries drawn from all segments of society as in Algeria. They fully realize that socialism does not represent the subjective interests of all groups in society. Certain classes are inevitably opposed to it, and thus must be excluded from the party.

The African Marxist-Leninists differ quite emphatically then from the earlier African socialists, not only by their belief in a single scientific socialism, class conflict, dictatorship of the proletariat and a small vanguard party to lead the revolution, but also by their acceptance of terror, violence or coercion as inevitable in the process of socialist transformation.

While none of the early African socialist and transitional leaders proposed a theory of coercion as a legitimate part of revolution, either to carry out their reforms or to repress their oppositions, the African Marxist-Leninists are much more ready to justify the use of coercion and even "terror" as a legitimate means of forcing along the revolutionary process.

By way of illustration, let us take the most dramatic example of Ethiopia, where Colonel Mengistu resorted to what he called "red terror" in order to crush a wide variety of his own personal as well as the revolution's numerous political enemies. Accusing them of employing "white terror" against the military government, he proclaimed: "It is an historical obligation to clean up vigilantly using the revolutionary sword. . . . Your struggle should be demonstrated by spreading red terror in the camp of reactionaries. Turn the white terror of reactionaries into red terror."[59]

This implies that to a very large extent, Marxist doctrine, coupled with historical circumstances, led to the glorification of victory through violent struggle. This can be confirmed once again by Mengistu's declaration to Fidel Castro in September, 1978. "Victory," he said, "is always the fruit of struggle. This is what Marxist-Leninist practice has taught us. This is what the great October (Soviet) Socialist Revolution has taught us."[60]

Surprisingly, President Didier Ratsiraka of the Malagasy Republic argued along the same lines when he remarked in early 1978 that "revolutionary violence is necessary to confront and defeat counter-revolutionary violence, in order to prevent the reactionaries from taking back control of the revolutionary power."[61]

To conclude this section it is important to acknowledge that between the African Marxist-Leninists and the early African socialists, there exist not only divergences as mentioned above, but also some similarities. These similarities are situated on the foreign policy level where "proletarian internationalism," on the one hand, and "Pan-Africanism" and "Third World nonalignment" on the other hand, express one and the same preoccupation.

Like Nkrumah in his later years, the African Marxist-Leninists see the world divided primarily between socialist and capitalist countries, anti-imperialist and imperialist ones. To this extent, nonalignment means primarily the struggle against "imperialism, neo-colonialism, and colonialism," evils they attribute solely to the West. Thus, nonalignment and proletarian internationalism are seen as going hand-in-hand without contradiction in purpose or objective.

PRESENT-DAY PERIOD: METAMORPHOSIS

A very quick look at the present-day reveals a great metamorphosis or "revival" of African socialism. In this regard, the four countries mentioned above are all the more interesting since they are extremely different from each other today.

Tanzania has remained relatively faithful, ideologically as well as politically, to the original concept of African socialism. Zambia, on the other hand, has strayed far away from it, to become basically a welfare state for the upper class. Algeria has turned into a highly centralized and bureaucratized country, single-mindedly pursuing a policy of industrialization. While it has rejected Marxism and extolled Islam, it is the most statist of all the early socialist countries. Guinea has become more Marxist in its ideology and continued to adhere to policies aimed at mobilizing the entire population. By creating the "party-state," however, Sékou Touré has opened the way for the eventual triumph of the state over the party, the very institution he had tried to build into the main pillar of his regime.

While it is quite difficult to reconstitute the different routes through which these countries have traveled in terms of their ideologies alone, it can be acknowledged, however, that Tanzania and Zambia are both prime examples of the African socialist ideology: Nyerere's *Ujamaa* and Kaunda's "Humanism" are almost indistinguishable from each other, yet the two countries have evolved into very different types of socioeconomic systems. Guinea is a perfect example of what we have called a "transitional" ideology, but the economic policies of the country do not reflect such a concept of socialism. Algeria, which has moved in the other direction, away from Marxism-Leninism, still is following a Soviet approach to economic development.

As a result, whatever their ideological similarities and differences, the four countries constitute today four quite distinct models of socialism in Africa: Zambia has become an example of perverse socialist development leading toward an "upper class welfare state,"[62] serving a small elite and presided over by a president who relentlessly exhorts his countrymen to behave in a manner to which they are no longer accustomed or motivated by any concrete rewards. Tanzania is a case study of "development without growth,"[63] stressing the equal distribution of wealth, the provision of basic needs to the poorest and the goal of national self-reliance. Algeria typifies a policy of "economics in command,"[64] emphasizing first and foremost a strategy for economic growth and for attaining economic independence: only secondarily can one talk of ideology and political mobilization. Finally, Guinea is the example of just the opposite, namely, of "politics in command"[65] in the sense indicated by Sékou Touré himself when he states: "If for some, politics is the art of playing, of deceiving, and of using other people, we do not view it in the same light. We define politics for our part as the science from which all other science originates, as essentially the capacity of making possible what is necessary for the people."[66]

In terms of concrete implications of all these metamorphoses, the African socialist experience reveals a set of crucial issues affecting the outcome of the socialist endeavor on the continent: "distortions" of one or another aspect of the African socialist ideal of participation, egalitarianism, and self-reliance.

Under the leadership of Kaunda, Zambia grew to become a society which was neither egalitarian, nor participatory, nor self-reliant. Nyerere made his Tanzanian society more egalitarian and marginally more collective, but he made a mockery of the principle of self-reliance in the process. Boumédiène's Algeria turned its back on self-management and participation, and sacrificed egalitarianism by neglecting the rural areas and allowing the growth of a bureaucratic and technocratic elite. But it did build a base for economic self-reliance through rapid industrialization. Finally, Sékou Touré may have checked capitalism and created a strong party, but his woeful neglect of the economy alienated a large portion of the population and eventually made Guinea into the epitome of the Third World country caught in the grip of multinational corporations.

With regard to the democratization process, the most striking distortion of the initial concept of socialism in all four countries has perhaps been the drift toward statism. The initial aspiration to create highly participatory democracies was embodied in institutions such as the village cooperatives in Zambia, the *Ujamaa* villages in Tanzania, self-management in Algeria, and the *Pouvoirs Révolutionaires Locaux* (PRLs) in Guinea.

Unfortunately, within a few years of experimenting with the approach to revolution and these kinds of institutions, all four countries reached a crisis point because of either apathy, mismanagement, or outright failure, and turned to the state for salvation.

The specific reasons why this trend toward statism emerged differ from country to country. In Zambia, it was related to the centralized nature of a copper-dominated, urban-oriented country and the total lack of "fit" between humanism and these conditions. In the case of Algeria, statism was a deliberate choice: the growth of a large bureaucratic class and the lack of political participation were a direct consequence of priority given to the rapid industrialization as a means of overcoming economic dependency. This concern led to centralized planning, the development of a technocratic elite, and increasing inequality between rural and urban areas. Finally, in both Tanzania and Guinea, statism emerged as a direct result of the failure of participatory schemes to spur lasting change. Both the *Ujamaa* villages in Tanzania and the PRLs in Guinea were intended to put power in the hands of the people and let them take responsibility for the economic and social transformation of the villages. But left on their own, the peasants did not take the initiative, and in the end the state stepped in to fill the vacuum.

Altogether, these distortions have risen from the lack of congruence among ideology, policy and conditions within the country; weaknesses caused by the lack of a solid economic base; dilemmas emerging from the impossibility of attaining all goals at once; and the difficulty of sustaining participation in the absence of any inherent, or for that matter artificially generated, dynamism in society. Underlying all these have been the omnipresent shortcomings of underdeveloped countries, such as the acute shortage of capital, personnel, and managerial experience and the strong proclivity toward elitism in a situation where anyone with a high school diploma, or even with a regular wage job, by definition, belongs to a privileged minority. This poses the question of democracy.

DEMOCRACY IN SOCIALIST PLANNING

We shall approach "democracy" in relation to the dangers inherent in socialist planning or--according to the expression--in a planned economy. In doing this, particular attention is to be focused upon what we shall call "democracy of labor." This is a part of "industrial democracy," which itself is a part of democracy or of government of/by/for the people.

Let us begin by defining first what we understand by socialist planning, which characterizes socialism today. It is difficult to speak of socialism today because it is at one and the same time both the master word for hundreds of millions of men and a formidable ambiguity[67] in modern economic and political language. Does one mean by "socialism" the program of Western socialist parties or the authoritarian phase of development in Eastern communism prior to the withering away of the state? Is it the vague demands of leftists around the world, or is it India and Guinea? What is the difference between socialism and neo-capitalism? Is socialism the doctrine of the "Founding Fathers" or the actual experience developed in the field? How can we avoid throwing together a reformist practice and revolutionary phraseology?

One might even be tempted to forego use of the term "socialism" on the grounds that it is worn out, that it is a part of the leftist logomachy, or that only worn out analyses are repeated in its name. But then we run the risk of "throwing out the baby with the bath water," the seed of hope with the chaff of words.

In order to explore the meaning of socialist planning, let us describe very succinctly its context, that is, socialism taken at its economic, socio-political and cultural dimensions.

At the economic level, socialism means simply a "planning." It involves to this extent the notion of "market economy," that is, an economy in which production and consumption are regulated by profits and monied needs, the notion of reference of the economic plan to "human need," and the notion of collective appropriation of the means of production.

These three elements or characteristics are joined in Paul Ricoeur's definition of socialism when he writes: "By socialism, we shall understand the transition from a market economy to a planned economy that is responsive to human needs and that is characterized by a transfer of the ownership of the means of production to collective or public entities."[68]

At the social and political level, socialism must be considered from the point of view of 'management', that is to say, of "the participation of the greatest number of individuals in economic decisions."[69] Therefore, this management must be "democratic" because at this level the question is one of the realization of democracy in the economy. This implies, in terms of goals, the reintegration of man into the economic and social mechanisms. Indeed the will to satisfy human needs in the most rational way is not enough to define socialism; we know full well that the often vague aspiration toward a more just, egalitarian, and communal society is the real soul of socialism. But this second goal lags far behind the first one. "Everywhere rationality is on the march," Ricoeur writes, "but nowhere is the participation of the greatest number in economic decisions making progress."[70] This is where socialism remains to be achieved.

Finally, at the third level, socialism is a "culture." This feature is the implication of the two preceding ones. Thereupon Ricoeur argues:

> If socialism gives precedence to real needs over profit and also over a pure technique of equilibrium and expansion, and if socialism implies the participation of the greatest number in economic decisions, then a whole conception of man is already traced out in this dual demand. It is in the 'humanism' of socialism that its most fundamental and most

stable aim lies.[71]

Ricoeur describes humanism through three themes. First, the theme of the "de-alienation of human work," that is the liberation of man from "the fetish of merchandise and of money"[72] which man has projected on his own existence. In other words, it concerns the liberation of man from Capitalism's power of alienation which lies in the fact that it has, "after having recognized the economic function of work, sacrificed its fundamental human meaning by subordinating it to the law of profit, to the law of things, to the power of money."[73]

Second, the theme of "man's control over economic phenomena," that is to say, "the triumph of human responsibility over blind mechanism, including those of politics, of administration and of bureaucracy."[74] For this reason precisely the de-alienation process must be extended by the 'socialization of the means of government'.

The third is the theme of "solidarity" which is the least technical and the closest to the "heart" of socialism. It follows that "more deeply than a technique, socialism is the cry of distress, the demand and the hope of the most humbled men."[75] To this extent, today one cannot separate socialism from solidarity with the most underprivileged fraction of humanity, with the misery of the underdeveloped peoples. If the socialist aspiration is not fundamentally linked with the revolt of the slaves, it is no more than a rational and dehumanized calculation, the specter of which has not yet ceased haunting us. "As if, Peguy said, the affairs of socialism never ceased to be the affairs of humanity."[76]

The weakness of the welfare state is the lack of a human perspective. The strength of the socialist camp is precisely the feeling of collective work being done; the friendship, irrespective of borders, for those who work and suffer; and the deep feeling of belonging to a single humanity. One can say that this is the role of utopia, and indeed it is. But "without utopia," Ricoeur states, "only calculation and technocracy remain."[77]

From the preceding description of socialism, we can draw some implications for the achievement of democracy. From its very beginning, socialism has opposed the administration of things by a technical *"oligarchy" à la* Saint-Simon and has aimed at a democratic administration of things, carried out in the name of the masses and controlled by them. Today we are much clearer in this respect, for we have before our eyes the various pathological expressions of planning, especially Stalinist planning.

One must measure carefully the political and human risks and costs of socialist planning. One must also reject the illusion that Karl Marx still cherished when he wrote *The Poverty of Philosophy* in answer to Proudhon's *The Philosophy of Poverty*, namely, that "the working class in the course of its development will substitute for the old civil society an association which will exclude classes and with it their antagonism; there will be no more political power as such since political power is precisely the official sum of antagonism in civil society."[78]

In a planned economy, on the contrary, economic decisions do not depend in the last resort on the possession of wealth; instead they are made by organizations representing the common interest whose fundamental purpose is the maximum satisfaction of real needs in the order of their urgency. Seen this way, Ricoeur notes, "socialism represents the conquest of the economy by rationality, by the same rationality that was previously at work in technology and in the sciences."[79] This is to say that in a planned economy, the economic reality is in a way "constructed" by foresight and decisions. It implies, therefore, some dangers for the achievement of democracy.

In effect, power is concentrated in fewer hands than in a capitalistic economy slowed down by its contradictions; everything in it is co-ordinated at the top, where the ultimate decisions are made by a limited number of men who have an almost limitless power over the collectivized wealth.

Furthermore, the material means of expression are in the hands of the ruling group. This group can impose a rigid orientation on labor and on the professions and exert a sort of authoritarian centralization of all choices. In order to assure itself of a long-term efficacity, the ruling group has the economic means to remove from itself the pressure of public opinion and mechanically to redirect public opinion itself.

These dangers--among others--pose acutely the problem of *industrial democracy* in Africa. The crucial questions here are: How can we avoid the creation of a new slavery through bureaucracy? How can we, on the one hand, assure the necessary stability and continuity of economic power and, on the other hand, assure the participation of the lower classes in decisions in ways other than through a fictitious and *a posteriori* control which, in the case of the People's Democracies, does nothing but ratify decisions which come from the top?

First of all, we should be tempted to suggest the implementation of *consociational democracy* as a possible solution for the evil of African "tribalism." To this extent, minority groups would be protected against arbitrary political measures backed by a "majority tribe," beyond the individualistic protection of a Human Rights bill. The minorities would not only be permitted to deal with their "internal" affairs autonomously, but certain positions in government would be reserved for them constitutionally.

Indeed, this is a fascinating perspective for poor African states, still engaged in the difficult process of nation-building, who are unwilling to waste human resources in "sterile" opposition politics but whose political culture favors broad consensus over the "game" of majority decisions. On the other hand, it is pure illusion to run a political system completely on the basis of the rule observed by Guy Clutton-Brock and according to which "the Elders sit under the big tree, and talk until they agree." That was impossible already in 1963 when Julius Nyerere chose these words as the motto for his pamphlet introducing the single-party system. Such a system cannot work in modern Africa.

Therefore, it is imperative to create representative organs for the discussion of fundamental choices. Political parties such as we know them today seem ill-adapted to this function, as they either represent special interest groups or combine divergent interests which neutralize each other, as in the case of the large American parties. It will be necessary to take a look at what the Yugoslavian producers' councils represent.

The creation of representative organs for the discussion of fundamen'al choices implies some economic policies articulated in terms of political strategies. On a lower level, the problem of the administration of the companies by the workers themselves must be posed. If the councils of workers do not have the power to accept or refuse higher production quotas, if no margin of choice in the direction of the company is left to them, if they have no *share* in the control over the director's execution of policies, one cannot really speak of *democracy of labor* in a socialist economy.

Ultimately, the goal of socialism is the right of each producer to decide how at all levels the surplus of his work will be distributed and used. To that extent socialism is the end of non-freedom which is represented by need and the conquest of the positive freedom constituted by participation in decisions at all echelons.

At this second level one can say that socialism is the system in which workers are the dominant social category; it is the system in which a democracy of labor exists side-by-side with planning. This second task must not be postponed in the name of the first, for the more powerful and extended the means of action available for the government of men, the more democratic the institutions and the customs should be.

The principal peril of a socialist economy is that its whole machinery may come under the control of a privileged and dominant minority. This danger can be eliminated only by a *radical socialization* in terms of *democratization* of the means of government themselves. This is contrary to the existence of a single party and to any system in which the trade unions are reduced to the simple function of diffusing propaganda or serving as a welfare office.

In our opinion, this radical socialization or democratization of the means of government requires ironing out misunderstandings and entrenched confusions about the proper role of political parties, on the one hand, and interest groups on the other. Interest groups are, and must be, more permanent. They must often *share* responsibility ("power") in one and the same institution, as is obvious in the case of work force and capital.

Therefore, conflicts among interest groups normally must be solved by compromise. Competition among them must be solved, for a limited period of time, by a majority decision. For this, all interest groups concerned must trust each other, for should this trust disappear not even the most elaborate consociational *Pacte National* can save the country from bloodshed.

This experience is always painful for some, but that cannot be helped. The only assurance necessary is the existence of a fundamental *consensus*. Consensus, in a democracy of labor and, by extension, in an industrial democracy, must exist on fundamental economic, social and political values as well as on procedure. It cannot be based on group interests or specific political strategies and decisions. To draw reasonable lines between these two realms is, indeed, essential.

It follows that a successful democracy of labor must be established on the basis of consensus about what is legitimate in the working place: which Human Rights, especially the right of work, are inalienable; to what extent individual freedom must be protected against governmental interference in matters of work; and how the people are supposed to control government in regard to labor. If and when consensus on these essentials withers away, the door opens for civil war; if and when the rigid claim to respect consensus is pushed too far, democracy of labor is lost.

To conclude, everywhere in Africa peasant farmers form the broad majority of the people, but hardly anywhere are they organized for efficient bargaining or for carrying any political weight. Every instance of emerging interest groups ready to bargain--be it market women, university students, or a small "labor aristocracy"--should be encouraged as a prerequisite for democracy.

Facultés Catholiques de Kinshasa   *The Catholic University of America*
Kinshasa, Zaire   *Washington, D.C.*

NOTES

1. J. Nyerere, *Ujamaa--Essays on Socialism* (Dar es Salaam: Oxford University Press, 1968), p. 11.

2. *Ibid.*

3. L.S. Senghor, *On African Socialism*, trans., Mercer Cook (New York: Frederich A. Praeger, 1964), p. 26.

4. *Ibid.*, p. 94.

5. K.D. Kaunda, *Humanism in Zambia, Part I* (Lusaka: Zambia Information Services, 1976), p. 69.

6. A.S. Touré, *The Doctrine and Methods of the Democratic Party of Guinea, Part II* (Conakry, N.D.), p. 26.

7. K. Nkrumah, *Revolutionary Party* (New York: International Publishers, 1973), p. 205.

8. J. Nyerere, p. 77.

9. *Ibid.*, p. 78.

10. A.S. Touré, p. 24.

11. K. Nkrumah, p. 436.

12. L. Diane, Interview with the *World Marxist Review*, 19 (n. 8, 1976), p. 110.

13. Afro-Shirazi Party Declaration to the 25th CPSU Congress, *World Marxist Review* 19 (n. 5, 1976), pp. 82-83.

14. K.D. Kaunda, p. 6.

15. J. Nyerere, p. 89.
16. *Ibid.*
17. A.S. Touré, p. 160.
18. K. Nkrumah, *Consciencism* (New York: Monthly Review Press, 1964), p. 79.
19. Idem, *Revolutionary Path*, p. 181 ff.
20. Idem, "African Socialism Revisited", *African Forum*, I, n. 3 (1966), in *Revolutionary Path*, p. 440.
21. *Ibid.*
22. *Ibid.*
23. *Ibid.*, p. 442.
24. *Ibid.*
25. *Ibid.*, p. 446.
26. K. Nkrumah, Extracts from *Class Struggle in Africa*, in *Revolutionary Party*, p. 489.
27. *Ibid.*
28. "Constitution of the Convention People's Party," in K. Nkrumah, *Revolutionary Party*, p. 59.
29. K. Nkrumah, p. 163.
30. *Ibid.*, p. 169.
31. K. Nkrumah, "The Myth of the 'Third World'," in *Revolutionary Path*, p. 436.
32. *Ibid.*, p. 438.
33. *Ibid.*, p. 439.
34. A.S. Touré, *Le Pouvoir Populaire* (Conakry: Imprimerie Patrice Lumumba, 1968), XVL, 161.
35. *Horoya-Special*, October 2, 1970.
36. *Horoya*, n. 2204, January 10, 1976.
37. *Ibid.*
38. Quoted by Lansana Diane, *World Marxist Review* 19, n. 8 (August, 1976), p. 109.
39. "Message from President Sékou Touré", in *Revolutions and Selected Speeches from the Sixth Pan-Africanist Congress* (Dar es Salaam: Tanzania Publishing House, 1976), pp. 16-17.
40. *Ibid.*
41. *Ibid.*
42. See Front de Libération Nationale, *La Charte d'Alger* (Algiers: Imprimerie Nationale Algérienne, 1964), p. 11.
43. Front de Libération Nationale, *Charte Nationale* (Algiers: Editions Populaires de l'Armée, 1976), pp. 26-27.
44. *Ibid.*, p. 46.
45. Speech of November 1, 1965 in *Les Discours du Président Boumédiène* (Algiers: Ministry of Information, 1966), p. 91.
46. M.S. Machel, Unpublished interview with David Martin of the London *Observer*, August 11, 1977.
47. Lucio Lara, in *The African Communist*, n. 74 (1978), p. 65.
48. Mohamed Siad Barre, in *World Marxist Review*, 19, n. 5 (May,

1976), p. 71.

49. *Central Committee Report to the Third Congress of Frelimo* (London: Mozambique, Angola and Guinea Information Center, 1978), p. 23 ff.

50. Amilcar Cabral, *Revolution in Guinea: Selected Texts* (New York: Monthly Review, 1969), pp. 56-75.

51. *The African Communist*, n. 74 (1978), p. 33.

52. Amilcar Cabral, p. 110.

53. Interview with Lucio Lara, *The African Communist*, n. 74 (1978), p. 33.

54. *Central Committee Report to the Third Congress of Frelimo*, p. 22.

55. *Ibid.*, p. 64.

56. *The African Communist* (n. 74, 1978), p. 31.

57. "Theses: What Are Their Objectives?," a document presented for discussion by Frelimo prior to the Third Congress, February 3-7, 1977, memo.

58. *Ibid.*

59. Speeches to the nation, November 13 and 14, quoted in Amnesty International, Swedish Medical Group, "Human Rights Violations in Ethiopia," 1977, p. 6.

60. "Fourth Anniversary of the Ethiopian Revolution," speech delivered by Lt. Col. Mengistu Haile-Mariam, September 12, 1978 (Addis Ababa: Ministry of Information), p. 8.

61. Interview with President Didier Ratsiraka, *Afrique-Asie*, n. 151 (December 26, 1977), p. 13.

62. Marina and David Ottaway, *Afrocommunism*, Second Edition (London: Africana Publishing Company; Holmes & Meier Publishers, 1986), p. 37.

63. *Ibid.*, p. 44.

64. *Ibid.*, p. 59.

65. *Ibid.*, p. 52.

66. Quoted in Claude Rivière, *Mutations Sociales en Guinée* (Paris: Marcel Rivière et Cie., 1971), p. 394.

67. Revmira Ismailova and Ursula Padel, "Zur Widerspiegelung der gegenwartigen Etappe der nationalen Befreiungsrevolution in der Sowjetwissenschaft. Literaturbericht", *Asien-Afrika-Latein-amerika* (Berlin: G.D.R., 1982), n. 2, pp. 217-224.

68. P. Ricoeur, "Le Socialisme aujourd'hui," in *Le Christianisme social*, 69 (1961), pp. 451-460; translated by Françoise Bien, "Socialism Today," in *Political and Social Essays by Paul Ricoeur*, collected and edited by David Stewart and Joseph Bien (Athens: Ohio University Press, 1976), p. 230.

69. *Ibid.*, p. 234.

70. *Ibid.*

71. *Ibid.*, p. 238.

72. *Ibid.*

73. *Ibid.*, p. 239.
74. *Ibid.*
75. *Ibid.*, p. 241.
76. *Ibid.*
77. *Ibid.*
78. Karl Marx, *The Poverty of Philosophy*, in D. Stewart and J. Bien, p. 235.
79. P. Ricoeur, in D. Stewart and J. Bien, p. 230.

PART III

RELATIONS BETWEEN CULTURES

CHAPTER XIII

SELF-KNOWLEDGE, SELF-IDENTITY

AND COOPERATION BETWEEN PEOPLES

GEORGE F. McLEAN

THE CONTEMPORARY PROBLEMATIC

A dialectic of the personal and the depersonalizing appears to be one of the paradoxes of recent experience. For a number of economic, educational and other reasons, the past decades have been marked in many parts of the world by a massive migration from the countryside into the towns and cities.[1] At first it was thought that the size of the town and of the factory would relieve the personal pressures of village life, for when the obligation of a more extended family and the all-seeing eyes of the neighbors were remote, persons and families could be truly free. Tolerance understood in this passive manner as non-interference--or was it non-caring?--was considered desirable and, indeed, appears to have constituted no small attraction drawing many young families to the city.[2] In fact, however, the problems of life are never so easily solved. Upon reflection, it can be seen that the attempt to dispense with so basic a dimension of the person as one's social character was doomed to failure, for it generated social dissatisfaction and deep loneliness--a living death.[3]

Further, the ever more close interaction of increasingly diverse peoples which has characterized modernization and nation-building could only exacerbate, rather than resolve, problems of living with others. As the level of work rises above a mute carrying out of orders, as parents begin to play an active role in planning goals for schools, as people take a more active role in a democratic system, and as all of these economic, educational and political decisions increasingly affect and are affected by national and international life, the level of interaction between persons increases geometrically. Decisions come to be made less individually and autocratically, and more through discussion in the home, the work-place, the community, the nation and the world. Indeed, T. Imamichi speaks of a basic inversion of practical reasoning reflecting the fact that the energy, transportation and communications provided by a developing technology are largely in common possession. It is not I but *we* who have these means; hence it is *we* who must choose; further, we must do so not only between means, but as regards the very goals to which they will be applied.[4]

In short, anonymity and disengagement from others is neither realizeable nor desirable. Modern life intensifies the need to interact positively with an ever expanding range of peoples traditions and interests, and this at ever more penetrating levels of one's life and work.[5] The problem is one of self-identity in interaction with others, of the auto-constitution of the human person in free and responsible interchange. Hence, growth in self-knowledge and self-identity is now required if we are to move from a passive posture of patience to a positive search and assimilation of additional views drawn from the experiences of others and to weld them into the complementary systemic relations required for modern living.[6]

But the issue is not merely one of missed opportunities. A brief catalogue of present tensions suggests the depth and difficulty of the problem of taking this step from passive to active tolerance. First, within the person there exist multiple tensions between, on the one hand, the traditional content of one's culture built upon community and, on the other hand, the cumulative and often depersonalizing demands of a life whose every phase is ordered according to the abstract rationalizations of industry, commerce, education and politics.

Secondly, within social, national and other groups and on the basis of the most subtle shadings of color or style of hair, birth or personal mannerism, one subgroup comes to be considered not merely slightly different, but somewhat threatening, and then markedly inferior. Even where no differences exist, some negative evaluation is imposed in order not fully to accept or recognize a group's freedom and dignity. Often the group resides in a distinct sector of a country or even of each town, surrounded by a climate of indifference or, more probably, of incipient antipathy. In some cases they are cast out to swell the growing tide of the world's 14,000,000 refugees, where they languish in camps, wander in hunger, and are indiscriminately exploited or even attacked. This is a primary problem of our time.

Thirdly, this phenomenon reappears between countries and continents; it shadows man's every advance. As the ability is developed to communicate and interact with peoples and cultures ever more distant and diverse, the modalities of alienation keep step, adopting ever more sophisticated and powerful economic and even military forms.

In this light the human travails entailed in establishing tolerance as a positive virtue appear to go far beyond commercial, territorial or ideological disputes--although any one of these can become the point around which coalesces a more perverse dynamism. What is at work is a humanly subversive process by which, in the search for self-identity and self-worth, the other--whether person or group, domestic or foreign--is looked upon as a threatening adversary, as unworthy of respect, and finally as an object of rejection or even of attack.

This is the lived dimension of the basic metaphysical problem of self-identity and hence of otherness. To ignore this fundamental character of the problem would restrict one's response to the level of compromises and accommodations possible in terms of the particular sciences, alleviating the symptoms while leaving the root problem unfaced. Such responses do little more than delineate the terms and plant the seeds for subsequent confrontation and conflict.

The real problems of interrelation between persons and cultural groups can be faced only by looking more deeply into the nature and origin of self knowledge and of self-identity to see whether this sets one against others or, on the contrary, unites persons; and if it does so whether this can ground the positive interaction or cooperation required by the tensions of our day.

PERSON AS GIVEN

One place to begin is with the person as a polyvalent unity operative on both the physical and the non-physical levels. Though the various sciences analyze distinct dimensions, the person is not a construct of independent components but an identity: the physical and the psychic are dimensions of myself and of no other. Further, this identity is not the result of my personal development, but was had from my beginning; it is a given for each person. Hence, while I can grow indefinitely, the growth will be always my own; it is the same given or person who perdures through all the stages of his or her growth.

This givenness appears also through reflection upon one's interpersonal relations. I do not properly create these, for they are possible only if I already have received my being and nature. Rather, relatedness is given with one's nature and received as a promise and a task; it is one's destiny. What depends upon the person is only the degree of his or her presence to others.[7]

Unfortunately, this givenness is often taken in one of the two senses associated with the terms 'datum' or 'data', the one hypothetical and the other evidential. On the one hand, in the hypothetical sense a given is a stipulation agreed upon by the relevant parties as the basis for a process of argumentation: Granted X, then Y. The premises of an argument or the postulates in a mathematical demonstration are such. On the other hand, in the evidential sense, data are the direct and warranted observations of what actually is the case. In both these meanings the terms 'given' or 'data' direct the mind exclusively toward the future or consequent as one's only concern. The use of the past participle of the verb stem (*data*) closes off any search toward the past so that when one given is broken down by an analysis new givens appear. One never gets behind some hypothetical or evidential given.

This closure is done for good reason, but it leaves a third --and for our purposes potentially important--sense of 'given'; this is expressed by the nominative form, 'donum' or gift. In contrast to the other two meanings, this would seem to point back, as it were, behind itself to its source in ways similar to the historians' use the term 'fact'. They note that a fact is not simply there; its meaning has been molded or made (*facta*) within the ongoing process of human life.[8] In this sense it points back to its origin and origination.

However, this potentially rich return to the source was blocked by the shift at the beginning of the 19th century from an empiricist to an anthropocentric view. In this horizon facts came to be seen especially as made by man, conceived either as an individual in the liberal tradition, or as a class in the socialist tradition--to which correspond the ideals of progress and praxis, respectively. Because what was made by man could always be remade by him,[9] however, this turned aside a radical search into the character of life as gift. Attention remained only upon the future understood simply in terms of man and of what man could do by either individual or social praxis.

There are reasons to suspect that this humanism is not enough for a positive sense of tolerance or cooperation with others. Without underestimating how much has been accomplished in these terms, the worldwide contemporary phenomenon of alienation from other cultures (not to mention one's own) suggests that something important has been forgotten. First, by including only what is abstractively clear it begins by omitting that which can be had only in self-knowledge, namely, one's self-identity and all that is most distinctive and creative in each people's heritage. Focusing only upon what is analytically clear and distinct to the mind of any and every individual renders alien the notes of integrity, wholeness and harmony. These characterize more synthetic philosophical and religious traditions and are realized in the self-knowledge of the seer[10] and under the personal guidance of a teacher or guru.[11]

Second there is danger that in concrete affairs the concern to build the future in terms only of what has been conceived clearly and by all will be transformed, even unwittingly, into oppression of self-identity and the destruction of integrative cultures both as civilizations and as centers of personal cultivation. Indeed, the charges of cultural oppression and the calls for liberation from so many parts of the world make one wonder whether the humanist notion of the self-given and its accompanying ideals can transcend the dynamics of power and leave room for persons, especially for those of other cultures.

Finally, were the making which is implied in the derivation of the term 'fact' from 'facere' to be wholly reduced to 'selfmaking,' and were the given to become only the self-given, it might be suspected that we had stumbled finally upon what Parmenides termed "the all impossible way" of deriving what is from what is not.[12] His essential insight--shared by Hinduism, Islam and the Judeo-Christian traditions--that all is grounded in the Absolute is a firm guard against undertaking such a route.

PERSON AS GIFT

It is time then to pursue the third meaning of 'given' and to follow the opening toward the source implied in the notion of gift. Above, we had noted some indications that self-identity and interpersonal relatedness are gifts (*dona*). Let us now look further into this in order to see what it suggests regarding the dynamic openness required for cooperation between persons and cultures.

First, one notes that as gift the given has an essentially gratuitous character. It is true that at times the object or service given could be paid for in cash or in kind. As indicated by the root of the term 'commercial,' however, such a transaction would be based on some merit (*mereo*) on the part of the receiver. This would destroy its nature as gift precisely because the given would not be based primarily in the freedom of the giver.

The same appears from an analysis of an exchange of presents. Presents cease to be gifts to the degree that they are given only because of the requirements of the social situation or only because of a claim implicit in what the other might have given me. Indeed, the sole way in which such presents can be redeemed as gifts is to make clear that their presentation is not something to which I merely feel obliged, but which I personally and freely want to do. As such then, a gift is based precisely upon the freedom of the giver; it is gratuitous.

There is here a striking symmetry with the 'given' in the above sense of hypothesis or evidence. There, in the line of hypothetical and evidential reasoning there was a first, namely, that which is not explained, but upon which explanation is founded. Here there is also a first upon which the reality of the gift is founded and which is not to be traced to another reality: it is the originating action precisely as free or gratuitous.

Further, as an absolute point of departure with its distinctive spontaneity and originality, the giving is non-reciprocal. To attempt to repay would be to destroy the gift as such. Indeed, there is no way in which this originating gratuity can be returned; we live in a graced condition. This appears in reflection upon one's culture. What we received from the authors of the *Vedas*, a Shankara or an Aristotle can in no way be returned. Nor is this simply a problem of distance in time, for neither is it possible to repay the life we have received from our parents, the health received from a doctor, the wisdom from a teacher, or simply the good example which can come from any quarter at any time. The non-reciprocal character of our life is not merely that of part to whole; it is that of a gift to its source.[13]

The great traditions have insisted rightly both upon the oneness of the absolute reality and upon the lesser reality of the multiple: the multiple is not The Reality, though neither is it totally non-reality. Anselm's elaboration of the notion of privation contains a complementary clarification of the gratuitous character of beings as given or gifted. The notion of privation was developed classically by Aristotle in his analysis of change, where privation appeared at the beginning of the process as the lack of the form to be realized. He saw this as more than non-being precisely in as much as it was a lack of a good which is due to that subject. Hence, in substantial change, because the basic potential principle is prime matter to which no specific form is due, privation plays no role.

Anselm extended this notion of privation to the situation of creation in which the whole being is gifted. In this case, there is no prior subject to which something is due; hence, there is no ground or even any acceptance. Anselm expressed this radically non-reciprocal nature of the gift--its lack of prior conditions--through the notion of absolute *privation*.

It is *privation* and not merely negation, for negation simply is not and leads nowhere, whereas the gift is to be, and once given can be seen to be uniquely appropriate. It is absolute privation, however, for the foundation is not at all on the part of the recipient; rather it is entirely on the part of the source.[14] This parallels a basic insight suggested in the Upanishads and perhaps the basic insight for metaphysics.

> In the beginning, my dear, this world was just being (Sat), one only, without a second. . . . Being thought to itself: 'May I be many; may I procreate.' It produced fire. That fire thought to itself: 'May I be many; may I procreate.' It produced water. . . . That water thought to itself: 'May I be many; may I procreate.' It produced food. . . . That divinity (Being) thought to itself: 'Well, having entered into three divinities [fire, water, and food] by means of this living Self, let me develop names and forms. Let me make each one of them tripartite. (*Chandogya Up., 6.1-3, 12-14.*)

To what does this correspond on the part of the source? In a certain parallel to the antinomies of Kant which show when reason has strayed beyond its bounds, many from Plotinus to Leibniz and beyond have sought knowledge, not only of the gift and its origin, but of why it had to be given. The more they succeeded the less room was left for freedom on the part of man as a given or gift. Others attempted to understand freedom as a fall, only to find that what was thus understood was bereft of value and meaning and hence was of no significance to human life and its cultures. Rather, the radical non-reciprocity of human freedom must be rooted in an equally radical generosity on the part of its origin. No reason, either on the part of the given or on the part of its origin makes this gift necessary; the freedom of man is the reflection of his derivation from a giving that is pure generosity: man is the image of God.

In turn, on the part of the gift this implies a correspondingly radical openness or generosity. The gift is not something which is and then receives; it was an essential facet of Plato's response to the problems he had elaborated in the *Parmenides* that the multiple can exist only *as* participants of the good or one. Receiving is not something they *do*; it is what they *are*.[15] As such they reflect at the core of their being the reality of the generosity in which they originate.

The importance of this insight is attested from many directions. In Latin America some philosophers begin from the symbol earth as the fruitful source of all (reflected in the Quechuan language of the Incas as the "Pacha Mama"). This is their preferred context for their sense of human life, its relations to physical nature, and the meeting of the two in technology.[16] In this they are not without European counterparts. The classical project of Heidegger in its later phases shifted beyond the unconcealment of the being of the things-in-time, to Being which makes the things manifest. The *Dasein*, structured in and as time, is able to provide Being a place of discovery among things.[17] Being maintains the initiative; its coming-to-pass or emission depends upon its own spontaneity and is for its sake. "Its 'there' (*Da-sein*) only sustains the process and guards it," so that in the openness of concealed Being beings can appear un-concealed.[18]

The African spirit, especially in its great reverence of family, community and culture, whence one derives one's life, one's ability to interpret one's world, and one's capacity to respond seems uniquely positioned to grasp this more fully. In contrast to Aristotle's classical 'wonder,' these philosophers do not situate the person over against the object of his or her concern, reducing both to objects for detached study and manipulation. They look rather to the source whence reality is derived and are especially sensitive to its implications for the mode and manner of one's life as being essentially open, communicative, generous and sharing.

IMPLICATIONS FOR A NEW NOTION OF TOLERANCE

Seen in terms of gift, person and community manifest two principles for tolerance in cultural interchange: complementarity which makes interchange positive, and generosity which induces its implementation. First, as participants in the one, self-sufficient and purely spontaneous source, the many are not in principle antithetic or antipathetic one to another. Rather, as limited images they stand in a complementary relation to all other participants or images. This is reflected in the enjoyment experienced in simple companionship in which, by sharing the other's experience of being, each lives more fully: the result is more than the sum of its parts. What is true here of individual persons in true as well both of groups of peoples and of the cultures they create through self-knowledge. It is this complementarity, derived from their common origin, which makes cooperation in work and decision making, whether in commerce or in culture, fundamentally possible and ultimately desirable.

This has two important implications for our topic. Where the Greeks' focus upon their heritage had led to depreciating others as barbarians, the sense of oneself and of one's culture as radically gifted provides a basic corrective. Knowing and valuing oneself and one's culture as gifts implies more than merely reciprocating what the other does for me. It means, first, that others and their culture are to be respected simply because they too have been given or gifted by the one Absolute source. This is an important step which Gandhi in calling outcasts by the name "harijans" or "children of God" urged us to take beyond any pride or isolation which would see others in pejorative terms.

But mere respect may not be enough. The fact that both originate from, share in and proclaim the same Self, especially as Good or Bliss, implies that in what they share of the good the relation between two cultures or integrating modes of human life is in principle one of complementarity. Hence, interchange as the effort to live this complementarity is far from being hopeless. In the pressing needs of our times only an intensification of cooperation between peoples can make available immense stores of human experience in living and sharing the good. A positive virtue of tolerance is our real basis for hope.

A second principle for interchange is to be found in the participated--the radically given or gifted--character of one's being. As one does not first exist and then receive, but one's very existence is a received existence or gift, to attempt to give back this gift, as in an exchange of presents, would be at once hopelessly too much and too little. On the one hand, to attempt to return in strict equivalence would be too much for it is our very self that we have received as gift. On the other hand, to think merely in terms of reciprocity would be to fall essentially short of my nature as one that is given, for to make a merely equivalent return would be to remain centered upon myself where I would cleverly trap, and then entomb, the creative power of being.

Rather, looking back I can see the futility of giving back, and in this find the fundamental importance of passing on the gift in the spirit in which it has been given. One's nature as given calls for a generosity which reflects that of one's source. Truly appropriate generosity lies in continuing the giving through participating, sharing or handing on this good to others. As this means being effectively concerned for the good of the other, it requires a vast expansion or breaking out of oneself as the only center of one's concern. It means becoming effectively concerned with the good of others and of other groups, for their promotion and vital growth.

The implications of such generosity are broad and at times surprisingly personal. First, true openness to others cannot be based upon a depreciation of oneself or of one's own culture. Without appreciating one's worth there would be nothing to share and no way to help, nor even the possibility of taking joy in the good of the other. Cultural interchange enables one to see that elements of one's life, which in cultural isolation may have seemed to be merely local customs and purely repetitive in character, are more fundamentally modes in which one lives basic and essential human values. In meeting others and other cultures, one discovers the deeper meaning in one's own everyday life.

One does more than discover, however. One recognizes that in these transcendental values of life--of truth and freedom, of love and beauty--one participates in the dynamism of one's origin and hence must share these values in turn. More exactly, one can come to realize that real reception of these transcendental gifts lies in sharing them in loving concern in order that others may realize them as well. To do this in reality means protecting and promoting what other peoples are and would freely become.

Finally, that other cultures are quintessentially products of self-cultivation by other spirits as free and creative implies the need to open one's horizons beyond one's own self-concerns to the ambit of the freedom of others. This involves promoting the development of other free and creative centers and cultures which, precisely as such, are not in one's own possession or under one's own control. One lives then no longer in terms merely of oneself or of things that one can make or manage, but in terms of an interchange between free men and cultures. Personal responsibility is no longer merely individual decision making or for individual good. Effectively realized, the resulting interaction and mutual fecundation reaches out beyond oneself and one's own culture to reflect ever more perfectly the glory of the one source and goal of all.[19]

This calls for a truly shared effort in which all respond fully not only to common needs, but to the particular needs of each. This broad sense of tolerance in a time of tension has been described by John Paul as a state in which violence cedes to peaceful transformation, and conflict to pardon and reconciliation; where power is made reasonable by persuasion, and justice finally is implemented through love.[20]

The Catholic University of America
Washington, D.C.

NOTES

1. Vance Packard, *A Nation of Strangers* (New York: McKay, 1972).

2. Richard Sennett, *Authority* (New York: Knopf, 1980), pp. 84-121.

3. David Russman, *The Lonely Crowd* (New Haven: Yale Univ. Press, 1961); J. B. Lotz *The Problem of Loneliness* (Staten Island, NY: Alba House, 1967).

4. T. Imamichi, "Problema Ethica et Eco-Ethica," *The Journal of the Faculty of Letters, The University of Tokyo: Aesthetics*, VI (1979), 5.

5. Peter Drucker, *The Age of Discontinuity* (New York: Harper and Row, 1968).

6. Imamichi, *ibid.*, pp. 4, 6 and 8.

7. Maurice Nedoncelle, "Person and/or World as the Source of Religious Insight" in G. McLean, ed., *Traces of God in a Secular Culture* (New York: Alba House, 1973), pp. 187-210.

8. Kenneth L. Schmitz, *The Gift: Creation* (Milwaukee: Marquette Univ. Press, 1982), pp. 34-42. I am particularly indebted to this very thoughtful work for its suggestions. I draw also upon my "Chinese-Western Cultural Interchange in the Future" delivered at the International Symposium on Chinese- Western Cultural Interchange in Commemoration of the 400th Anniversary of the Arrival of Matteo Ricci, S.J., in China (Taiwan: Fu Jen Univ., 1983), pp. 457-72.

9. Karl Marx, *Theses on Feuerbach*, nos. 6-8 in *F. Engels, Ludwig Feuerbach and the Outcome of Classical German Philosophy* (New York: International Publishers, 1934), pp. 82-84. Schmitz, *ibid.*

10. A. S. Cua, *Dimensions of Moral Creativity: Paradigms, Principles and Ideals* (University Park, PA: Pennsylvania State Univ. Press,

1978), chaps. III-V.

11. W. Cenkner, *The Hindu Personality in Education: Tagore, Gandhi and Aurobindo* (Delhi: South Asia Books, 1976).

12. Parmenides, *Fragment* 2.

13. Schmitz, 44-56.

14. Anselm, *Monologium*, cc. 8-9 in *Anselm of Canterbury*, eds. J. Hopkins and H. W. Richardson (Toronto: E. Mellen, 1975), I, pp. 15-18. See Schmitz, 30-34.

15. R. E. Allen, "Participation and Predication in Plato's Middle Dialogues" in his *Studies in Plato's Metaphysics* (London: Routledge, Keegan Paul, 1965), pp. 43-60.

16. Juan Carlos Scannone, "Ein neuer Ansatz in der Philosophie Lateinamerikas," *Philosophisches Jahrbuch*, 89 (1982), 99-116 and "La Racionalidad Cientifico-Technologica y la Racionalidad Sapiencial de la Cultura Latino Americana," *Stromata* (1982), 155-164.

17. William J. Richardson, *Heidegger: Through Phenomenology to Thought* (The Hague: Nijhoff, 1967), pp. 532-535.

18. Joseph Kockelmans, "Thanksgiving: The Completion of Thought," in Manfred S. Frings, ed., *Heidegger and the Quest for Truth* (Chicago: Quadrangle Books, 1968), pp. 175-179.

19. Schmitz, 84-86.

20. John Paul II, "Address at Puebla," *Origins* VIII (n. 34, 1979), I, 4 and II, 41-46.

CHAPTER XIV

UNIVERSALISM AS THE MEANING

OF RECENT HISTORY

DEVELOPMENTS IN THE MARXIST
THEORY OF FORMATION

JANUSZ KUCZYNSKI

The topic of this paper is both difficult and extensive. The author's aim is to discover the significance of the Western world as a culture and history in general, and of their relationship as regards mankind. In the final part of this paper I would like to propose a certain ensemble of norms deduced from the concept of universalism which is under construction.

I propose the following definition of terms:

1. "Dialectics" is understood essentially in the classical manner, i.e., that of Hegel and Marx, although in view of the object I was forced to supplement it slightly. I refer to dialectics because the complexity of the object, its inner, multi-level contradictions, and the unique dynamics of development call for the use of this method;

2. As in my earlier works,[1] I consider "meaning" to correspond to "essence," and therefore to be the cognitive and creative bond between the subject and the object, and subsequently the sum of value;

3. "Essence" is a condensed form of all relations linking a given object with the world, which can be captured in a single category or statement, that is, the relations determined by the object's construction, the laws of development and the necessary traits which occur in all of its manifestations;[2]

4. "The West" denotes the civilization and culture born in ancient Greece which today includes the North American continent, Europe and the USSR;

5. Authentic universalism, as understood here, is a philosophy of "mankind-for-itself," a self-knowledge of mankind which at present is taking on a concrete form.

All these descriptions are of an introductory character and will be developed in the course of the analysis and new proposals. Their common premise is a philosophy of meaning which makes it possible to grasp the essence of the reality under examination and builds the presuppositions for the transformation of reality. Meaning is determined in a twofold manner. As a correlate of essence it has an objective foundation in the object itself; nevertheless, the way of seeing the object depends upon the historical and personal situation of the subject, as well as upon his knowledge, activity and creative attitude. The meaning of one and the same reality is thus partially different in every interpretation, but what is common for all results from its being objectively rooted in the essence. The philosophy of meaning must begin therefore from examining the essence and may be in position to construct norms.

The question concerning meaning pertains also to the creative correlate of "essence"; it deals not only with what is, but also with what we can create from essence. This is particularly evident when in the object and between a given object (and its essence) and other objects there appear contradictions such that it is no longer possible to retain the object in its former state, namely, when crises threaten the object itself with annihilation.

This is the present situation of the West which finds itself in a growing collision with other civilizations. It is in an unstable position in an equally unstable international order, torn by intensifying internal contradictions. The West is experiencing a crisis of violent changes. A United Nations University paper even mentions "the failure of the Promethean civilizational project."[3] This is a thesis with which I should like to argue, although I do not disregard its great impact both as inspiration and as warning.

The main inner contradiction to be found in practically the whole world is that between two systems: capitalism and socialism. I shall present the hypothesis that its solution is possible only through a "forward movement," that is, through its abolition in a new synthesis or new formation. As we shall see, this is not a revival of the convergence theory, nor do I have in mind a "post-industrial society." I am concerned with interpreting the essence of the contemporary situation of the West, with co-endowing the West with a new meaning and with solving contradictions at a most explosive moment. These undertakings are the duty and mission of Western intellectuals, and require comprehension of the process of shaping mankind-for-itself, whose correlate could be an authentic and creative universalism.

THE DEFINITION OF A NEW UNIVERSALISM: A PROJECTION

The word "universalism" (from the Latin word: *universalis*) means "striving to disseminate a given opinion, to include all people in a certain activity, to embrace a given entity." In philosophy this term was used to describe all attitudes and views which recognize the domination of the whole over its parts or over the individuals, etc. According to this meaning, universalism is usually understood as the opposite of different varieties of individualism. In theology (particularly Catholic) the term "universalism" denotes the global nature of the Church, the exclusive truth of a faith open for all.

This study is not intended to present a review of the various concepts of universalism, but only to suggest an introductory proposal for a new universalism. At the end of my paper I shall depict the features of this universalism obtained from analysis and deduction. At this point I should like to mention certain aspects of the problem.

First, in relation to the meaning of history, I wish to deduce the new universalism not only from facts concerning the history and elements of various doctrines, but also from the process of development and its rules. Universalism is understood here as a philosophy which results from the objective situation as determined by the laws of development. It grows out of various "universalities" and "specificities."

Second, universalism is understood as a projected philosophy of mankind, that is to say, mankind is its object and its group subject.

Third, universalism is not as yet a fact, although one could indicate the many tendencies and elements which co-create it. It is undergoing a process of creation, and my reflections are also intended as an attempt at becoming aware of, or even gaining self-awareness concerning the process or movement which constitutes universalism.

The new universalism is to be the first truly all-embracing theoretical correlate of mankind which today finds itself in a transition from a mankind-in-itself towards a mankind-for-itself. It has to be open in order to sum up dialectically common values and be tolerant towards differentiated and antagonistic values.

THE THEORY OF SOCIO-ECONOMIC FORMATIONS AS THE FOUNDATION OF UNIVERSALISM

The fundamental question which appears here, concerns the field in which we are to conduct comparisons. They are not possible in any specific field because such comparison immediately places it in an hegemonic position over all others. No field of a given universal feature, e.g., science, nature, market, can be sufficient since it pertains only to a chosen sphere. Hence we must discover a truly universal field which would be all-embracing and neutral, i.e., which would be the meta-field. It is my opinion that for this the best and only such field today is the theory of socio-economic formations and the diachronically universal and concrete totalities of social life.

The meta-field in which comparisons can be made is in reality built "from the bottom," in a succession of dialectical generalizations of empirical data.[4] The procedure of supersession (*Aufhebung*), regardless of its sources in Hegelian epistemological realism, has its initial empirical and factual basis in axiological nominalism. *Aufhebung* occurs within the creation of formations--not only during transitions between them, but during the emergence of what is specific, i.e., the new elements of universality.

The material needs of people and their fulfillment constitute a foundation of individual and social life and of the regeneration and reproduction of human nature. From this point of view, these needs are the primary universal element common to all people. The ways in which those needs are satisfied are diverse and consist of the various modes of production which seem to form a link between people in time through particular levels of development and the increasingly rational and successful modes of production.[5]

A temporal and historical entity or formation includes also an enormous number of specifics, e.g., states and nations. They are distinguished predominantly by their cultural and political differences. Within each formation the mode of production and the productive relations join everyone together, while the awareness of those aspects of production expressed in culture is a factor of differentiation. Power-politics, on the other hand, inevitably continues to divide people and set them against each other.

Unity-definite formation thus is constituted primarily by a balanced level of the productive forces and the system of productive relations, i.e., the mode of production. This, however, is a unity of only one of the four strata mentioned by Abel-Malek, and differs from the cultural and political strata. The cultural stratum unifies social life into the forms of consciousness, the political one into the forms of power, and the economic stratum into the mode of production. These three various strata and the three different forms and contents of social life constitute a mixture of specificity and historical universality.[6] In short periods of time the forms of political totalization appear to be decisive. The time of economic totalization is longer, but it can be defined and is relatively constant within a formation. The paradox that the greatest permanence is had by the most transitory forms, i.e., forms of consciousness in the cultural stratum, consists in the fact that in contrast to the two earlier ones, they reflect abstract aspects and not concrete totalities and things.

Culture, however, is also subject to universalization. The fundamental difference from economy is that there does not appear to be a leveling unification. Cultural values, by becoming universal, i.e., as if stemming from a given specificity and attaining the rank of a universally recognized phenomenon, do not lose their individuality and remain themselves un-interchangeable (in contrast to e.g., cars, money, radios, etc.). In contrast to the political sphere, the promotion of culture to universality does not mean winning an hegemoneous position, the subjection or enslavement of others. It signifies a "pure" recognition, unconnected with compulsion.

In social life as a whole all the three spheres are so intertwined that it is difficult to perceive processes of unification. This situation becomes increasingly complicated during the course of historical progress. Marx wrote that:

> In general outline, the Asiatic, feudal and contemporary bourgeois modes of production can be designated as successive epochs of the economic social formation. Bourgeois productive relations appear as the last antagonistic form of the social process, antagonistic not in the sense of individual antagonism, but in the sense of an antagonist arising from the social conditions of the life of individuals; but the productive forces emerging in the bosom of bourgeois society will also create the conditions for the resolution of this an-

tagonism. Hence with the bourgeois social formation the prehistory of human society comes to a close.[7]

In other words, the historical accomplishment of capitalism is that it ended the dissemination and disintegration of mankind into mutually independent individuals. An objective, socio-economic foundation of unity came into being accompanied by a material-social premise for authentic universalism.[8]

The Soviet scholar, Yu. I. Semenov, writes that:

In contrast with all previous history, the replacement of feudalism by capitalism took place not only at the level of human society as a whole, but also inside every social organism. The world capitalist system was the first which, for all practical purposes, drew every social organism on earth into its own sphere of influence. In this sense, global history in a literal sense only began with socialism.[9]

In this way, mankind-in-itself originated. All societies were drawn into the network of basic economic relations, providing the primary and fundamental premise for the unity of mankind. At the same time there appeared also contradictions between regional societies which increased together with the development of their self-knowledge, i.e., of the cultural and political spheres. If one were greatly to simplify the problem and do justice to only one of its aspects, one could say that the awareness of economic inequalities (and the scale of comparisons is discovered at the moment of entering into the same formation) found its patriotic forms of expression in culture and its nationalist forms in politics.[10]

Capitalism created a global history, but did not produce a global society, understood as a community. On the contrary, it gave rise to a large number of increasing contradictions. Unification became objectively possible and universalism could appear and did so in at least two forms, those of ecumenism and internationalism.[11] Self-annihilation, however, still remains a danger.

Ernest Gellner emphasizes the fact that Marxism is evolutionary and writes that "evolutionism is a stress on endogenous development as the main and crucial process in human history."[12] This can be understood in two ways: (a) "if we exclude extra-terrestrial intrusions" (Gellner, p. 69), and (b) as a "purely" internal development of a given civilization, uninfluenced by other significant civilizations.

The first sense applies to mankind as a whole--as Gellner explains in more detail--adding that Marxism includes evolutionism together with functionalism which starts "from the sometimes conspicuous fact of stability or stagnation."[13] Only in the second sense can it be applied to a mankind composed of various societies.

In conclusion to the first problem, one can say that Marxism considers the culture of mankind to be wholly endogenous, that it includes cultures endogenous in varying degrees, and that we can also observe instances of stagnation, isolation and diffusion. For all practical purposes, this is an assertion of an existing fact, but with important theoretical and even ideological consequences.

What is the relation between cultures which remain at different levels of development? All theories of universalism, including internationalism, ecumenism and the concept of *specificité-universalité* of Abdel-Malek (which stems from the practical aspects of the international cooperation of men of letters and science) can be understood fully and reasonably only in the widest possible "geographical" and historical context, i.e., in the light of the philosophy of economic and social formations. The meaning of history constitutes the foundation of all foundations. Understood in this context, the meaning of history is our meta-field.

The meaning of history is not "given" from the outside, as the main thesis of Lessing's well-known book proclaims,[14] nor can we accept the statement made by Husserl who used quotation marks for the "meaning" of history.[15] This meaning is first deducted from praxis, from empirical material, and then constituted.

Geoffrey Barraclough writes that:

> Comparative history is the modern answer--the preferred method of approach of contemporary historians--to the question of the meaning of history. It seeks meaning not, like universal historians, in a continuous narrative of human development, not, like meta-historians, in a comprehensive, overall pattern, but in elucidating the nature of the perennial problems which have assailed mankind throughout its history. That it does so by organizing the past in the paradigms and categories.[16]

In the same work we come across extensive acknowledgement of the importance of Marxism as one of the most fundamental premises of universalism:

> At the present time one 'philosophy of history' alone retains its vigor and heuristic potency, and that, of course, is Marxism. As we have seen, Marxism is a powerful intellectual force not only in the Communist countries of the world, but throughout Asia, and its impact in the non-Communist west is scarcely less powerful. Few modern writers of stature, even among those who profoundly disagree with his analysis, have failed to pay tribute to the seminal influence of Marx's philosophy of history. Of all 'great sociological theories of history', writes Isaiah Berlin 'Marxism is much the boldest and the most intelligent.[17]

CENTER-PERIPHERIES

The second problem of the theory of formation as interpreted by Semenov and Gellner, and which at this stage appears to be particularly acute, concerns the relationship between the center and the peripheries. Semenov wrote that:

> It appears as a characteristic trait of every world system which constitutes a center of pan-global development, that it expands at the cost of retarded social organisms, which are drawn into the orbit of its influence. Not infrequently these societies provide the base for the emergence of social organisms of a new type, which then also enter the world system. The enlargement of the world system is accompanied by a further extension of the zone of its influence. More and more social organisms, belonging to lower types, are drawn into it.[18]

This problem was examined very extensively by E. Gellner who introduced the terms:

> the torch relay view of history, and what may also be called the displacement effect, or the doctrine of the essential periphery. This historic periphery, one might say, is a subject not object of history in Semenov's view: during various crucial transitions, i.e., the asiatic slave and the slave/feudal, it played a crucial role in the attainment of the next historic step.

Though Semenov does not really spell this out, the same would now seem to be true for the capitalism/socialism transition. Gellner continues:

> The fact that historic leadership is displaced, that the torch is passed sideways, that its new erstwhile retarded recipients are also essential for further progress, dispenses both them and their predecessors from that irksome theoretical obligation to pass through all stages . . . . If the participation of the periphery was essential for the attainment of the next stage, then parts of the old center not affected by the agency of the newly active periphery are ipso facto debarred from being the originators of the next round, the next set up. Some transitions positively require a radical change of world leadership, it would appear.[19]

This is an extremely optimistic view as regards all specificity. It somewhat recalls the Hegelian conception of "historical nations,"[20] but seems to be much more just and gives more opportunities for the more and more numerous peripheries. Considering the formation of a number of greatly differentiated economic, political and cultural centers, Gellner's opinion appears to be even more interesting. Sometimes all the three spheres join together, at other times a certain center of a given area dominates only politically, and not economically, etc.

Historical periphery/center transitions were connected with transitions from one formation into another. "But the feudal/capitalist transition is exceptional: it is so to speak, a center-preserving transition, and this is quite idiosyncratic. . . . The last transition, which is yet to come, will also be unique, in that it will be neither center preserving nor center-displacing, but center-dissolving."[21]

We must examine this problem in more detail. Gellner writes that:

> The diversity and plurality of nations and cultures is not a contingent accident, a by-product of the isolation and hence of the linguistic and other idiosyncracies of primitive communities, but an essential fact, without which the whole process of world history could not work. This seems to follow, if from nothing else, from the crucial role played by peripheral nations on those three supremely important occasions in world history. If a backward and distinct periphery is essential for some steps forward, there could be no progress in a world with one nation only.[22]

I think that this is a particularly powerful theoretical and historical defense of specificity based on the theory of formations and the resulting center-periphery conception. It both reflects the cruelty of the actual course of history and opens up a broad path to be followed by all contemporary nations. At the same time, it does not hide actual facts, or seek refuge from the most complicated problems of hegemony. It wishes to change them into "leadership" which is not identified with hegemony, thus introducing an additional note of optimism. Summing up this theoretical line of thought, Gellner writes:

> A western anthropologist who dared speak, without irony, of the 'mission civilisatrice' or of the 'white man's burden', would be more or less ostracized by his professional community. Semenov has no hesitation in using the notion of differences of level of development and referring to the obligations of global leadership which this carries.[23]

The theory of formations proves to be the most extensive premise of the conception of the meaning of history and, as a result, also of the new universalism. The defense of specificity is correct, just and noble, but it will always remain a defense of a certain element of entity. In order to understand specificity we must "raise ourselves" theoretically to the meta-level of entity, and then to all levels of historical development. To understand the meaning of a certain element one must also refer it to other elements, and subsequently to the ultimate explanation within a historical totality.

The theory of formations provides us with much more than the essentially Platonic instrument of consecutive epochs, their inner rules co-determined by internal contradictions. We are able to understand the formation of consecutive entities and horizons of meaning, and their mutual relations. The theory of formations, as interpreted by Semenov and Gellner, gives an explanation of the particularly important problem of endogenous cultures, especially when compared to the center/periphery issue. This also broadens the conception of "strategic comparatism," since it supplies us with the most extensive historical and contemporary basis for comparisons and even for evaluations.

In reality, however, it is extremely difficult to apply the theory of formations to scientific projects. One simply has to use it as a whole, and not selectively. It becomes a truly universal hermeneutics when interpreted in a comprehensive way. It not only explains facts and laws, but also makes it possible to make predictions. Although it often seems that this ability to predict fails, the fault lies with those who do not see the problem clearly enough, or try to exploit Marxism as a tool of empty ideological phraseology.

The factor which complicates the opportunities for realistic predictions is the growth of the role of consciousness. Although this growth is taken into consideration by the law of development of socialist formation, praxis proves that it enlarges the scale of difficulties. Nevertheless, hope accompanies those difficulties since more and more depends upon the intellect and will of all people. This means that we are truly passing from a kingdom of necessity to--let us modify Engels--an all-human republic of reason and of meaning.

VALUATIONS OF CULTURES AND THEIR DIFFERENCES

I am concerned here with the equality of cultures based on their specificity and with the conclusion that differences should not be evaluated. This opinion expresses a noble attitude but it remains objectionable, not only for evident reasons, but because of more profound axiological considerations. I would reinforce the view which I intend to question by citing Malraux's opinion that the Pieta by Michelangelo is by no means artistically more valuable than a ritual mask from Africa. This example can be defended, but its message cannot. Obviously, within a single culture there are distinct valuations and a hierarchical order. Actually, every culture influences the others as a rule from a position of superiority. This is a universal fact and forms the condition of a meaningful evaluation which has to be related to a scale of values. Rejection of these facts stems from a fear that the differences in the scale of values would be transformed into an instrument of domination and exploitation as was the case many times over, and even into a tool of extermination, e.g., in genocidal ideologies.

There are several fields, I believe, for the evaluation of cultures and cultural phenomena.

1. Epistemological--the cognitive values of various cultures are strikingly unequal. This concerns not only the obvious superiority of the

West in exact sciences, but also the supremacy of Buddhism in the field of the intuitive cognition of subjectivity (*Satori*) or the ancient Chinese knowledge of certain physical properties of the body and its practical application (acupuncture, *kung fu*);

2. Aesthetical--in the past and at present we encounter valuations of works of art from the point of view of their cognitive values, force of expression, novelty, etc., and even from the point of view of their moral message. This is obvious within cultures, but the situation becomes different when dealing with the sphere between cultures. Would we be questioned if we introduced the concept of "meta-culture"?

3. Ethical--true, comparative intercultural valuation is, essentially, a failure. This is where certain complexities of the problem are to be found. Given the unequal value of cultures let us set aside for a later examination the question how to maintain the equality of the rights of their collective subjects, how to build unity out of this actual and axiological diversity, how to emphasize the meaning of the West, e.g., in its Latin American reception, how to search for universality on the aforementioned three planes and how to intensify it, while retaining full specificity?

TOWARDS AN AUTHENTIC AND CREATIVE UNIVERSALISM

This discussion is focused on the problem of relationship between specificity and universality. I should like to develop the conception of an authentic and creative universalism.

If we accept the Aristotelian understanding of truth as a reflection of reality, we must regard it in the social sciences, and especially while studying the problem of universalism, as an element of conformism or even conservatism. If we require a sociological-philosophical thesis to retain its veracity (I will not discuss the great difficulties in ascertaining such a thesis which, however, ought to be feasible by adopting the principle of verifiability), then we can demand logically only that theory should follow facts or comply with facts of the same kind. In social life this would mean a denial of opportunity for theoretical prediction and scientific projection with respect to the vast, and perhaps the most important, areas of qualitatively new phenomena. Marxism in particular, while adopting verifiability as a starting point and a foundation, must add the principle of creativity.[24]

Hence, a true universalism should have a number of characteristics.

1. In its ontology and epistemology it should express the whole complexity of the diversified world and of its unifying forces, its differences, specificity, universalities, various universal elements, levels, tendencies and needs. It must provide the ability to recognize and understand them;

2. In its axiology it should contain all diverse values wherever and whenever they might have been products; moreover, it should perceive all hierarchies of value as well as their worth and openness;[25]

3. In its philosophy of history it should present the world in historical dynamics, in authentic dialectical development, and, while co-creating the meaning of history by deriving it from the past and the present, impart this meaning in a developed form to the future.[26]

4. It should not relinquish valuation, but free this from attempts at domination and violence. The recognition of the superiority of some element of a given culture, e.g., with regard to cognitive abilities, practical, economic efficacy, and even the extent of aesthetic acceptance, in relation to the comparable element of other cultures simply means rendering justice to definite accomplishments. Day to day praxis actually achieves this, but we ought to recognize such superiority more openly and honestly without attempting to subordinate some cultures to others. After all, even messianism does not have to be connected with chauvinism.

5. Authentic and creative universalism should become a correlate of the transformation of a mankind-in-itself into a mankind-for-itself. This means the departure of the old and the birth of a new humanity, which should be aware of itself and united. It will be omnipotent as a result of dialectically embracing all values, and it will be above antagonistic contradictions which it will transform into creative tensions.

6. The essence of this new mankind will be in the mutually enriching dialectics of the individuality of individuals, of groups, of nations and of an all-embracing community. I predict flourishing of differences when such a unity is achieved.

7. Universalism as a correlate of such humanity must rise above, rather than oppose, the present differences and even their theoretical, philosophical totalizations. This will become possible when such totalizations are freed from serving antagonistic classes, and in this sense universalism must be a meta-philosophy. Moreover, it is necessary to rise above the manifestations and concepts of a struggle, above the victory of one culture over others, and to strive for the supplementation of one culture by another.

8. Just as socialism has its premises in capitalism, so universalism as a theory has its premises in contemporary universalities, e.g., in science, logic, sport, technology and predominantly in the similarity and frequently even identity of the tragedies of human existence, as well as in cultures and communities.

9. In its axiology and normative message, universalism has to advocate the solidarity of all peoples and nations rooted in our common human fate and in our joint struggle against the ever more numerous and greater threats, including the nuclear suicide of mankind.

10. Universalism will remain authentic and creative as long as it is realistic and optimistic, although it is also fully conscious of the drama of the inevitable "exclusion" of certain values at the expense of others in the numerous situations which demand that such a selection be made. This optimism is justified by the historical premises of universalism and by the goodness and rationality of human nature which reveal themselves

in full under appropriate social conditions. Authentic universalism is turned towards the future, although it remains rooted in past premises and revolutionizes contemporaneity.

Each of the points presented above justifies my polemical remarks addressed to the contention made by Habermas at the Berlin Conference of the United Nations University, that the existence of various universalisms is a paradox. Actually, there have been many universalisms, poorly or better substantiated, even contradictory in many points. This is not a paradox; I would even say that every specificity-for-itself strives to become a universalism. The problem lies therefore not in the hierarchical arrangement of universalisms in history, but in the attempt to "neutralize" them in a new and truly global universalism. The previous universalisms also contained some truths though absolutized into totalities with a tendency towards dominating and destroying others.

Scholars, and above all philosophers, should become the collective subject of the new universalism. Their responsibility is undeniably the greatest, whereas their situation remains very difficult because of ideological divisions which express objective contradictions between classes, and at times also between cultures. If philosophers manage to reach an agreement without relinquishing their distinct views, the greatest obstacle will be removed.

The decision-making center remains in the sphere of politics, but scholars are co-responsible. There is no world government now, and none in the foreseeable future. Already, however, scholars govern through a ministry of souls among the intellectuals of the world. To those who are able to learn history in the perception of life (*historia est magistra vitae*), it teaches that mankind not only remembers, but also knows scholars better than politicians and rulers. Even the greatest politicians drop away, while philosophers from centuries and millennia past are not only retained in the memory of mankind, but continue to function today.

Uniwersytet Warszawski
Warsaw, Poland

NOTES

1. Those conceptions of mine were presented in *Culture and Thought*, ed. Anisuzzaman and Anouar Abel-Malek (London: The UNU and Macmillan, 1983), Cf. also J. Kuczynski, "The Meaning/Sense of the Word--the Meaning/Sense of Being," *Dialectics and Humanism*, 7 (19-80), pp. 167-181.

2. The Soviet five-volume *Filofskaya Entsiklopediya* gives a slightly different definition: "Essence describes the actual contents of the object, expressed in the unity of all various and contradictory forms of its existence." This is followed (vol. V, p. 186) by a definition of phenomenon: "A phenomenon is a certain 'revelation' of the object, its em-

pirically ascertained external form of existence. In thought, categories of essence and phenomenon express the need to transit, and the transition itself from the variety of the existing (literally--ready) forms of the existence of the object to its inner contents and unity in a concept. The task of science is to penetrate the essence of the object."

3. The United Nations University, Sub-Project: Endogenous Intellectual Creativity (EIC), *IV Regional Symposium: Crisis, Culture and Innovation in the Western World (Europe and North America)*, Fondazione Feltinelli, Guideline, p. 8.

4. *Wielka Encyklopedia Powszechna PWN* (The Polish Scientific Publishers Great Encyclopedia), vol. II, p. 818. Neither in the Soviet nor in the English language philosophical encyclopedias does "universalism" appear separately. The situation in philosophical dictionaries is equally unsatisfactory. For example, R. Eisler writes in *Wörterbuch der Philosophischen Begriffe* (Berlin: Mittler, 1930): "Universalismus (ethischer) ist der ethische standpunkt, nach welchem als das Objekt des sittlichen Handelns nicht Individuen als solche, sonderb eine Gemeinschaft (Volk. Staat. Menschheit) erscheint (sozialer, politscher, nationaler, humaner.") In A. Lalande, *Vocabulaire technique et critique de la philosophie*, we find: "Universalism--Doctrine ou croyance suivant la quelle tous les hommes sont destinies finalement au salut. Universalité--Allgemeinheit, Allheit, Gesamtheit, Universality--charactere de ce qui est universel. Universel--Qui s'étend a l'Univers entier."

In a review of historiosophic attitudes concerning primarily the problem of the political unity and diversity of the world (*Geschichtsphilosophie und Welburgerkrieg* [Heidelberg: Winter Verlag, 1959], pp. 306-307), Hanno Kesting wonders: "Ist die Zweiheit Ubergang zur Einheit oder zur Vielheit?", and contrasts universalism as an ideology of unity, with pluralism, the ideology of plurality.

The Integration of Political Communities, ed. by P.E. Jacob and H.V. Toscano (New York: 1964), p. 203: "Particularism, the opposite of universalism, applies only to certain groups and areas. Freedom from want for every human being anywhere in the world is clearly a universalistic goal. Many religious imperatives are universalistic. Incidentally, the history of religions has shown that the particularistic religions were inevitably replaced by the universalistic ones."

5. A. Abdel-Malek, *The Concept of Specificity: Positions* (The United Nations University, 1979), pp. 3-5; this paper was presented in Tokyo in 1977 and at the Ninth World Congress of Sociology, Uppsala, 1978.

6. I do not mention the stratum of reproduction and sexual life, because as an absolutely and globally universal nature it can be inserted into the first stratum.

7. K. Marx, Preface to "A Contribution to the Critique of Political Economy," in K. Marx and F. Engels, *Selected Works* (Moscow, 1973), I, 504.

8. Despite the fact that Marx and Lenin made the assertion of the

capitalistic unification of the world into one of the main trends of their theories and included predictions and postulates for the creation of an international solidarity, to be followed by the unity of mankind, the awareness of this situation of mankind appeared in non-Marxist historiography much later. G. Barraclough *Main Trends in History* (New York: Holmes & Meier, 1979), p. 153 writes: "As early as 1936, the great Dutch historian, Huizinga, pointed out that 'our civilization is the first to have for its past the past of the world, our history is the first to be world-history; subsequent events have only confirmed his verdict. As since 1945 the world has moved into a new phase of global integration, the demand for a history which reflects this new situation has become more insistent."

9. Yu. I. Semenov, "The Category 'Social Organism' and Its Significance for Historical Scholarship," *Voprosy Istorii* (1966).

10. Despite a frequent identification of those two concepts in English and French, one also encounters their contraposition, e.g., Johan Huizinga, "Patriotism and Nationalism in European History," in *Men and Ideas* (New York: Meridian Books, 1959), p. 95: "In the ominous present there are two forces that, for good or evil, are straining and convulsing the world organism like a fever. One of them is patriotism, the will to maintain and defend what is one's own and cherished, a will that, at present, is everywhere and every day being put to the most severe test, in violent combat and patient service. The other is nationalism, the powerful drive to dominate, the urge to have one's own nation, one's own state assert itself above, over, and at the cost of others. Patriotism, says the fool within us all, is our virtue, and nationalism is the vice of others." Cf. J. Kuczynski, *Indywidualnosc i Ojczyzna. Filozoficzna problematyka kwestii narodowe* (Individuality and Fatherland). The Philosophical Problems of the National Question (Warszawa, 1972). The contraposition between those two concepts is emphasized particularly strongly in the copious Soviet works on the subject: Cf. a summary of the problem in: P.N. Fyedoseyev, *Komumunizm i Filosofia* (Moskva, 1971).

11. "Oikoumene" appeared already in the Hellenistic period, and the problem itself, according to certain scholars, in the Bible. Cf. G. Viatte, *Oecuménisme* (Paris: Casterman, 1964), p. 15: "Quand nous ouvrons la Bible, nous sommes immédiatement placés dans des perspectives universalistes." Let us draw attention also to the fact that Viatte interprets universalism as a result of monotheism and stresses that: "Le messianisme chrétien est foncierement universalité. Il y a là, à premiere vue, un contrast saissant avec l'exclusivism du judaisme" (p. 28). The ecumenical movement as an answer to the disintegration of Christianity appeared during the period of capitalism. Cf. G. Tavard, *Petite histoire du movement oecumenique* (Paris: Fleurus, 1960).

12. *Soviet and Western Anthropology*, ed. by Ernest Gellner (New York: Columbia Univ. Press, 1980), p. 65.

13. *Ibid.*, p. 69.

14. T. Lessing, *Geschichte als Sinngebung des Sinnlosen* (2nd edi-

tion; Hamburg: Rutten & Loening, 1962).

15. E. Husserl, *Cartesianische Meditationen*, marginal note 182. The variety of other definitions of meaning, e.g., empirical and objective, does not change the basically idealistic attitude, i.e., the endowing of meaning, which was expressed so vividly in *Idea*, I.

16. G. Barraclough, 170.

17. *Ibid.*, p. 164.

18. *Soviet and Western Anthropology*, p. 50.

19. *Ibid.*, pp. 68-69.

20. More precisely--"welthistorischen Volk." The paradox of Hegel's historiography is the statement that "one cannot learn anything (from such nations) as regards the political system principle, the principle of our times" (*Philosophy of History*).

21. *Soviet and Western Anthropology*, pp. 77-78.

22. *Ibid.*, pp. 78-79.

23. *Ibid.*, p. 82.

24. I wrote about this extensively in my polemics with the Hegelian vision of philosophy in *Homo Creator* (Warszawa, 1976, 2nd edition 1978).

25. K. Mushakoji, writing about the importance of the topic of the Kyoto symposium for the United Nations University Programme said that: "A new international order cannot be only globalist, i.e., it should not be based on a uniformizing cosmopolitism. It should rather encourage the participation of different cultural traditions in the common task of building a global order based on endogenous intellectual creativity." *Intellectual Creativity in Endogenous Culture*, Papers of the Asian Regional Symposium, Kyoto, November 1978, ed. by Anouar Abel-Malek, co-edited by Amar Nath Pandeya (Tokyo: The United Nations University, 1981), p. 22.

26. Cf. the earlier use of the theory of formations as a foundation for the meaning of history.

CHAPTER XV

THE UNIVERSE OF HUMAN THOUGHT

KRZYSZTOF TUREK*

> *Twenty three centuries ago there lived a man who demanded only an immovable fulcrum to move the earth from its orbit, his name was Archimedes.*

There are three characteristic attitudes in relation to the forces of nature. In the first one tries to protect oneself from natural forces or to live with them in a kind of symbiosis, in the second one attempts to escape from them, and in the third one tries to become master of the power accumulated in nature. The first attitude is easily recognizable in primitive religions in which nature itself and its forces are deified. An attempt to protect oneself against these deified forces takes the form of religious rites and sacrifices. As a place of escape Plato pointed to the eternal world of ideas which could be attained by contemplation. According to Plato the power of nature and the world of things as its effect is a kind of illusion unworthy of consideration by a mind which has discovered what is eternal.

Completely opposite the contemplative mode of life ('vita contemplativa') recommended by Plato is the active life. This has made possible the creation of our scientific-technological civilization in which the forces of nature are under human control. Men born as products of forces stored in the natural environment are able to use these forces to liberate themselves from the Earthly environment to which they were supposed to be bound forever, to control these forces and to use them to create an artificial environment.

By tearing themselves from Earth and reaching the Moon, they have proven that they can overcome the limitations of their Earthly condition. The feelings of exultation, pride and power when man first put his foot on the Moon was high reward for all those past or present who chose the active life of developing science and technology. Step by step this process has unveiled the universal laws and forces. Their power to use these even for a brief period of time in shaping the face of Earth has enabled them to liberate themselves from Earth.

Hannah Arendt concludes in her analysis of the active life as the condition for science and technology that by discovering universal laws and forces and using them to develop space technology man proved to be a child of the universe rather than of the Earth. Having made an Archimedean point of the universe with its universal laws and forces, we are able now to look upon Earth from the point of view of the universe. This is true not only while standing on Moon, but even while sitting in a chair and solving such theoretical problem as the proportion of the Earth's mass which should be changed into energy according to Einstein's law (E = mc^2) for launching Earth from the Solar system. Hence, in the world of universal laws and forces we have found an Archimedean point which makes lifting the Earth at least theoretically possible.

Two inventions abolished the picture of the world created by people contemplating a heaven of eternal ideas and wondering about things just as they are. The telescope revealed the immensity of the universe, the microscope exhibited the minute parts of the Earth's bodies. The medieval hierarchic and spatially conceived world in which everybody had his or her proper place, both on Earth in the hierarchical medieval society and after death in a sphere of heaven or hell or purgatory, was demolished as the two abysses, infinity and nothingness, opened before our astonished eyes and minds. The world view sanctified by tradition and Church as a main pillar of medieval culture was broken, and with it the medieval world also began to break apart. Exiled from the familiar harmonious world of Dante with earth at its physical center and with its spiritual dimension ordered by a conceptual theological framework, people had to create a new culture.

Passage to this culture in the Baroque age was painful. Characteristically, it was an age of fear and alienation because people could not find themselves in the new world. This fear was best expressed by Pascal, who, being conscious of being tossed between two infinite abysses, felt like a reed swaying in wind:

> We are floating in a medium of vast extent, always drifting uncertainly, blown to and fro; whenever we think we have a fixed point to which we can make fast, it shifts and leaves us behind; if we follow it, it eludes our grasp, slips away, and flees eternally before us. Nothing stands still for us. This is our natural state and yet the state most contrary to our inclinations. We burn with desire to find a firm footing, an ultimate, lasting base on which to build a tower rising up to infinity, but our whole foundation cracks and the earth opens up into the depth of the abyss.

At the same time, the discovery of the double infinity inspired in Descartes a quite opposite way of searching for what Pascal considered impossible, namely, "a firm footing, an ultimate, lasting base on which to build a tower rising up to infinity." His certain and secure foundation on which to build was the "thinking self" and its corresponding method of doubt. Through doubting all that could be doubted, and treating all provisionally as false, he wanted to prepare for the erection of a tower in the human mind, convinced that certain knowledge is possible only where the mind is treated according to its own forms and formulas. The Cartesian "thinking self," together with his rule: "de omnibus dubitandum est," was the Archimedean fulcrum for shaping modern thought. Hannah Arendt writes: "In modern philosophy and thought, doubt occupies much the same central position as that occupied for all the centuries before by the Greek *thaumazein* or the wonder at everything that is as it is."

Einstein's particular and general theory of relativity is considered one of the most magnificent steps in the ascent of the human mind because he pointed to a new Archimedean point outside the universe. From this point it became possible to trace the history of the universe and to create for it different theoretical models, thus bringing human thought to the point which till then had been reserved for God. Once in possession of this new Archimedean point cosmologists learned to reproduce with amazing ease the history of the universe from its early beginning to an unimaginably distant future. Astronomers, armed with powerful telelescopes and radiotelescopes have found traces of this history in the universe and a sophisticated space telescope soon will be able to look 14 billion light years into space, seven time deeper then is now possible--so distant that even the limits of Einstein's universe may be observed.

In exploring the abyss of space after the discovery of the telescope astronomers expected to find there other celestial bodies like the Sun or Earth, but no one had an idea of what was to be found by the microscope in the abyss of nothingness. What was found in the deepest levels of the microworld would probably deepen Pascal's fear. The world of atoms and elementary particles revealed by physicists since the beginning of the twentieth century has proven to be, in its most minute objects, incomparably smaller then the smallest objects seen by the best optical microscopes. Quantum mechanics has proven to be the Archimedean standpoint for controlling this amazing world. Moreover, this theory has made it possible to control light in new and extraordinary ways. Chip micro-processors and lasers are among the most spectacular effects of the new micro-technology.

Both Archimedean points--the theory of relativity and quantum mechanics--endowed man with a basis for investigating the universe and becoming masters of that small part called Earth. Nevertheless the process of life itself which imposes upon mankind the most serious constraints remained beyond its control. The turning point in the process of uncovering the mystery of life was the discovery of the structure of DNA by Francis Crick and James Watson in 1953. Just as a perforated tape instructs a computer aided machine regarding what shape it is to cut from a piece of metal, long-chained particles of deoxyrybonucleid acid control the activity of cells in living organisms. The information on how to process the material is contained on the tape in the spacial configuration of holes. In DNA information on the sort of biological molecules (proteins) what is to be fabricated is coded in the sequence of molecular bases. Slowly scientists learned how to cut the genetic tape into pieces, introduce new segments, and then join them together again, programming in this way new living organisms. In this man discovered a new Archimedean point and became master of life, a position which for ages also had been reserved for God--men became 'children of Frankenstein'.

The invention of the computer and then the home computer liberated the human mind from the shackles imposed upon it by the human brain's capacity for calculating and processing information. In a kind of symbiosis with this unique artifice, men rapidly enlarged their intellectual power, developing a new branch of science, artificial intelligence, in order to create objects having some features of human intelligence. To profit as much as possible from this symbiosis man developed different artificial languages and other means for dialogue with their intelligent creature. They also tried to teach it their own language, learning themselves in the process much about this basic tool of interhuman communication. Moreover some new creatures can recognize patterns, trace moving objects or produce the sounds of speech. Creating intelligent objects men found another Archimedean fulcrum which made them masters of their own intelligence and were able to release intelligence outside the brain. Once more men transcended the limitations imposed on them by the life process which created their brains.

Tracing the ascent of human being we have found Archimedean standing points outside Earth, outside the universe, outside life and outside intelligence. Ascending to these points men discovered--and are still discovering--a great deal about earth, about the universe, about life and about intelligence. This ascent of man has taken place in the culture dominated by the active mode of life (*vita activa*). The moving spirit of this attitude is the presupposition that men are able to understand only what they themselves have made especially in the process called experimentation. Its presupposition is that every truth is revealed in an experiment and is confirmed by technology.

THE ARCHIMEDEAN POINT FOR SHAPING THE WORLD OF CULTURE

Western culture has also another attitude founded on the presupposition that the deepest layers of truth are revealed in the contemplative life (*vita contemplativa*). According to Plato, who first pointed to this as the supreme mode of life, contemplation lifts the human mind to the farthest expanse of the world of eternal ideas and eternities. For ages contemplative life was accepted as the supreme mode of life in Christian culture. At the bottom of the cover of J. Mark's book, entitled *Science and the Making of the Modern World*, there sits a woman--probably the ancient goddess of wisdom, Sofia--pointing with her left hand toward heaven to which her face is lifted. She is surrounded by wise men, some of whom contemplate models of a geocentric universe and of the harmony of the spheres. The minds of the others are on the world of eternal truth as can be deduced from the upward turn of their faces. Just behind this world of contemplation, in the upper part of the picture, is the world of the *vita activa*. In this world the space shuttle is launched, but the society immersed in contemplation does not see it.

The contemplative mode of life dominated the intellectual culture of the Middle Ages. Of course, people lived actively, waging wars, taking part in crusades, travelling European routes of pilgrimage and building cathedrals, but all these activities were treated as handmaids of contemplation. In contrast, the hierarchy of values in contemporary Western culture places the active mode of life in the highest position which, several centuries ago had been occupied by the *vita contemplativa*. A mode of life different from that characteristic of our culture is usually given lower value. Because the mode of life of human beings is one of the most important dimensions of a culture, we evaluate cultures or sub-cultures in terms of their mode of life--especially in nonpluralistic societies, "other" means worse.

Let us now make the following mental experiment: let us place before our minds different modes of life--different philosophical and theological systems--just as the the contemplative and active life were put before our eyes in the above example. Moreover, let us try to suspend judgment on the value of these different constituents of the various cultures. In doing so one finds oneself at a new Archimedean standpoint, which might be called the universe of human thought. If from this point we inspect our own cultures we find that each of them puts different limitations upon our minds. Moreover, we discover that prior to reaching this point we really were not able to shape our mind, which is shaped by the culture in which we live. Prior to the moment of transcending Earth and finding themselves to be children of the universe rather than of earth, men were not capable of using universal forces effectively to change their earthly condition. Similarly, without tracing the universe of human thought men were not consciously able to shape their minds, their modes of life and consequently their cultures and subcultures.

With the transformation which takes place in preferring the active to the contemplative mode of life, reality ceased to be accepted "as it is"; it became for Western consciousness only a stage of further development under the human control. Firmly grounded upon this Archimedean standpoint men became increasingly skilled in using natural laws and forces for their own needs. Logically the experience of the human power to control matter awakens a desire to find the Archimedean point for controlling history. This inspiration came from Darwin, whose idea of natural development through natural selection or the survival of the fittest in the struggle for life was projected in terms of Marx's concept of society as the product of a gigantic historical movement proceeding according to the law of class-struggle. Darwin's and Marx's theories were used as the basis of two great totalitarian movements, Nazism and communism, both shook the world by using terror to accelerate the movement of history, eliminating unfit races in the case of Nazis and dying classes in the case of communism. These totalitarian movements turned away from the Cartesian standpoint, and sentenced the thinking and doubting self to death. The new immovable fulcrum was ideology which, supported by terror, imprisons the human mind in a rigid framework of concepts supposed to be beyond any doubt. Thus, a culture based upon ideology must be quite opposite in character to modern Western culture built upon standpoints such as that of Descartes. A totalitarian culture looks for self affirmation, whereas, as noted by Leszek Kolakowski, the unique feature of European culture is its ability to criticize itself, to doubt its own values.

Whereas the spokesmen of ideologies claim to have the total knowledge of the laws which rule history, scientists working on a Cartesian basis and accumulating more and more knowledge about the world and about the methods of developing science have become increasingly convinced that it is impossible to have any total knowledge of reality. In addition to criticism, this attitude toward the world is guided by two other values: pluralism and tentativeness. Scientists recognize both the tremendous effort required to estimate even a minute piece of the truth of the world, and the tentative character of the majority of scientific hypotheses which compete mutually in the process of formulating more firmly established theories. Thus, it becomes manifest that the Cartesian standpoint has as its internal structure three values: criticism, pluralism and tentativeness.

Reaching the Archimedean point in the universe of human thought men become masters of their minds and really free. From the point of view of the universe of thought, every philosophical and theological system is only a mental experiment in which we discover a part of truth about ourselves and about the world. The works of great European philosophers should be treated in this way. Every mode of life, every culture or subculture has its unique value as an experiment which reveals a part of the truth about man. But from this point of wiew it appears also that every culture places upon the minds of its participants strong limitations, among which the stereotyping and ideologization of thought are the most important. To this is added the danger of imprisoning the mind in the history of a given culture.

TO THE CASE OF POLAND

The Polish consciousness is deeply historical. Poland had a glorious period of history in the 15th and 16th centuries under the rule of the Jagiellonian dynasty. At this time Polish culture, broadly understood and in its political form, was so attractive that it was possible to create in its framework a union of nations. Polish, Lithuanian and other smaller nations joined the union freely and without force. It was a golden period during which the gentry--12% of the whole population--created the democratic Gentry Republic with elected kings, whose power was restricted by special rules and by a parliament. In this period the concepts of freedom, democracy and tolerance developed in Poland. It would be interesting to compare the concept of freedom in Poland during these centuries and that in the USA at the present time for it was not by chance that two members of the Polish tradition of freedom, Kosciuszko and Pulawski, are heroes both of the USA and the Polish nation.

At the end of 18th century Poland was divided between three states--Austria, Prussia and Russia. Though Poland disappeared from the maps of Europe for about 125 years, surprisingly it is just during that period of the partition that Polish culture flourished with works which even now stimulate creative Polish artists and Polish thinkers. Thanks to this strong cultural tradition Poles were able to preserve their identity during the occupation.

Beside the castle of Polish kings on the Wawel Hill in Krakow stands the old Cathedral. In its center is the grave of St. Stanislaw, the martyr from the early days of Polish state, who lives in the memory of Poles as the first fighter for human rights against tyranny by the monarch. In this Cathedral where kings were crowned and buried are found the graves of great Polish poets. Stanislaw Wyspianski located the plot of his play "Acropolis" in this national shrine. One night he awakened some of the stone statues inside the Cathedral to play the mysteries of the drama which took place in the minds of Poles during the captivity. Wyspianski clearly recognized the danger of imprisoning the Polish historical and cultural consciousness in the past. In a very impressive scene trumpets sound and bells ring when Christ as Apollo comes to the Wawel in streams of lights to destroy this great Polish sanctuary with its graves of the kings in order to free the Polish mind from the shackles of its own culture and turn it toward the future.

CONCLUSION

Having found an Archimedean point beyond the native cultures, we can launch our mind to a point in the universe of human thought from which we can see all cultures as more or less minute planets at which different modes of life and different hierarchies of values are cultivated. The night after July 20, 1969, when Neil A. Amstrong and Edwin Aldrin left the first footprints on the moon, I looked for a long time at the moon trying to guess the thoughts and feelings of astronauts at seeing their homeland, Earth, as a beautiful blue but fragile bubble in the black and barren abyss of space. Was this a feeling of pride, of power, of freedom or of Pascalian fear? Whatever they felt, I was sure that they could never be the same persons they had been upon leaving Earth. They would be always alone with their unearthly experience, forever alienated from their Earthly household.

Is not the mind which reaches the Archimedean point in the universe of human thought and looks back at his own culture in a position similar to those who have seen the Earth from the Moon? Such a person, at least at the present stage, cannot live for long in un-earthly conditions, but must return. Similarly one is unable to drift for long outside his own culture, but must return to it, so as not to become a homeless wanderer in the universe. Nonetheless, he may have found there the freedom and stimulus to reshape creatively his own culture as an alternative to remaining alone with his extracultural experience. On the other hand, he could try to escape from his newly discovered freedom, to forget where he was, to lose the real Archimedean point, and return to the culture of his homeland as the prophet of a new ideology.

Our way to the universe of human thought passed through Archimedean points. Reaching them men were able to develop science into a power capable of harnessing the forces of nature in the service of people. We traced this route to the utmost limits of the universe, that is, as far as is possible without going beyond the limits of philosophy. We found the Cartesian standpoint with its three values of criticism, pluralism and tentativeness to have fundamental meaning.

But our way is by no means unique. Certainly there are other values which are guiding points to the furthest expanse of the universe of human thought. Discovering them is the most exciting adventure on the long, perhaps endless, way to the unification of different cultures without losing their real values.

AGH and
The Pontifical Academy of Theology
　　Krakow, Poland

*See Discussion VI.

CHAPTER XVI

TWO DIMENSIONS OF CULTURE

KRZYSZTOF TUREK*

ENCOUNTERS

There are many kinds of human encounters. Some are intimate with persons in a family, others are with friends, acquaintances, nature and culture; there are encounters with God. An encounter differs substantially from knowledge of things. What is encountered acts on our consciousness much more intensively than do mere objects of knowledge. The encountered reality seems to speak in us. We met a friend and are in sympathy with his problems for a while. A mother and her children share the mystery of motherhood in the encounter with husband and father. We play with a child whose unusual world suddenly opens to us, just as a patient's pain makes itself felt in a physician. Mountains tell us about eternity with their firm and invariable persistence, while a cemetery's mystery of death asks us about the sense of life. We go into ecstasy over a work of art; in the silence of a temple we listen to the voice of God.

In the encounter my self disappears and makes room for what is encountered. The reality encountered does not appear as a thing or an arrangement of things, for the encounter is a prereflective contact of a man with reality, a primary experience of self, the world, other men and God. The Cartesian thinking and doubting self is not yet present, nor are the concepts prepared for grasping what is given in the encounter.

Speech originates in an encounter. At the beginning a man opens in silence to his own self, nature, another person, the world of culture . . . God. Silence here means withdrawal to a space not ordered by preconceptions, concepts and judgments. In this space we must await the encounter, but are never sure it will really appear, because the encounter is a fully spontaneous event. We can prepare ourselves for it, we can accept or reject it, but we cannot control it.

One night the Pharisee Nicodemus came to Christ and heard words which astonished him. Christ said to him: "Verily, verily, I say unto thee, except a man be born of water and the Spirit, he cannot enter into the kingdom of God. That which is born of the flesh is flesh, and that which is born of the Spirit is spirit" (John 3: 1-6). Nicodemus's astonishment was founded on his experience: a man is born from the mother's flesh; how can the man be born again when he is old? Our scribe notices in himself only natural man; Christ pointed to the existence of another man under the cover of flesh whom Paul of Tarsus called the inward or spiritual man (see Romans 7, 22-23; Corinthians 2, 14-15).

In contemporary philosophical terminology we would speak of two selves. The natural self is closed in oneself and egoistic, controlled from one side by the requirements of flesh and from the other side by the requirements of reason. Consequently, we have two extreme philosophical expressions of the natural self: Freudianism and rationalism. Where Freud in his philosophy exposed the role of flesh, especially of sexual urges, rationalists emphasized the role of reason. For the source of human speech Freud pointed to the subconscious. Fascination with dreams and passions as the speech originating from this source gave strong impulse to the development of a new mode of expression, namely, surrealism. Rationalists have questioned the importance of spontaneous streams of speech, especially of their content which does not fit the categories of reason.

We must look for a spiritual self beyond the natural one, and thence for a personal self beyond the two extremes. This personal self is the proper subject of encounter, both with one's own self and also with other personal selves.

Most phenomenological analyses of encounter are devoted to meetings of persons; some philosophers would even reserve the philosophical term 'encounter' for that phenomena. I am not in position to summarize here the works devoted to analyses of the encounter with other persons. For our purposes it is important to point to encounter as the source of speech, of which the encounters by great poets as reflected in their poems are the most spectacular examples.

During the period of partition of Poland in the XIXth century, the most creative Poles lived in France. The youngest of them, the poet Cyprian Norwid, outlived the others, some of whom he met just before their death. He recorded the memory of these meetings in his essay "The Black Flowers," which describes, among others, his meeting with Chopin in his flat in Paris when Chopin had a deadly disease.

> So I entered the room adjoining the drawing-room, where Chopin had his bedroom, feeling very grateful that he wished to see me, and found him dressed but half-reclining on the bed, his legs swollen, which I could discern at once because of the shoes and stockings he was wearing. The artist's sister sat at his side, strangely like him in profile. . . . He, in the shadow of a deep bed with curtains, propped up on a pillow, and wrapped in a shawl, looked very beautiful, as always, displaying in the most mundane movements something of perfection, something of a monumental outline . . . something which either Athenian aristocracy could have adopted as a cult during the most beautiful epoch of Greek civilization--or that which an artist of dramatic genius portrays, for instance, in classical French tragedies, which because of their theoretical polish in no way resemble the world of antiquity, but can nevertheless, thanks to the genius of a Rachel, become naturalized, credible and truly classical. . . . Chopin possessed such naturally idealized perfection of gestures, wherever and however I saw him . . .

So--his voice interrupted by coughing and choking--
he began to complain that I had neglected him so long; then
he began to banter and tried to accuse me in a most innocent
manner of mystical tendencies, which, since it gave him
pleasure, I allowed; then I conversed with his sister--there
were intervals of coughing; then came the moment to leave
him in peace so I began to say goodbye, and he gripping my
hand and shaking his hair from his brow, said: 'I'm moving
out! . . .' and began to cough, which having heard, and
knowing that it was good for his nerves sometimes to con-
tradict him strongly, I employed just such artificial tone and
kissing him on the arm said, as one does to a person who is
strong and manly: '. . . You keep moving out every year . . .
and yet, God be praised, we still see you alive.'

To which Chopin, concluding the words interrupted
by the cough, said: 'I'm saying that I am moving out of this
apartment to the Place Vendome. . . ."

This was my last conversation with him, for shortly
afterwards he moved to the Place Vendome and there died,
but I did not see him again after that visit in the rue Chail-
lot.[1]

After Chopin's death Norwid wrote one of his greatest poems:
"Chopin's Piano," the first three stanzas of which echo his last meeting
with Chopin.

There are many records of encounters with God in culture. Let us
mention only a few of these which had significant influence on European culture. There were the great encounters of Patriarchs, prophets and
authors of the psalms. There are records of the encounters of the Apos-
tles with Christ, of which that of St. Paul on the way to Damascus is the
most famous. The streams of speech which originated in these meetings
are recorded in the books of the Old and New Testament.

The vivid book of martyrology recorded speech originating in
encounters of Christians with Christ in the Roman Empire-- speech so
strong that its consequence was death.

The speech which sprang from encounters of the Fathers of the
Church transformed the ancient culture into a Christian one. Monastic
culture was the expression of monks' encounters with Christ in a desert
and in St. Benedict's monasteries. Encounters with Christ by mystics like
Eckhard, J. Tauler, St. John of the Cross, found their expression in
mystic literature. Encounters by Luther and Loyola originated the
streams of speech which changed the shape of Christianity and European
culture in the Baroque epoch.

In European culture among the most famous encounters with nature, with sun, moon, stars and sky, are those of St. Francis of Assisi. In
his hymn to the sun he calls these pieces of God's work of creation:
brothers and sisters.

For the Silesian shoemaker, philosopher and visionary, Jacob Bohme, everything had its spiritual core which expresses itself in the speech of nature. Bohme understood the material qualities of things as the sounds of that speech.

Freidrich Schelling described opening to this speech of the world as an insight into the internal spirit of nature which acts within things, and which speaks by their form and shape as by symbols. For the romantics this meeting with nature was a kind of mystical experience. Novalis claimed that nature can be grasped only as the result of contemplation, because only thus can one enter into immediate contact with it.

That the attitude to nature of Francis, Bohme or the romantics in which natural beings are equal or even higher in dignity than man is rare in our age. Now the dominant attitude is that of science and technology in which nature is conceived as material for scientific investigations and technical manipulations.

TWO ATTITUDES TO NATURE: CONTROL AND ENCOUNTER

There are two opposed attitudes to nature: on the one hand, in terms of the tiny human shapes set into majestic and mysterious landscapes as in the pictures of Casper Friedrich; and, on the other hand, that of physicists who release nuclear energy from an objectified world. The two approaches exclude each other. The romantics show that the strangeness between a man and nature can be canceled if one avoids imposing forms, especially the form of things, upon it. Overcoming the desire to control nature is the necessary condition for hearing its speech. But this means that in order to hear the speech of nature we have to leave aside what, in my other chapter, I termed the Archimedean points of science; we must put aside the basic tool for controlling the world, namely, physics, for most systematically among all sciences physics drowns the speech of nature and deprives it of its beauty. The world of physics is one without brilliance and darkness, songs of birds and the roar of sea, the majesty of mountains and the peace of meadows and fields. It is a world of silent networks, of relations called structures, which are represented in the heavy texts of theoretical physics. Grasped in the form of things, the world loses its subjectivity; it becomes a thing subject to being changed and transformed. This attitude, which constrains the richness of the world to the skeleton of its structure, is followed by the positivist and structuralist reductions of meaning to a place occupied in that closed weave or framework of relations.

In contrast, an inner trembling and emotion, a sense of something unusual, ecstasy, fascination and a feeling that something new is being born are often signs of an encounter. These feelings fill us in the presence of the masterpieces of art or literature which crown human culture. When contemplated in silence, their creativity strikes us as a gift of heavenly generosity. Paul III fell praying on his knees before Michelangelo's Last Judgment. The Holy Roman Emperor, Charles V, spent his last two years in semi-monastic seclusion with Titian's painting of the same scene.

C.E.M. Joad wrote: "It is difficult for any of us in moments of intense aesthetic experience to resist the suggestion that we are catching a glimpse of a light shining down to us from a different realm of existence." An aesthetic experience is a kind of encounter and, in the language used in that essay, the glimpses of light are the source of speech, that is, the phenomena which originate in an encounter and are expressed in language, art, literature, behavior or acts.

Often simultaneous encounters of different sorts take place. In beautiful scenery one usually meets not only nature, but a moving aesthetic experience which opens one to his personal self, to other persons or to God. This trembling expression of simultaneous encounter with nature and with one's own self can be found in Czeslaw Milosz's poem: "Gift":

A day so happy
Fog lifted early, I worked in the garden
Hummingbirds were stopping over honeysuckle flowers.
There was no thing on earth I wanted to possess
I knew no one worth my envying him.
Whatever evil I had suffered, I forgot.
To think that once I was the same man did not embarrass me.
In my body I felt no pain
When straightening up, I saw the blue sea and sails.[2]

For many people natural scenery is the place in which God reveals himself. There are numerous records of encounters with nature followed by encounters with God. One of these is that of Gerard M. Hopkins, expressed in his poem "Hurrahing in Harvest":

Summer ends now; now, barbarous in beauty, the
stocks rise
Around; up above, what wind-walks! what lovely behavior
Of silk-sack clouds! has wilder, wilful-waiver
Meal-drift moulded ever and melted across skies?

I walk, I lift up, I lift up heart, eyes.
Down all that glory in the heavens to gleam our Saviour;
And, eyes, heart, what looks, what lips yet gave you a
Rapturous love's greeting of realer, of rounder replies?

And the azurous hung hills are his world-wielding shoulder
These things, these things were here and but the beholder
Wanting; which two when they once meet,
The heart rears wings bold and bolder
And hurls for him, O half hurls earth for him off
under his feet.

SPEECH AND MACHINE INTELLIGENCE

Stages of Speech and Structures of Language

As the speech of nature has a temporal structure, one can distinguish stages in its occurrence. At first one opens oneself to an encounter with his egoistic or personal self, with another person, with nature or with the world of culture. If an encounter really takes place it gives birth to a stream of speech. In the second stage, different streams of speech which originated in those encounters are integrated in what can be called preconceptual thinking. At that stage one awaits in silence an effect of the opening which took place in the encounters. This is the basic condition for shaping the human interior and the reason why Pythagoras ordered his followers to keep many years of silence and why mystics point to the desert as the symbol of remaining in silence before God. The fruitful silence in which the man allows for speech of nature to mature in him is totally distinct from that silence caused by thoughtlessness, fear, desire of revenge or hate.

At a third stage speech meets the deep structure of language. The modern understanding of language systems originates from Noam Chomsky's concept of generative grammar. According to him language consists of deep structure which corresponds only to meaning and surface structure which relates directly to sound. These structures are related by certain operations called grammatical transformations. Consequently, a language system or the grammar of a language has three components, namely, the subsystem of rules which characterize the deep structure, the analogous subsystem which controls the surface structure and the subsystem of transformational relations between the two structures. To accommodate the creative aspect of language a system has to be able to create an infinite domain of paired deep and surface substructures.

Structures of Language, Thinking and Reality

Until now we have discussed the activation of a language system by streams of human speech originating from encounters. That process takes place within the person, but the language system can be activated also by a social environment and various human activities, among which science and technology are the most important. Conventional sentences spoken in everyday life to communicate our needs, requests and interests to others or to exchange information, routine sentences spoken in office work are the examples of the language system being activated by the social environment. Here the extreme example is the language of propaganda consisting of single words, phrases or sentences and impressed upon human minds by continuous repetition. These elements can be joined into a more or less self-consistent ideological system by a tiny group of people and often is enforced by terror as the obligatory linguistic model.

Ideology is a denial of human speech originating in encounters. No closed language system is capable of grasping human speech which springs from an infinite number of human encounters. Real speech bursts every conventional system of expression as is best seen in works of great poets, mystics, dramatists, artists and novelists. Often they break out of accepted forms of expression to find another which better fits the streams of speech born within them. This opening to new forms of language is the living character of language which continuously changes as new generations try to externalize in language the speech originating in their own encounters.

According to B. Whoof the grammar of language is a system of textual structures which reflects the way of thinking and seeing the world by a given society. Language is seen as constraining human thinking, directing it into prepared channels which emphasize some aspects of reality and reason and neglect other aspects which are exposed by other languages. An individual is unconscious of that structure and incapable of overcoming it. Like a marionette, his or her language behavior is determined by unconscious patterns. Moreover, not only the individual's language behavior, but also his whole experience of the world is mediated by the language habits of the society to which he belongs. Whoof's lingual determinism, though much more deeply argued than that of advocates of ideology, absolutizes the constraining aspects of language. He did not recognize the power of authentic human speech to transform any language into a flexible tool for expressing the source-experience in encounters.

Scientific theories are specific language constructs which are more or less formalized. The most formalized usually are physical theories; for example, quantum theory is formalized in the framework of the mathematical structure called Hilbert space. But if the scientific theories are language constructs and if Chomsky's description of language is correct, then the formal structure of a theory has to be the deep structure of language. Moreover, the theories have their confirmation in experiments and technology, in the human ability to control the material world of things. To explain that amazing ability of controlling the world with the aid of scientific theories it seems necessary to assume that the theories have something in common with material things. What is common is the structure, in other words, the deep structure of physical theories is identical with the structure of the material world. The language of the theories and material world are two different representations of the same fundamental ontological component, the structure.

Chomsky in his philosophical considerations came to the conclusion that structures of language are structures of thinking. I would use here the term "reasoning" instead of "thinking," because I previously called thinking the search by the mind for an adequate deep structure for a stream of speech. Because the stream of speech is non-structural in its essence, thinking in my interpretation involves both structural and nonstructural components whereas reasoning is rather the structural activity.

Now we can take one further step and identify three structures: the structure of reasoning with that of language, and both of these with the structure of material reality. This identity seems to take place in the case of the structure of a true scientific theory that is one which is confirmed by experiments and technology. The structure then has both mental representation and material realization. Usually, as the full structure of a scientific theory is not realized materially, there is room for mental representation of fragments of the structure which have not been materially realized and in the process of experiment and technology that mental representation is transformed into material realization.

The Nature of Machine Intelligence

In his essay, "The Formal Nature of Language," Chomsky sketched a perceptual model which incorporates the grammar of a language, which acts as a switch receiving signals as "input" and assigning various grammatical substructures as "output." This presumes that language perception takes place in a particular structural framework which can be discovered. This idea has made possible the progress in natural language computer processing stimulated by the development of multiprocessor computer technology. The assumption that the structures of natural language are sufficiently recognized to implement them effectively on computers is essential for Japan's Fifth Generation Project to provide facilities for natural language communication between human and machine.[3] The fifth generation machines are expected to understand continuous human speech and respond intelligently to users giving the spoken language. Moreover, a machine translation sub-project is being released initially between English and Japanese. As people work out the fifth generation machines their creations will become more similar to human beings.

D. Norman and D. Rumelhart from the University of California, San Diego, together with the LNR research group have developed Pylyshyn's hypothesis that the same deep structure is common both for language and visual data.[4] The Fifth Generation Project includes as its goal machines which would process pictures and images intelligently and contribute to computer-aided design and manufacture. Such an image processing system would consist of feature extractors to distinguish, for example, the boundaries of objects, display generators and an image data base. The Japanese intend to develop in the framework of their project a computer knowledge-base capable of storing the entire *Encyclopedia Britannica*. The organizational structure of that base can be conceived as the deep structure of the system, while the structures of the lingual and image processing systems could be accepted as the surface structures of language and vision respectively. Thus the fifth generation computer has as its main goal intelligent creation which might see, talk and perform many intellectual tasks much more efficiently than the human brain and be capable of storing in its memory huge amounts of knowledge. In the not too distant future we can expect robots which can see, hear, speak, understand and act under novel circumstances. These will exist not only in science-fiction books and movies, but in the real world.

CULTURE, THE LIMITS OF MACHINE INTELLIGENCE AND THE DISTINCTIVELY HUMAN

The world of culture is derivative of human beings, who differ substantially from the world of nature. At present the world created by man is being increasingly filled with more and more "intelligent" creations: computers, personal computers, intelligent communication networks, smart weapons and, in the near future, "smart" robots. In that process the world of culture itself becomes intelligent. In this it follows the world of nature which gained intelligence with the arrival of creatures possessing brains and improved its intelligence through the process of evolution to produce that most intelligent of creatures, man. In turn, human intelligence has continuously transformed the world of nature into one of culture. Finally, man unleashed intelligence from his brain and transplanted it to machines. That artificial intelligence not only transforms the world of nature more intensively but influences the human psyche. As the creation of an intelligent environment was made possible through the discovery of the structures of language, reasoning and reality, it is reasonable to call this area of culture its structural dimension, which, in turn, corresponds to the natural human self.

The neural sciences explore neural networks in order to learn their organization and manner of operation. Neural networks are the parts of living organisms which support intelligence as electronic circuits support artificial intelligence. From the point of view of these sciences neural centers are multi-processor like systems which were created in the process of evolution. We can say that these centers of intelligence located in neural centers of the human body are evolving to become the fundamental feature of the non-life, feelingless, emotionless and sexless world of human artifices. That intelligent world of culture amazes both its creator and participants, giving them a sense of unusual power. Expanding very quickly, it seems to surpass other less expansive dimension of human culture.

CULTURE AND THE LIMITS OF MACHINE INTELLIGENCE

The designers of the Japanese automatic translation program promise that their machine will translate texts between English and Japanese with 90% accuracy; the remaining 10% must be processed by human beings. There are two possible explanations of that 10% error. At first, one can say that the structures of the languages are not fully recognized and the hardware of translation machine is not yet perfect. Thus, the percentage of error could decline as the system approaches its perfection. The second explanation is deeper: that there are non-removable mistakes in the automatic translation which result from the nature of human speech. Human speech which originates in encounters often breaks lingual structures in search of the best form, as often happens in poetry. These deformations of lingual structures are a kind of warning signal that the text cannot be understood solely in the framework of linguistic structures, but must be related with the unanticipated it encounters. The experience of encounter cannot be computerized because of its originality, non-repeatedness and unstructural character. By that unique ability for encountering other persons, oneself, God, nature and the world of culture, humans transcend the computerizable world of structures.

Language is only one of the forms in which speech expresses itself. That is why such phrases as: body language, the language of feeling, of actions or of art are met in natural language. Poetry, literature, prayers, works of mystics, religious activity and art originate in encounters as non-structural dimensions of human culture.

We found previously that the structure of reasoning and the deep structure of language are the same for all human beings. That is the reason why expanding the structural dimension of culture by developing science and technology standardizes all cultures.

In contrast, different ethnic or social groups cultivate various kinds of encounters in different scales. There is also no one-to-one correspondence between speech originating in the encounters and its expressions. Thus, the broadening of the non-structural dimension of human culture by different groups has to lead to differentiation of cultures.

Is the Japanese goal of 90% accuracy for an automatic translation program realistic? The accurate translation of a text is possible only if the text is understood by the translator. For the texts from the structural dimension of a culture the meaning of substantives can be grasped by putting forward the distinctive semantic features from a general list. Such a list could contain for example the following features: abstractness - concreteness, vitality - non-vitality, personality - un-personality, collectivity - element, plant - information, institution - tool, liquid machine - material part. The meaning of the verb is defined as a network of relations in the deep structure. For example, the meaning of a clause with the verb "sell" involves more than seventy structural elements.[5]

As it follows from the investigation of the LNR research group the number of structural elements which have to be kept in the computer memory increases rapidly together with the complexity of the world which has to be "understood" by the computer--very quickly exceeding the capacity of existing hardware.[6] Taking into account the development of multi-processor technology, the Japanese Fifth Generation Program has a chance of success in manufacturing hardware capable of storing and processing the extraordinary large number of the structural elements required for intelligent translation of texts belonging to the structural dimension of human culture. However, there is no prospect for automatic translation of texts from the non-structural dimension, such as that quoted above, for such texts can be understood only in relation to the non-structural experience of encounter.

Thus, it probably will be possible to manufacture machines which surpass the human power of reasoning, at least in certain areas, just as they now surpass human calculating and often information processing capacities. But the human capacity for thinking which cannot be reduced to reasoning will continue to transcend intelligent artifices. From this it follows that the sources of human uniqueness and hence dignity should be sought in the non-structural dimension of culture among those encounters which originate non-structural mental activity.

AGH and
The Pontifical Academy of Theology
Krakow, Poland

NOTES

*See Discussion VI.

1. Cyprian Kamil Norwid, *Poems*, A. Czerniawski, trans. (Krakow: Wydawnictwo Literackie, 1986).

2. Trans. from Polish by Cz. Milosz.

3. E. Eignenbaum and Pamela McCorduck, "Land of the Rising Fifth Generation" in Tom Forester, ed., *The Information Technology Revolution* (Cambridge: MA: M.I.T., 1985), p. 71.

4. Z.W. Pylyshyn, "What the Mind's Eye Tells the Mind's Brain," D. Norman, D. Rumelhart and the LNR Research Group, *Exploration in Cognition* (San Francisco: Freeman, 1975), pp. 21 and 281.

5. *Exploration in Cognition*, p. 273.

6. *Ibid.*, p. 373.

CHAPTER XVII

LEARNING TO PARTICIPATE

HUMANISTIC AND PRAGMATIC EDUCATION

FOR A MULTICULTURAL COMMUNITY,

POLITY AND WORLD

TIMOTHY READY

Is it possible for schools in multicultural polities to educate youths in a way that respects the various cultures, yet simultaneously instills the common values and requisite skills that are necessary to function in the society at large? Can an educational program which must socialize youths to roles in a mass society do so without undermining local cultures and communities or causing youths to become alienated from them? The answers to these questions depend upon:

1. definitions of the concepts of culture, education, community and society; and
2. the manner in which the above concepts are related to each other in implicit and explicit theories of education.

COMMON HUMANITY AND CULTURAL VARIABILITY

Many people consider the development of the concept of culture within anthropology to be the most outstanding contribution of that discipline to the understanding of humankind. Differences exist, however, regarding the definition of this concept. Indeed, many anthropologists do not employ the concept of culture, at all, preferring to focus on the structure and function of society (e.g. the British tradition of social anthropology)[1] or upon modes of production (the Marxian tradition).[2] Those anthropologists who do employ the concept of culture seldom agree upon what a culture is. Some define it as "a way of life" (e.g., A.L. Kroeber),[3] including social organization, meaning system, language, implements, etc. Others see culture exclusively as a meaning system[4] that is shared by members of a society and which is passed on from generation to generation. Among those who define culture as a meaning system, some emphasize the manner in which language encodes meaning;[5] others study key excerpts of cultures as texts, using literary analysis as a model for the search for central themes within the culture.[6] In contrast, cultural ecologists such as Julian Steward[7] and Marvin Harris,[8] and cultural evolutionists like Leslie White,[9] primarily have viewed culture as humankind's mode of physically adapting to the environment, with technology

as the primary determinant of social and political formations and their corresponding ideologies.

I am among those anthropologists who consider culture to be a useful concept. Culture, like all concepts, however, should be considered a tool--a means of assisting in the study and understanding of meaningful social action.[10] If the concept of culture is to be of value then, like all tools, it must be used with caution and precision. The concept of culture came into prominence in anthropology in the first decades of the twentieth century when Franz Boas[11] promoted the term to replace race as the key explanatory concept for human behavior. Promotion of the concept of culture has been important in combatting racist thought in intellectual circles during this century. It did this by disaggregating explanations of human belief and behavior from the phenotypic traits of peoples. Although the concept has been useful in this regard, I would suggest that an over-reliance on culture as the core concept in contemporary social studies has the potential of misleading and even dehumanizing our understanding of humankind.

Reliance upon culture as an explanatory tool can be misleading for various reasons. First, there is the problem of the reification of the concept, thereby attributing to the concept of culture a concreteness which is not warranted. Particularly in complex social systems (which are becoming the norm in the modern world), how does one recognize a specific culture? Where does Culture A begin and Culture B end? Should culture be considered an independent or dependent variable in relation to social action, the economy and politics?

I prefer to view culture from a phenomenological perspective similar to that elaborated by Peter Berger and Thomas Luckmann in their book, *The Social Construction of Reality*.[12] They view culture as the result of a dialectical process which involves three phases: (1) the exteriorization of (unstated) human strivings and needs through action and symbolic expression; (2) the objectification of those symbolic forms into a cultural reality that is common to society; and (3) the selective internalization of that cultural reality by members of a society according to their position in that society. Phase 3 leads once again to the channelling of individual strivings and urges for creative symbolic expression. This phenomenological perspective on culture accomplishes the task of reincorporating thinking, feeling, passionate human beings into social studies. It thereby addresses a deficiency that has existed in a variety of perspectives, including the Marxian, the positivistic and culturalist.

A limitation of this phenomenological perspective, however, is that the manner in which objectification or institutionalization occurs during the second phase of Berger & Luckmann's dialectical process is not fully developed. This weakness in the phenomenological perspective can be addressed by considering several other social theories, including Anthony Giddens,[13] theory of structuration. The first and third phases of Berger & Luckmann's social construction of reality, however, are the ones that are of primary concern here.

From the perspective taken here, then, culture can be seen as composed of a body of conventional knowledge, values and aesthetic forms available to members of groups, communities and societies. These conventional forms begin to be transmitted at birth, if not before, as the infant externalizes its need for food, warmth, and tactile stimulation (dare I say love?) and meets with the culturally patterned modes of response of the mother and other caretakers. Cultural learning continues during early childhood as the child slowly learns to talk and otherwise attempts to gain control of that which he or she wants. *What* the child wants, of course, becomes increasingly influenced by conventional cultural values and understandings. As the process of learning and growing continues, so does the process of cultural differentiation and personality development. As all individuals within a culture are not totally alike in their values and understandings, it is apparent that cultural learning differs according to the idiosyncratic experiences of the individual as well as the experiences that individuals share with limited numbers of others, e.g., in members of family, religious sect, gender, class, locality, etc.

Cultural variation is not infinite, however. As argued by Clyde Kluckhohn and H.A. Murray,[14] in some ways each human being is like all other people, some other people, and no other person. There remains a core of commonality of humanity that makes meaning across cultures possible. Of course, precisely to define what that core of common humanity is, (i.e., human nature, or the human condition) is very controversial and difficult. Certainly it is beyond the scope of this paper to comprehensively examine the issue. I would like to offer a few comments, however, on what some of these common denominators may be. First, Paul Ekman[15] has found through scientifically controlled cross-cultural studies that facial expressions of emotions such as happiness, anger, grief and sadness are almost universally understood. John Bowlby,[16] Mary Ainsworth[17] and others, working with infants cross-culturally, found that there are great similarities in the processes of bonding between infants and mothers, and that infants exhibit similar sequences of behavior as they react to the absence of their primary caretaker. Thus, studies with infants suggest that certain emotions may be common to all, and that a common, biologically based urge for attachment, bonding, or social belonging may be universal.

Common denominators of human nature are much more difficult to identify after infancy, as diffuse and unspecific urges and strivings are channelled through specific cultural and social forms. I will mention a few possible common denominators which are relevant to the understanding of phases one (externalization) and three (interiorization) of Berger and Luckmann's social construction of reality. The first common denominator is that proposed by Walter Goldschmidt.[18] He has suggested that the desire to enhance the self is equally common to all. But this does not mean that human beings are necessarily selfish or dedicated to individualistic pursuit. Indeed, self enhancement may imply just the opposite in those circumstances in which one's evaluation of self worth is contingent on conforming to cultural norms, religious precepts, or sacrificing one's material interests or even one's life for a cause such as country or religion. Thus, enhancement of the self in the sense that individuals seek to maintain self respect and, not coincidentally, the respect of other members of communities to which one belongs is fundamental to our humanity.

Next, I cite the work of the Israeli medical sociologist, Aaron Antonovsky,[19] who discusses the concept of coherence in the context of social and psychological influences upon health. He argued that the quest for coherence is universal, and that the absence of coherence is associated with ill health. Essentially, coherence is comprised of the evaluation of one's circumstances such that one believes (correctly or incorrectly) that one understands what one needs to know about one's social and physical surroundings and that, based on this understanding, things will turn out alright.

That which constitutes "all right," of course, is one of the most difficult problems in postulating human common denominators. Evaluations of what is desirable or good are largely determined by cultural values. However, if there were no common evaluation of good, it would then be impossible to consider principles of ethics that could transcend specific cultural traditions. To address this problem I refer briefly to an intriguing book by J. van Baal,[20] entitled *Man's Quest for Partnership: The Anthropological Foundations of Ethics and Religion*. As implied by the title, van Baal argues that the good can be defined cross culturally as meaningful participation in a community. It is not unlike Martin Buber's[21] discussion of *agapé*. It entails concern for others and a sense that others care about you. It entails being recognized as worthy and welcome, and feeling that one is a part of something larger than oneself. Partnership, he argues, necessarily entails some compromise of hedonistic gratification for the benefit of ongoing participation in which one is motivated to conform or excel in terms of the values of one's community. Partnership cannot be achieved through asocial hedonistic pleasure seeking. Nor can it be found (or at least sustained) by conforming or identifying with totalitarian visions in which the value of the contributions of individual participants is not appreciated. It is derived from ongoing participation in a community in which one is appreciated and welcomed.

EDUCATION IN COMPLEX SOCIETIES

So far, we have discussed the concept of culture, and proposed some common denominators of human nature or the human condition that limit the range of cultural variability. It was necessary to address these issues in order to explain the remaining concepts introduced at the start of the paper, namely, education, community and society, and the models by which they may be related to each other in order to produce a humane and effective education.

Let us now address the question posed at the start: Is it possible to provide culturally sensitive education in a complex, multicultural society and still educate youths for the effective enactment of economic and political roles, i.e., the roles of a citizen in a mass society? First, let us discuss what we mean by education. Education is a type of cultural learning (enculturation). It exists in virtually all societies, as it is the deliberate and systematic attempt to transmit skills and understandings, habits of thought and deportment required by the group of which the learner is a novice member.[22] While education may be found in all societies, however, schooling is not. Schooling denotes institutionalized education in which one learns vicariously in roles and environments defined as distinct from those in which the learning eventually will be applied. Education in mass societies, then, is typically handled through the institution of schooling. Education in a small scale society would likely be intimately related to the life of the community to which one belonged. Schooling in a mass society in contrast requires the learning of knowledge and values which not only are dissociated from the context in which they will be applied, but which for youths in certain circumstances may also have little apparent relevance to themselves either now or in the future.

Ivan Illich[23] and Paulo Freire,[24] among others, have criticized schooling in mass societies as being inherently alienating. Illich notes that schools deliberately prepare youths to function in large, bureaucratic institutions over which they tend to have little control. These institutions of mass society draw youths away from the local communities in which they could realistically expect to participate meaningfully (c.f. van Baal). This withdrawal implies the loss of competency on the part of individuals and groups personally to address their own needs, rather than having to rely upon bureaucratically controlled institutions, be they state controlled or corporate. Although many people would consider Illich's radical antimodernism impractical for this last decade of the twentieth century, his criticism of mass education is not inconsistent with that of other critics of modern state institutions. Most notable among these is Peter Berger,[25] who proposed the concept of mediating structures. Like Illich, Berger has argued that the large scale institutions of modern societies do not promote participation or identification with a genuine community. Because of this absence of participation and local community control, there is little allegiance to behavioral norms and values proffered by those institutions. This tends to result in psychological alienation, lack of adherence to the dominant culture of the institution, and the possibility of social deviance of one form or another. Extending the critique of Illich to the realm of social policy, Berger would have the state promote small scale institutions (including schools) in which members of local communities would have a say and could meaningfully participate.

This problem of a lack of identification with, and participation in, educational institutions is particularly acute when the curriculum is set by dominant sectors of society which have a culture or subculture different from the students' home community. The result is that youths from minority groups, particularly those that historically have been relegated to inferior socio-economic status, do not succeed to the same degree as members of the dominant culture in mastering the cultural agenda both of the formal school curriculum and of the informal school culture. Consciously or unconsciously, minority youths are more likely than others to conclude that to risk their self esteem in the present, and to invest their hopes for the future by aspiring to prestigious social statuses associated with the dominant culture is a high risk strategy unlikely to be personally satisfying. Research I conducted[26] several years ago in Corpus Christi, Texas, confirmed this to be so and for at least two reasons:

(1) Succeeding in terms of the norms and values of the school, which were consistent with those that would be necessary to occupy high status positions in adult society, seemed to many Mexican-American and Black youths to necessitate the abandonment of their customary modes of speech (including accent), and aesthetic preferences in music, clothes, etc. That is, it seemed to these youths that succeeding in terms of the "official" culture would require them to abandon their own culture which provided meaning and fulfillment in the context of family and peer group relations. In other words, it would mean "turning their backs" on themselves, their families and their communities.

(2) Despite the fact that minority youths were equally if not more likely than others to state when asked that they considered it important to do well in school, these youths were faced with a less favorable opportunity structure. That is, they were confronted with a configuration of more obstacles (e.g., monetary deficiency, fewer social contacts in potentially useful situations, cultural biases) and fewer resources (e.g., monetary, role models, potential patrons). Thus, while identifying with the goals of 'official' culture as portrayed by the school, a relative lack of means to achieve those goals led to a refocussing of personal interest in activities and issues other than those associated with success in school (e.g., alternative peer cultures, employment, sports, etc.).

Because of the high risk to self esteem and the potential for alienation from one's own community associated with identification with the "official" culture as articulated by the schools, approximately half of the minority secondary students dropped out of school before graduating. In part, the high drop-out rate can be considered a manifestation of the psychological defense mechanism of withdrawal from a social context in which one is evaluated unfavorably. It is interesting to note that a similar process of withdrawal by many Mexican-American and Black youths due to alienation from "official" school culture occurred even in schools in which most of the teachers and administrators were from backgrounds similar to those of the students. Many youths saw little relationship between the lessons learned in school and the practical problems of everyday life in their communities. Success in school implied "getting ahead" of the disvalued status that the students, their families, friends and community currently occupied in society.

Another consequence of this withdrawal from, or rejection of, the "official" school culture is identification with youths having a subculture and a corresponding pattern of social interaction that is different from, if not inconsistent with the "official" school culture. In a sense, these youth subcultures can be considered as adaptations to a sociocultural milieu in which minority youths perceive that the cards are stacked against them. Although there is not a one to one correspondence between identification with a particular youth subculture and socioeconomic status (SES), race or ethnicity, it was certainly true that low SES minority youths were more likely to identify with subcultures that were inconsistent with the successful enactment of valued social roles within the context of the dominant culture. It is likely that this process of alienation from the dominant culture and corresponding identification with various youth subcultures was playing an important part in the replication of pre-existing patterns of social stratification in yet another generation of youths. I wish to emphasize, however, that this process of identification with alternative cultures takes place in the context of opportunity structures that vary enormously in relation to SES, ethnic and gender status.

An alternative model of education in multicultural contexts is represented by The Multicultural Career Intern Program (MCIP), a high school serving recent immigrant and refugee youths residing in Washington, D.C. Most of the 250 students who attend the school are of extremely limited economic means. About two-thirds of the students are Latin American or from the Caribbean, with the greatest number of these having fled the violence and disorder in El Salvador. Among the 25 countries represented at the school, there are also large numbers of students from Ethiopia, China, Haiti, The Dominican Republic, and Guatemala. MCIP explicitly promotes appreciation for the many cultures represented at the school through the curriculum in social studies, literature, the arts and extracurricular activities. Celebrating as an asset the cultural diversity represented by the student body not only serves to promote intercultural understanding, it also means that the school strives to demonstrate vividly the relevance of the academic lessons within the context of a variety of cultures and communities, rather than from the point of view of conformity to one cultural model.

Thus, in addition to the seemingly idealistic emphasis upon multiculturalism as an asset, the school is, in fact, unrelentingly pragmatic. It tailors instruction so that it addresses the frame of relevance of a diverse student body, many members of which could easily decide that schooling is a luxury they cannot afford given their economic, social and political circumstances. Besides respecting cultural diversity, MCIP is sensitive to how education for an economically insecure population must be of demonstrable use in making a living. Thus, the MCIP model of education emphasizes the relationship of academic learning to earning a living. All students are placed in internships related to career interests. The students thereby acquire, through personal experience and observation, a first hand understanding of the skills, knowledge, norms and values required in what, to the students, is the unfamiliar culture of the American workplace.

MCIP simultaneously respects and encourages the maintenance of the various cultures of the students, while promoting the assimilation of the knowledge and values necessary to successfully live and work in the United States. To put it differently, the school teaches the students the knowledge and values necessary to participate in, and contribute to, American society, but does so with the basic premise that society can, should, and to some extent, does tolerate cultural diversity. To a large degree, MCIP functions in a manner not unlike Berger's mediating structure. It is a small, nurturing social institution with which the students strongly identify and within which they can participate meaningfully. In the tolerant and supportive school environment, the students are less likely to feel rejection from peers and teachers for an inability or unwillingness to conform to cultural norms unrelated to those of their own communities. Tolerant of cultural diversity and various levels of preparedness to master academic lessons, the school creates an attractive culture in which youths of diverse backgrounds participate in a real community. The school culture emphasizes respect for self and others, tolerance for differences in values and perspectives, and a hopeful common purpose of acquiring the knowledge and skills which will enable them to live and work in what previously may have been perceived as a strange and somewhat frightening new society.

HUMANE AND PRAGMATIC EDUCATION
in Culturally Diverse Societies and
an Increasingly Interconnected World

As we approach the end of the twentieth century, it is clear that the degree of isolation of the peoples of the world has been greatly diminished. No one's life remains unaffected by the actions of people, distant or near, who are culturally different from themselves--even though many may not understand the nature of this interconnection. Trade, jet airplanes, and the mass media are among the factors that have contributed to the emergence of a global society, albeit extremely heterogeneous, incomplete, and disturbingly unruly. Not only are the various nations and regions of the world being drawn into increasing interdependence, culturally diverse people increasingly are being drawn into personal contact with each other. This occurs not only in relatively elite circles of higher education, commerce and politics, but also at the grass roots level as peoples migrate to distant locations within nations and internationally in search of employment. As documented by Eric Wolf[27] in his book sardonically entitled, *Europe and the People Without a History,* this process has been occurring on an increasingly large scale since the 18th century. The emergence of capitalism as the predominant mode of production has created a truly international division of labor. Individuals and families living in parts of the world in which the global economic system offers few jobs are migrating to foreign nations where the prospects for making a living are better. The challenge for education in such increasingly heterogeneous societies is simultaneously to provide youths the skills meaningfully to participate in the larger society, while maintaining respect for one's own cultural heritage, and developing an appreciation for the common humanity shared with others manifesting other cultures. In addressing this challenge, educational institutions also will be building the ethical foundations for the emerging global society.

No society can exist, be it local, regional, national or global, without a corresponding culture to imbue social interaction with meaning, logic, order and purpose. At the very least, culture must provide a common core of understandings, rules and norms for the various parties involved in the shared system of interaction if each is to be able to peaceably pursue their own interests. As J. van Baal has argued,[28] such a system of "minimal ethics" must exist to assure the basic rights of each person and to prevent violence. A system of minimal ethics alone, however, probably is not enough to ensure the ongoing functioning of either small or large scale social systems. A deeper and more profound sense of ethics that transcends "live and let live" is required to assure that individuals and groups can peaceably pursue their interests. An ethical system which evokes a sense of belonging and partnership is of crucial importance in the maintenance of an ongoing system of social interaction in which individuals and groups from all backgrounds can participate meaningfully.

Van Baal calls this deeper ethical system "natural ethics."[29] He argues that although natural ethics are most visible as the foundation of kinship based primitive societies, they must also exist to some extent even in bureaucratically organized mass societies. Natural ethics can be understood as similar to Martin Buber's discussion of agapé as a commitment and concern for the well being of others. In kinship based societies, social interaction occurs among people who know each other in a variety of contexts. Unlike in modern societies outside the domain of the family and friends, social ties among people in primitive societies transcend specific instrumental purposes. They extend beyond economic interdependence to a shared commitment to a coherent and comprehensive system of beliefs and values. In multicultural nation states, natural ethics are evoked through symbols such as the flag and participation in national rituals such as the celebration of holidays, and in national sporting events. The power to elicit a sense of meaningful participation and belonging of such symbols and rituals, however, is limited. This is especially true for cultural minorities and others who may be cut off from more substantive participation in the major institutions of society.

The emerging global society has not yet firmly established a system of minimal ethics, let alone natural ethics. As neither is well established, ethnic, sectarian, class and nationalist ideologies legitimize actual and potential violent conflict on a scale that is unprecedented in the history of the world. The underdevelopment of an ethical dimension of culture corresponding to global society also legitimizes disinterest in issues such as famine, ecological crisis, and other threats to the health and well being of people outside of one's own group.

Education can help to address the need for an ethical system for an increasingly interdependent world by pursuing objectives similar to those of the Multicultural School (MCIP) of Washington described above. Educational programs preparing youths meaningfully to participate in a culturally heterogeneous world might share the following objectives:

- Create a learning environment such that the students identify with local community values and norms and develop concern for the welfare of their fellow students at the school. Create an atmosphere in which the student feels at home, but is also challenged to contribute to something that is larger than oneself.

- Promote respect and appreciation for the variety of cultures represented in the social system, but focus the curriculum upon the needs and interests of each of the culturally diverse communities that is served.

- Educate about broader patterns of interdependence among the peoples of the community, region, nation and world, and promote identification with values and norms that could motivate a sense of commitment and belonging to the emerging "global village."

- From the culturally familiar base of the school in which students feel "at home," provide instrumental linkages to the economic, social and political institutions of the wider society. Equip and motivate the student to participate and contribute to broader systems of social interdependence.

By promoting these objectives, it is argued that schools will enable their students to learn to participate as capable and ethical citizens in the emerging global society. Of course, there are limitations to the extent that education can facilitate the development of an ethically sound global culture or promote effective participation of youths in the economic, social and political institutions of the broader society. Educational institutions do not exist in a vacuum. To educate for mutual understanding and respect within the context of societies in which the basic human rights of others are abused poses obvious difficulties. To ignore them would be the same as educating youths to participate in a fairy tale world. However, to the extent that leaders of economic, social and political institutions are willing and able to cooperate in facilitating the participation of persons from a variety of cultural and economic backgrounds, then such educational programs are more likely to be effective. It is beyond the scope of this paper to address the question of the role of education in societies in which basic human rights are denied. I wish to

conclude simply by arguing that an education which emphasizes participation and partnership within ever broadening circles of social interaction (within corresponding, nonexclusive cultures--not unlike Janusz
Kuczynski's[30] image of layered cultural allegiances) is the general principle that I propose as the cornerstone of an education that is humane,
pragmatic and appropriate for our times.

The Catholic University of America
Washington, D.C.

NOTES

1. A.R. Radcliffe Brown, *Structure and Function in Primitive Society* (New York: Free Press, 1952).
2. Eric R. Wolf, *Europe and the People Without a History* (Berkeley:
University of California Press, 1982).
3. A.L. Kroeber, "The Superorganic," *American Anthropologist*, 19
(1917), 163-213.
4. Clifford Geertz, "The Impact of the Concept of Culture on the
Concept of Man," in *The Interpretation of Cultures* (New York: Basic
Books, 1973).
5. Dell Hymes, "Introduction," in *The Functions of Language in the
Classroom*, Courtney Camden, Vera P. John, & Dell Hymes, eds. (New
York, Teachers College Press, 1972).
6. A.L. Becker, "Text Building, Epistemology, and Aesthetics in
Javanese Shadow Theatre," in *The Imagination of Reality: Essays in
Southeast Asian Coherence Systems*, A.L. Becker & Aram Yengoyan, eds.
(Norwood, NJ: ABLEX, 1979).
7. Julan Steward, *Theory of Culture Change: The Methodology of
Multilinear Evolution* (Urbana: University of Illinois Press, 1972).
8. Marvin Harris, *The Rise of Anthropological Theory: A History
of Theories of Culture* (New York: Crowell, 1968).
9. Leslie White, *The Science of Culture: A Study of Man and Civilization* (New York: Farrar, Strauss, 1949).
10. Anthony Giddens, *Central Problems in Social Theory* (Berkeley, University of California Press, 1979).
11. Franz Boas, *Anthropology and Modern Life* (New York: Dover,
1986).
12. Peter Berger and Thomas Luckmann, *The Social Construction
of Reality: A Treatise in the Sociology of Knowledge* (Garden City, NY:
Anchor Books, 1967).
13. Anthony Giddens, *op. cit.*
14. Clyde Kluckhohn and H.A. Murray, "Personality Formation:
The Determinants," in C. Kluckhohn & H.A. Murray, eds., *Personality in
Nature, Society and Culture* (New York: Knopf, 1949), p. 35.
15. Paul Ekman, "Universals and Cultural Differences in Facial
Expressions of Emotions," in J.K. Cole, ed., *Nebraska Symposium on*

Motivation (Omaha: University of Nebraska Press, 1972).

16. John Bowlby, *Attachment and Loss* (New York: Basic Books, 1973), vol. II.

17. Mary Ainsworth, "Attachment and Exploratory Behavior of One-Year Olds in a Strange Situation," in B.M. Foss, ed., *Determinants of Infant Behavior* (London: Methuen, 1969), vol. IV.

18. Walter Goldschmidt, "Ethology, Ecology and Ethnological Realities," in George Coelho, David Hamburg & John Adams, eds., *Coping and Adaptation* (New York: Basic Books, 1974).

19. Aaron Antonovsky, *Health, Stress and Coping* (San Francisco: Jossey-Bass, 1979).

20. J. van Baal, *Man's Quest for Partnership: The Anthropological Foundations of Ethics and Religion* (Assen, The Netherlands, 1981).

21. Martin Buber, *Between Man and Man* (New York: Scribner, 1970).

22. Judith Friedman Hansen, *Sociocultural Perspectives on Human Learning: An Introduction to Educational Anthropology* (Englewood Cliffs, NJ: Prentice-Hall, 1979).

23. Ivan Illich, *Deschooling Society* (New York: Harper & Row, 1971).

24. Paulo Freire, *Education for Critical Consciousness* (New York: Seabury Press, 1973).

25. Peter Berger, "In Praise of Particularity: The Concept of Mediating Structures," *The Review of Politics*, 38 (1976), 399-410.

26. Timothy Ready, "Being a Teenager in Corpus Christi," in Timothy Ready, *An Investigation of Biological, Psychological and Sociocultural Influences Upon the Blood Pressures of Adolescents in Corpus Christi, Texas* (Doctoral Dissertation; East Lansing, MI: Michigan State University, 1981), pp. 172-241.

27. Eric Wolf, *op. cit.*

28. J. van Baal, *Man's Quest for Partnership*, pp. 257-317.

29. *Ibid.*

27. Janusz Kuczynski, "For a New Universal Order," *Dialectics and Humanism*, 4 (1986), 171-176.

CHAPTER XVIII

MYSTICAL TEXTS

AS AN ENTRY INTO

THE CROSS-CULTURAL STUDY OF RELIGION

*JAMES R. PRICE III**

My thesis, in brief, is that the praxis of mysticism gives rise to a grammar of mystical interiority which can function metalinguistically to critically ground and explain the religious claims of various mystical traditions.

I will unfold this thesis through the analysis of two mystical texts, the *Cloud of Unknowing*[1] and Patanjali's *Yoga Sutras*.[2] I will begin with an analysis of the *Cloud*, showing that a principle intention of the work is to develop a critical grammar of mystical interiority. After transposing the *Cloud* from faculty psychology to intentionality analysis, I will then more briefly analyze the *Yoga Sutras*.

"THE CLOUD OF UNKNOWING"

The *Cloud of Unknowing*, a 14th century work by an anonymous Englishman, has long been recognized as a masterpiece of Christian mysticism. Along with the spiritual wisdom of the text, commentators regularly have drawn attention to the language of the *Cloud*. They have commended the author for the freshness and vigor of his prose, for his clarity, for his wit, and for the simple beauty of his style. In this chapter, however, I wish to highlight an aspect of his language which has received scant attention.

Specifically, I intend to examine the procedure employed by the author to explain, clarify and safeguard the meaning of his spiritual language. My contention, phrased in the terminology I will develop later, is that the author of the *Cloud* presents his reader with a critical grammar of mystical interiority. Not only, it seems to me, is this mystical grammar the key to reading his text but, as I will argue in section II, it provides an important entry into the cross cultural study of religion.

The author's concern for language and for a proper understanding of his text appears at the outset of the *Cloud*. In the first words of his prologue, he implores ("with all the power and force that the bond of charity can command") anyone tempted to read the book in a careless and shallow way simply to put it down rather than to fall into error and misunderstanding (p. 101). The author wants to bring his reader to an explicit understanding of a spiritual experience which he refers to alternately as a "simple reaching out to God" and a "simple stirring of love."

His concern regarding the issue of understanding is real and suffuses the text. Repeatedly, he warns that a misunderstanding of his spiritual language can lead in practice to physical trauma, distorted imagination, even madness. Whereas understanding opens up the possibility of union with the divine, misunderstanding risks falling into the hands of satan (IV.127; XLV.205; LI.219).

Thus, to forestall misunderstanding his language the author of the *Cloud* employs a linguistic device common to most mystical texts: the use of paradox. His concern is that the "simple reaching out to God" will be interpreted falsely in a literal, "physical way" and he uses paradox in a "negative" fashion to preclude this. For instance, the author stated that while the experience of "a simple reaching out to God" is indeed a "reaching out" and a "stirring," it is nevertheless not a movement. It is a rest, but not a stopping (LIX.237); it is a nowhere that is nothing (LXV-III.252).

As useful as paradox might be, its limitation is that it is not explanatory. To state that the "simple reaching out to God" is a rest but not a stopping may provide a helpful clarification, but it does not explain what is this "simple reaching." Thus, it remains strictly supplemental to the author's principal linguistic concern.

In order to explain his spiritual language, the author develops a linguistic device which I referred to earlier as a grammar of mystical interiority. Speaking broadly, his procedure is to correlate such terms as the "simple reaching out to God" and the "cloud of unknowing" with the inner experience of the contemplative, which in turn he objectifies in terms of a psychology of the spiritual faculties. This provides him with a critical grammar which enables him to specify precisely the meaning of his spiritual language.

Basic to this grammar is a set of distinctions which the author draws in terms of the three potential "foci" which can occupy the mind. Thus, for the author, when the mind is occupied with material things one is "beneath and outside oneself." When the mind is occupied with "the intricacies of the powers of the soul" one is "within and on par with oneself." Finally, when the mind is occupied with "the substance of God himself" one is "above oneself and under God" (LVII.249). It is the middle level, the level of the power of the soul, that the author of the *Cloud* takes as the explanatory key to spiritual language. In his own words, "[Anyone] who is ignorant of the Powers of his own soul, and the way in which these powers operate, can very easily be deceived in his understanding of words which are set down with a spiritual meaning" (LXV-II.250).

Having advanced this interpretive principle, the author goes on briefly to distinguish the various powers of the soul in terms of a faculty psychology. He distinguishes the principal powers of mind, reason and will, and the secondary Powers of imagination and sensuality. The imagination is the power by which we generate the images of things we think about and claim to know (LXV.246). Reason is the power by which we distinguish the good things presented by the imagination from the bad (LXIV.244). Sensuality operates in the sphere of sensation and affect; it is therefore linked to the imagination through the perception of the senses, but more fundamentally to the will through feelings of pleasure and repugnance (LXVI.247). The will is the power by which we choose the good which has been ascertained by the reason, with sensuality providing the power of affect which orients those choices (LXIV.245). The mind is the power which in itself does not act, but rather "contains and comprehends within itself (the other) four powers and their activities" (LXIII.243).

In his brief exposition the author is both dependent upon and presumes familiarity with the medieval tradition of faculty psychology; there are, for instance, echoes of Richard of St. Victor in his treatment. However, neither a more detailed exposition nor a critical assessment of his position is necessary at this point. What is of concern here is the way in which he employs his faculty psychology to give explanatory precision to his mystical language. As a way of focusing this concern, I propose in what follows to ask a question which can be answered in terms of the author's grammar of mystical interiority, i.e., What does the author mean when he speaks of a "simple reaching out to God"?

A first step toward answering this question is to notice that in the following texts a "simple reaching out to God" emerges as a key term functionally related to two others: a "cloud of unknowing" and a "cloud of forgetting."

> When you first begin to undertake [this exercise], all that you find is a darkness, a sort of cloud of unknowing; you cannot tell what it is, except that you experience in your will a simple reaching out to God (III.120).

> If ever you come to this cloud, and live and work in it as I bid you, just as this cloud of unknowing is above you, between you and your God in the same way you must put beneath you a cloud of forgetting, between you and all the creatures that have ever been made (V.128).

That the author locates the "simple reaching out to God" in the "will" will be discussed below. Here it is important to notice that the simple reaching out to God is directly correlated with the second key term, the "cloud of unknowing." To reach out to God is to experience a cloud of unknowing. Directly correlated with this is the third key term, the "cloud of forgetting." For to experience a cloud of unknowing "above" oneself is simultaneously to experience a cloud of forgetting "beneath" oneself. Thus, to experience a simple reaching out to God is to experience a cloud of unknowing which is also to experience a cloud of forgetting. The three are different facets of the same experience.

The significance and purpose of this functional relationship is that an understanding of the "simple reaching out to God" can be gained through an understanding of the "cloud of unknowing." This is how the author seeks to communicate this experience. After pointing out that he is not referring to either a physical or an imagined cloud, he specifies his meaning: "When I call this exercise a darkness or a cloud . . . I mean a privation of knowing" (IV.127-128). This means that the "simple - reaching out to God" has nothing to do with the powers of sensation, imagination, or reason. It involves an experience of unknowing in which none of them are operative. As the author puts it, "take care in this exercise and do not labor with your senses or with your imagination in any way at all. For I tell you truly, this exercise cannot be achieved by their labor; so leave them and do not work with them" (IV.127).

To leave the sense and imagination is not only to find a cloud of unknowing "above," but a cloud of forgetting "beneath." In the cloud of forgetting any object ("creature") which can be sensed, imagined or known by the powers of the soul is "forgotten" when those powers become quiescent in the simple reaching out to God. Again, in the author's words: "not only the creatures themselves, but also their works and circumstances . . . should be hid under the cloud of forgetting. I make no exceptions" (V.128).

This includes even the most basic experience of the self:

> So you must destroy all knowing and feeling of every kind of creature, but most especially of yourself. For on the knowledge and experience of yourself depends the knowledge and experience of all other creatures. . . . You will find (that) what remains between you and your God is a simple knowing and feeling of your own being. This knowing and feeling must always be destroyed before it is possible for you to experience in truth the perfection of this exercise (XLIII.202).

The author, then, does not give a direct definition of the simple reaching out to God. Rather, he defines it indirectly by identifying it in relation to the key terms which admit of direct definition, the cloud of unknowing and the cloud of forgetting. These terms are directly identifiable, of course, because they pertain to the middle level, the level "within and on par with oneself" which focuses on the powers of the soul. These are used to identify a state which is "above" the mind.

A simple reaching out to God, then, is to be understood and identified as that state in which there is no object of understanding because all the powers of the mind are inoperative. In this context, it becomes clear that the word "simple" is also a technical term for the author. It refers to the mind in a state devoid of any mental operation. Thus, in the citation above, when the author speaks of "a simple knowing and feeling of your own being" he is referring to an experience of one's mind, which, though devoid of gross mental content, is nevertheless identified as one's own. In relation to the simple reaching out to God, this simple sense of self is an "object" which must disappear beneath the cloud of forgetting.

A final step remains. Given that the simple reaching out to God is not a knowing, what does it mean that the author locates this experience in the will and associates it with love? He refers to the simple reaching out to God as "a simple stirring of love in the heart," adding with typical caution, "I do not mean in your physical heart, but in your spiritual heart, which is your will" (LI.218). In this regard, the author maintains that "it is love alone that can reach God in this life, and not knowing" (VIII.139). Refocused in this way, our question becomes: What does the author mean by a "simple stirring of love"?

Predictably, he specifies an answer in terms of an analysis of the powers of the soul, and his principle concern is to point out that the stirring of love is not a feeling. For just as the cloud of unknowing "prevents you from seeing [God] clearly by the light of understanding in your reason," so it prevents you from "experiencing him in sweetness of love in your affection" (III.121). It is not simply the knowing of all objects that must be placed under the cloud of forgetting, but all the feelings associated with such knowing that must be placed beneath it as well (XLIII.202).

The author makes this point in extended fashion by recommending that the contemplative play with God a game in which the contemplative would hide his or her desire for God. He recommends this so that the contemplative's desire does not become confused falsely with sensual feelings. As he puts it: "I want you to put [your desire] down into the depths of your spirit, far from any ignorant contamination with any sensible thing which would make it less spiritual, and in that way, so much farther away from 'God'" (XLVII.211).

In short, the author identifies the "simple stirring of love" in the same way and in the same terms in which he identifies the "simple reaching out to God." Functionally, he relates it to the cloud of unknowing and the cloud of forgetting, making clear that it has nothing to do with the feelings associated with the soul's power of sensuality. Just as the "simple stirring of love" is an unknowing, so it is to be understood and identified as an unfeeling. It is a "simple" experience in which none of the powers of the soul are operative, neither sensuality, imagination, reason nor will. It is an experience devoid of an "object" of consciousness.

In this way, then, the author fulfills the primary intention of his text. By correlating a number of functionally related technical terms with the inner experience of the contemplative, the author develops a grammar of mystical interiority which enables him both to explain and control the meaning of his spiritual language. With this intention now clarified, it is appropriate to examine the limits the author places upon it.

First, it will be clear to those familiar with the *Cloud* that its focus is intentionally narrow. The book was written for a person in the process of discerning a call to the contemplative life (I-II.115-119). Though not a book for the beginner in the Christian spiritual life, it is a book for the beginner in contemplation. As a result, the author's intention is limited (in terms of the grammar he develops) to explaining the basic contemplative experience of the simple reaching out to God. Hence, the *Cloud* is not a book which deals in detail with the steps of the spiritual life preceding the entry into contemplation. Imaginative meditation, for instance, is acknowledged but quickly set in its place beneath the cloud of forgetting (XXXV.187-189).

Nor does the author extend his mystical grammar to those experiences which emerge after the cloud of unknowing has been entered. Entry into the cloud of unknowing is not entry into a void, and the author acknowledges that mystical knowing and feeling take place in the context of the simple reaching out to God, but he refuses to speak about these:

> Perhaps it will be his will to send out a ray of spiritual light, piercing this cloud of unknowing between you and him, and he will show you some of his secrets. . . . Then you shall feel your affection all aflame with the fire of his love, far more than I know how to tell you or may wish to at this time . . . and to put it briefly, even though I dared so to speak I would not wish to (XXVI.174-175).

Although the author refuses to explain these experiences, this refusal itself highlights the explanatory value of his grammar of mystical interiority. In the absence of this grammar, all we can say is that mystical knowing and feeling take place which have nothing to do with the powers of the soul in their ordinary operation. What is a knowing beyond imagination and reason? What is a feeling beyond sensation and will? The answer to these questions lies in an extension of the grammar of mystical interiority.

Second, given the author's focus on the basic experience of contemplation, he is not concerned principally with the question of religious doctrines. It is significant, however, that to the extent that the author does deal with doctrines, he correlates them with his grammar of mystical interiority. For example, the doctrine of original sin is correlated with the experience of disharmony in the powers of the soul (X.141). Union with the divine nature of Christ is correlated with the entry into the cloud of unknowing (IV.125; XVI.155; XXV.171-172), as is union with God:

> Whenever you are aware that your mind is occupied with no created thing, whether material or spiritual, but only with the substance of God himself, as indeed the mind is and can be in the experience of the exercise described in this book; then you are above yourself and under God.
>
> You are above Yourself because You are striving by grace to reach a point to which you cannot come by nature;

that is to say, to be made one with God in spirit and in love and in oneness of wills. You are beneath your God: for though it can be said that during this time God and yourself are not two but one in spirit, . . . nevertheless you are still beneath him. For he is God by nature from without beginning (LXVII.249-250).

The significance of this passage is that it illustrates that the grammar of mystical interiority can also provide an explanatory basis for the use of doctrinal language. The author identifies union by correlating it with the interior state of "simple reaching out to God." No material object is present in the mind, nor is there a spiritual object, which would include the simple experience of the self mentioned earlier.

The author, however, does not explain fully. Due to his own circumscription of the topic, he does not explain the interior conditions which would correspond to the doctrinal claim that even though there is "a oneness of wills" there is nevertheless "a difference in natures." He simply asserts it as a doctrinal claim. In principle, however, it seems to me that a more fully developed grammar of mystical interiority could specify these conditions. This, in turn, would have significant implications for inter-religious dialogue, but that is the subject of the next section.

INTENTIONALITY ANALYSIS AND "THE CLOUD OF UNKNOWING"

In the first section I argued that the principal concern of the author of the *Cloud of Unknowing* is to develop a critical grammar of mystical interiority. In this section I wish to make the larger claim that a focus on the critical grammar of mystical interiority offers not only an interpretive key to the *Cloud of Unknowing*, but a potentially fruitful approach to the cross cultural study of religion.

My claim rests upon two assumptions, both of which I feel can be substantiated. The first, quite simply, is that the *Cloud* is not alone. Other texts from other religious traditions, such as Patanjali's *Yoga Sutras*, also develop and present grammars of mystical interiority. Like the *Cloud*, the intention of these texts is to aid their reader in the attainment of a particular mystical experience or pattern of consciousness. As we have seen, to accomplish this it is necessary to be able to communicate and explain precisely what the particular experience is. Thus, the authors develop grammars of mystical interiority, technical spiritual vocabularies which they correlate critically with the dynamics of human consciousness.

My second assumption is that the dynamics of human consciousness are common across cultures and religious traditions, and that this commonality can provide an explanatory basis for the cross cultural study of religion, a basis which can in principle explain both the similarities and differences of the various traditions.

Several precisions are in order on this point. First, I am not asserting in advance that the various traditions are either similar or different. Rather, I am proposing a method for making those determinations. Second, I do not deny that the doctrinal and spiritual terms employed by mystics in their grammars of mystical interiority emerge from and are specific to their cultural and religious traditions. My point is that these terms are both employed in an effort to identify and explain certain operations of consciousness and that they receive their precision from these operations. In other words, there is a mutually critical correlation between the terms and the operations. Thus, to the degree that the operations of consciousness are cross-cultural, the referent of the particular terms will be cross cultural.

Third, it is possible that different traditions (or different mystics within the same tradition) focus on different spiritual experiences and hence different patterns of consciousness. In this case, attention to the appropriate grammars of interiority would clarify these differences and the attendant doctrinal and religious differences. Similarly, it is also possible that different traditions (or mystics within the same tradition) focus on the same spiritual experiences and patterns of consciousness. In this case, attention to the appropriate grammars would not only clarify the similarities but provide a basis for assessing the relative adequacy of the attendant doctrinal and religious claims.

In this essay, however, I can attempt only to clarify and argue for the methodological adequacy of my proposal. The application of this method to some of the larger questions in the cross-cultural study of religion indicated above must await book length treatment. In what follows, therefore, I will suggest that to develop a grammar of mystical interiority appropriate to the cross-cultural study of religion, the faculty psychology employed by the author of the *Cloud* must be transposed into the terms and relations of intentionality analysis. In section III, I will offer a brief comparison of the grammar of the *Cloud* with that of Patanjali's *Yoga Sutras* on the basis of this transposed grammar.

The reasons for a transposition from faculty psychology to intentionality analysis are several. The first is the theoretical reason which led to the demise of faculty psychology in general. Faculty psychology, with its emphasis on the powers of the soul, presents a static theory of the mind which abstracts from the dynamic operations of consciousness. Intentionality analysis is articulated in terms of those operations.

The second reason is theological. Though this is clearly not a problem for the best faculty psychologists, nevertheless, because the powers of the soul are conceptualized as static there is a tendency for what might be called a fallacy of misplaced concreteness. That is to say, when it is forgotten that terms like "reason" and "will" are abstractions, there is a tendency to think of them as though they were specific "parts of" or "places in" the soul. It seems to me that something like this can easily happen when disputes arise over whether union with God takes place in the will, as the tradition of Augustine and Richard of St. Victor asserts, or whether it takes place in the intellect, as Pseudo-Dionysius and Aquinas hold. The shift to intentionality analysis can clarify and dissolve these disputes.

The third reason is intra-textual and pertains to the *Cloud of Unknowing* itself. As is evident from the discussion in section I, the author of the *Cloud* aligns himself within the tradition of Augustine and Richard of St. Victor by locating the simple reaching out to God in the will. I think the inheritance of this tradition leads the author to be inconsistent in his use of terminology.

The difficulty is this. If the simple reaching out to God entails the quiescence of all the powers of the soul, including the will, how can union with God take place in the will? Given his faculty psychology, it seems to me that the more appropriate power with which to associate the union of God is "mind." It contains the will and all the other powers, it would seem that when those powers are quiescent the mind is what remains. Indeed, there is evidence that on this point the author of the *Cloud* regards the mind and the will as equivalent terms (LXVII.249-250).

To move from faculty psychology to intentionality analysis is to change one's basic terms from powers of the soul to operations of consciousness. The following presentation, which will be rather condensed, involves two steps. First, the correlation of the operations of consciousness as articulated by intentionality analysis with the faculty psychology of the *Cloud*, and then an exposition of the mystical grammar of the *Cloud* in terms of intentionality analysis.

Following Lonergan's objectification of the operations of consciousness, which the reader is invited to identify in operation in his or her own consciousness, the basic operations can be sketched as an interlocking sequence of experiencing, understanding, judging, deliberating, evaluating and deciding. Each operation in itself is conscious and a particular manifestation of consciousness.[3]

Comparing this sketch to the faculty psychology presented in the *Cloud*, the power of reason corresponds to the operation of deliberation and the power of will corresponds to decision. As articulated in the *Cloud*, the power of sensuality combines the operations of experiencing and evaluating. The power of imagination combines understanding and judging, and the power of mind corresponds to consciousness itself. In this comparison, then, another inadequacy of the *Cloud*'s faculty psychology becomes apparent. Its conflation of distinct operations of consciousness into one power in the case of sensuality and imagination render it insufficiently precise.

It will be recalled that the grammar of mystical interiority in the *Cloud* identifies a simple reaching out to God as corresponding to an interior state in which all the powers of the soul are quiescent and in which there is no object, either material or spiritual, occupying the mind. To transpose this into the terms and relations of intentionality analysis requires the clarification and functional relation of four terms:

consciousness, intentional consciousness, mystical consciousness and the ground of consciousness.

"Intentional consciousness" is a pattern of operations (e.g., experiencing, understanding, judging, etc.) by means of which a subject seeks to understand, know and evaluate a particular object--where "object" is defined functionally as whatever is intended by those operations. The intentional object, therefore, may be a tree or consciousness itself. Knowing and valuing *per se* are acts of intentional consciousness.

In contrast, "consciousness" refers to the experience of being present to oneself as conscious. This is not another intentional operation. The term "consciousness" refers to that awareness which is immanent in all intentional operations. Taken in this sense, consciousness is not an object; it is the ground or possibility of conscious intentionality. Thus, whereas consciousness can be known "as object" through intentional inquiry, it is experienced "as consciousness" through a heightened awareness of one's own awareness, that is, of the ground of one's intentional operations.

The third term, "ground of consciousness," is functionally related to "consciousness" as the source of its possibility. In doctrinal language, it is referred to in the *Cloud* as "God." The question as to whether or how the "ground of consciousness" is identical to, or different from, "consciousness" itself is the sort of question to be worked out through the analysis of grammars of mystical interiority.

The fourth term, "mystical consciousness," may be introduced by noting that mystical consciousness is related to "consciousness" as consciousness is related to intentional operations. That is to say, if "consciousness" entails a heightened awareness of the ground of "intentional consciousness," "mystical consciousness" entails a heightened awareness of the ground of awareness, of the "ground of consciousness." Thus, mystical consciousness differs from the ground of consciousness in that it refers to the experience by which one is present to that ground.

Specified in the language of the *Cloud*, (1) "intentional consciousness" corresponds to the powers of the soul, and hence, in its absence, both to the cloud of unknowing and to the cloud of forgetting. (2) "Consciousness" corresponds to the power of the mind. (3) The "simple" sense of self or mind corresponds to an experience in which the individual simply experiences his or her own "consciousness," both apart from any particular operation of "intentional consciousness" and yet not explicitly aware of the "ground of consciousness." (4) The "ground of consciousness" corresponds to what the author of the *Cloud* means by God. (5) "Mystical consciousness" corresponds to the simple reaching out to God, the awareness of God that emerges when intentional consciousness is inoperative (the cloud of unknowing) and the "simple" sense of the self has been transcended. The correspondence of this grammar to Patanjali's *Yoga Sutras* is the subject of the next section.

"THE YOGA SUTRAS"

As the *Cloud of Unknowing* is a classic of Christian spirituality, so the *Yoga Sutras* are a classic of Hindu spirituality. They are similar in that both present grammars of mystical interiority; they differ in the scope of their treatment. The *Cloud* is a text for the beginner in contemplation; its focus is narrow. The *Yoga Sutras* is a text for an adept contemplative. The *Cloud* is therefore also expansive and repetitive regarding its subject, whereas the *Yoga Sutras* consists in a highly condensed, functionally related technical vocabulary threaded together in 196 *sutras*. In what follows, then, I will first sketch the scope of the *Yoga Sutras* and then focus on the point in which the two texts meet.

Patanjali divides the *Yoga Sutras* into four sections. The first section, called *Samadhi Pada*, is designed to answer the general question: What is Yoga? The second section, called *Sadhana Pada*, has two parts. The first part gives an analysis of the conditions of human life; the second part deals with the first five, or preliminary practices of Yoga. The third section, called *Vibhuti Pada* also has two parts. The first deals with the three remaining practices of Yoga which culminate in "samadhi," the contemplative state sought by Yogis. It is this part which corresponds to the principal focus of the *Cloud*. The second part of the third section deals with the powers or "siddhis" which are acquired in the course of contemplation. The fourth section, called *Kaivalya Pada*, deals with the philosophical problems which are involved in the study and practice of Yoga.

The claim I wish to advance here is that when the author of the *Cloud* speaks of the "simple reaching out to God," he is referring to the same inner experience of which Patanjali speaks of in the *Yoga Sutras* when he refers to an experience of "nirbija samadhi." What does Patanjali mean by "nirbija samadhi"? Like the author of the *Cloud*, he explains both "nirbija" and "samadhi" by correlating them with the operations of consciousness.

"Samadhi" is one of the basic terms in the *Yoga Sutras*. Patanjali employs it to designate a particular state of contemplation. In order to specify it accurately, he defines it in relation to two other terms, "dharana" and "dhyana." "Dharana" refers to a state of concentration on an object in which the mind may wander occasionally to other objects (III-1.275). "Dharana" refers to a deepened state of concentration in which there are no distractions at all (II1-2.278). "Samadhi" refers to a still deeper state in which not only are there no distractions, but there is no awareness of the mind or of consciousness itself. As Patanjali puts it, "when there is consciousness only of the object of meditation and not of itself (the mind) there is *samadhi*" (III-8.281). Clearly, the three terms refer not to different techniques, but to a deepening state of concentration. Considered together, Patanjali refers to the dynamic process of *dharana-dhyana-samadhi* as "samyama" (III-4.286).

It is obvious from the preceding discussion that the state of samadhi is attainable in relation to any number of objects. In fact, Patanjali distinguishes four principal classes of objects upon which "samyama" can be performed (I-41-50). The term he uses to refer generally to these types of *samadhi* is "sabija samadhi," that is *samadhi* with an object or "seed" (I-46.114). He designates a more advanced state of contemplation, however, with the term we have already met, "nirbija samadhi." This is "seedless" *samadhi*, or *samadhi* without an object (I-51.122-124;III-8.-292). It is the state of *samadhi*, which opens upon the experience of enlightenment or liberation, which Patanjali refers to as "kaivalya" (II-25.198;III-51.365;III-56.372).

Patanjali, in fact, extends his grammar of mystical interiority to discriminate several factor related to *nirbija samadhi* and *kaivalya*, but since the author of the *Cloud* chose not to do the same, these distinctions will not detain us here. What is of importance is the comparison of the grammars of mystical interiority presented by Patanjali and the author of the *Cloud*. For when "nirbija samadhi" is compared with "a simple reaching out to God," by correlating both with the terms drawn from intentionality analysis a striking similarity emerges.

First, the fact that "nirbija samadhi" is without an object or seed, indicates that there is a quiescence of intentional consciousness, an entry into the clouds of unknowing and forgetting. Second, the experience of consciousness itself, which the *Cloud* refers to as the "simple" experience of the self, is also transcended. By definition, *samadhi* is a state without awareness of the mind. Thus, in a state of seedless *samadhi*, even an awareness of consciousness without an object disappears. Hence, third, *nirbija samadhi* is the opening up of mystical consciousness, aware of its transcendent ground. This corresponds to the state of a "simple reaching out to God" in the *Cloud* and marks a state of union of wills with the divine. Patanjali identifies it as "kaivalya," the state of liberation.

Clearly, there is much work to be done in developing a comprehensive grammar of mystical interiority and in the careful analysis of mystical texts. However, if the foregoing argument is sound, then I think it evident that the study of mystical texts presents a promising entry into the fascinating and important discussions associated with the cross cultural study of religion.

The Catholic University of America
Washington, D.C.

NOTES

*See Discussion VII.

1. *The Cloud of Unknowing*, edited, with an introduction by James Walsh, preface by Simon Tugwell (Ramsey N.J.: Paulist Press, 1981).

2. *The Science of Yoga*, translation and commentary by I.K. Taimni (Wheaton, Ill.: Theosophical Publishing, 1961).

3. Bernard Lonergan, *Method in Theology* (New York: Herder and

Herder, 1972), chapter 1.

THE UNITY OF HUMAN NATURE

AND THE DIVERSITY OF CULTURES

KENNETH L. SCHMITZ

Two intersecting problems which are as old as philosophy itself are the problems of the one and the many and of the same and the different. Nowadays, however, they intersect with unprecedented frequency and intensity. One of the factors that contributes to the intensity is the increasing experience of what I will call *cultural pluralism*. Let me say what I mean, first taking the terms separately and then together.[1]

The human community may be viewed in several ways; among them are the political, social and cultural. I will use the term *culture*, not in its aesthetic sense but primarily in its anthropological sense. That is, culture is the distinctive ensemble of more or less stable and general ways in which a community and its members act, an integer of customs, values and traditions, usually bound together by a common language and often by common group memories.[2] The political domain, on the other hand, is the organization by which group decisions are arrived at and carried out; the concrete network of relationships which carries the cultural heritage and which grounds the political structure comprises the social body. On this understanding, the term *political* is meant to designate the group's power of decision and action, the *social* stands for the matrix of the common life, and the *cultural* refers to the manner or mode of that life. In this sense, the cultural taken in itself is always an abstraction from the social matrix in which it is embedded and which it helps to form and animate. The general term "culture", then, is a rough, variable, vague term, to be used more in pointing to specific cultures than in defining them exactly. Undeniably, there *are* specific cultures and, equally undeniably, there is a *diversity* of them, usually designated by differences of language and organization, and less obviously by differences of custom and tradition.

By the term *pluralism*, however, I do not mean simple plurality, the mere co-existence of different versions of something. Thus, for example, a plurality of philosophical positions is not philosophical pluralism, and a mere variety of cultures is not cultural pluralism. Pluralism rests upon a direct experience of otherness which is of such an impact that it is difficult to remain indifferent to it or relate to it as something quite outside our concern. That is why, for example, philosophical pluralism requires us to relativize our own philosophy; we must internalize other philosophical positions by considering our own not as absolute, but instead as placed within the context of other positions which are not without their own measure of truth. This does not surrender the hegemony of truth to mere relativism; on the contrary, it demands that we submit our own philosophical judgments to the sole interest of true knowledge. Such submission takes the form of criticism from others, further reflection on our own part, and a ready openness to further truth. In a word, we are forced to distinguish between our own philosophy and philosophy itself, and between full truth and our incomplete understanding of it.[3] For all the differences between philosophy and culture, a similar readjustment is required of us by cultural pluralism.

CULTURAL PLURALISM

Cultural pluralism, in the sense in which I mean it, then, consists of the recognition: (i) that human life has taken shape among groups organized according to more or less distinct sets or ensembles of ways, customs, techniques and traditions; (ii) that these ways form more or less loose, more or less consistent totalities (even with internal contradictions) which, taken as a whole, are radically diverse from one another; and (iii) that no one culture exhausts the possibilities of being human or the human possibilities of group life. Each culture is in some sense a whole, though it may be a porous one. That is to say, the recognition of the specificity and diversity of cultures does not require the denial of interaction between them, or of the cross influences that alter them, or of the internal and external forces that contribute to their birth and rise or to their decline and death.

Let me here suppose a theory of culture-formation, intended to suggest two general sources of cultural diversity. Since our empirical and pre-historical knowledge is as yet imperfect, my suppositions must remain somewhat speculative and had best remain as simple as possible--simple, to be sure, but not overly simplified for the present purpose. I assume the following: that in the early development of the race humans lived together in small bands, largely separated from one another for purposes of adequate feeding-range and that they gradually spread out into new environments. As their concentration must have been upon meeting survival needs, external conditions must have played a dominant role. Nevertheless, in speculating about human beings it would be foolhardy to assign to such a *search for survival (esse)* the sole cause of diversity.

As survival needs were more or less successfully met, a second source of diversity (undoubtedly always there, since we see faint anticipations of it among the primates) increasingly made its demands. I will call it a *search for meaning (bene esse)*, hoping that the term will not be mistaken for some exotic and ethereal enterprise, but will be understood instead to be the exercise of human intelligence as it combines a particular curiosity regarding details at hand with a general wonder regarding natural and human events, including those of life and death. The presence of this search is indicated by the improvement in techniques, by the early graves and cult objects, and eventually by the myths and rituals.

With this second source of culture formation the human imagination comes into play, drawing upon feelings, memory and intelligence. This second source of diversity was wont to be called the human spirit, but with the current emphasis upon hermeneutics, it may be more easily recognized under the name of *interpretation*. With the imagination, there breaks open a field of possibilities that, combined with the differences of physical conditions among the various bands or groups, has led to the variety of social organization and cultural pattern which is so marked a feature of human existence. It is not relevant to our topic to generalize further concerning the development of cultures, especially since the remarkable variety of conditions would require detailed studies within which various tribes and nations (in the cultural not the political sense) are formed. It is enough to recognize that most cultures, if not all, embrace and animate a variety of communities which share a common language and common customs, experiences and memories.

Now, cultural pluralism is an *attitude* toward other cultures, but even more it is an attitude towards one's own. For it relativizes one's own culture by situating it within the broader indefinite context of cultural diversity. Moreover, the relativization must be so thorough that no specific culture can claim to be the absolute centre among the various cultures, in the way in which Hegel, for example, thought of Northern European culture as the best realization of human possibilties. It follows from this that we are required to renounce the attitude of cultural imperialism whose slogan is: "We the Greeks" and the rest "the *barbaroi.*" Admittedly, it is very difficult--perhaps impossible--to relativize our own culture in so thorough-going a manner. Only the rarest among us has no remnant of the attitude expressed by the English lady travelling abroad for the first time. When reminded that she was now a foreigner, her eyes blazed as they swept the alien crowd, and in shocked tones she protested: "But *they* are the foreigners." What is more, it may not be desirable--always and for everyone--to relativize one's culture so thoroughly. Given our imperfections, it is difficult to retain pride in one's own cultural heritage without absolutizing it, on the one hand, and, on the other, to cultivate a critical spirit towards it without abandoning it for nihilism.

Cultural pluralism, then, is an attitude toward a specific sort of difference. It accepts the fact that humans have organized themselves in radically different ways and that no one way recommends itself as the *only* adequate human way, or even as the best possible way. Whether gladly or with reluctance, the cultural pluralist accepts the condition of being human as one of enculturation, and accepts the fact that the enculturation of the human race is radically multiform--no matter how adaptible, shifting and obscure the exact boundaries might be that differentiate cultures in any region or at any time. Nor is the attitude of cultural pluralism without an added risk; for, in the face of the bewildering complexity of human diversity, it is easy to lose sight of the features common to the face of humanity, and to let them dissolve into a plethora of variety. An antipathy towards what is common led Nietzsche to re-mark that the differences within humanity are greater than the differences between man and beast. The suspicion grows that the unity of being human is more apparent than real. Yet these cultures are one and all *human*. As they are totalities of organization brought about by human agency, there is at the very least an implicit unity in the diversity. We have come, then, to the topic of the present enquiry: the unity of human nature and the diversity of cultures. It is, as I have said, a specific form of the ancient problem of the one and the many, and of the same and the different: How are we to understand the diversity of cultures *and* the unity of humanity?

MODERN UNIFORMITY AND HUMAN UNITY

The question: whether and in what sense humanity is one? is a question that rebounds upon the questioner, and even upon humanity itself. It is important to ask whether the unity of being human is a hollow mask, for if it is it would not be possible to speak on behalf of *man as such* a word that counts and is no bare verbalism. Humanism, both theistic and atheistic, would prove to be an empty shell. To be sure, in Western philosophy--and also within some religious philosophies of the Orient, as well as in many pre-literate myths--there is an explicit or at least implicit sense of the unity of mankind, but it has not usually taken full account of human diversity. Then, too, the question is not one only for philosophers or for intellectuals. It is also answered in various ways in the *fora* of human life: more or less explicitly by those who advocate human rights, by those who seek to strengthen international law, by many who protest nuclear war, and by those who cross boundaries of class and nation to remedy conditions of poverty and human misery. It is answered more or less implicitly by those engaged in trade, in communi-cations and in travel, in scientific and cultural exchanges; and in nega-tive ways--sadly--even by those who wage war against their fellow humans, since, strictly speaking, wars are waged principally by humans, allegedly for humans, against humans.

Of course, in the present situation there is not only diversity; there are forces of unification working towards the interdependence of hu-mans. International and inter-cultural meetings are a feature of what has been called "modernity." Closely associated with "modernization" is the spread of scientific technology, which provides the impetus for industri-alization, mechanization, urbanization and systemic interdependence. Like most human movements, this massive force which is constituted of a series of revolutions in sources of energy, techniques of production, modes of transportation and possibilities of communication, is ambiva-lent with regard to the advantages and disadvantages it has brought humankind. Western society has committed itself so unreservedly to the process--and seems likely to carry other societies a considerable way with it--that it is unrealistic to speak of turning back, even if that were desirable, which I am convinced it is not.

But modernization can become more than a process. Although unremitting and unambiguously beneficent "progress" has been rejected *as an idea* in many quarters today. Nevertheless, it still operates within the process of modernization as a good or ideal for humanity as such. The unity it offers *in its present state*[4] consists in a rather restrictive uniformity.[5] The reason for this is that the forces of modernization have to do basically with time and motion. In standardizing the processes of production, exchange and consumption, the systemic interdependence which modernity fosters cannot easily brook different qualities of time and movement, cannot tolerate slower or faster rates of movement which are out of synchronization with the demands of the system. But, precisely, the customs and institutions of many traditional cultures are especially sensitive to the quality of time, movement and periodicity; and when they do not "come on line," when they do not fall in with the current technological rhythm, it is easy to look upon them as impediments to be swept away in the name of the advantages of modernization. Such standardization is characteristic of the present form of the processes of modernization.

To be sure, there are indications, admittedly slight as yet, of a will to restrict the indiscriminate application and to modify the uniformity of modernization. The growing awareness of the related problems of pollution and exhaustion of resources has encouraged a moment of reflection within the so-called advanced industrial societies on the part of some of their members and even very slightly of society as a whole. Such a reflection takes shape through the formation of new social movements of concern. It is possible, too, that the as yet largely untried resources of other cultures may lead to a containment and a modification of these massive forces. But in their present form and in respect to the traditional cultures, these forces posit a countervailing force which often amounts to a counter-culture. That counter-culture contains within it a more or less definite sense of human unity that is at odds with radical cultural diversity.

It is by no means obvious that such uniformity is the appropriate cultural expression of the unity of humankind. Is there, however, a modern unity compatible with its age-long diversity? The question is a real one, especially given the resilience with which some traditional cultures have tried to insist upon their own values and ways. Unfortunately, that insistence takes shape too often as an ineffectual rear-guard action, or as an indiscriminate reaction against all things modern. But, to the extent that such cultures are influenced by modernization, they receive more than consumer products; they also ingest modern attitudes towards work and play, towards individuality and sociality, towards the relation between the sexes, and a wide range of other attitudes. They also learn to prefer purely technical solutions to human problems. Above all, they receive historical consciousness, i.e., a sense of rupture and loss of direct communion with their immediate past, in part because of the rapidity with which the social environment changes. For better and for worse, the past loses authority over the present and the future. As a result, being unable to be defended today by an appeal to tradition, traditional cultures are bereft of their surest power. But neither can nostalgia bridge the gulf, since its unreal quality only empties traditional cultures of their seriousness and reduces them to costume dancing and exotic cuisines, an intermittent fringe upon the allegedly "serious" core of modern life.

In sum, modernization in its present form, while it often does increase differences among individuals, works at a deeper level towards an ideal of unity that requires standardization in fundamentals. The question now becomes: Is the unity of humankind compatible with the non-uniformity of cultures? The question calls for an enquiry into the relation between what is individual and what is common to humans. As so often, I find a turn to Aristotle makes a good beginning.

HUMAN COMMONALITIES AND CULTURAL SPECIFICITY

In speaking of the entities or ontological units which he thought primary, Aristotle never separated their common basis or *commonality* from their individuality, though he distinguished these two features and made them constitutive of the primary entities.[6] I say "constitutive" not "compositive," in order to insist upon the originality and primacy of the whole entity, whose principles of individuality and commonality are neither prior to, nor consequent upon, its integrity. Among the terms Aristotle used to designate the primary entities is an especially apt one: *tode ti,* "this something of a certain kind." Although he *distinguished* the two factors expressed by this term, he never *separated* them from one another, since there could be no "this" (*tode*) without a nature of some "kind" (*ti*). We might ask, then, in the case of human beings what this "kind" (*ti*) might be. If we remain within the illumination provided by Aristotle's thought, without pretending to repeat his explicit teaching, a development of the meaning of *ti* recommends itself that is not incompatible with his thought and yet suggestive for ours.

The *tode* indicates the individuality or singularity that characterizes Aristotle's primary entities. But it is not an isolated individuality; and a moment's reflection upon the physical make-up of the human individual confirms his or her dependence upon other human beings, as well as upon a suitable natural, technical and social environment.[7] Moreover, as I have already mentioned, recent anthropological study of early humans suggests that human individuals lived in small bands, perhaps of forty to fifty individuals of varying age, from infancy to seniority, so that the human *this* (*tode*) is deeply embedded in group-existence. Indeed, the lone man is not only an abstraction from, but is usually a tragedy in, the real order. The inseparability of the *this* (*tode*) that is distinguishable but not separable from the *kind* (*ti*) becomes in the real situation of human beings the ineradicable interdependence of the individuals with each other in the context of the kind. With this in mind we might look again at the *ti*.

The primary sense of the *ti* is factoral.[8] It is the basis for answering the question: What is it (*ti esti*)?, and constitutes *what* the individual is. First of all, taken in its most general sense, it ranges the human alongside other types of substance, as a distinctive kind of substance. Next, taken in its biological sense, the human *ti* names the species, and situates the whole of humanity in relation to other biological genera and species.[9] When philosophy learned to speak Latin, the term *natura* came to be taken as more or less equivalent to the Greek term *physis*; indeed, the term *physis* is derived from *phuo*: "to grow," even as *natura* is derived from *nascitur*: "to be born." Nevertheless, the emphasis, usage and application of the two terms differ, especially in relation to their cognate terms within their respective cultures. In some instances, where the Greeks preferred to use the terms *ousia* and *eidos* to answer the question *ti esti*?, the Latin usage preferred *natura* or the neo-logism *essentia* to answer the question *quid sit*? And so even the gods and God were said in Latin to possess a "nature." In this sense, then, essence and nature came to designate the same factor within a being, but with the term "essence" emphasizing the kind, and the term "nature" emphasizing that which followed from the kind.[10] We are still, however, within the broad suggestive light of Aristotle's *ti*, as we try to bring to further determinate expression the commonality shared by human individuals.

For the sake of consistency, then, I use the term "human nature" to indicate the kind (*ti*), the term "being human" to indicate the ontological mode of human existence, the term "human being" to indicate a concrete human individual (*tode ti*), the term "humankind" (and occasionally "human race") to indicate the unity of all past, present and future human beings *in their concrete unity*, but also with reference chiefly to actually existing humanity. Finally, I use the term "humanity" indefinitely to mean several of the above senses at the same time or to express an unrestrictedly general sense. It is in this ancient Graeco-Latin context, with nuances which still reverberate in Western philosophy, that I put the question about the unity of humankind in the face of the diversity of human cultures: What is the being, essence or nature of humanity that has realized and expressed itself in a diversity of cultures?

There is more meaning in the human kind, the human *ti*, of course, than its being ranged alongside other kinds of substances and other animate species. Indeed, several further meanings of commonality suggest themselves. First of all, Aristotle appreciated full well the distinctive social nature of human beings, and held the conviction that human life could be lived fully only in the *polis*, that strange institution which was neither a city nor a state in our sense of the word. And it remains true that human beings are communitarian: they are meant to live (*esse*) and can live humanly (*bene esse*) only within or in relation to a community. Now, the warp and woof of a society and its specific culture are made of the commonplaces shared among the people of that culture: their values, customs and memories. But the social fabric also includes many special roles, offices and institutions which take their meaning from the society and its culture as a whole, so that they too are commonalities. That is, both the commonplaces and the special institutions are not merely structures or modalities possessed by the culture, but are realities and idealities shared and sustained within it.

As long as we attend to a single specific culture, these commonalities may be designated as *intra-cultural* universals. Such essential commonalities include the way in which the acquisition and distribution of the food supply is organized, some recognition of what constitutes membership in the society, some more or less determinate accommodation between the sexes, some arrangement for the nurture and enculturation of the young, some specification of what constitutes a crime against the society or its members, etc. The commonalities vary in content, specificity and application, not only from one specific culture to another, but also within the same culture, either over the course of time or even over different regions pervaded by the same culture. Still, to the degree to which the culture constitutes a more or less effective whole, particular modifications reflect the total culture within which they are situated.[11]

The culture is often open to alien influences, adaptable both from within and without, but its commonalities or universals together constitute a cultural totality which may be considered as a cultural type, such as the French or Japanese. How are we to understand the character of the unity that stamps such a cultural type? To the degree that an individual is enculturated in a specific culture, she or he participates in its essential commonalities. However, to "participate in" a culture does not mean primarily to receive an individuating property or attribute that marks a person as belonging to a type, as we might speak of a Percheron draught horse or a Canadian Grizzly bear. Rather, participation in a culture means living with other members of the culture in the atmosphere of its pervasive and dynamic commonalities.

Now, as soon as the diversity of cultures is taken seriously and recognized as the age-long condition in which human nature has existed and continues to exist, then the concept of a specific cultural type falls short of what is needed in order to account for the unity of human nature. For there is no one cultural type, at least not yet, and the differences of culture may be too great to be retained within a single super-culture.[12] Even if a single world-culture is presently forming under the impetus of modernization--which I hold to be a dubious assertion, given the determination of various cultures to continue in existence--the super-culture would have to relate to the existing diversity in one of two ways: either it would have to depreciate the importance of the differences and ultimately eradicate them, or it would have to recognize their importance and somehow accommodate them. It is the meaning of the "somehow," then, that is the focus of the question.

THE PRESENCE OF HUMAN NATURE
IN DIFFERENT CULTURES

The situation may be put thus: human cultures are diverse, human nature is somehow one. Of course, how we put the question may already dispose us towards an answer. If we put the question as follows: *Despite the diversity of cultures, how is human nature one?* then the adversative clause turns us in a quite different direction than if we were to ask: How, *in and through* the diversity of cultures, is human nature one? I will put the question in this latter form, for three reasons. First, the opening word "despite" in the first formulation does not merely accentuate the diversity, it suggests that it is an obstacle, whereas the opening word "how" in the second formulation accepts the possibility that the diversity can be the means for securing the unity. Secondly, we have known no other human condition than a diversity of cultures, so that the factual evidence (though it does not establish necessity in the future) bids us to work with the materials provided us. Thirdly, I give credit to the intuition that a single uniform culture, being limited, would be less abundant in its resources and possibilities than a variety of cultures is likely to be. I favor this intuition because it seems to me that we need a variety of human resources for the solution of problems and the enrichment of the quality of human life. This intuition or supposition bears a predilection towards plenitude, a bias towards diversity, and entertains the conviction that, even if the physical conditions of human existence come to be more or less standardized, the imaginative and interpretive energies could still seek to express, not only individual peculiarities, but also distinctive social and cultural totalities, sustained by language, history, traditions and a particular arrangement of values. At any rate, instead of simply letting the forces of unity and diversity contend, it seems to me to be worthy of philosophy in the present situation to try to determine in what way, if any, human nature may be one *in* the diversity of cultures. Let me look at three answers which might be given.

The concept of *family resemblances (Familienaehnlichkeiten)*[13] in which a member of a family resembles one member in certain ways but still another member in other ways--fits the situation in regard to certain interrelated particular differences among cultures. What is more, the concept can be therapeutic against a notion that would represent human nature as a static and unreal eternal essence. But it does not seem to me that such a chain of family resemblances--in which one culture is like another in one respect, and like still another culture in another respect--is strong enough to establish either the pervasive commonality that constitutes a specific culture, or the commonality of a human unity that may be found to underly all cultures. It seems to me that, while the concept of family resemblances preserves the differences admirably, it does not account sufficiently for the solidarity implied by the idea of humankind and even required as the basis of the rights and responsibilities which are associated with being human and which are implicit in many cultures and encoded in many civilizations.

The unity of mankind is not simply a descriptive term, it is also value-laden. The sense of *non-otherness* must be sufficiently strong to accommodate the almost instinctive response to other humans that marks our conduct in regard to them, and distinguishes it from our conduct with regard to other kinds of beings. That distinctive unity must be strong enough to ground the sense of sayings such as Hemingway's: "Ask not for whom the bell tolls, it tolls for thee"; or such as Terencius': "Nihil humanum mihi alienum est." Indeed, even in intensely negative moments of conflict, such as war, there is the recognition of a strong value-laden relationship. Nor is it a fatal objection to this felt unity to point out that human beings too often have identified--and too often still identify--"being human" (or at least, being "fully" human) with their own group and their own culture, and have accorded full rights only to those who are members of their group. For all that, the exclusive limitation--against the stranger, the aborigine, the Jew, the Black or the Catholic, against women or against the very poor--has often betrayed an uneasy suspicion that the outcast is really one of us. An ancient Egyptian priest wrote of the foreign Hyksos conquerors: "People who are not people are invading our country." The ambiguous struggle with cultural specificity and human universality is evident in the phrase: "people who are not people." But even today, we ought not to congratulate ourselves too easily, as though we are entirely free of the inclination to marginalize.

A second attempt to understand the unity of human nature within the diversity of cultures is provided by *analogy*.[14] Human nature can be understood univocally, i.e., as a type-term which is uniformly predicable of every individual human. In this sense, "human nature" is the *ti* in Aristotle's *tode ti*. Moreover, such a *ti* can be expanded beyond the conception of a natural species (whether physical or also biological) to include the social dimension of human life (the *polis*), so that a specific social and cultural milieu can itself be understood as one type among a variety of other social and cultural types. In this usage, the term "human nature" is used *univocally*.

If, on the other hand, we expand our consideration in order to seek out the unity of being human in the face of the diversity of cultures, then we need to go beyond univocal types. In order to appreciate the full force of analogy, we must get beyond the mistaken notion that analogous usage is primarily a form of identity-predication. Quite the contrary, it is an attempt of the mind and the word to situate commonality within radical diversity. Thus, for example, to cite the loosest and most fragile form of analogy: metaphorical or "improper" analogy--the dictionary will tell us that the word "wing," used of a bird and of an aeroplane, is used analogously. Such a metaphor does, indeed, find a commonality in respect to two such totalities which are as diverse as a feathered organism and a mechanical contrivance: they both sustain flight. The unity then can be siphoned off as an abstract meaning: "sustenance of flight." Ah! but what different flights! For in the concrete situation, their commonality cannot be separated out from their diversity, as one might pluck the feathers from a chicken or render pure gold from an alloy. Thus, analogical usage in general is a strategy for preserving the diversity of meaning even while it recognizes a certain unity of meaning inseparable from that diversity.

Nevertheless, metaphorical analogy will not suffice, unless, of course, human beings are only metaphorically one. So we turn to proper analogy. Consider the term "unity" and its derivatives. We can and most often do use the term univocally, as when--faced with a multiplicity of results as diverse as productions of agriculture, industry and culture--we compute products in terms of some standard of economic value (GNP, etc.). Such uniformity is required by the mathematical concept of unity, and is obviously of the greatest utility. But, if we go a little more deeply into the way in which things *are* one, we find a surprising non-uniformity. A dozen eggs, a painting by Matisse and the consensus of a nation are all in very diverse senses actually and properly one. But apart from a very general formula: "undivided being" (*ens indivisum*), which must itself be "cashed out" analogously, i.e., variously, neither the meaning nor the actuality of the way in which eggs form *a* dozen, colours blend into *a* painting and a nation comes to *a* consensus is detachable from the eggs, the Matisse or the nation. Proper analogy consists then of the recognition of a commonality that is *present and operative* in two or more diverse situations, yet is *inseparable* from each.

There are several forms of analogy, two of which may serve our consideration. First of all, there is the analogy of reference or *pros hen* equivocation (and its later modification as the analogy of attribution). In Aristotle's text on health[15] the organism is the primary analogue of medicine and exercise, of complexion and urine, all of which can quite properly be called "healthy." Each of these latter is related to health in the organism either as means to it or as sign of it. Such an analogy is teleological in character; and traditionally, i.e., in Aristotle and in a somewhat different way in Thomas Aquinas, such an analogy is grounded in substance or being, and ultimately in the divine being. In our present enquiry, however, we are looking for a more proximate ground: the unity of human nature in terms of humanity itself. Now, cultural pluralism has already set aside the supremacy of a single culture among the various cultures, as though it could be the central referent, as, for example, a Euro-centrism. That leaves human nature as the central referent of unity in the diversity of cultures. But human nature does not exist as such; it exists only in the different encultured individuals. That is to say, the human nature that is present and operative in all cultures is not something real in itself, since it is real only in its dispersal among the various cultures.

It is here that the analogy of proper proportionality[16] comes into play, since it does not require a real single primary referent, but rather recognizes a relation or proportionality of differing proportions between human nature and its diverse cultural realizations. Thus, to recall the example of analogous unity given above, the unity of a dozen eggs is proportioned to the collectedness of a heap, the unity of the Matisse to the harmony of an artefact, and the unity of a national consensus to the convergence of minds, wills and hearts. Similarly, one should expect that a human being will relate to language, to work, to the community, etc., in ways proportioned to and pervaded by the character of his or her culture. The advantage of this analogous strategy is that it helps us to understand the unique totality of each culture, while preserving the unity of being human among the diversity of cultures. The unity possessed by each encultured human is a "being related to a specific culture. . . ." But the disadvantage of analogy is its inability to further determine the real unity present in the diversity.

To recapitulate: In asking about the unity of human nature I began with the classical notion of universality: a meaning is universal if it can be said to hold for all instances; and necessarily so, insofar as it is what is essential to the kind or type. I softened up the notion of unity of type by suggesting the limited use of the concept of family resemblances, since it stresses the differences among the units. But because--or so it seems to me--such a concept does not give sufficient strength to the unity implied in the concept of humanity, I went on to analogy. The first proper mode of analogy, that of reference, stresses the unity of human nature, but--unlike the central referent in Aristotle's example, in which the healthy organism is an actual entity separable in reality from its food and medicine--there is no human being who exists without one or another or a mixture of cultural types. On the other hand, the second mode of analogy, that of proper proportionality, does stress the inseparability of the unity of human nature from its embodied diversity, but it fails to determine the unity *qua* human in a fully actual way.

We need, therefore, to pass on to another, more concrete mode of universality, and this passage implies a redirection of metaphysics and epistemology. Moreover, the direction of the quest renders the value-laden character of human unity explicit, and thereby discloses that the question all along has not been a disinterested question that is supposedly value-neutral. We have come more clearly in recent times to surmount the modern attempt to separate objective fact and subjective value, a pseudo-distinction of which the ancients were innocent. We have come to see that objectivity is itself value-laden. Indeed, truth itself is something worthy, without thereby having only subjective import. In using the term "value," then, I am conscious of the charges of subjectivism made against the term, stemming in part at least from its post-Kantian history; and I wish to discharge my own use of the term from such subjectivism. What I mean by value is primarily the ontological *worth* of anything (*Wert, virtus, arete*).

CONCRETE MODES OF COMMONALITY

A meaning may be said to be universal if it is referrable or applicable to a plurality; and a reality may be said to be universal if it is found or realized in many. We are asking, given the plurality of cultures, in what sense if any human nature is one and universal. Throughout the present essay I have used the term *commonality* to suggest that culture is not an ordinary universal property, such as the colour of one's eyes. Instead, culture is universal in the sense that it points to a pervasive and integral characterization of an individual, group or society. Indeed, it can be torn away from them, if at all, only in the very desperate situations which reduce human beings to the most elemental state of penury, and displace them to extreme marginality. The reality of culture is communal in that it draws the individual into a dynamic participation in a specific social and cultural milieu which is constituted by commonalities such as a shared language and a common heritage. The term "commonalities" is meant to indicate that these aspects are lived out with others and lived in common with them. A culture is universal in that many humans share in its determinate unity.

In order to throw light upon the sense in which human nature is one and universal, then, I turn to a further sense of commonality, and a different mode of universality. It has been present in philosophy for a long time, but it was Hegel who first gave it its most explicit attention. It is that sort of universality that does not attain its commonality by abstraction from the differences among its instances in the manner of a type-universal. For that reason it has been called an *embodied* or *concrete* universal. Although the latter designations are not quite satisfactory, they do stress the inclusion of differences *within* the universal itself, unlike the type- or class-universal whose instances are external to and abstract from it; and so it might also be called an *inclusive* universal. Such universality does not arise from the mere possession of the common type, in the way that adult male foxes, those solitary beasts, possess the same nature as others of their kind. Instead, it is closer to the universality of the herd, which anticipates (in however unflattering a manner) the social need of humans. A culture is universal not so much by reproduction and instantiation as by *participation*. The *ti* in this sense, then, is the universality of the band and of the *polis*, the commonality of the community. Here is universality not of type (*eidos*), but of totality (*Totalitaetsbegriff*).[17]

Now, within any society there are institutions that are universal and common in this way; they are *intra-cultural* universals. Since they impinge always or sometimes upon the life of all or most of its members, and with respect to the life of society as a whole, they are *communitarian* universals. Thus, in every society there is some arrangement for the exchange of goods between individuals and between groups. This, then, is a commonality. As anthropologists also tell us that it is an institution, we may speak of them as *institutional* universals because they are commonalities in which all or most members of a society and culture share, however occasionally or unequally. Now, it is in just this orientation towards the concrete that the question of the unity of *human nature* becomes the question of the unity of *humankind*. So, the question may be rephrased: How are we to understand the unity of *humankind* in the face of the diversity of its cultures? With this question we pass beyond the sphere of intra-cultural universals to the question of *inter-cultural* universals. How are we to understand these inter-cultural commonalities?

FROM INTRA-CULTURAL COMMONALITIES TO INTER-CULTURAL COMMONALITES

We may begin by observing that there are at least three different ways in which institutions play the role of inter-cultural commonalities. I shall set them out in the order in which they move more fully towards inter-cultural commonality. The first sort function as intra-cultural universals, but they are not specific to one culture, inasmuch as they are institutions which, though they may be invented in one culture, are reproduced in other cultures; they are universal by replication. Striking modern examples include hospitals, schools and universities, national airlines, standing armies, police forces, etc.

The second sort of inter-cultural universal is that of a single institution in which various cultures participate. By their very nature these institutions have a high degree of organization. Examples include the United Nations (including the full range of its activities in UNO, UNESCO, WHO, FAO, the World Court, etc.), the Roman Catholic Church, FISP (Fédération internationale des sociétés de philosophie), etc. These latter are in some sense trans-cultural, not that they are beyond all culture but that their principal *raison d'etre* is not simply embedded in any one specific culture. On the contrary, much of their influence is exercised in the inter-cultural sphere with respect to their principal purpose.[18]

These unique institutions closely approach the final sort of institutional universals, which I will call: *contextual* universals. They bear directly upon the question of the unity of mankind in the face of the diversity of its cultures. Unlike the second sort of institutional universal, such as the Church or the United Nations which act in their own names, these are joint ventures that exist *only* in the relation *between* cultures. In that sense, they are not culture-specific, though they are cultures-dependent. Examples are many and of very different character and unequal worth: war is one of them, though happily institutions need not be eternal; of necessity, from very early times and increasingly, international trade is another; more recently still, with both its educative value and its artificiality, tourism is yet another; so too are telecommunications. Nor can we forget the many causes and movements, such as that of the conservation of planetary resources and that of human rights; finally, there are meetings of intellectual, cultural and scientific character. I call these joint commonalities "contextual universals" because participants from a variety of cultures can share in the opportunities for which these universals provide the context.

It would be a mistake, however, to look upon the context as a merely external framework whose significance is exhausted by the efficiency of its organizational techniques and attention to administrative details. To be sure, these are the important *technical values* to be realized in such contexts, but there is much more. In intellectual, cultural and scientific meetings, for example, the selection and division of themes, the invitation of speakers, the arrangements for discussion should meet the demands of honesty and fairness, of openness and respect, of readiness to listen and to grow. These are deeply human values, and in the planning and execution of such inter-changes these values are put to the test and extended in a way quite other than in meetings within one's own culture. These are the *moral values* inherent in the contextual universals.

What is distinctive about them in these contexts is that the moral values are no longer simply ideals within one's conscience, nor embodied in the familiar conditions of one's own culture. Instead, they show up with strange faces, speaking in tongues other than one's own, carrying unfamiliar inheritances of memories and aesthetic sensibilities. In such contexts we are stretched to recognize--not simply the technical and the moral--but what I can only call the *anthropological values* of humankind as such. For there are in these contexts values that can be found only in the uncharted gaps *between* cultures, in which we glimpse the face of mankind as a whole. It is a face that cannot be detached like a mask from the diversity of humankind. Nor can it be compressed into a single shape by the imposition of a monoform culture, at least not yet and--I suspect--not without great pain and loss. In the human interval between the cultures, dynamic commonalities open up a space and sustain it for inter-action and inter-communication. In that space we may experience a bewilderment in the face of radically different attitudes and responses. The challenges of diversity, however, also contain within them the opportunities for developing the commonalities that are required if we are to build the actual unity of mankind in and among the diversity of its cultures. The unity of human nature has always existed as a type with its propensity for building a specific culture; but now the unity of humankind exists as a real possibility.

So understood, the *ti* of Aristotle is both a type and a work. The realization of the unity of mankind is the task of realizing a unity that is in accordance with, but not simply that of, type nor even only of analogy. It is instead the task of the actual and concrete realization of the interdependence of the whole of humankind. This unity of humankind lies before us as a still unrealized, or at best only partially realized, task. It is on the basis of the type (*ti*)--our need for social living--and within the analogous diversity of cultures--which has no single culture as its centre--that we are called to this unprecedented opportunity to realize the unity of humankind. These contextual universals, then, are in the nature of a Kantian regulatory ideal, but with this grave qualification: Kant thought of humanity in terms of the high European culture of his time. We, on the other hand, are being forced by fast-moving events to recognize that the reality of humankind will have to shape itself *in and through, between and among* the diversity of cultures. For the unity of human nature is no mere essence realized only in individuals and formed within specific cultures; it must also become a concrete interdependent reality that is to be realized as the joint product of the diverse cultures. That reality is taking shape even now; the task is to give it a human and not a de-humanized face.

Great forces of modernization are already carrying the work of unification forward. If it is not to culminate in the uniformity of a standardized culture with all the loss which that would entail, then thought and word and will need to be given-not merely to the preservation of the diversity extant in traditional cultures, for this would merely make a fetish out of difference--but to the positive opportunities the *space between* offers us: the opportunity to sift what is essential and what is best and best loved in one's own culture, to sift it from what needs eradication, correction or development, and to respect that process in others. The diversity of cultures will survive only if each culture carries out a critical reappropriation of its heritage and its as yet unfulfilled promise within what I have called the emerging contextual universals made possible by modernization. This will require more than submission to the pressures of modernization or subscription to the ideal of "modernity." It will require understanding, research, reflection, deliberation, judgment and the will to action. But it is a noble work in which human nature meets the openness of its historical existence.

The task will be helped, no doubt, by dialogue such as that which occurs at scientific and cultural meetings, not only in the formal sessions but in the informal conversations as well. But the exchange calls for listening as well as speaking, for we are being called to venture out into relatively unexplored seas, into unknown space between the cultures, in which we must recognize the freedom of others to contribute to what can only be the *joint* building up of the unity-in-diversity of humankind. Only such a joint undertaking will allay the mis-givings of a Buddhist colleague who once remarked in an inter-religious meeting that dialogues were inventions of the Christian and secular West, the last vestiges of the will to dominance. His suspicion is not without warrant.[19] Turning it upon myself, I must now relativize what I have just said, especially about contextual universals. I have presented them out of my own cultural situation as a Canadian and a Catholic.[20] I now make them as an offering towards a larger truth.

Trinity College
    University of Toronto
    Toronto, Canada

NOTES

1. A version of this paper was read at the International Congress of Philosophy in Cordoba, Argentina, September 1987.

2. See A. L. Kroeber and C. Kluckhohn, *Culture* (New York: Vin-

tage, n.d.), especially the emphasis upon rule or way (p. 95) and structure or pattern (p. 118).

3. See "Philosophical Pluralism and Philosophical Truth," *Philosophy Today*, 10 (1966), 3-18.

4. This took its fundamental shape during the 17th and 18th centuries, chiefly in France and England. See my "Enlightenment Criticism and the Embodiment of Social Values: The Hegelian Background to a Contemporary Problem," *Indian Philosophical Annual*, 18 (Madras: Radhakrishnan Institute for Advanced Study in Philosophy, 1985-86), 32-53.

5. The sophistication of developments in mathematics may help to mitigate the cruder forms of standardization associated with the earlier mathematization--or more precisely, mechanization--of science.

6. See "Community: the Elusive Unity," *Review of Metaphysics*, XXXVII (1983), 243-264.

7. Whatever juridical and political use the social contract theory might have, if one were to mistake it for an ontological statement about man--viz., that society is formed originally by contractual consent among fully developed adults--its artificiality would become immediately apparent. What is significant is the continuing, though decreasing, strength of its hold on many Western thinkers.

8. *Ti* is, in Aristotle, also the basis for the formation of what he called "secondary substances" (*deuterai ousiai*). We recognize them as abstract universals designating the logical species and genera of substances. But I set this meaning aside, since it is derivative from and rests upon the primary ontological sense.

9. This does not commit us to a doctrine of eternal species, since the human *ti* is capable of development within its boundaries or thresholds, and at one time did not exist (even the Greek myths spoke of that).

10. Cicero and Boethius played major roles in the translation of Greek terms into Latin. Heidegger has voiced his criticism of the results in *Einfuehrung in die Metaphysik*. Cf. also, Rainer Schuermann, *Heidegger on Being and Acting: From Principles to Anarchy*, tr. from the French by C.-M. Gros (Bloomington, Ind.: Indiana University Press, 1987); especially Part III, pp. 97-151. For my own understanding of principles (*archai*), see "Metaphysics: Radical, Comprehensive, Determinate Discourse," *Review of Metaphysics*, XXXIX (1986), 675-694.

11. Colin Turnbull, *The Mountain People*, has described the decline and death of a culture, brought about by internal failure of will and deliberate loss of social memory, as well as by desperate external pressures--a loss that affected all aspects of the culture.

12. Some indication of an over-extension of a single culture may find an analogue in the centrifugal tendencies of the English language brought about by its rapid world-wide diffusion, whereby it acquires differences of syntax as well as of vocabulary. This is a phenomenon exactly opposite to the relative isolation which in the past consolidated different dialects within a language.

13. See L. Wittgenstein, *Philosophical Investigations* (New York:

Macmillan, 1953), nn. 66-67 (pp. 31-32). Cf. *Blue Book* (Oxford: Blackwell, 1960), pp. 17-18.

14. For a profound yet general discussion of analogy with references to Aristotle and Thomas Aquinas, as well as to modern scholarship, see Gerard Smith and Lottie Kendzierski, *The Philosophy of Being* (New York: Macmillan, 1961), pp. 180-217.

15. *Metaphysica*, Book IV (Gamma), 2, 1003a34ff.

16. See Smith, *op. cit.*, pp. 208-210.

17. It is refreshing to remember that Aristotle's term for the universal (*katholou*) is used both for the conceptual whole grasped by the intellect (*Posterior Analytics* II, 19, l00a9-b3) and for the concrete whole which is apprehended by sense perception (*Physics* I, 1, 184a24-26). The concrete universal developed in this essay arises out of the modern problematic but also recalls the interplay between these two Aristotelian senses.

18. Multi-national commercial corporations and international labour unions are other examples.

19. Let me point out the promising work of a young French-Canadian philosopher, Jacques-Bernard Roumanes, who insists that we must go even beyond dialogue to something like what he calls "antithetic." If I have understood him, dialogue remains too close to monologue; see "Passer la pensée," forthcoming in the publication of the Second Bulgarian-Canadian Philosophical Colloquium, Varna, 1987.

20. My own country is, from its roots, the political union of two nations, two cultures, two languages: French and English. Within an even larger context, which includes the original peoples--the Dene and the Inuit--as well as the Metis, there must also be placed the later immigrants who brought something of their cultures (separated however from the primary institutions which fostered them). The task within Canada is to build up in the Canadian milieu what I have called contextual universals.--In a quite different sense, the multi-cultural character of the Roman Catholic Church calls for an analogous task. In this regard, it is interesting that the present Pontiff, who has written on philosophical anthropology, has set up a papal *Concilium pro cultura*.

DISCUSSION

A number of issues are involved in determining whether this study of problems regarding the relations between cultures should focus upon: (a) relations between cultural and ethnic groups, (b) modernization, as the progressive rationalization of the lives of ethnic groups, or (c) the relation between these two.

From the 1950s there has been a renewed and increasing sensibility by the various groups to their cultural and ethnic identity. Hence, the increasing rationalization of life does not necessarily correspond to a lessening of ethnic or cultural sensibilities.

When attention is directed primarily not to the economic or political dimension, but to cultural or ethnic identity the central issue becomes the components of each group's distinctive identity and the development and evolution of that cultural content in the form of a tradition. While keeping in view these issues of cultural content and boundaries, given the progressive involvement of smaller groups in ever larger units, it is helpful to consider such factors in analogous terms as a proportion of proportions, that is, to look at persons in relation to their ethnic group in a manner similar to the relation of the ethnic groups to such larger entities as nation or total cultural unit.

In this context a major issue is how the retention and promotion of ethnic identity can contribute to cooperation with other ethnic units in broader national or international contexts.

Alienation is an opposite phenomenon. Among other causes, this arises from colonization, oppression by dominant groups and the impact of cultural change or modernization through the development of abstract scientific knowledge and technical competencies. If alienation should prove to be an essential component of development, its role in the evolution of the major and sub units would need to be better understood. Case studies in the various cultural regions as well as in the areas of language, family and education could also prove helpful.

In sum, the issues to be explored include:

(a) the nature of cultural identity and identification,

(b) the causes and nature of inter-cultural conflict, and

(c) the resources for cultural complementarity, peace and progress.

These problems are experienced both by each culture in relation to their own processes of modernization, and between cultures the achievements of modernization bring them into greater contact/competition.

I. PERSONS, COMMUNITIES AND CULTURES
(See Chapter II)

Person bespeaks: (a) uniqueness: in contrast to a problem which can be solved and done away with, the person is a mystery; (b) integrity, which integrates all levels of reality; (c) understanding and behavior; and (d) a dynamic and enduring identity.

Relation: The person is relational. This is true with regard to world and to others, whether family or society, with whom we must be attuned.

Indian thought stresses the importance of avoiding selfish or egoistic affirmation and domination, and of affirming *sattva* or goodness as the principle of knowledge and equanimity.

Community: To be is to be with others; thus self-conciousness includes consciousness of others (and vice versa) for the person can exist only through a person. This implies the importance of availability. Hence, there is a contrast between: the I-it relation as experiencing and using others, which is marked by eros or selfish love; and the I-thou relation which is mutuality and presentness to others, and is marked by agapé or unselfish love. Community is neither I nor thou, but in between as "we". As this implies mutual respect and concern, human destiny and salvation lie in mutuality. Morality then means self-actuation with responsibility.

Building Community: The above qualities of dignity, uniqueness and goodness can be developed only through living for others in mutuality and trust. Intimacy is distinct from the two opposites: privacy which is seen more as a lack or a deficiency and is hence pejorative, and familiarity which is only a knowledge of details. Intimacy is openness to other's most profound and hidden meaning. This requires trust, both because only by self-disclosure can the other be aware of my most personal self, and because one cannot scrutinize every facet of the other: one must be willing to accept his basic openness to the good. Hence, the challenge is both to respect the other's privacy and to be willing to accept intimacy when the other is willing to reveal him or herself.

The Buddhist sense of community is strongly marked both by a sense of respect for the dignity of oneself and of others, and by compassion and willingness to be for the other. This is reflected in the Buddha's rejection of any vow of obedience in order that one not be the master of another. Yet, according to the Boddhisatva ideal, even after achieving enlightenment one might remain in the world in order to serve others.

II. THE NATURE AND ORIGIN OF A CULTURAL TRADITION
(See Chapter I)

Culture is created by the person, but the locus of culture is the community. It is important to avoid a restrictive sense of culture by which one might limit one's community according to a single aspect, e.g., one's religion. A broader sense of community with nature and of mankind as needed. This requires searching within one's culture for elements of transcendence by which one can open one's sense of community to other people and to union with all of nature.

The etymology of the term "culture" may be derived from:

(1) "Cultivation," as in agriculture, stressing that a person must be prepared carefully if he or she is to be creative in character, taste or judgment (see *paidea, bildung*), or

(2) "Civilization" as stressing that one must be a member (*civis*) of a group in order for such cultivation to take place. This sense can have positive overtones, as when "tradition" is treated as it is below, or nega-

tive overtones of exclusion and disdain (*barbaroi*).

While it is the person who acts, to act precisely as a person is to act in terms of one's capacity for self-consciousness and self-determination. If, however, the *self* must be understood in relation to *group,* then self-consciousness is developed in terms of group-consciousness and group-determination which, in turn, is passed on as "tradition." In a pluralistic context the existence of multiple traditions constitutes the issue of relation between cultures.

The human self has not merely an animal awareness bound to, and by, the physical environment; it is able to take up this environment in a manner that is self-conscious or self-aware (knowing that one knows), possessing it as a right rather than merely as a physical fact, and hence being able to shape it through the creative production of food, clothing and shelter. This self-consciousness and self-determination is enmeshed and coordinated, not only with physical nature, but with our human environment, i.e., with others who are similarly conscious and free. This takes place on a number of levels, each one included successively and cumulatively in those that follow.

Hence, before birth one's life is synchronized with the rhythm of the life of one's mother. In infancy one is at home in one's family, and thereby able to develop self-confidence and self-expression. In childhood one learns behavior and language whereby one receives an elaborate pattern for interpreting and evaluating. In sum, one is born not into chaos, but into a cosmos, family and community that is intimately coordinated and delicately delineated.

Experience over extended time enables a group to learn what is good and important for it and for others, not only in terms of tactical adjustments for pragmatic purposes, but in terms of the real meaning of life and of values worthy of commitment. This is done freely and responsibly. Hence, "history" as including the bad (a Simon Legree) as well as the good (a Lincoln) must be distinguished from "tradition" which consists of what has been consciously interpreted and freely accepted, embraced, affirmed and cultivated.

Through their balanced realization of the values of their tradition one or another exceptional individual can become a classic instance of a culture. In turn, they may even become symbols (and myths) as they come to express, not only the partial tentative affirmations of meaning and value possible in their time (e.g., Lincoln's concrete decisions), but the fullness of those values which a people has accepted as principles upon which to build their community (e.g., Lincoln as enshrined in his Memorial).

In sum, the cultural component of ethnic identity arises through conscious and free choice from the experience of a people, and expresses their sense of meaning and values through symbols and myths. As will be noted below, these evoke in the members of the group a new awareness of the beauty of a tradition and a new response to its attractive power; in this way traditions can come to constitute norms for future action.

A cultural tradition is not then a set of past facts, but the effect of human consciousness as it responds freely to history and progressively articulates lessons learned regarding the meaning of life. Tradition is not distant or past oriented, but lives in the lives it inspires and judges. We do not reconstruct it, but belong to it as the ultimate community of human striving in which we are situated and on the basis of which we interpret our situation and respond to the challenges of life.

Hence, tradition as cultural model is not in the order of techné, an abstract complete and fixed ideal which is simply to be repeated in various circumstances. Rather, it is a guide in changing times to help human consciousness find an appropriate response which will unfold or supply more of the meaning of the vision of life, namely, the culture discovered through long experience. This is not to compromise, but to perfect and complete the tradition which lives and develops in new ways in each generation.

III. THE MEETING OF CULTURES AND OF PEOPLES
(See Chapter I)

Development of a culture requires prudence (*phronesis*) or choice adapted to the circumstances, which generally include other cultures. It requires also sagacity (*sunesis*) as the ability to share or experience concern for the difficulties of others. A failure of *sunesis* in one who nonetheless has some understanding of the situation results in a "terrible" person (Aristotle), i.e., one who can manipulate others for selfish and destructive purposes. Are the sole alternatives to *sunesis* either: destructive self-assertion in adversarial, even "cut-throat" competition, e.g., in business relationships, fundamentalist religious intolerance, balkanization of the intellectual life, commercial strife and even genocide; or homogenization which would abandon one's self-identity and produce the truly "terrible" specter of successive generations without heritage, dignity, norms or compassion? If so then our future would be bleak indeed.

To respond to this threat a number of notions must be clarified. First of all the person's "horizon" is universal, or all of being, but precisely as this can be seen from the vantage point of one's cultural heritage. This is not a blinder but a lens, ground through centuries of experience, which enables those born and educated within it to see with discernment and to respond humanely. It is necessary to "de-absolutize" and with self-awareness consciously to situate this lens in order to be open and to relate to the achievements of other cultures using other lenses.

A number of factors make possible such de-absolutizing and openness:

- the nature of human consciousness as able to take up, inspect and respond to options;
- increased communication and contact between cultures in our days;
- the development of new paradigms and even of new Archimede-

an vantage points (see the papers of Prof. C. Turek) not only for abstract models of techné but for ethics and aesthetics;
 - religious perspectives which relativize all human achievements in relation to the really absolute.

The *logic* of this process of opening is that of being questioned. This supposes that though one's mind is open to all, one's sensibility is always limited and in part distorted. Therefore, one's attitude should not be that of argument or opinion to defend one's position and suppress all other vision. Rather, one needs to promote the expression of views which will challenge one's own cultural tradition and thereby make possible one's own liberation, not from one's own tradition which is the indispensable basis or lens for one's vision, but from the limitations and/or distortions of that lens. This is able to be realized most fully and profoundly through attentive dialogue with members of other groups with whom I am in contact, and perhaps especially with those least integrated into, or even "marginalized" by, nation or state.

The basic attitude here is that my heritage has something new to say to me. That is, our search is not to find something exotic or alien which at best with difficulty, and only to a limited degree, can be integrated into one's life and vision. Rather, through being questioned, one is enabled to reach more profoundly into one's own heritage of wisdom in order to draw out the new applications required for our day. Paradoxically, this ability to reach into one's own culture is convergent with openness to dialogue with other cultures. This may indicate that such extrinsic factors as prophetic religions, intercultural exchange and even clashes may be not entirely negative, but required as catalysts for cultural growth.

Transcending One's Ethnic and Cultural Identities

The unique intensity and depth of meaning of ethnic identity appears in the impact of an ethnic slight; this is felt more strongly and forgiven less readily than an insult received as an individual. This sensitivity and passionate involvement extends to the group's history in which one takes pride or experiences hurt, and through which one is committed to certain ideals and burdens. Hence, the history of one's ethnic group is very important and a serious factor in interaction. Further, it would be incorrect to consider ethnic sensibility a waning holdover from the past. If anything, it is a special phenomenon of our times or at least has achieved a new consciousness in recent decades.

In view of all this it could be suggested that it be assured that the various ethnic groups simply be left untroubled. But this was the rationale for the Indian reservations in the U.S. and for the homelands in South Africa. Even if honestly proposed and, above all, freely accepted, the commercial and other dynamics of modern life appear to be moving the various groups inevitably into ever more intense interaction.

It could be feared that any type of categorization is limiting and that to be identified ethnically could be restrictive. This would be true only if ethnic identity were asserted in a reductive manner, that is, if one's culture were taken as a limiting rather than an enabling base.

Nevertheless, given the passionate character of ethnic involvement and the tensions which can arise within countries due to resultant clashes of cultural groups, some consider it necessary to transcend ethnic identification. Noting the ability of the human person to be many things, some think it better to base one's primordial attachments simply upon common geography: a new nationality for immigrants; upon needs, interests and aspirations: a new city for those who move for career opportunities; or upon language: even if this be an adopted or a neutral one such as English in Nigeria or India. Thus, for instance, it might be thought desirable for an Ibo from Eastern Nigeria to be able to be assimilated to the way of life in Lagos in Western Nigeria, though this is the geographical and cultural region of the Yoruba. To some degree this is characteristic of urbanization and of emigration to other cultural areas--not to mention the human experience of escaping earth and looking back upon it from space. Different countries reflect different degrees of cultural continuity and sensitivity.

However, there are many dangers in bypassing identification in terms of one's cultural values and attempting to substitute merely geographic or pragmatic identities. The idea of transcending one's culture seems unthinkable outside of an elite (e.g., a university) group which already has been transplanted geographically and intellectually. Even in such cases one's cultural identity remains, e.g., it is precisely as an Ibo that a person from Eastern Nigeria undertakes with gusto and confidence the task of adapting and succeeding in life in Lagos; he would not cease to identify himself as Ibo.

Adaptation can have many meanings and corresponding evaluations:

(1) If taken in the sense of merely forgetting the appreciation of human dignity had by one's forebears in the hope that one's descendants might take up the appreciation of human dignity had by another group, there might be some hope of success by the next generation particularly if this were the case of one person (a wife) entering a fully specified cultural context, such as the family of her husband.

(2) If taken in the sense of transplanting a new set of values (e.g., a Christian ethic) at the cost of, and in the place of the traditional ethic, many now conclude from experience that this produces new generations with no profound values whatsoever (see the dissertation of H. Kenote, Univ. of Nairobi, 1986). The current broad and intensive concern for inculturation reflects the breadth and depth of this conclusion.

(3) If taken in the sense of desensitizing future generations to that acquired wisdom and humane commitment in which their culture and that of their forebears most fundamentally consists it would be a very costly homogenizing and dehumanizing solution to the problem of ethnic rivalry. In Biafra the threat of such a mental lobotomy generated a war

of secession; in South Bronx it produced rapacious gangs echoing the invasion of the proverbial vandals.

(4) If taken in the sense, not of stripping families of cultural values, but of developing an openness between peoples and cultures which mutually enrich each other, then the roots for this must be, not foreign, but deeply within one's own culture. More properly this might be called, not transcending, but developing one's identity through relations or dialogue between cultures, as indicated by a developmental approach.

To conclude: in view of the depth, the importance and the felt commitment to one's cultural identity as the essential articulation of one's humanness, transcending or deadening it would appear neither feasible nor desirable. Instead one might follow a developmental approach. This would mean not being immutably fixed upon one or another particular property of a culture, as if these were of absolute value, but focusing rather upon the reality of being born into, and growing within, a group. In this way, rather than abstracting from one's roots and the wealth of human experience and commitment which that entails, one could draw as richly upon this as would be helpful in the development of one's life and in facing the challenges this entails. This would imply that one's horizon be not a set of blinders, but a particular perspective or even vantage point on the basis of which one is enabled to face new issues and meet new peoples and circumstances. In this the image of a net might be of special help, for it consists of many strands, each of which interconnects with many others, and all of which continually adjust in proportionate unison in response to new and changing circumstances and tasks.

IV. GROUP IDENTITY AND CULTURAL TRADITIONS
(See Chapter IV)

Identity itself is basic and is not reducible to any set of factors or properties. Hence, logically, it can be stated by "A is A," but not by "3+1 = 4." It is expressed through a number of elements: language, work, values, etc.

The study of groups has moved from typologies, through Barth's work on contrasts between groups, to the present sense of interaction between individual and group, as each generates the other. Groups can be ordered progressively according to the number of elements and the number of people involved. The number of elements increases as one moves from, e.g., a football team which occupies only a few hours a week and touches only one dimension of a person's life, through a subculture such as a school in which a person might remain for a few years or a professional association or social club which might be more continuous, to an ethnic group in which one lives all the stages of one's life and which influences one's spirit and values, one's economic and social relations. Hence, a nation might be described as an ethnic group with political power.

Conversely, beyond the ethnic group the number of elements might decrease while the number of people involved increases. Thus, for example, the number of elements involved formally in the state is fewer (law, territory and symbols); this number decreases further as the territory expands to such geographical units as a Central America or Latin America.

The ethnic group is the strongest sense of group. Ethnicity is not just one of many distinguishing factors (A.P. Royce), for it concerns the identity itself of all its members who cannot drop their identity without destroying themselves.

Each group has a characteristic set of elements (traditions, clothing, architecture, form of work, social organization) which make possible an empirical identification of the members of the group. These elements are not the group's identity, which is within the group and cannot be defined by any extrinsic elements. While all of these elements support the group and pertain to the culture, not all are distinguishing elements. Indeed, in the concrete these latter are determined by the group.

The central issue is not ascription or differentiation from other groups, as stressed by Barth, but the selection of the characteristics, symbols and answers to problems. Four elements appear to be necessary and sufficient for a group:

1. Biological continuity: this is not race or blood, but the fact of being born inside a group (or, in the case of a spouse, being assumed into a group by marriage).

2. Means of communication: language or symbols.

3. A scale of aesthetic, moral and political values: what is important here is less the values themselves than sharing the same scale of values: inasmuch as this generates the same cosmovision or interpretation of society, and hence the unity of the group.

4. Membership: the capacity to distinguish those who are within the group from those outside it.

A group is strongly synchronic. It can change under the impetus of an individual leader, but only if that person is accepted by the group; otherwise the person loses his or her leadership role. The relation to resources, i.e., to the means for cultivating, working and producing artifacts, is so important that disruption of this relationship is deeply disruptive of the group, and for that reason will be resisted passionately.

In anthropology concepts serve as tools which are developed in particular contexts and for particular tasks. Their content is not fixed and might be changed, not only from one period of time to another, but from one context to another. Hence these concepts may be understood better as serving heuristically to bring various aspects to one's attention, than as fixed or necessary definitions or divisions of concepts.

The term 'state' can be used for different types of englobing structures. As 'empire' it would include multiple ethnic groups. In a case such as Switzerland it could include a number of 'nations' in a federation. The term 'nation' generally bespeaks an ethnic group which is to some degree politically autonomous. In Japan only one ethnic group has full political autonomy. More often there are a number of ethnic groups in a state, which groups constitute nations if they retain some degree of political autonomy, as do the four ethnic groups in the Swiss confederation.

V. THE DEVELOPMENT OF ETHNIC CONSCIOUSNESS
SINCE 1960 (See Chapter V)

Evidence of Recent Development in Ethnic Consciousness:

Instruments developed for work in this field include tests for the degree of one's personal identification in ethnic terms, a scale of such relationships, and a set of criteria for ethnic studies. A recent development in related studies has been the realization of detailed historico-sociological studies of single neighborhoods.

The bibliography on the subject has been subject to exponential explosion. Frameworks and categories for using this bibliographical material can be drawn from Carter and Bentley, *Ethnicity and Nationality: A Bibliographic Guide* and from Thernstrom's *Harvard Encyclopedia of Ethnic Groups in America*

The volume of ethnic heritage studies is not constant but subject to periodic increases and decreases (Glazer), e.g., in the U.S. such studies were not continued by the States with funds from block grants. This phenomenon needs to be understood in order to be ready for the next wave.

Conclusion: the development of ethnic consciousness in the last 35 years has been a feature of our times.

Explanation of the Development of Ethnic Consciousness

Fundamentally the rise in ethnic consciousness seems to be an integral and fundamental aspect of the search for meaning. This has a number of factors:

- The general search for meaning in the wake of an era marked by existential meaninglessness and the absurd from the 30s to the 50s.
- The break-up of the empires at the end of the Second World War and the process of nation-building have raised the level of national ethnic consciousness. This has included also the immigration of ethnic groups into multi-ethnic or other ethnic contexts, thereby raising the issue of self-identity.
- A serial effect seems to have been generated in the U.S. by the civil rights movement. In asserting black identity it moved other groups to a clear sense of their own self-identity.
- The social sciences have been affected by this search for meaning and self-identity, moving researchers beyond ideals of abstract objectivity in a shift of paradigms.
- With the developing sense of person and hence of culture, increasingly the term 'ethnic' has broadened into the whole range of factors relating

to the person.

- Historical studies have begun to include micro or detailed investigations of particular villages or neighborhoods tracing the development of particular populations. Geographical differentiations within the same ethnic group have received more attention (Boston Irish/Philadelphia Irish, etc.).

The Nature of Ethnic Consciousness

On the one hand, the similarity between members of the same group is often perceived in terms of differences from members of other groups. Further, as ethnic identity is so deeply felt and an object of such passionate commitment, conflict on ethnic grounds can be vastly more intense than conflict on ideological grounds.

On the other hand, differences between members of the same group are appreciated only from within the group. This directs attention to the illegitimacy of stereotyping; in the extreme it raises the question of whether the process of ethnic generalization is based upon lack of knowledge and experience.

On the personal level, ethnic consciousness is a matter of both ascription and self-understanding: (1) Ascription: presence in an ethnic group is not a matter of personal choice; rather one is born into the group and of necessity belongs to it. In this sense one's ethnic history is part of one's personality. (2) Self-understanding: people vary in the degree of the importance which consciousness of their ethnicity has in their self-understanding.

The penetrating and quasi-religious character of this consciousness was noted inasmuch as it relates to one's basic identity and hence is a context of ultimate meaning and concern. It is consciousness of a special type, different from understanding and more related to aesthetic awareness. In contrast to the nature of scientific understanding, we have comparatively little understanding of how this consciousness works, though it has been experienced as waves of immigrants have entered into political competition and successively gained their standing in multi-ethnic contexts.

In some countries, with literally hundreds of ethnic groups and proximate memories of the most serious conflicts, the development of ethnic consciousness could be explosive and detrimental. Nevertheless, ethnic consciousness is a fact which could not be done away with without serious damage to one's self-identity and sense of personal and group dignity. Consequently, it needs to be dealt with creatively and turned into a positive force for personalized political expression and interaction. This, of course, supposes some overarching context of unity for mutual respect and cooperative, albeit competitive, interaction. Abuses of ethnic consciousness include: a. romanticizing, b. commercializing, c. politicizing, d. polarizing, e. manipulating ethnic sensibilities for various extraneous gains, and f. mythologizing, e.g., attributing all problems to the majority culture.

Politics and Ethnic Consciousness

Politics understood as the search for an equitable utilization of resources and a peaceful resolution of conflict is crucial to ethnic relations. These interchanges cannot be administered out of existence by theories of conflict or methods of cooperation; they must be worked with.

As they generally concern the disposition of resources, convergent forces must be found for the resolution of conflict. In this there are three sectors: (1) government, (2) private enterprise, and (3) community and neighborhood-based ethnic groups. The third sector has the capability of balancing the concerns of the first two with those of the community by energizing people from below and developing the networks essential for the proper delivery of services by the governmental and the private sectors.

The distinctive identification of this third sector is sometimes difficult in the U.S. where many public factors are under private auspices. However, the third sector can be described as: (1) non-profit, (2) community based, (3) expressive of the peoples' desire to help themselves and change their social standing, and (4) person-centered. Often it is manifested in work to elect its members to political positions, in the establishment of credit unions, in housing projects, etc.

Ethnic consciousness can be the basis for effective political action among immigrants when the sense of ethnicity appears to wane after a few generations and the groups become increasingly dispersed geographically. This may not be a problem, however, where elements of racial discrimination or economic depression contribute to binding the group together.

The development of interaction of the third or neighborhood sector with the other two sectors is important both (1) to the degree that mega-government and corporations make it necessary for people to reassess their identity and affirm their ethnic, basically their personal, identity, and (2) in order for the other two sectors to act effectively. Only by a partnership of the public with the neighborhood or community sector has improvement been realized in neighborhoods. This implies nothing less than a total restructuring of society with a realignment and sharing of power. It is no small project.

VI. SCIENCE, PERSON AND RELIGION AS CULTURAL FACTORS
(See Chapters XV and XVI)

Science as Search for an Archimedean Fulcrum

Classically there have been three attitudes toward natural forces: (1) symbiosis: the effort of tribal religions to achieve a positive and protective relation to nature, (2) escape: Plato's orientation toward contemplation, and (3) mastery: science's effort to control nature through taking an active attitude.

With the breakup of medieval culture two abysses opened before man: infinity symbolized by the telescope, and nothingness symbolized by the microscope.

Archimedean fulcra were provided successively by: (1) Descartes' method of doubt as shaking all human thought, (2) Einstein's general theory of relativity as taking human vision beyond the universe, (3) quantum mechanics as taking man into the abyss of nothingness to control the universe, (4) Crick and Watson's discovery of the structure of DNA as opening control of life, and (5) the invention of the computer as liberating man from the limitations of the human brain.

This manifests an ascent of man by means of his active life as things are revealed in experience and confirmed by technology. This contrasts to the contemplative mode of life which tends to look at others in a perjorative light. To shape our culture and not only be shaped by it we need to transcend it via a new Archimedean fulcrum. (False fulcra have been provided by such ideologies as communism and Naziism which destroy the world in order to move history.)

An authentic fulcrum is provided by the Cartesian doubt as this leads to self-criticism with its values of pluralism and tentativeness. In this light every philosophy and theology is a mental experiment. Considered positively, each culture reveals a part of the truth. Considered negatively, however, it limits the mind by stereotyping, ideologizing and imprisoning the mind in the history of a particular culture. It was in this later sense that the Polish poet Wyspianski drew the image of the destruction of the tombs of the kings in order to free the Polish mind from the shackles of its culture and open it to the future.

One needs to escape one's culture by the scientific attitudes of criticism, pluralism and tentativeness which gave one the freedom of a new Archimedean point, in order to be able to question and reshape that culture.

The Relation of Science to Human Cultivation

Technology has contributed to the development of life, including its personal expression and interrelation; none would agree to do without it. We do not have nature as untouched by human technological intervention; if that was a paradise it has been irretrievably lost. No rejection of technology as such can be considered authentic while we continue, inevitably, to employ it.

Its specific danger is expressed, then, not by the term "technology" as a tool which can be used for many goals, but by the term 'technocracy' by which man is subsumed by the technology and reduced to a tool for whatever--even the highest--achievement.

Perhaps an even greater danger is that the combination of mathematicized science with technocracy might simply merge both man and nature into an abstract or artificial structure. Heidegger noted that when the Romans built the first bridge across the Rhine it was an act of respect for the river and for nature, whereas our building an electrical plant there simply ignores the river and the contours of nature.

A response to both of these dangers will require:

(1) reaffirmation of respect for the person;

(2) recognition of the person as mystery, i.e., that, being self-conscious and free or self-determining, he or she is not reducible to the empirically observable or the mathematically calculable objects of science, but rather is a unique and limitless expression of Being breaking into time; and

(3) extension of this sense of mystery to nature as the human environment, as did Buber in considering the I-thou relation not merely as between persons, but also as of persons with plants and animals when one takes account of their entire and unique being.

Science and Cultural Specificity

On the one hand, there are reasons to think that science can break beyond culture: (1) culture can be changed by outside factors as was illustrated by the impact of Christianity upon Roman culture; and (2) the present situation is distinctive in that the development of communications and interaction makes manifest the limitations of a culture. These reasons suggest that one can find in science and its ability to submit all to doubt an Archimedean point for directing the movement of history.

On the other hand, it might be asked whether what is generally referred to as science is itself culture-free, or instead essentially an expression of Greco-Western history and culture. If that were the case its approach would constitute, not an Archimedean fulcrum outside of cultures, but a cultural imperialism. A number of factors suggest this to be the case.

The history of science traced by Prof. Turek is distinctively the history of developments in the West. The view reflected would seem to be that of science as dominating and subduing nature.

The approach supposed for science is analytic and reductivist according to which all is to be understood in terms of minimal forces and fields; any element of conscious response or free decision is not only irrelevant but disruptive. In this sense, while hoping to be culture-free, in fact it would reflect a distinctive cultural pattern and constitute thereby a cultural imperialism. By systematically ignoring the formative elements of a culture, it would undermine control by its own culture. Thus there emerges the pervasive specter of technocracy enslaving man.

The fact that other cultures approach reality in a synthetic rather than an analytic manner suggests that there can be dramatically different scientific paradigms. Departments, e.g., of "non-western" medicine in universities in some cultural regions and such practices as Chinese acupuncture indicate that this knowledge can have its structures, its technology and its verification. Approaches, e.g., of an African mind in terms, not of minimal particles, but of life forces may be more adaptable to understanding which takes account of personal and cultural values and goals.

Such synthetic systems manifest an ability to integrate persons' constitutions and activities themselves and with nature. This, along with the distinctive success of such systems in the practical order, as, e.g., the Japanese industrial effort, suggests:

(a) that "Western" science, rather than constituting an Archimedean fulcrum outside of culture, is an integral component of Western culture and shares its limitations;

(b) that through interchange with other cultures this can be made at once both less humanly damaging and more productive; and

(c) that it can be important to look within Western culture for its own resources of unity and synthesis.

Religion, Culture and Change

There is a certain sense in which modern scientific and technological capabilities transcend culture and provide capabilities which all cultural areas need in this period of increasing economic interaction and competition. If, however, these capabilities were to delineate a new common culture this would be in danger of being a technocratic suppression of the humane.

Hence, along with interchange and communication of technology, there is need for other dimensions of meaning beyond reductionist Western rationalism. This would have a number of characteristics.

First, a sense of mystery would need to be saved from being interpreted as arbitrary and unfounded so that it can be appreciated as taking one beyond the practical desire to dominate, manage and manipulate, to an attitude of respect for nature, persons, communities and their culture.

Second, a sense of contemplation would need to be freed from being interpreted as escapism in order that it include attention to the earth, understood also as a field of divine and human activity. In this sense P. Teilhard de Chardin saw science as leading to, and being integral with, contemplation; and Jesuit spirituality speaks of contemplation in action.

Third, religion as a "standing out" or "ecstasis" provides an Archimedean fulcrum for valuing and evaluating the world and its cultures. It does this, however, not through a dehumanizing abstraction from culture as the reflection of man's conscious effort toward self-realization. On the contrary, religion enters most deeply into conscious reflection upon the source of the human effort, and hence into the deepest significance and highest goals of humankind's multiple (cultural) routes to recognize, realize and fulfill this work. In this light cultures should be forces not of inertia, but of change.

Dissatisfaction with the world is a common human phenomenon; it can be found, e.g., in Lucretius. In the modern West the impetus for change came, not simply from alchemy and Bacon's notion of knowledge as power, but also from the religious thrust to search out the knowledge needed to transform the world from its present state to the heavenly Jerusalem. This Augustinian vision provided the inspiration and orientation for the key rationalists of the 16th through the mid-19th centuries.

Implementations of the desire for change can be undertaken in various ways. It would seem destructive to turn away from most of the imaginative capabilities of man's aesthetic dimension in favor merely of that which can be articulated mathematically. This would not escape imagination, but merely reduce all to one of its modes. On the contrary, it is the poetic and aesthetic imagination, as enabled by the resources of a culture, which is able to envisage alternatives and provide vision for the emancipation, transformation and promotion of a culture through changing historical circumstances.

VII. CROSS-CULTURAL STUDIES AND RELIGIOUS EXPERIENCE AT THE ROOT OF CULTURES (See Chapter XVIII)

A more perennial position on cross-cultural studies, typified by Huxley, holds that all mystical experience is of the same nature, with differences arising only in attempts to express their content. A more recent position, reflecting the thought of Kant and Wittgenstein, holds that there is no unmediated experience. The doctrines held by a person enter into the very make-up of one's experience. This implies such a radical pluralism and relativism that no comparison or evaluation of these experiences is possible.

The paper of Prof. Price differs from both of the above positions by proceeding, not from the content of the experience, or from the metaphysical position of the one who has the experience, but conversely from the experience as giving content to, and critically grounding, the doctrine. This approaches a field in terms, not of its object or of the content of reflection, but of what the person does, i.e., the dynamics of consciousness in doing science, poetry, etc. Thus, it avoids imposing a doctrine on a text and is more faithful to the method of the mystics themselves. Concretely, the investigation of Prof. Price consists of a comparative analysis of texts from two traditions for a grammar of mystical interiority via a correlation of mystical terms with the inner experience itself of the contemplative. In contrast, the classical analyses of these experiences has objectified in them a psychology of spiritual faculties.

Two assumptions are operative here: that there are texts in various cultures which develop grammars in order to help the reader attain specific patterns of consciousness (e.g., mythical texts which develop grammars of mystical interiority); and that across cultural traditions the dynamics of consciousness are common and as such provide explanatory bases for cross-cultural studies.

This implies that we must not assume, but develop a method for deciding whether there are ambiguities and/or differences between traditions. While terms are distinctive of a culture, they are employed to identify and explain operations of consciousness; hence they receive their precision from these operations. There is then a mutually critical correlation between terms and operations: if the operation is cross-cultural so too will be the referent of the terms.

Different traditions can focus on different spiritual experiences and patterns of consciousness. Hence attention to the appropriate grammar of interiority should clarify these differences (and related doctrinal and religious differences). Conversely, where different traditions focus on the same spiritual experience or pattern of consciousness the appropriate grammar of interiority should clarify their similarity, and thereby found an assessment of the relative adequacy of doctrinal and religious claims. This paper tests these assumptions and implications.

The Cloud of Unknowing points out that the key to understanding spiritual language is to focus not upon what is outside and below the self, i.e., the material world, in relation to which it speaks of a "cloud of forgetting"; nor upon what is above the self, i.e., God, in relation to which it speaks of a "cloud of unknowing"; but upon what is within or on a par with the soul, i.e., a "simply reaching out to God."

This simple stirring of love is defined not positively and conceptually, but negatively in contrast to, e.g., the senses as "unfeeling." It is knowledge beyond imagination and reason, and feeling beyond sensation and will. In this state our present type of consciousness is not operative; this state is another mode of experience which, when arrived at, we call God. Religious doctrines enter only inasmuch as they are correlated with mystical interiority and thereby find some explanatory basis.

Transposition of the mystical grammar of the *Cloud of Unknowing* from faculty psychology into the terms of intentional analysis implies:

- that the powers of the soul would correspond to intentional consciousness, i.e., the experiencing, understanding and judging by which we evaluate an object. Conversely, the absence of these constitute the clouds of forgetting and unknowing;

- that the powers of the mind would correspond to an inmost-awareness in which one's consciousness is experienced without the particular operation or object which was had in intentional inquiry; and

- that God corresponds to the ground of consciousness, the source of the very possibility of consciousness.

NB: the distinction between 2 and 3 is the point of potential contribution by an analysis of the grammars of mystical interiority. "Simply reaching out to God" takes place when intentional consciousness is inoperative via the cloud of unknowing, leaving a simple sense to the self as being transcended. This entails a heightened awareness of the ground of consciousness by which one is present to that ground.

The *Yoga Sutras* by Patanjali reflects a similar dynamic in its treatment of *nurbya samadhi*:

- quiescence of intentional consciousness corresponds to entry into a cloud of forgetting;

- transcending the experience of self in consciousness without an object (or seed) corresponds to the simple experience of the self; and

- the opening of a mystical consciousness to awareness of its transcendental ground constitutes a state of liberation which corresponds to the simple reaching out to God in a state of union with the divine.

Method: Abstract and Concrete Levels of Analysis

Symbols can be analytic or descriptive. Analytic symbols tend to see the transcendent as coming to us and reflect an explanatory and quasi-scientific type of insight and mentality. This requires a certain transcendence of the situation in order to inspect it and categorize it. In this it reflects the breakthrough in Athens that made possible analytic thinking; in this it is the bearer of a specific cultural heritage. It should not be ruled out, however, that multiple cultures could develop similar capabilities. Descriptive symbols tend to reflect the person as reaching out to the transcendent. They are poetic rather than analytic, and are used by many mystics. The *Cloud* and the *Yoga Sutras* both use this explanatory mode.

Grammar and semantics: to the contrast of grammars between the *Cloud* and the medieval scholasticism should be added semantic considerations, because of itself the relatively abstract analysis of grammar does not produce new or exact meaning. This leaves one floating in a paradox, not only between two cultures but within each culture, though paradox can be useful in opening up levels of consciousness.

Deep language structure (Chomsky) might be looked to as a way of developing cross-cultural comparison and communication through a structure that is common to all languages. However, while deep structure as purely logical would assist in translation between languages, it cannot serve mystical language, the content of which contains feeling and free personal commitment. Chomsky distinguishes between language as static and speech as dynamic. As this reflects the person, it is important not only to read a person's text, but to see and hear him/her.

This limitation of abstractive knowledge for analyzing the relation between cultures is illustrated by the way in which people who recognize themselves easily as in one or another group (e.g., Polish, French, etc.) do not recognize themselves as ethnic, for the latter bespeaks, not only the concrete people in terms of which they find concrete identity, but the abstract notion of "groupness."

Cross Cultural Comparison and Communication

Given the distinctive character of a language and the primitive role this plays in experience, is it possible to expect that texts from two different language areas would refer to the same reality. E.g., can union with Christ in the *Cloud* and Buddhistic *nirvana* be expressions of comparable realities? The answer to this can admit of a cautiously positive answer if one considers the type of texts (in this case, both texts are in mystical traditions), what the texts are dealing with (in this case, not an external reality, but the dynamics of human consciousness), and what these dynamics are attempting to achieve (namely, not an imaginative representation of an external object, but a transcendence of imagination and conceptualization).

Given all of these provisions, the fear might remain that the one who compares the two might be more influenced by one of the two texts, even if this be taken as testimony of the consciousness had in one cultural tradition. To this one response might be to consider as ideal a comparative reading by someone who belongs to neither tradition or to approach this by focusing upon critical grammar (J. Price). An alternate approach (e.g., H.G. Gadamer) would be to recognize that one is always immersed in a culture and located in time, and then to make the most of this. By recognizing one's own horizon and approaching a text as a dialogue with another horizon one can search for expansion of one's horizon making it more rich as a fusion of both. (See Chapter XIII.)

Efforts at cross cultural communication need to take into account the characteristics of the overarching or undergirding vision of the culture in order to avoid attempting to identify what in reality are different concerns. Nevertheless, if these are taken into account, the capacity of the human mind to transcend any limited horizon--even its own--can engender some comprehension for the project of the other. This can be done even while recognizing its distinctiveness and one's inability to appreciate it exhaustively from without even more than from within. By drawing positively on the strengths of each culture in a process of dialogue, each interlocutor can be freed from some of his or her limitations and enriched by dimensions of the experience and vision evolved by other cultures. Such contribution could be made, for example, by:

- the Chinese emphasis upon harmony with nature, which has often been overlooked in the process of industrialization and commercial exploitation;
- the Buddhist emphasis upon states of consciousness, which could be very helpful if another culture were to look into its states of consciousness; and
- the Yoga system's attention, not necessarily to a transcendent being, but to the various dimensions of one's physical and spiritual development in a particularly comprehensive and integrating manner.

Each of these--and others as well--can make important contributions if drawn upon in an open and integrating spirit.

Person and Culture

The text of *The Cloud* distinguishes between the will and the mind, suggesting by the latter a deeper more central point of the person in which the various faculties are rooted and which might be a point of union with the divine in a way that the intellect or will could not be. This suggests an important facet not so much in faculty psychology as in a "faculty" metaphysics done in terms of substance and accidents. Namely, it is not the faculties which act (the voice which sings), but the person who acts (and sings), etc. This could help to understand the mystical experience as the deepest involvement of the person in inter-personal commitment. Given the importance of an analysis of consciousness and its rich contribution, it is important to remember that it is not separated consciousness but persons who sense, observe, feel, react and respond. It is a community of humans, not of spirits, which needs to be built with all the dimensions and problems of human persons, as well as their needs and capacity for overcoming physical limitations and hardships.

Some would draw a parallel distinction between personality and the person. According to this the former would be culturally specified and differentiated, whereas the latter would be more profound and the point of intercultural communication, understanding and empathy. On the other hand, this model of the person might imply too great a separation between person and culture, in the same manner as the view commented upon above. Just as it is not possible to think of a singer except in terms of a person who arranges notes in a pattern which is easily distinguishable as to its culture and perhaps even its year, so it would be difficult to consider a person who can communicate except in terms that are specified culturally. It may be more helpful that the culture, while possessed of a specific identity, is not for that reason closed from others; rather it is a unique mode of expression and interpretation which enables me to see all, but to do so in a special manner and hereby to be able to play a distinctive role in the human community and in human history.

Community and Conflict

In his analysis of the human condition J. Van Baal notes the need to feel part of something larger than self. Just as the infant looks to the family, the growing and grown person needs affinity with others. This also provides individuation through enabling one to establish oneself as a person who can act efficaciously. It constitutes a point between the extremes of being cut off, on the one hand, and, on the other hand, being reduced to a mere part of a collectivity. It can also be a basis for a person's relation to the natural and the supernatural.

Victor Turner sees two different levels for considering this social life. In terms of *civitas* one has a set status with roles and obligations logically worked out. If this be the only consideration it can lead to abuses of one's position and hence to discord in society. In terms of *communitas* one takes account of the meaning of one's life with others, its motivation and hence its emotional content. This is a different and deeper mode of knowing than is *civitas*, and may be grounded in or oriented toward the mystical dimension described above.

The religious bonds of a community (*communitas*) generate emotional ties and symbols which establish one's relations with nature, other persons and the superhuman. Thus, the religious doctrine one brings to an interchange between groups shapes the whole. In principle this should contribute an ability to appreciate the importance of the individual, an attitude of simplicity in the use of material goods, and a positive attitude of concern and compassion for others.

If the above is a true articulation of a phenomenological search into the depths of human consciousness, then the sources of conflict must lie in such other dimensions of human consciousness as power or pleasure, the drive to know or the search for meaning. There is then dire need for a theory of the person as conscious in history and culture. This, in turn, would make it possible effectively to comprehend the nature and dynamics of breakdowns in relations between cultural groups, to respond wisely thereto, and to build a future for mankind marked by freedom, progress and a transcending peace.

G. McLean

A BIBLIOGRAPHY ON

PHILOSOPHY AND CULTURE

GEORGE F. McLEAN

I. The Nature of Culture

    A. Culture: General Nature
    B. Philosophy and Culture
    C. Culture and Religion
    D. Civilization

II. Diversity and Cultures

    A. Pluralism
    B. Relativism
    C. Historicity

III. Culture and Social Life

    A. Culture and Social Life
    B. Cultural Crisis, Critique, and Change

IV. Regional Cultures

    A. Early Cultures
    B. Contemporary European and Technological Culture
    C. Hispanic Cultures
    D. African Cultures
    E. Asian Cultures

THE NATURE OF CULTURE

Culture: General Nature

Anderson, A.R. and Moore, O.K. Toward a Formal Analysis of Cultural Objects. *Synthese* 14 (62) 144-70.

Beck, M. The Independence of Culture from Race. *Soc Rev* (London) 30 (38) 49-62.

Bello, A.A. Life and Culture in the Analysis of Man and Nature. In A.T. Tymeniecka, ed., *Phenomenology of Man and the Human Condition.* Dordrecht: Reidel, 1983.

Berger, P. Walter Benjamin: Contribution a une theorie de la culture contemporaine. *Rev Esth* 1 (81) 21-28.

Bernard, P. L'avenir de la culture. *Diogene* 66 (69) 120-40.

Bernard, J. Observation and Generalization in Cultural Anthropology. *AJS* 50 (45) 284-91.

Bidney, D. The Two Sources of Culture and Ethics. *Monist* 47 (63) 625-41.

Bidney, O. On the Concept of Culture and Some Cultural Fallacies. *Am anthropologist* (Phil) 46 (44) 30-44.

Bongioanni, F. *Gusto e cultura.* Torino: Accame, 1939.

Boullart, K. Art in Culture: Arbitrariness and Ambiguity. *Commun log* 17 (84) 47-56.

Bridel, Y. Pierre Thevanaz, et le probleme de la culture. *Rev Theol Phil* (75) 189-97.

Brightman, E.S. Three Conceptions of Culture. *P* 2 (37) 146-58.

Brozi, K.J. The Cultural Standard. *Dialec Hum* 10 (83) 703-16.

Carpenter, R.B. 'Ontological Naivete' and the Truth of Myth. *Personalist* 44 (63) 189-221.

Chenu, M.D. Maritain, J.: "Humanisme intégral." *BT* 5 (38) 360-64.

Crollins, A.A.R. Inculturation and the Meaning of Culture. *Gregorianum* 61 (80) 253-74.

Curren, H. New Cultures: A Challenge to Universities. *Gregorianum* 63 (82) 507-23.

De Gre, G. The Sociology of Knowledge and the Problem of Truth. *J Hist Ideas* 2 (41) 110-15.

Derisi, O.N. Espiritu y cultura. *ITA Humanidades* 9 (73) 17-28.

Derisi, O.N. Cultura y valor. *Sapientia* 16 (61) 243.45

Dumont, F. *Le lieu de l'homme: la culture comme distance et mémoire.* Montréal: HMH, 1968.

Eliot, T.S. *Notes Toward the Definition of Culture.* New York: Harcourt, Brace 1949.

Feldman, F. The Principle of Moral Harmony. *J Phil* 77 (80) 166-79.

Ferrandis Torres, M. *Historia general de la cultura.* Valladolid: Prieto, 1934.

Frank, J. *Fate and Freedom.* New York: Simon & Schuster, 1945.

Frobenius, R. *La cultura como ser vivente. Contornos de una doctrina cultural y psicologica.* Madrid: Espana-Calpe, 1935.

Frome, E. Le drame fondamental de l'homme: naître à l'humain. *Age Nouveau* 13 (59) 42-47.

Gadol, E. The Idealistic Foundations of Cultural Anthropology: Vico, Kant and Cassirer. *J Hist Phil* 12 (74) 207-25.

Garces, V.G. Tiempo y espacio de la cultura. *Revista Mexicana de Sociologia* T5 n 1.

Geertz, C. Common Sense as a Culture System. *Antioch Rev* 33 (75) 5-52.

Gheorghe, E. Culture from the Angle of Action and Creativity. *Phil log* 25 (81) 95-103.

Ghise, D. La continuité authentique de la culture. *Rev Esth* 25 (72) 307--

13.

Goel, D. Culture and Reality. *Visva Bharati J Phil* 4 (67) 62-68.

Goran, I. Anthropologie et culture. *Phil log* 27 (83) 116-22.

Golubovic, Z. Culture as a Brdige Between Utopia and Reality. In M. Muckorri, ed. *Praxis*. Dordrecht: Reidel, 1979, 167-81.

Gorki, M. *La culture et le peuple*. Paris: ESI, 1938.

Granell, M. Existencia y cultura. *Cuad Filosof* 14 (74) 30-37.

Gross, D. Culture and Negativity: Notes Toward a Theory of Culture. *Telos* (78) 127-32.

Gulian, C.I. Sur la structure dialectique de la culture. *Phil log* 18 (74) 3-16.

Gupta, R. A Note on the Definition of Culture. *Indian Phil Quart* 10 (82) 65-84.

Harris, W.H. Human Value in a Non-Technical Culture. *Main Currents* 14 (57) 27-30.

Heiddeger, M. *Carta sobra el humanismo*. Madrid: Taurus 1966.

Henle, R. *Language, Thought and Culture*. Ann Arbor, 1958.

Hooker, C.A. and Spivak, G. Explanation and Culture. *Human Soc* 2 (79) 223-44.

Howard, A. and Scott, R.A. Cultural Values and Attitudes Toward Death. *J. Existent* 6 (65-66) 161-74.

Jonsen, A.B. The Reality of Culture. *Mod Sch* 35 (57) 52-59.

Kearney, M. *World View*. Novato: Chandler and Sharp, 1984.

Kemal, S. Aesthetic Necessity, Culture and Epistemology. *Kantstudien* 74 (83) 176-205.

Konczewski, C. Les conditions de la creativité des peoples. *Rev Met Morale* 72 (67) 206-15.

Kraft, J. The Paradoxes of Culture. *Ratio* 4 (62) 16-21.

Kreyche, G.F. Culture, the Humanities and Personhood. *Listening* 18 (83) 158-71.

Krieger, L. The Autonomy of Intellectual History. *J Hist Ideas* 34 (73) 495-516.

Kroeber, A.L. and Kluckhohn, C. *Culture: A Critical Review of Concepts and Definitions*. Toronto: Random, 1963.

Kroeber, A.L. *The Nature of Culture*. Chicago: University of Chicago Press, 1952.

Kuninski, M. and Kadenacy, T. The Methodological Status of Cultural Sciences According to Heinrich Richert and Max Weber. *Rep Phil* (79) 71-85.

Laird, J. *Limits of Speculative Humanism*. London: Oxford, 1940.

Lambek, C. *Growth of the Mind in Relation to Culture*. London: Williams Norgate, 1936.

Leclercq, J. *Culture et personne*. Tournai: Casterman.

Lesser, A. Research Procedure and Laws of Culture. *Phil of Sc* (Baltimore) 6 (39) n 3.

Lidden, J.E. Appraisal of Cultural Norms. *Ethics* 59 (49) 143-45.

Lindsay, J. *A Short History of Culture*. London: Gallancz, 1939.

Linton, R. *The Cultural Background of Personality.* New York: Appleton, 1945.

Lopez Quintas, Alfonso. Art and Culture. *Int Phil Quart* 24 (84) 273-82.

Makeel, H. A Psychoanalytic Approach to Culture, Character and Personality. *Personalist* 5 (37) 267-84.

Malinowski, B. *A Scientific Theory of Culture and Other Essays.* Chapel Hill: University of North Carolina, 1944.

Malinowski, B. *Man and Culture.* London: Routledge, 1957.

Malinowski, B. Culture as a Determinant of Behavior. In *Factors Determining Human Behavior* (Harvard Tricentinary Conference). Cambridge: Harvard, 1937.

Margolis, J. Nature, Culture and Persons. *Theor Decis* 13 (81) 311-30.

Maritain, J. *True Humanism.* New York: Greenwood, 1970.

Markus, G. The Soul and Life: The Young Lukacs and the Problem of Culture. *Telos* (77) 95-115.

Matrai, L. Uber eine strukturelle definition der kultur. *Akten XIV Intern Kongr Philos IV* 454-56.

McNutt, H. An Event Theory of Culture. *Phil Phen Res* 19 (58) 65-73.

Meister, R. Seinsformen der Kultur. *BDP* 17 (43) 361-79.

Millet, R. L'Anthropologie moderne. *Etudes* 327 (67) 163-69.

Mondin, B. La Cultura: definizione, proprieta principali e element costitutivi fondamentali. *Sapienza* 33 (80) 261-69.

Moock, W. *Aufbar der Kulturen.* Paderborn: Bonifacius, 1937.

Mueller, G.E. Style. *J Aes Art Crit* 1 (41) 105-22.

Noland, R.W. T.H. Huxley on Culture. *Personalist* 45 (64) 94-111.

Norbeck, E. Cultural Anthropology Views of Man and Culture. *Thought* 39 (64) 253-72.

Ortega y Gasset, J. Von der Lebensfunktion der Ideen. *Europa Rev* 13 (37) 40-51.

Pace, E. Inversione e significato della cultura. *Aut Aut* 103 (68) 7-13.

Paelien, G.A. The Meaning of Culture. *Indian Phil Cult* 10 (65) 18-22.

Pagot, C. *Les bases de la culture générale.* Paris: Oeuvre des etudes, 1945.

Perricone, C. George Santanyana's View of the Place of Art in a Cultural World. *SJ Phil* 21 (83) 547-64.

Pieper, J. *Leisure, the Basis of Culture.* London: Collins, 1965.

Piettre, A. Pour une nouvelle esperance. *Rev univ sc mor* 1 (65) 27-29.

Plott, J. Art as the 'Soul' of Culture. *J W Vir Phil Soc* (76) 7-9.

Pro, D. Contenido del concepto cultura. *Philosophia* (Mendoza) 1 (45).

Reiser, B. De legibus culturae. In *Miscellanea Philosophica R. P.J. Gredt.* 1938, 269-94.

Ries, R.E. Rationality, Culture and Individuality. *Ethics* 74 (64) 121-25.

Roemer, R.E. The University and the Cultural Complex. *J Thought* 14 (79) 249-54.

Roheim, G. *The Origin and Function of Culture.* (Nervous and Mental Disease Monographs, n 69, 1943).

Rotenstreich, M. On Levi-Strauss' Concept of Structure. *Rev Metaph* 25

(72) 489-526.

Russell, L.J. and Macbeath, A. Is Anthropology Relevant to Ethics? *Aris Soc* 20 (46) 61-84.

Sanyal, B.S. *Culture: An Introduction.* New York: Asia 62.

Savile, A. Tradition and Interpretation. *J aes art crit* 36 (78) 303-16.

Scannone, J.C. Hacia una pastoral de la cultura. *Stromata* 31 (75) 237-259.

Schachter, C. Contributo all'analisi del concetto di cultura. *RF* 28 (37) 289-97.

Sepich, J.R. *Sobre inteligencia y cultura.* Buenos Aires: Cultura Catolica, 1938.

Simon, P. Frommiskeit und Kultur. *TG* 33 (41) 301-11.

Stepa, J. Methodes des recherches scientifiques et l'esprit de la culture. *Collect Theologica* (Lwow) 18 (37) 565-615.

Strenski, I. Reductionism and Structural Anthropology. *Inquiry* 19 (76) 73-89.

Talbutt, P.C. Motives, Reasons and Culturation. *Phil Res Arch* 9 (83) 245-64.

Tanase, A. Culture, Humanisme, Personalité. *Phil log* 25 (81).

Tejera, V. Cultural Analysis and Interpretation in the Human Sciences. *Man World* 12 (79) 192-204.

Thiel, M. Kultur und Sittlichkeit. *DTF* 19 (41) 49-74.

Tigner, H.S. *Our Prodigal Son Culture.* Chicago: Willett, 1940.

Timivella, G. *La liberta della cultura e la cultura come liberta.* Milano: Bocca, 1939.

Titze, H. Transzendental, Existentiell und Strukturell.

Triandis, H.C. Social Psychology and Cultural Analysis. *J Theor Soc Behav* 5 (75) 81-106.

Tung-sun, Chang. Thought, Language and Culture. *Sociological World* 10 (38) 17-57.

Verene, D.P. Cassirer's Concept of Symbolic Form and Human Creativity. *Ideal St* 8 (78) 14-32.

Vermeersch, E. Some Remarks on the Analysis of the Culture Concept. *Stud Phil Gand* 3 (65) 161-213.

Volpicelli, L. Lavoro e culturi. *Scuola e lavoro* (Brescia: La Scuola, 1942).

Vycines, V. *Our Cultural Agony.* The Hague: Nijhoff, 1973.

Wagner, R. *The Invention of Culture.* Englewood Cliffs: Prentice Hall, 1975.

Wallton, R.J. Cultura, existencia y logica trascendental: apofantica formal y material en la fenomenologia. *ITA Humanidades* 9 (73) 41-60.

Weintraub, K.J. *Visions of Culture.* Chicago: Univ of Chicago Pr 1966.

Wermlund, S. Culture, Behavior and Patterns of Behavior. *Theoria* 17 (51) 276-90.

Wiser, C. *Man and Culture.* New York: Crowell, 1938.

Zollschan, J. *Le rôle du facteur racial dans les questions fondamentales*

de la morphologie culturelle. Paris: Rousseau, 1934.
Zvorikine, A.A. Some Problems of the Theory of Culture. *Cahiers d'histoire mondiale* (Neuchatel) 10 (67) 346-92.

Philosophy and Culture

Abellan, J.L. *Mito y cultura.* Madrid: Seminarios y Ediciones, 1971.
Alonso, L.G. Vision filosofica de la cultura deste la perspectiva actual. *Logos* (Mexico) 12 (84) 121-27.
Bagolini, L. Mito y cultura en la tradicion y en el proyecto social. *Humanitas* (Mexico) 21 (80) 229-39.
Baldini, M. La dimensione ideologica dell'epistemologia di Karl A. Popper. *Sapienza* 27 (74) 129-54.
Banfi, A. Concetto, metodo, probleme di una filosofia della cultura. *Congres Descartes* X (37) 156-62.
Bedard, M. Philosophie et culture générale. *Philosophiques* 5 (78) 381-96.
Bohr, Niels. Natural Philosophy and Human Cultures. *Nature* 143 (39) 268-72.
Borne, E. Pour une philosophie de la culture. In *Savior et vulgarisation.* Paris: Fayard, 1962.
Bougle, C. *Humanisme, sociologie, philosophie: remarques sur la conception française de la culture générale.* Paris: Hermann, 1938.
Brennan, R.E. The Thomistic Concept of Culture. *Thomist* 5 (43), 111-136.
Brennan, R.E. The Thomistic Concept of Culture. *Thomist* 5 (43) 111-36.
Brennan, W. Myth and the Revitalization of Metaphysics. *PACPA* 45 (71) 52-57.
Campanelli, A. *Problemi scolastici e culturali dell'ora attuali.* Mirandolo: Grilli, 1942.
Carr, D. Husserl's Problematic Concept of the Life-World. *Am Phil Quart* 7 (70) 331-39.
Cassirer, E. *An Essay on Man: An Introduction to the Philosophy of Human Culture.* New York: Yale, 1944.
Cassirer, E. *Naturalistische und humanistische Begrundung der Kulturphilosophie.* Goteborg: Wettergren und Kerber, 1939.
Cassirer, E. *Zur logik der kulturwissenschaften.* Goteborg: Elander, 1942.
Caturelli, A. Para una filosofia de la cultura. *G Meta* 18 (63) 54-61.
Cauchy, V. Culture et verité chez Aristote. *Diotima* 12 (84) 41-47.
Cohen, J.W. The Role of Philosophy in Culture. *Phil East West* 5 (55) 99-112.
Copleston, F.C. *Friedrich Nietzsche: Philosopher of Culture.* New York: Barnes & Noble, 1975.
Cullen, C.A. Ser y estar: Dos horizontes para definir la cultura. *Stromata* 34 (78) 43-52.
Damian, Cornel. Ontological Significations of the Humanization Process. *Phil Log* 26 (83) 285-92.
De Kuyer, K. The Problem of Ground in the Philosophy of

M. Heidegger. *Thomist* 47 (83) 100-17.

DeAlejandro, J.M. Semiotica y cultura. *Pensamiento* 31 (75) 43-53.

Derisi, O.N. *Filosofia de la culture y de los valores.* Buenos Aires: Emece, 1963.

Dersi, O.N. Persona y Cultura. *Sapientia* 25 (70) 251-56.

Devaraja, N.K. *The Philosophy of Culture: An Introduction to Creative Humanism.* Delhi: Katab Mahal, 1963.

Dondeyne, A. Qu'est-ce que la philosophie? *Sapientia* 26 (71) 103-20.

Doyle, D. The Symbolic Element in Belief: An Alternative to Tillich. *Thomist* 45 (81) 449-71.

Dupre, W. The Hermeneutical Significance of Culture. *PACPA* 47 (73) 12-20.

Eco, U. Looking for a Logic of Culture. Lisse: de Ridder, 1975.

Edel, A. The Status of Key Concepts in Ethical Theory. *Phil Rev* 54 (45) 260-70.

Eliade, M. Simbolos y culturas. *Revista de educacion* 4 (59) 645-48.

Fancelli, M. La misura dell'uono e la filosofia della cultura. *Logos* 3 (71) 401-16.

Feibleman, J.K. Culture as Applied Ontology. *Phil Quart* 1 (51) 416-22.

Fekete, J. Benjamin's Ambivalence. *Telos* (78) 192-98.

Fernandez del Valle, A. Basave. Filosofica de la cultura. *Humanitas* (Mexico) 17 (76) 13-22.

Freyer, G. *Theorie des objecktiven Geistes: Ein Einleitung in die Kulturphilosophie.* Darnstadt: Wissenschaft, 1966.

Fruchon, P. Hermeneutique, langage et ontologie: un discernement du Platonisme chez H.G. Gadamer. *Arch Phil* 37 (74) 353-75.

Garcia, A. Filosofia y cultura. *Annales U Central* (Quito) 60 (38) 89-98.

Gibson, M. The Meeting Ground of Philosophical Anthropology and Cultural Anthropology. *Human Context* 6 (74) 296-305.

Hall, D.L. Whitehead's Theory of Cultural Interests. *SJ Phil* 7 (69-70) 457-72.

Hall, D.L. *The Civilization of Experience: A Whiteheadian Theory of Culture.* New York: Fordham, 1973.

Hartshorne, C. Analysis and Cultural Lag in Philosophy. *SH Phil* 11 (73) 105-12.

Hinman, L.M. Gadamer's Understanding of Hermeneutics. *Phil Phen Res* 40 (80) 512-35.

Hogan, J. Gadamer and the Hermeneutical Experience. *Phil Today* 20 (76) 3-12.

Hussain, S.S. Philosophy and Culture. *Pakistan Phil Congr* 15 (68) 206-209.

Ives, M.C. *The Analogue of Harmony: Some Reflections on Schiller's Philosophical Essays.* Pittsburgh: Duquesne, 1970.

Keable, G. The Renewal of Myth. *Theor Theor* 10 (76) 113-24.

Kirsch, D. Philosophy in Human Sciences. In *The Need for Interpretation: Contemporary Conceptions of the Philosopher's Task.* M. Rosen, ed. London: Athlone, 1983, 11-32.

Klemm, D.E. *The Hermeneutical Theory of Paul Ricoeur: A Constructive Analysis.* Lewisburg: Bucknell U Pr, 1983.

Klocker, H.R. Philosophy in a Cultural Context. *Teach Phil* 1 (75) 147-51.

Krawczyk, Z. The Ontology of the Body: A Study in Philosophical and Cultural Anthropology. *Dialec Hum* 11 ((84) 59-74.

Lauer, E.F *Kulturphilosophie.* Koln: Wienand, 1970.

Lawrence, F. Gadamer and Lonergan: A Dialectical Comparison. *Int Phil Quart* 20 (80) 25-47.

Levi, Albert W. Hegel's *Phenomenology* As a Philosophy of Culture. *J Hist Phil* 22 (84) 455-70.

Lindley, T.F. Moore's Nominal Definitions of Culture. *Phil Sci* 20 (53) 335-38.

Lorite-Mena, J. Objectividad deseo de verdad y hermeneutica. *Pensamiento* 39 (84) 3-32.

Maritain, J. Humanisme et Culture. *EC* 2 (35) 94-130.

Markus, G. Die Seele und das Leben: der 'Junge' Lukacs und das Problem der Kultur. *Rev Int Phil* 27 (73) 407-38.

McClain, E.G. A New Look at Plato's *Timaeus. Music Man* 1 (75) 341-60.

McKeon, R. Fact and Value in the Philosophy of Culture. *Akten XIV Intern Kongr Philos IV* 503-11.

McMahon, F.E. Metaphysics and Culture. *PACPA* 16 (40) 123-29.

Mohan, R.P. *The Thomistic Philosophy of Civilization and Culture.* Washington: CUA, 1948.

Morelli, Mark D. *Philosophy's Place in Culture: A Model.* Lanham: UPA 1984.

Morra, G. La riscoperta del mito. *Stud Betavina* 16 (69) 503-509.

Morris, B. *Philosophical Aspects of Culture.* Yellow Springs: Antioch, 1961.

Nayan, K. Oswald Spengler: Philosophy of Man and Culture. *Indian Phil Quart* 11 (84) 101-18.

O'Farrell, F. Man's Metaphysical Dimension. *Rev Port Filosof* 25 (69) 135-39.

Ortez-Oses, A. Modelos Hermeneuticos y Mitologicos. *Rev Port Filosof* 40 (84) 291-306.

Paim, A. Culturalismo e conscienia transendental. *Rev Bras Filos* 21 (71) 9-14.

Pro, D.F. Entre la ontologia y la antropologia filosoficas. *Sapientia* 33 (78) 39-54.

Radest, H. B. Ethical Culture and Humanism: A Cautionary Tale. *Relig Hum* 16 (82) 59-70.

Reiser, B. De cultura et de philosohia culturae. *Aug* 14 (37) 355-416.

Ricoeur, P. Ideology and Utopia as Cultural Imagination. *Phil Exch* 2 (76) 17-28.

Roberts, C. Husserlian Phenomenology and Parsonian Functionalism in Juxtaposition. *Dialogue* 18 (76) 60-65.

Romero, F. *Los problemas de a filosofia de la cultura.* Sancta Fe: Edc univ del Litoral, 1938

Romero, F. *La filosofia de la cultura.* Medellin: Univ de Antioquia, 358.

Rossi, I., ed. *The Logic of Culture: Advances in Structural Theory and Methods.* South Hadley: Bergin, 1982.

Rowinski, C. Tradition and Culture. *Dialec Hum* 10 (83) 231-44.

Saci, E. Fenonenologia e antropologia culturale. *Aut aut* 77 (63) 9-11.

Saksena, S.K., Moore, C.A. and Mei, Y.P. Cohen on the Role of Philosophy in Culture. *Phil East West* 1 (51) 38-49 (Saksena); 113-24 (Moore); 137-48 (Mei).

Saleem, M. Philosopher as a Physician of Culture. *Pakistan Phil Congr* 10 (63) 463-66.

Sebba, G. Symbol and Myth in Modern Rationalistic Societies. In *Truth, Myth and Symbol.* J.J. Altizer et al (ed). Englewood Cliffs, N.J.: Prentice Hall, 1962, pp. 141-68.

Severino, E. La terra e l'essenza dell'uomo. *G Crit Filosof Ital* 22 (68) 339-40.

Smith, P.C. H.G. Gadamer's Heideggerian Interpretation of Plato. *J Brit Soc Phen* 12 (81) 211-30.

Stace, W.T. The Place of Philosophy in Human Culture. *Philos* 12 (37) 302-16.

Veit, Walter. The Potency of Imagery - The Impotence of Rational Language. (Ernesto Gressi's Contribution to Modern Epistemology). *Phil Rhet* 17 (84) 221-39.

Verene, D.P. The Philosophy of Culture and the Problem of Human Existence. *Akten XIV Intern Kongr Philos IV* 497-502.

Weigert, A. A Cultural Aspect of Thomistic Ethics. *Rev Univ Ottawa* 35 (65).

Wojcieckowski, J.A. Philosophie de la culture. *Rev Univ Ottawa* 43 (73) 145-51.

Zilarosa, G.R. L'existenzialismo e le possibilita di apertura culturale nel mondo contemporaneo. *Inc Cult* 2 (69) 421-30.

Culture and Religion

Abel, W. and Reincke, G. Religion, Myths, Kultur. *Bib Philos Clas* 23 (38) 218-37.

Acton, H.B. Religion, Culture and Class. *Ethics* 60 (50) 120-30.

Adams, J.L. *Paul Tillich's Philosophy of Culture, Science and Religion.* New York: Harper & Row, 1965.

Adams, J.L. *Paul Tillich's Philosophy of Culture, Science and Religion.* Washington: UPA, 1982.

Albino, E.M. Di un umanesimo cristiano. *CC* 2 (35) 292-98.

Ayala, F.J. Man in Evolution: A Scientific Statement and Some Theological and Ethical Implications. *Thomist* 31 (67) 7-20.

Bell, D. Reflections on Culture and Religion in a Post-industrial Age. In M. Kranzberg (ed) *Ethics in an Age of Pervasive Technology.* Boulder: Westview, 1980, 34-55.

Bell, D. The Return of the Sacred: The Argument About the Future of Religion. *Zygon* 13 (78) 187-208.

Belletti, B. Fede, cultura e storia in O. Kohler. *Sapienza* 36 (83) 60-65.

Borgmann, A. Christianity and the Cultural Center of Gravity. *Listening* 18 (83) 93-102.

Botez, A. Creation in the Dynamics of Cultural Paradigms. *Phil Log* 27 (83) 122-35.

Brennan, W.T. Myth, Culture and Catholicism. *Listening* 18 (83) 19-31.

Brunner, H.E. *Christianity and Civilization*. New York: Scribners, 1948.

Bulman, R.F. *A Blueprint for Humanity: Paul Tillich's Theology of Culture*. East Brunswick: Associated U Pr, 1981.

Burkoe, R.W. What Does Determine Human Destiny: Science Applied to Interpret Religion. *Zygon* 12 (77) 336-89. Bustamente, N. Approccio alla nozione di cultura nel magistero di Giovanni Paolo II. *Doctor Communis* 35 (82) 317-326.

Cappello, G. Umanesimo e scolastica: Il Valli, gli umanisti e Tomasso d'Aquino. *Rev Filosof Neo Schol* 69 (77) 423-42.

Carrier, H. Chiesa, cultura e sviluppo. *Gregoranium* 62 (81) 661-79.

Cavadi, A. Sulla Cultura in quanto mediazione tra fede e prassi politica. *Sapienza* 33 (80) 356-61.

Chenu, M.D. Humanisme chrétien et culture classique. *Rev Dominicaine* (Montréal) (34) 461-67.

Chifflot, D. The Cultural Responsibility of Christians. *Blackfriars* 26 (45) 403-405.

Cobb, John B. *Beyond Dialogue: Toward a Mutual Transformation of Christianity and Buddhism*. Philadelphia: Fortress, 1982.

Cochrane, C.N. *Christianity and Classical Culture*. Oxford: Clarendon Press, 1940.

Conio, C. Alcune Osservazione sul rapporto culturi e religione. *Rev Filosof Neo-Scolas* 68 (76) 509-12.

D'amore, B. Cultura e civilta cristiana in una visuale Tomistica. *Sapienza* 34 (81) 150-59.

Dawson, C. *Religion and Culture*: Gifford Lectures, 1947. New York: AMS, 1979.

Dawson, C. *Progress and Religion, An Historical Enquiry*. London: Sheed and Ward, 1937.

Dawson, H. *Fondements d'une culture chrétienne*. Paris: Bloud et Gay, 1934.

Dawson, H. *Progrès et religion*. Paris: Plon, 1935.

de Lubac, H. *The Drama of Atheist Humanism*. Gloucester: Smith, 1964.

DeCorte, M. Conception catholique et tendances actuelles de la culture. In *Actes du VI Congres Cath de Malines* 5 (36) 21-28.

DeCorte, M. Catholicisme et cultures contemporaines. *Orientations Relig* 10 (37) 272-88.

Derisi, O.N. Humanism y transcendencia. In *Actas de las sez jorn univ de humanidades*. Mendoza: Inst de Filos, 1964, pp. 79-83.

Devaraja, N.K. *Philosophy, Religion and Culture: Essays in Search of Definitions and Direction.* Delhi: Macmillan, 1975.

Dhavamony, M. Phenomenology of Religion. *Heythrop J* 17 (76) 64-67.

Dourley, J.P. Jung, Tillich and Aspects of Western Christian Development. *Thought* 52 (77) 18-49.

Dupré, L. Religion, Ideology and Utopia in Marx. *New Schol* 50 (76) 415-34.

Dupre, W. Mirror and Enigma: The Meaning of God on Earth. *Listening* 20 (85) 65-83.

Eibl, H. Religion und Kultur. *SZ* 137 (40) 137-43.

Feaver, J.C. & Horosz, W., eds. *Religion in Philosophical and Cultural Perspective: A New Approach to the Philosophy of Religion Through Cross-disciplinary Studies.* Princeton: Van Nostrand 1967.

Ferreira da Silva, V. Origem religiosa da cultura. *Convivium* (Sao Paolo) 1 (62) 32-41.

Gera, L. Cultura y dependencia, a la luz di la reflexion teologica. *Stromata* 30 (74) 169-93.

Griffiths, P., and Lewis, D. On Grading Religions, Seeking Truth and Being Nice to People. A Reply to Prof. Hick's "On Grading Religions." *Relig Stud* 19 (83) 75-80.

Hartt, J. Theology of Culture. *Rev Metaph* 6 (53) 501-10.

Hay, G.C. The Christian Philosopher and Cultural Decadence. *Phil Stud* (Ireland) 28 (81) 140-48.

Humanisme scientifique et humanisme chrétien. *Et Francisc* 19 (69) 367-82.

Hunermann, P. Iglesia y cultura: Reflexiones teologicas sobre su interdependencia. *Stromata* 33 (77) 195-233.

Jaeger, W. *Humanism and Theology.* Milwaukee: Marquette University Press, 1943.

Kroner, R. *Culture and Faith.* London: Cambridge University Press, 1952.

Labowitz, M. On Tradition, Belief and Culture. *JP* 40 (43) 100-105.

Ladrière, J. Le chrétien et la culture. *Essais sur l'homme* 1945, pp. 33-34.

Lauer, Quentin. Religion and Culture in Hegel (Comment by R. Bernascomi). In L. Stepilevich (ed) *Hegel's Philosophy of Action.* Atlantic Highlands: Humanities Pr, 1983, pp. 103-124.

Laviosa Zambotti, P. Origen y difusion de la civilizacion. Barcelona: Omega, 1958.

Lebowitz, N. On Tradition, Belief and Culture. *J Phil* 40 (43) 100-105.

Lindsay, A.D. *Religion, Science and Society in the Modern World.* New Haven: Yale, 1943.

Loisy, A. La valeur humaine du christianisme. *RMM* 41 (34) 531-33.

Lynch, W.F. Culture and Belief. *Thought* 25 (50) 441-63.

MacCormac, E.R. Religious Metaphors: Mediators Between Biological and Cultural Evolution that Generate Transcendent Meaning.

Zygon 18 (83) 45-65.

Maistriaux, R. *Les humanistes classiques et l'humanisme chretien.* Bruxelles: Cité chrétienne, 1937.

Malevez, L. La philosophie chrétienne du progrès. *NRT* 64 (37) 377-85.

Maritain, J. *Religion und Kultur.* Freiburg Pr: Herder, 1936.

Mel'nikova, A.V. Atheism and the Area of Spiritual Culture. *Soviet Stud Phil* 4 (65-66) 13-23.

Molitor, A. *Culture et christianisme ou le tourment de l'unité.* Tournai: Casterman, 1944.

Mondin, B. Culture and Christianity. *New Schol* 53 (79) 191-205.

Montanari, F. Religione e cultura. Roma: Studium, 1938.

Morgan, J.H. Religious Myth and Symbol: Convergence of Philosophy and Anthropology. *Phil Today* 18 (74) 68-84.

Niebuhr, H.R. *Christ and Culture.* New York: Harper, 1951.

Nowaczyk, M. John Paul II's Concept of Culture. *Dialec Hum* 10 (83) 169-82.

Panikkar, R. Aporias in the Comparative Philosophy of Religion. *Man World* 13 (80) 357-84.

Panikkar, R. Hermeneutics of Comparative Religion. *J Dharma* 5 (80) 38-51.

Paulus, R. Zur Krisis des idealistischen und christlichen Geistes. *TB* 16 (37) 47-60.

Pelikan, J. *Human Culture and the Holy: Essays in the True, the Good and the Beautiful.* London: SCM 1959.

Phillips, D.Z. The Devil's Diagnoses: Philosophy of Religion: 'Objectivity' and 'Cultural Divergence.' *Philosophy Supp* (84) 61-78.

Pollock, R. Catholic Philosophy and American Culture. *Thought* 17 (42) 60.

Pushparajan, A. The Christian Perspective of Worship and Culture. *J Dharma* 3 (78) 373-94.

Rademacher, A. *Religion and Bildung. Eine kulturphilosophische Betrachtung.* Bonn: Hanstein, 1935.

Rodriguez Carro, V.J. Los presupuestos antropologicos y culturales del culto religioso. *Pensamiento* 30 (74) 173-89.

Rougier, L. *La civilisation chrétienne.* Quebec: Le Canada Fr. (32) n. 6.

Scannone, J.C. Vigencia de la subiduria cristiana en el ethos cultural de nuestra pueblo: Una alternativa teologica. *Stromata* 32 (76) 253-89.

Sibley, J.R. A Christian Theology of Culture. *Quest* 8 (64) 50-64.

Sigmond, R. Cultura e culture alla luce della "Gaudium et spes." *Sapienza* 20 (67) 17-29.

Simon, H. *Le problème de la culture chrétienne,* 1934.

Spera, S. Cristianismo e cultura. *Aquinas* 25 (82) 553-68.

Spiegler, G. *The Eternal Covenant: Schleiermacher's Experiment in Cultural Theology.* New York: Harper & Row, 1967.

Spirito, U. *La Vita como amore. Il tramonto della civilta cristiana.* Firenze: Sansoni, 1970.

Tanase, A. The Concept of Creation in the Light of the Philosophy of Culture. *Phil Log* 23 (79) 13-23.

Tillich, P. *Theology of Culture.* (Ed. R.C. Kimball.) New York: Oxford University Press, 1959.

Toynbee, A.J. *Christianity and Civilization.* Wallingford, PA: Pendle Hill, 1947.

Van Melsen, A. Science and Christianity as Universals of Culture. *Thomist* 31 (67) 137-58.

Van Baaren, Th. & Drijvers, H.J.W. (eds.) *Religion, Culture and Methodology.* The Hague: Mouton, 1973.

Varillon, F. Culture humaine et renoncement chrétien. Problème et solutions. *Et* 223 (35) 151-70.

Veuillot, F. *Civilisation et sainteté.* Paris: Beauchesne, 1945.

Wei, Tam Tai. *The Worth of Religious Truth Claims: A Case for Religious Education.* Washington, UPA 1982.

Williams, L.P. Cultural Crisis and the Absolute. *J Thought* 9 (74) 216-18.

Wood, H.G. *Christianity and Civilization.* London: Cambridge, 1942.

Civilization

Battaglia, F. Cultures y civilizaciones. *Anu Filos Der* 12 (66) 25-35.

Bouvier, R. Civilisation: le mot et l'idée. *Bull Intern Com of Hist Sc* (Paris) 11 (39) 56-66.

Brameld, T. Philosophy of Culture: Implications for Philosophy of Education. *Educ Theor* 6 (56) 158-69.

Brameld, T.B.H. *Patterns of Educational Philosophy: Divergence and Convergence in Culturological Perspective.* New York: World, 1950.

Brucculeri, A. La civilta e le sue moderne involuzioni *CC* 2 (39) 110-20; 311-24; 396-403.

Cazeneuve, J. *Bonheur et Civilisation.* Paris: Gallimard, 1966.

Ciaramelli, Fabio. Le rôle du Judaïsme dans l'oeuvre de Levinas. *Rev Phil Louvain* 81 (83) 580-600.

De Constantim, Y. *Enquête sur l'homme: I. les problèmes de civilisation.* Paris: Buchet-Chastel, 1966.

De Corte, M. Morale et culture. *TP* 3 (41) 97-122.

Delos, J.T. *Le problème de la civilisation.* Montréal: La Nation, 1944.

di Gandia, Culture y civilizacion. *Estudios* (Buenos Aires) 28 (37) 175-80.

Emmet, D.M. A Philosophy of Civilization. *HJ* 32 (34) 175-83.

Fancelli, M. *Educazione dell'uomo e filosofia della cultura.* Rome: Bulzoni, 217.

Ferrero, G. Civilisation et Progrès. *Cent Int de Synthèse,* 1938.

Fischer, H. *Vernunft und Zivilisation, die antipolitik.* Stuttgart: Seewald, 1971.

Foroughi, A.H. *Civilisation et synthèse.* Paris: Alcan, 1936.

Fuentes Castellanos, R. Concepto integral de civilizacion. *Eca* 16 (61)

227-31.

Galli, D. Spirito critico e civilta. In *Mem XIII Congr Intern Filos VI*, 279-82.

Gooch, G.P. *The Unity of Civilization.* London: Ethical Union, 1934.

Hajko, D. Zivilisation, Kultur und Kulturellen Wert. *Deut Z Phil* 26 (78) 1509-16.

Handlin, O. *John Dewey's Challenge to Education: Historical Perspectives on the Cultural Context.* New York: Harper, 1959.

Heard, G. *The Source of Civilization.* London: Cape, 1935.

Huguet, J. *La culture face aux civilisations.* Paris: Silvaire, 1963.

Huntington, E. *Mainsprings of Civilization.* New York: Wiley, 1945.

Johnson, A.H. *Whitehead's Philosophy of Civilization.* Boston: Beacon, 1958.

Kaestle, C.F. Moral Education and Common Schools in America: A Historian's View. *J Moral Educ* 13 (84) 101-11.

Khalaf, S. The Growing Pains of Arab Intellectuals. *Diogenes* 54 (66) 59-80.

Kotarbinski, T. L'analyse et la construction de la notion du sujet agissant et de la civilisation. *Mem XIII cong intern filos VI*, 317-24.

Kunhan, Raji C. Elements in Human Civilization, Materialistic and Spiritual. *Aryan Path* 14, n 5.

Leclercq, J. *Nous autres civilisations.* Paris: Fayord, 1967.

MacIver R.M. *Civilization and Group Relationships.* New York: Harper, 1945.

Malinowski, B. *Freedom and Civilization.* New York: Roy, 1944.

Marrou, H.D. Culture, civilisation, décadence. *RS* 15 (38) 133-60.

Murray, G.G.A. *Anchor of Civilization.* Oxford: Oxford U Press, 1943.

Nef, J.U. *A Search for Civilization.* Chicago: Regnery, 1962.

Nogueira, Lavandeira A. Algunos comentarios sobre los conceptos de civilizacion y cultura. *Mirador Cultural* (Mexico) 1 (62) 189-203.

Onkeley, H.D. Nationalism and Civilization. *The Contemporary Review*, 166 (1944) 95-99.

Pascadi, I. L'art entre culture et civilization. *Phil Log* 19 (75) 341-47.

Pegand, G. *Culture et civilization dans l'impasse.* Paris: Courrier du livre, 1966.

Pepper, C., et al. *Civilization.* Berkeley: University of California, 1942.

Petruzzellis, N. Cultura filosofia e educazione. *Sapienza* 31 (78) 170-86.

Phillips, D.C. "Post-Kuhnian Reflections on Educational Research." In J.F. Soltas, ed. *Philosophy and Education - 80th Yearbook NSSE.* Chicago: U of Chicago 1981, pp. 237-61.

Punki, H.H. Vested Interests and Civilization. *JP* 42 (45) 533-36.

Quigley, C. Cognitive Factors in the Evolution of Civilization. *Main Currents* 29 (72) 69-75.

Richardson, D.B. Toward a Formal Model of Civilizational WorldStyles. *Scientia* 109 (74) 509-26.

Richardson, D.B. Are Civilization and Culture Really Different? *New Schol* 32 (58) 373-82.

Robinson, E.A. Ethics and Civilization. *J of Lib Rel* 6 (45) n 4.

Royce, N.J. R.S. Peters and Moral Education: The Justification of Procedural Principles. *J Moral Educ* 12 (83) 174-81.

Santangelo, P.E. *Il mito della civilta*. Torino: Subalpina, 1939.

Seignobos, Ch. Histoire des conditions générales de la vie civilisée chez les peuples. *RCC* 37 (35) 110-21; (36) 511-24, 163-76, 453-65.

Semerari, G. Civilta dei mezzi e civilta dei fini. *Aut aut* 17 (63) 12-26.

Tats, D. Civilisation et culture. *Rev Univ Bruxelles* 12 (59-60) 434-53.

Thurnwald, R.C. Civilization and Culture. A Contribution Toward Analysis of the Mechanism of Culture. *Am Soc Review* 1 (36) 387-95.

Tsanoff, R.A *The Moral Ideals of Our Civilization*. New York: Dutton, 1942.

Van Breda, H.L. *Culturphilophie*. Leuven: Warny, 1943.

Virion, P. *Civilisation, notre bien commun*. Paris: Etude Corporatives, 1943.

Von Grunebaum, G.E. *Islam: Essays in the Nature and Growth of a Cultural Tradition*. London, 1961.

Warden, C.J. *The Emergence of Human Culture*. New York: Macmillan, 1936.

Wirsing, M.E. *Teaching and Philosophy: A Synthesis*. Boston: Houghton Mifflin, 1972.

DIVERSITY AND CULTURES

Pluralism

Ajmal, M. & Hamid-ud-din, M. Individual and Culture. *Pakistan Phil Congress* 7 (60) 127-32.

Alcorta, J.I. Una nueva vision de la filosofia. *G Metaf* 28 (73) 465-79.

Alston, W.P. Internal Relatedness and Pluralism in Whitehead. *Rev Metaph* 5 (52) 535-58.

Anderson-Gold, S. Cultural Pluralism and Ethical Community in Kant's Philosophy of History. *Grad Fac Phil* 9 (82) 67-77.

Appleton, N. Democracy and Cultural Pluralism: Ideals in Conflict (B. - Sarlos, Response to Prof. Appleton). *Proc Phil Ed* 38 (82) 151-58.

Appleton, N.R. On the Cogency of Cultural Pluralism. *J Thought* 18 (83) 10-28.

Appleton, N. Cultural Pluralism: Must We Know What We Mean? *Rev J Phil Soc Sci* 1 (80) 54-66.

Arrupe, P. Pluralismo delle culturi e cristianesimo. *Sapienza* 20 (63) 7-16.

Awerkamp, D.R. Religion in a Pluralistic Age. *Relig Hum* 11 (77) 60-68.

Barnard, F.M. & Vernon, R.A. Pluralism, Participation and Politics: Reflections on the Intermediate Group. *Polit Theor* 3 (75) 180-97.

Bekker, S. Pluralism and Conflict Regulation. *Phil Papers* 6 (77) 33-55.

Beltram, G.A. Confluents de cultures en anthropologie. *Diogene* 47 (64) 3-15.

Bharati, A. Culture and Cultures: A Linguistic Approach. *Akten XIV Itern Kongress Phil IV* 447-219.

Bird, O. *Cultures in Conflict: An Essay in the Philosophy of the Humanities.* Notre Dame: U of Notre Dame Press, 1976.

Broudy, H.S. The Public School in a Fragmented Culture. *J of Thought* 10 (75) 253-61.

Burke, T.E. The Limits of Relativism. *Phil Quart* 29 (79) 193-207.

Burns, W.H. et al. How (If at All) Should Religion be Taught in a Society in Which There Are People of Many Faiths? *Theor Theor* 10 (71) 243-47.

Capek, M. Bergson, Nominalism and Relativity. *SWJ Phil* 9 (78) 127-33.

Caturelli, A. Pluralismo culturale y sabduria cristiana. *Humanitas* (67) 113-45.

Caws, P. On the Teaching of Ethics in a Pluralistic Society: A Groundwork for a Common Morality. *Hastings Center Rep* 8 (78) 32-39.

Coward, H.G. Theologizing in a World of Pluralism. *J Sharma* 6 (81) 343-51.

Currie, A.W. On Translating from Another Culture. *Dalhousie Rev* 47 (67-68) 567-75.

Danielou, J. Le Pluralisme de la pensée. *Sapienza* 19 (66) 11-23.

Dasgupta, P. An Essay Toward Cultural Autonomy, *Indian Phil Quart* 11 (84) 437-60.

De Degan, G. Pluralismo e unita della cultura cristiana. *Sapienza* 20 (67) 112-18.

de Smaele, F. Pluralisme éthique et verité. *Rev Phil Louvain* 66 (68) 661-87.

Dechert, C.R. A Pluralistic World Order. *PACPA* 37 (63) 167-86.

Derisi, O. La cultura y las cultures. *Sapienta* 18 (63) 38-45.

Derisi, O.N. Multiplicidad material y unidad spiritual meditacion sobre la situacion de la cultura en nuestro tiempo. *Sapientia* 18 (63) 3-6.

Eisele, C. Dewey's Concept of Cultural Pluralism. *Educ Theor* (83) 149-56.

Elders, L. Saint Thomas et la diversité des opinions philosophiques. *Doctor Communis* 28 (75) 171-89.

Ericson, E.L. A Dynamic Diversity. *Humanist* 37 (77) 37.

Etcheverry, R. *Le conflict actuel des humanismes.* Rome: PUG, 1964.

Etcheverry, A. The Present Diversity Among Humanisms. *Phil Today* 3 (59) 268-76.

Farber, M. Remarks About Pluralism. *Rev Metaph Morale* 75 (70) 350-53.

Fatula, M.A. Dogmatic Pluralism and the Noetic Dimension of the Unity of Faith. *Thomist* 48 (84) 409-32.

Fisher, G. International Negotiation: Cross-Cultural Perception. *Hu-*

manist 43 (83) 14-18.

Flewelling, R.T. Mediating Concepts in Contrasting World Cultures. *Personalist* 28 (47) 5-20.

Fontaine, W.T. The Means and Relation and Its Significance for Cross-cultural Ethical Argument. *Phil. Sci* 25 (58) 157-62.

Francis, M. Multiculturalism: A Sixth Ideology of Cultural Diversity. *Proc Phil Educ* 37 (81) 291-97.

Freyre, G. Ethnic Groups and Culture. *Diogenes* 25 (59) 41-59.

Frost, M. Some Doubts About the Pluralist Enterprise. *Phil Papers* 6 (77) 51-61.

Geymonat, L. L'impossible neutralité. *Scientia* 107 (72) 753-63.

Gironella, J.R. El pluralismo teologico ante la filosofia y ante el filosofia del lenguaje. *Espiritu* 24 (75) 47-86.

Gispert-Sauch, G. The Dynamics of Cultural Pluralism and Worship-patterns. *J. Sharma* 3 (78) 350-63.

Gleiman, L. Violence in a Pluralistic Society. *PACPA* 37 (63) 88-96.

Goldstone, P. The Metaphysics of Teaching: Nature and Artifact/Unity and Plurality. *Proc Phil Educ* 39 (83) 83-96.

Gualtieri, A.R. Landscape Consciousness and Culture. *Relig Stud* 19 (83) 161-74.

Gunther, G.M. Sympathy in Plotinus. *Int Phil Quart* 24 (84) 395-406.

Hammer, J. Il pluralismo culturale e la chiesa. *Sapienza* 19 (66) 24-33.

Harris, J. A Paradox of Multicultural Societies. *J Phil Educ* 16 (82) 223-33.

Harvanek, R.F. Philosophical Pluralism and Catholic Orthodoxy. *Thought* 25 (50) 21-52.

Hearn, T.K. On Tolerance. *SJ Phil* 8 (70) 223-32.

Heelan, P. Emotions Across Cultures: Objectivity and Cultural Divergence. *Phil Supp* (1984) 21-42.

Hick, J. On Conflicting Religious Truth-Claims. *Relig St* 19 (83) 485-92.

Hick, J. *God Has Many Names.* Philadelphia: Westminster, 1980.

Hopkins, P. *World Culture.* Pasadena: Freedom, 1945.

Hountondji, P. Pluralism--True and False. *Diogenes* (73) 101-18.

Itzkoff, S.W. Cultural Diversity and Democratic Prospect. *Rev J Phil Soc Sci* 1 (80) 35-53.

Itzkoff, S.W. The Sources of Cultural Pluralism. *Educ Theor* 26 (76) 231-32.

James, W. Pluralism and Religion. *Hibbert J* 50 (52) 324-28.

Johnson, C.D. The Morally Educated Person in a Pluralistic Society. *Educ Theor* 31 (81) 237-50.

Johnstone, H.W. and Marienthal-Maschler, C. Skepticism and Inferior Knowledge: A Note on Aristotle's Pluralism. *Phil Phen Res* 22 (62) 472-80.

Kallen, H.M. *Cultural Pluralism and the American Idea.* Philadelphia: U of Penn, 1951.

Kariel, H.S. *The Decline of American Pluralism.* Stanford: Stanford

University Press, 1961.

Klein, J.T. Value Choices and Pluralism: Rejoinder to Rozychi. *Educ Theor* 29 (79) 71-72.

Klein, J.T. Cultural Pluralism and Moral Education. *Monist* 58 (74) 683-93.

Kliever, L.D. Authority in a Pluralistic World. *The Search for Absolute Values*. New York: ICF Pr 1977.

Kluckhohn, C.K. The Special Character of Integration in an Individual Culture. *Main Currents* 7 (50) 102-106.

Koenigsberger, D. *Renaissance Man and Creative Thinking: A History of Concepts of Harmony 1400-1701*. Atlantic Highlands: Humanities Press, 1979.

Koertgi, N. Theoretical Pluralism and Incommensurability. *Philosophica* 31 (83) 85-108.

Kolenda, K. Globalism Versus Consensual Pluralism. In M.B. Storer (ed) *Humanist Ethics*. Buffalo: Prometheus, 1980.

Kronenberg, A. Where are the Barbarians: Ethnocentrism versus the Illusion of Cultural Universalism. The Answer of an Anthropologist to a Philosopher. *Ultim Real Mean* 7 (84) 233-36.

Kruger, L. Unity of Science and Cultural Pluralism. In R. Hallen (ed), *Science and Ethics*. Amsterdam: Rodopi, 1981.

Kuntz, P. Philosophy as the Discovery of Orders. *Teach Phil* 3 (79) 65-81.

Labarrière, P.J. Pluralisme, pluralités, unité. *Etudes* 346 (77) 773-86.

Lahbabi, M.A. Cultural Pluralism and Human Civilization. *Personalist* 40 (59) 246-59.

Lahoz Lainez, B. *El distino humano en el realismo introspectivo*. Madrid: Estudios 1963.

Lamont, C. Pluralism, Chance and Freedom. *Humanist* 8 (48) 1220.

Langevin, G. Le pluralisme en matiere spirituelle et religieuse selon Karl Rahner. *Laval Theol Phil* 29 (73) 3-17.

Latora, S. Quale pluralismo. *Sapienza* 28 (75) 74-79.

Leontif, W. Note on the Pluralistic Interpretation of History and the Problem of Interdisciplinary Cooperation. *J Phil* 45 (48) 617-123.

Lesser, G. & Kandell, D. Cross Cultural Research: Advantages and Problems. *Human Context* 1 (69) 347-76.

Lindgens, G. Pluralismus und Christentum: Studie zur Katholischer Theorie uber das Verhaltnis von Pluralismus und Wahrheit. *Frei Z Phil Theol* 29 (82) 465-87.

Luce, R.A. Jr. Existential Symptom and the Cultural Conflict. *J. Existent* 2 (61) 49-70.

Lustgarten, L.S. Liberty in the Culturally Plural Society. In A.P. Griffiths (ed.) *Of Liberty: Supplement to 'Philosophy 1983.'* Cambridge: Cambridge University Press, 1983, pp. 91-108.

Machamer, P. The Harmonies of Descartes and Leibniz. *Midwest Stud Phil* 8 (83) 135-42.

Magid, H.M. *English Political Pluralism, The Problem of Freedom and*

Organization. New York: Columbia University Press, 1941.

Martin, R. & Hanson, F.S. The Problem of Other Cultures. *Phil Soc Sci* 3 (73) 191-208.

Martin, M. Theoretical Pluralism. *Philosophia* (Israel) 2 (72) 341-50.

Marty, F. Le pluralisme. *Etudes* (76) 773-88.

Maruyoma, M. Paradigmatology and Its Implication to Cross-Disciplinary, Cross-Professional and Cross-Cultural Communications. *Dialectica* 28 (74) 135-96.

Maxcy, S.J. Horace Kollen's Two Conceptions of Cultural Pluralism. *Educ Theor* 29 (79) 31-39.

Maxcy, S.J. Ethnic Pluralism, Cultural Pluralism and John Dewey's Program of Cultural Reform: A Response to J. Christopher Eisele. *Educ Theor* 34 (84) 301-305.

Mazrui, A.A. World Culture and the Search for Human Consensus. S.H. Mendlovitz (ed). *On the Creation of a First World Order.* NY Free Press, 1975.

McBride, W. and Schrag, C.O., eds. *Phenomenology in a Pluralist Context.* Albany: SUNY, 1983.

McKeon, R. Conflicts of Values in a Community of Cultures. *J Phil* 47 (50) 192-209.

McMurrin, S.M. Metaphysical Diversity and Cultural Disposition: A Case Study in Philosophic Difference. *Phil Phil E & West* 17 (67) 97-106.

Merrill, R. Philosophical Monism, Hermeneutic Pluralism and the Decline of the Humanities. *Human Soc* 3 (80) 335-49.

Miri, M. and Miri, S. Unity in Diversity. *Indian Phil Quart* 10 (83) 425-48.

Murray, J.C. The Problem of Pluralism in America. *Thought* 29 (54) 165-208.

Myers, H.A. *The Spinoza-Hegel Paradox: A Study of the Choice Between Traditional Ideologies and Systematic Pluralism.* Ithaca: Cornell, 1944.

Myers, H.A. *Systematic Pluralism: A Study in Metaphysics.* Ithaca: Cornell, 1961.

Nédoncelle, M. Brevi osservazioni en la pluralita dei tempi. *Filosofia* 28 (77) 201-208.

Nelson, A.M.C. Unity versus Diversity. *Zygon* 13 (78) 53-64.

Newman, J. Foundations of Religious Tolerance. Toronto: University of Toronto, 1982.

Newman, J. The Idea of Religious Tolerance. *Amer Phil Quart* 15 (78) 187-95.

Nichols, D. *Three Varieties of Pluralism.* London: Macmillan, 1974.

Nichols, D. *The Pluralist State.* London: Macmillan, 1975.

Nicholson, L. Multiculturalism and the G.E. Moore Fallacy. *Proc Phil Educ Supp* 37 (81) 45-48.

Nitta, Y. Singularity and Plurality in Husserl. In A.T. Tymeniecka (ed), *Soul and Body in Phenomenology.* Dordrecht: Reidel, 1983.

Northrop, F.S.C. & Livingston, H.H. (eds) *Cross-Cultural Understanding: Epistemology and Anthropology.* NY: Harper & Row, 1964.

Oliver, Jr. H.M. Von Mises on the Harmony of Interests. *Ethics* 70 (60) 282-90.

Osgood, C.E., Narz, W.H., Miron, M.S. *Cross-cultural Universals of Affective Meaning.* Urbana, Ill: Univ of Illinois, 1975.

Owens, J. The Grounds of Ethical Universality in Aristotle. *Man World* 2 (69) 171-93.

Perelman, C. The Philosophy of Pluralism. *Phil Exch* 2 (78) 49-56.

Perelman, C. The Foundations and Limits of Tolerance. *Phil Forum* (Pacific) 2 (63) 20-27.

Pereza, C.C. Pluralismo y democracia, valores politicos. *Logos* (Mexico) 8 (80) 21-30.

Perkinson, H.J. Education and the New Pluralism. *Rev J Phil Soc Sci* 1 (80) 1-14.

Peters, K.E. Modern Science and Religious Pluralism. *Nat Forum* 63 (83) 15-16.

Pingel, M. The Lost Key: A Study in Intercultural Symbology in XIII congr intern filos. 373-87.

Pratte, R.N. Cultural Pluralism and Its Relativistic Component. *Rev J Phil Soc Sci* 1 (80) 15-34.

Pratte, R.N. Five Ideologies of Cultural Diversity and Their Ramifications. *Proc. Phil Ed* 35 (79) 264-78

Pratte, R.N. Five Ideologies of Cultural Diversity and Their Curricular Ramifications. *Rev J Phil Soc Sci* 5 (80) 79-96.

Pratte, R.N. Cultural Pluralism and Its Justification. *J Thought* 18 (83) 29-36.

Pratte, R. The Concept of Cultural Pluralism. *Proc Phil Educ* 28 (72) 61-77.

Pucciarelli, E. El pluralismo en filosofia. *Cuad Filosof* 18 (78) 5-22.

Rawls, J. Social Unity and Primary Goods in A. Sin, *et al* (eds.) *Utilitarianism and Beyond.* London: Cambridge U, 1982, 157-86.

Reagan, T. Competing Cultural Ideals for the School: Liberal Education and Multicultural Education. *Phil St Educ* (83) 63-71.

Rintelen, F.J., von. El encuentro entre las culturas. *Fol Hum* 9 (71) 481-500.

Robert, J.D. Trois principes épistémologiques pour une recherche dialogale. *Rev Phil Louvain* 76 (78) 205-17.

Roubinet, P. Métaphysique et pluralisme: la métaphysique générale de G. Martin. *Arch Phil* 32 (69) 314-35.

Rozycki, E.G. Rationality and Pluralism. (Response by F.T. Villeman). *Proc Phil Educ* 35 (79) 195-204.

Ruja, H. & Shapiro, M.H. The Problem of Pluralism in Contemporary Naturalism. *Phil Phen Res* 10 (49) 65-72.

Sarlos, B. Cultural Pluralism in a New Key. *Proc Phil Ed* 38 (82) 159-62.

Scannone, J.C. Sabiduria, filosofia e inculturacion. *Stromata* 38 (82)

317-27.

Schmitz, K.L. Philosophical Pluralism and Philosophical Truth. *Phil Today* 10 (66) 3-18.

Schmitz, K.L. Community: the Elusive Unity. *Rev Metaph* 37 (83) 243-64.

Schneider, H.W. & Broyer, J.A. Creative Intercultural Relations in *Creative Interchange*. J. Broyer (ed). Carbondale: S. Illinois University Press, 1982.

Schurr, A. Réflexion philosophique et pluralisme. *Arch Phil* 38 (75) 61-78.

Scruton, R. The Significance of Common Culture. *Philosophy* 54 (79) 51-70.

Sheldon, W.H. Professor Maritain on Philosophical Co-Operation. *Mod Sch* 22 (45) 88-97.

Sidorsky, D. Contextualism, Pluralism and Distributive Justice. *Soc Phil Pol* 1 (83) 172-95.

Skillen. J.W. Societal Pluralism: Blessing or Curse for the Public Good. In F. Canavan (ed) *The Ethical Dimension of Political Life*. Durham: Duke University, 1983.

Skovira, K.J. Cultural Pluralism, Categories of Identity and Definitions of Ethnicity in Educational Discourse. *Phil Stud Educ* (78) 64-71.

Smart, N. *Worldviews: Crosscultural Explorations of Human Beliefs*. New York: Scribner's, 1983.

Spassov, D. Once Again Monism or Pluralism. *Rev World* 19 (76) 23-33.

Spassow, D. Zur Kritik des Modernen Philosophichen Pluralismus. *Deut Z Phil* 25 (77) 1508-12.

Stengren, G.L. The Possibility of a Single Ethics in a Pluralistic World. *PACPA* 37 (63) 84-87.

Tauber, K.P. Anima, D'versiones on Cultural Absolutism. *Ethics* 61 (51) 225-28.

Thomas, W.J. The Comparative Study of Cultures. *Am J of Soc* (Chicago) 42 (36) 177-85.

Tracy, D. Theological Pluralism and Analogy. *Thought* 54 (79) 24-36.

Vasseur, L. *Le congrès planétaire de l'unité de culture*. Paris: Soc Ed d'Enseignement 1966.

Walsh, P.D. Value Education in a Pluralist Society: A Reply to R.M. Hare. *Proc Phil Educ Soc* GB 10 (76) 24-33.

Walzer, M. *Spheres of Justice: An Inference of Pluralism and Equity*. New York: Basic, 1983.

Watson, W. *The Architectonics of Meaning: Foundations of the New Pluralism*. Albany: SUNY, 1985.

Weiss, P. Toward Unity of Culture: A Program for a Program. *Zygon* 2 (67) 223-30.

Whitson, R.E. American Pluralism: Toleration and Persecution. *Thought* 37 (62) 492-526.

Wiese, L. The Social, Spiritual and Cultural Elements of the Interhuman Life. *Soc Rev* (London) 29 (37) 136-53.

Wilson, J. Art, Culture and Identity. *J Aes Educ* 18 (84) 89-98.
Wolff, R.P., Moore Jr., B. & Marcuse, H. *A Critique of Pure Tolerance.* Toronto: Saunders, 1965.
Wolin, S.S. The American Pluralist Conception of Politics in *Ethics in Hard Times.* A.L. Caplan *et al* (eds). New York: Plenum, 1981.
Yoshikawa, M.J. Culture, Cognition and Communication. *Commun Log* 17 (84) 377-86.
Yudkin, M. A Cross-cultural Plight. *Phil Invest* 2 (79) 9-12.
Zappone, D.G. Un dibattito sul pluralismo culturale. *Sapienza* 79 (66) 5-10.

Relativism

Alexander, C. Cultural Transmission and Economic Development: Critique of Educational Positivism. *Educ Theor* 31 (81) 351-58.
Bernstein, R.J. *Beyond Objectivism and Relativism: Science, Hermeneutics and Praxis.* Philadelphia: Univ of Penn Pr, 1983.
Bidney, P. Cultural Relativism and the Value of the Human. *Humanitas* 15 (79) 153-60.
Blasco, J.L. Compromiso Ontico y Relativdad Ontologica. *Teorema Mono* (75) 131-46.
Briskman, L. Historicist Relativism and Bootstrap Rationality. *Monist* 60 (77) 509-39.
Chattopadhyaya, D.P. Relativity of Language and Culture. *Indian Phil Quart* 3 (76) 183-93.
Coburn, R. Relativism and the Basis of Morality. *Phil Rev* 85 (76) 87-93.
Copleston, F.C. The History of Philosophy: Relativism and Recurrence. *Heythrop J* 14 (73) 123-35.
Crittenden, B. Sociology of Knowledge and Ethical Relativism. *St Phil Educ* 4 (66) 411-18.
Crowley, D.J. Aesthetic Judgment and Cultural Relativism. *J Aes Art Crit* 17 (58) 187-93.
Cunningham, F. & Goldstick, D. Marxism and Epistemological Relativism. *Soc Prax* 6 (78) 237-54.
Darvos, W.R. Verdad y relativismo segun el pensamiento de Tomas de Aquino. *Sapientia* 34 (79) 231-54.
De Marneffe, J. Cultural Relativism. *Indian Phil Quart* 1 (74) 313-23.
Diorio, J.A. Cognitive Universalism and Cultural Relativity in Moral Education. *Educ Phil Theor* 8 (76) 33-52.
Doppelt, G. Kuhn's Epistemological Relativism: An Interpretation and Defense. *Inquiry* 21 (78) 33-86.
Drange, T.M. A Defense of Metaethical Relativism. *J W Vir Phil Soc* 9 (75) 20-23.
Durka, G. Relativism in Philosophy. *Aitia* 3 (75) 20-23.
Dye, J.W. Cultural Relativity and the Logic of Philosophy. *Tulane, St Phil* 16 (67) 37-52.
Evans, J.D.G. Aristotle on Relativism. *Phil Quart* 24 (74) 193-203.

Ferg, S. Plato on False Statement: Relative Being, a Part of Being, and Not Being in the *Sophist*. *J Hist Phil* 14 (76) 336-42.

Fopp, R. Cultural Relativism Re-examined - A Response to F.C. White's "Knowledge and Relativism." *Educ Phil Theor* 16 (84) 37-42.

Fuchs, J. The Absoluteness of Moral Terms. *Gregorianum* 52 (71) 415-58.

Gardiner, P. German Philosophy and the Rise of Relativism. *Monist* 64 (81) 138-54.

Gardner, M. Beyond Cultural Relativism. *Ethics* 61 (50) 38-45.

Gordon, D. Is Relativism Dishonest? *Analysis* 39 (79) 223.

Gramsci, A. Une Pensée située. *Etudes,* n. 76 459-86.

Griffioen, S. Marx and the Relativity of Philosophy. *Phil Reform* 43 (78) 168- 82.

Harman, G. Moral Relativism Defended. *Phil Rev* 84 (75) 3-22.

Harman, G. Relativistic Ethics: Morality vs Politics. *Midwest St Phil* 3 (78) 109-21.

Harrison, G. Relativism and Tolerance. *Ethics* 86 (76) 122-35.

Hartung, T.E. Cultural Relativity and Moral Judgments. *Phil Sci* 21 (54) 118-26.

Hauptli, B.W. Quinean Relativism: Beyond Metaphysical Realism and Idealism. *SJ Phil* 18 (80) 393-410.

Hiley, D.R. Relativism, Dogmatism and Rationality. *Int Phil Quart* 19 (79) 133-49.

Howard, V.A. Do Anthropologists Become Moral Relativists by Mistake? *Inquiry* 11 (68) 175-89.

Israel, J. Cultural Relativism and the Logic of Language. *Diogenes* 113-14 (81) 107-26.

Jacobs, R.H. Karl Manheim's Search for a Philosophy of Education Consistent with Relativism. *Stud Phil Educ* 7 (72) 190-209.

Kahn, C.H. *Linguistic Relativism and the Greek Project of Ontology in M. Sprong (ed) The Question of Being*. University Park: Penn State University Press, 1978, pp. 31-44.

Knight, S. Three Varieties of Cultural Relativism. *Educ Phil Theor* 16 (84) 23-36.

Kohlberg, L. Indoctrination versus Relativity in Value Education. *Zygon* 6 (71) 285-310.

Ladd, J. The Issue of Relativism. *Monist* 47 (63) 585-609.

Lazari Pawlowska, I. On Cultural Relativism. *J Phil* 67 (70) 57783.

Lopez, A.I. Relatividad, Conocimiento y realdad. *Rev Filos* (Costa Rica) 18 (80) 1-30.

Lukes, S. Relativism: Cognitive and Moral. *Aris Soc* 48 (74) 165-89.

Mandelbaum, M. Subjective, Objective and Conceptual Relativism. *Monist* 62 (79) 403-28.

Margolis, J. Robust Relativism. *J Aesth Art Crit* 35 (76) 37-46.

McCarthy, T. Rationality and Relativism in Habermas' Critical Theory. *Nous* 14 (80) 75-76.

McClintock, T.L. The Argument for Ethical Relativism from the Diversity of Morals. *Monist* 47 (63) 528-44.

McClintock, T.L. The Definition of Ethical Relativism. *Personalist* 50 (69) 435-47.

McHoul, A.W. Ethnomethodology and the Position of Relativist Discourse. *Theor Soc Behav* 11 (81) 107-24.

Meiland, J.W. On the Paradox of Cognitive Relativism. *Metaphil* 11 (80) 115-26.

Meiland, J.W. Concepts of Relative Truth. *Monist* 60 (77) 568-82.

Meiland, J.W. Cognitive Relativism: Popper and the Argument for Language. *Phil Forum* (Boston) 4 (73) 406-21.

Newman, J. Metaphysical Relativism. *SJ Phil* 12 (74) 435-48.

Nielsen, Kai. On Locating the Challenge of Relativism. *Second Order* 1 (72) 14-25.

Nielsen, Kai. Varieties of Ethical Subjectivism. *Dan Yrbk Phil* 7 (70) 73-87.

Nielsen, Kai. Rationality and Relativism. *Phil Soc Sci* 4 (74) 313-31.

Nordenbo, S.E. Pluralism, Relativism and the Neutral Teacher. *J Phil Educ* 12 (78) 129-39.

Nowell-Smith, P.H. Cultural Relativism. *Phil Soc Sci* 1 (71) 1-18.

Perkins, R.L. Conceptual Relativism and Europocentrism. The Reply of a Philosopher to an Anthropologist. *Ultim Real Mean* 7 (84) 237-40.

Piovani, P. Antirelativismo, pluralita dei valori, restaurazioni universalistiche. *G Crit Filosof Ital* 53 (74) 321-42.

Postow, B.C. Dishonest Relativism. *Analysis* 39 (79) 45-48.

Quantz, R. Concepts of Relativity in Multicultural and Multiethnic Education. *J Thought* 19 (84) 35-48.

Quesada, R. Identidad y relatividad. *Teorema Mono* (75) 89-106.

Rabossi, E.A. Relativismo: Diversidad de sistemas moral y conducta racional. *Cuod Filosof* 10 (70) 307-22.

Ramsperger, A.G. Absolute Truth, Relative Reality, and Meaningful Events. *J Phil* 48 (51) 29-33.

Reid, C.L. Popular Subjectivism and Relativism. *J Crit Anal* 2 (70) 36-42.

Reznek, L. A Note on Relativism. *Phil Papers* 8 (79) 69-71.

Rorty, R. Pragmatism, Relativism and Irrationalism. *PACPA* 53 (80) 719-38.

Rotenstreich, N. Relativity and Variety of Philosophical Systems. *Phil Phen Res* 41 (80) 182-203.

Ruben, D.H. Social Relativism and the Theory of Right. *Analysis* 34 (74) 167-73.

Sadiq, K.G. Cultural Relativism and Morality. *Pakistan Phil Congr* 12 (65) 60-80.

Sapire, D. Metaphysical Relativism: The Universe as a Bottomless Pit. *Phil Papers* 8 (79) 66-88.

Schmidt, P.F. Some Criticisms of Cultural Relativism. *J Phil* 52 (55)

780-90.

Schutte, A.G. Phenomenology and the Problem of Relativism in Social Science. *Phil Papers* 8 (79) 21-28.
St. Hilaire, G. Cultural Relativism and Primitive Ethics. *Mod Sch* 36 (59) 179-96.
Szobo, M.C. Variable Truth. *Z Math Log* 30 (84) 401-14.
Tennekes, J. *Anthropology, Relativism and Method: An Inquiry into the Methodological Principles of Science of Culture.* Assen: Van Gorcum, 1971.
Todd, W. Relationism. *Method Sci* 9 (76) 174-94.
Volpati, F.M. L'ontologia fra 'assoluto' e 'relativo'. *Teoresi* 33 (78) 315-22.
Weinstein, M.A. The Problem of Relativism. *Human Context* 7 (75) 422-25.
Wellman, C. The Ethical Implications of Cultural Relativity. *J Philos* 60 (63) 169-84.
Westie, F.R. and Hummel, R. Normative Absolutism vs Sociological Relativism. An Investigation of Two World Views. *Educ Stud* 11 (80) 25-36.
Westphal, M. Donagan's Critique of *Sittlichkeit.* Ideal Stud 15 (85) 1-17.
White, F.C. Knowledge and Relativism: An Essay in Philosophy of Education. Assen: Van Gorcum 1983; *Educ Phil Theor* 14-16 (82-84).
Williams, B.A.O. The Truth in Relativism. *Proc Aris Soc* 75 (7475) 215-28.

Historicity

Anderle, O. The Revolution in the World-View of History. *Diogenes* 9 (55) 43-54.
Arroya Ochoa, S. La historicidad del hombre en la filosofia de André Marc. *Logos* 3 (75) 9-41.
Bannan, J.F. Truth and Historicity. The Community Dimension. *PACPA* 43 (69) 148-54.
Beraldi, P. Moralita e storicita. *G Crit Filosof Ital* 52 (73) 444-51.
Blanchette, O. Language, the Primordial Labor of History: A Critique of Critical Social Theory in Habermas. *Cult Herm* 1 (74) 325-82.
Braybrooke, D. Refinements of Culture in Large-Scale History. *Hist Theor* 9 (69) 39-63.
Brown, H.I. For a Modest Historicism. *Monist* 60 (77) 540-55.
Burrell, D.B. Truth and Historicity: Certitude and Judgment. *PACPA* 43 (69) 44-55.
Capalbo, C. L'historicité chez Merleau-Ponty. *Rev Phil Louvain* 73 (75) 511-35.
Chartschew, A.G. and Ivanow, W.G. Uber den Historismus in der Ethik. *Sowjet Ges Beitr* 9 (69) 947-52.

Chastel, A. and Klein, R. Humanism, Historical Consciousness and National Sentiment. *Diogenes* 44 (69) 1-18.

Ciardo, M. Storicismo - liberalismo - socialismo. *Rev Stud Croce* 16 (79) 223- 36.

Collier, C. History, Culture and Communication. *Hist Theor* 20 (81) 150-67.

Colucci, F. Marxismo e storicismo. *Riv Stud Croc* 11 (74) 76-84.

De Waelhens, A. Note sur les notions d'historicité et d'histoire chez M. Heiddegger. *Arch Filosof* 2 (71) 117-24.

Eicher, P. Der Geschichtliche Mensch - Karl Rahner's Philosophische Reflexion zur Geschichlichkeit. *Frei Z Phil Theol* 16 (69) 197- 221.

Fagone, V. Storicismo e romanticismo. *Civ cat* 115 (64) 222-35.

Fernandes, S. Acronia e historicidade. *Rev Bras Filos* 19 (69) 287-304/-421-46.

Friess, H.L. Historical Interpretation and Culture Analysis. *J Phil* 49 (52) 340-49.

Gedoe, A. Die einheit von Geschichtlichkeit und Objectivitaet der Erkenntnis. *Deut Z Phil* 18 (70) 825-42.

Gerlach, H.M. Metaphysik oder Geschichtlichkeit: zu einem Gruenddilemma Spatburgerlicher Philosophigeschichte. *Deut Z Phil* 27 (79) 420-31.

Giroux, L. L'historialité chez Heidegger et son rapport à la philosophie de la vie de W. Dilthey. *Dialogue* 15 (76) 583-94.

Goldman, M. Le concept de structure significative en histoire de la culture. In *Sens et usages du terme structure*. 124-35.

Grene, M. The Paradoxes of Historicity. *Rev Metaph* 32 (78) 15-36.

Gruner, R. Historicism, Its Rise and Decline. *Clio* 8 (78) 25-39.

Guzzo, A. Scetticismo, relativismo, storicismo. *Filosofia* 26 (75) 123-28.

Hall, E.T. *The Dance of Life: The Other Dimension of Time.* Garden City: Anchor, 1983.

Heller, A. Historicity and Consciousness. *Phil Soc Crit* 7 (80) 1-16.

Henriot, P. Procès de l'historicisme ou procès de la philosophie? *Rev Métaph Morale* 81 (76) 262-70.

Herbert, G.B. Human Rights and Historicist Ontology. *Phil Forum* (Boston) 9 (77) 26-41.

Jannazzo, A. Il carattere radicale dello storicismo. *Rev Stud Croce* 7 (70) 152-55.

Jung, H.Y. The Life-World, Historicity, and Truth: Reflections on Leo Strauss's Encounter with Heidegger and Husserl. *J Brit Soc Phen* 9 (78) 11-25.

Kuderowicz, Z. Husserl as a Critic of Historicism. *Rep Phil* (78) 19-29.

Kuntz, Paul G. The Dialectic of Historicism and Anti-Historicism. *Monist* 53 (69) 656-69.

Laird, A. Historicism and Historical Laws of Development. *Inquiry* 11 (68) 155-74.

Lakebrink, B. Metafisica e historicidad. *Ethos* (1974-75) 91-107.

Langan, T. Historicity and Metaphysics. *PACPA* 48 (74) 1-13.

Ligota, C.R. and Strassfeld, R. Bibliography of Works in the Philosophy of History. *Hist Theor Beiheft* 18 (79) 1-111.

Liveanu, V. Sur l'historicisme marxiste. *Phil Log* 24 (80) 205-15.

Llompart, J. La historicidad de los derechos humanas. *An Cated Suarez* 12 (72) 131-60.

Loewith, K. Warheit und Geschichtlichkeit. *Universitas* 25 (70) 1077-89.

Lubbe, H. Der Kulturelle und Wissenshaftstheorie ord der Geschichtswissenshaft. *Conceptus* 10 (76) 49-56.

Mandelbaum, M. The Presuppositions of (Metahistory). *Hist Theor* 19 (80) 39-54.

McMullin, E. The Ambiguity of Historicism. In *Current Research in Philosophy of Science*. P Asquith (ed.). Ann Arbor: Edwards, 1979, 55-83.

Morrison, J.C. Husserl's 'Crisis'; Reflections on the Relationship of Philosophy and History. *Phil Phen Res* 37 (77) 312-30.

Moutsopoulos, E. Historiologie philosophique et philosophie de l'histoire. *Diotima* 6 (78) 151-53.

Moutsopoulos, E. Modèles historiques et modèles culturels. *Humanitas* (81) 19-24.

Murphy, M.G. Toward an Historicist History of American Philosophy. *Trans Peirce Soc* 15 (79) 3-18.

Northrop, F.S.C. The Philosophy of Culture and Its Bearing on the Philosophy of History. *Phil Phen Res* 9 (44) 568-75.

Olivier, P. Historicisme et métaphysique chez Croce. *Rev Stud Croce* 8 (71) 260-68.

Ott, H. L'herméneutique de la societé: le problème de l'historicité collective. *Rev Int Filosof Diritto* 48 (71) 240-60.

Poggeler, O. 'Historicity' in Heidegger's Late Work. *SWJ Phil* 4 (73) 53-73.

Prestipino, G. Historicisme et phénoménologie chez Banfi. *Diotima* 6 (78) 26-29.

Richardson, D.B. The Philosophy, History and Stability of Civilizations. *Thomist* 20 (57) 158-90.

Ricoeur, P. History and Humanities. *J Phil* 73 (76) 683-94.

Riedel, M. Historizismus und Kritizismus: Kant's Streit mit G. Forster and J.G. Herdin. *Kantstudien* 72 (81) 41-57.

Riedel, M. The Normative Understanding of History versus Historicism. *Ideal Stud* 8 (78) 1-13.

Seifert, J. Truth and History: Noumenal Phenomenology. *Diotima* 11 (83) 160-81.

Stokes, W.E. Truth, History and Dialectic. *PACPA* 43 (69) 85-90.

Urbach, P. Is Any of Popper's Arguments Against Historicism Valid? *Brit J Phil Sc* 24 (78) 117-30.

Vass, G. On the Historical Structure of Christian Truth. *Heythrop J* 9

(68) 129-42.

Walton, C. Bibliography of the Historiography and Philosophy on the History of Philosophy. *Int Stud Phil* (77) 135-66.

White, H.V. Historicism, History and the Figurative Imagination. *Hist Theor Beiheft* 14 (75) 48-67.

Wolterstorff, N. On Avoiding Historicism. *Phil Reform* 45 (80) 178-85.

Wren, T.F. Heidegger's Philosophy of Time. *J Brit Soc Phen* 3 (72) 111-25.

Wrolblewski, J. L'ambiguita dei diritti fondamentali tra esistentialismo e storicismo. *Rev Int Filos Diritto* 55 (78) 359-62.

CULTURE AND SOCIETY

Culture and Social Life

Adams, G.P. et al. *Knowledge and Society: A Philosophical Approach to Modern Civilization*. New York: Appleton-Century, 418.

Alisjahbana, S.T. *Values as Integrating Forces in Personality, Society and Culture: Essay of a New Anthropology*. Kuala Lumpur: Univ of Malaya Press, 1966.

Astrada. *Humanismo y dialectica de la libertad*. Buenos Aires: Dedafo, 1960.

Barry, V. *Personal and Social Ethics: Moral Problems with Integrated Theory*. Belmont, Ca: Wadsworth, 1978.

Betruzzellis, N. Cultura e democrazia. *Ras Sc Filos* 22 (69) 145-46.

Bidney, D. On the Philosophy of Culture in the Social Sciences. *J Phil* 39 (42) 449-57.

Bynack, V.P. Noah Webster and the Idea of a National Culture: The Pathologies of Epistemology. *J Hist Ideas* 45 (84) 99-114.

Campanini, G. Cultura: incontro del singolo con la societa. *Humanitas* 18 (63) 47-57.

Cotta, S. Dimensioni culturale della politica o dimensione politica della cultura? *Sapienza* 33 (80) 280-97.

Culea, H. Cadres socio-culturels du genre commm de connaissance. *Phil Log* 16 (72) 417-23.

de Soignie, P.R. *Culture et milieux populaires*. Tournai: Casterman, 1944.

de Mello-Kujawski, G. Cultura e liberdade I-II. *Convivium* SP 3 (63) no. 6: 29-63; no. 7: 8-32; no. 10: 3-16.

Dewey, John. *Freedom and Culture*. New York: Putnam, 1939.

Dewey, J. *Freedom and Culture*. London: Allen & Unwin, 1940.

Dollard, J. Culture, Society, Impulse and Socialization. *AJS* 45 (39) 50-63.

Du Bois de Marneffe. *Culture et Civilisme*, Tournai: Casterman, 1944.

Duran de Seade, E. State and History in Hegel's Concept of People. *J Hist Ideas* 40 (79) 369-84.

Eco, U. Cultura di massa ed evoluzione della cultura. *De Homine* 21

(63) 288-316.

Georgel, G. *Les rythmes dans l'histoire. Les rythmes dans la vie des peuples. La synthèse dans l'histoire et l'évolution cyclique des civilisations.* Paris: Régionalisme, 1939.

Gheorghe, E. Social and Individual Demands in the Sphere of Culture. *Phil Log* 27 (83) 48-52.

Ghurye, G.S. *Culture and Society.* Bombay: Oxford nd.

Gilson, E. *La Societe de masse et sa culture.* Paris: Vrin, 1967.

Glenn, J.D., Jr. *Marcel and Sartre: Philosophy of Communion and of Alienation* in P.A. Schelpp, ed., *The Philosophy of Gabriel Marcel.* LaSalle: Open Court, 1984, 525-52.

Gluck, P.G. Quality versus Ideology: A Note on "Elitism" and "Cultural Democracy." *J Aes Educ* 18 (84) 77-84.

Griffin-Collart, E. L'égalité: condition de l'harmonie sociale pour J.J. Rousseau. *Rev Int Phil* 25 (71) 298-311.

Gulian, C.I. Sociétés et cultures. *Phil Log* 18 (74) 111-20.

Gulian, C.I. La sociologie de la culture (des orgines jusqu'à Hegel). *Phil Log* 16 (72) 351-67.

Hollhuber, I. The Metasociological Background of Modern Integral Culture. *Akten XIV Intern Kongr Philos VI* 239-95.

Imam, G. The Problem of National Character. *Pakistan Phil Congr* 8 (61) 113-17.

Imbert-Nergal, R. Que peut apporter le rationalisme a l'humanité. *Cahiers rationalistes* n 182 (59) 250-66.

Jones, R.A. and Kuklick, H., eds. *Knowledge and Society: Studies in the Sociology of Culture Past and Present V* 4. Greenwich: Jai Pr, 1983.

Jules-Rosette, B. The Politics of Paradigms: Contrasting Theories of Consciousness and Society. *Human St* 1 (78) 92-110.

Kann, Mark E. The Political Culture of Interdisciplinary Explanation. *Human Soc* 2 (79) 185-200.

Kockelmans, J. Toward an Interpretative or Hermeneutic Social Science. *Grad Fac Phil* 5 (75) 73-96.

Lacroix, J. La démocratie et le droit à la culture. *Comprendre* (Venice) 33-34 (69) 50-61.

Laloire, M. Culture et communauté. *VI* 57 (38) 349-58.

Lamont, W.D. Politics and Culture. *Philos* 20 (45) 39-58.

Masini, G. A Bridge for the Present Crisis in Culture and Society. In *The Search for Absolute Values.* New York: ICF Pr, 1977.

Meadows, P. The Cultural Organization of Action. *Phil Sci* 13 (46) 332-38.

Miscol, O. Social Conditioning and Liberty in the Perspective of Cultural Integration. *Phil Log* 23 (79) 25-30.

Morris, B. Democracy and Culture. *Ethics* 66 (56) 87-91.

Mukerjee, R. Conscience and Culture: A Biosocial Approach to Morals. *Ethics* 60 (50) 178-87.

Mumford, L. *Stadskultur.* Stockholm: Forbundets, 1942.

Northrop, F.S.C. *Ideological Differences and World Order: Studies in the Philosophy and Science of the World's Cultures.* New Haven: Yale, 1949.

Ohe, S. Nature and Culture in Human Freedom. *Ethics* 77 (67) 314-18.

Petruzellis, M. La funzione sociale della cultura. *Sapienza* 33 (80) 385-412.

Piotrowski, A. A Sociological Theory of Culture. *Dialec Hum* 10 (83) 163-68.

Pithod, A. Sociedad, cultura y personalidad como objectos reales y como sistemas de accion. *Ethos* (74-75) 127-43.

Raulet, G. Le rôle des "Sciences de la culture" dans une science sans domination. *Petite Rev Phil* 5 (84) 89-104.

Redfield, R. The Folk Society and Culture. *AJS* 45 (40) 730-42.

Simon, Y.R. *Work, Society and Culture.* New York: Fordham, 1971.

Smith, E.V. Four Issues Unique to Socio-Cultural Indicators. *Soc Indic Res* 5 (78) 111-20.

Sorokin, P.A. *Society, Culture and Personality: Their Structure and Dynamics.* New York: Harper, 1947.

Tanase, A. La signification et l'efficience sociale de la culture. *Rev Filozof* 29 (82) 449-52.

Thomson, D. The Cultural Efforts of National Self-Sufficiency. *HJ* 37 (38) 135-41.

Tijcrino, R.A. *Libertad y cultura.* Medellin: Univ de Antioquia n 65.

Toynbee, A.J. Feibleman's Exposition of the Indivisibility of Human Affairs. *Stud Gen* 24 (71) 652-59.

Trigg, R. Reason, Commitment and Social Anthropology. *Phil* 51 (76) 219-22.

Van Dyke, V. The Cultural Rights of Peoples. *Univ Human Rights* 2 (80) 1-21.

Varma, V.P. The Political Philosophy of Rabindranath Tagore. *Visvabharata Quart* 26 (60) 93-127.

Vasoli, C. *Tra Cultura e ideologia.* Milan: Lerici, 1961.

Williams, R. *Culture and Society 1780-1950.* London: Chatto and Windus, 1958.

Woodward, J.W. Cultural Evolution and the Social Order. *J of Soc Phil* 4 (39) 4.

Zivotic, M. Socialism and Mass Culture. *Praxis* 1 (65) 318-28.

Cultural Crisis, Critique and Change

Abbate, M. *Liberta e societa di massa.* Bari: Laterza, 1967.

Adams, E.M. Philosophical Education as Cultural Criticism. *Teach Phil* 3 (79) 1-11.

Adorno, T.W. Critica della cultura e societa. *De Homine* 2 (63) 391-410.

Bell, D. The Cultural Contradictions in Capitalism (critique) J. Bensman, "The cultural contradictions of D. Bell". *J Aes Educ* 6 (72) 11-38.

Berger, H. Jr. Outline of a General Theory of Cultural Change. *Clio* 2

(72) 49-63.

Bien, J. Lukacs on Culture and the Primacy of the Economic. *J Thought* 9 (74) 28-36.

Bogolyabova, J.F. The Development of the Concept of 'culture' in the Soviet Literature on Historical Materialism. *Deut Z Phil* 30 (82) 255-58.

Bondy, A.S. Filosofia de la dominacion y filosofia de la liberacion. *Stromata* 29 (73) 393-97.

Camacho, L.A. Desarrollo y cultura: Enfoques y disemfoques. *Rev Filos* (Costa Rica) 22 (84) 31-38.

Cauchy, V. Culture and Human Deviancy. *Dialec Hum* 11 (84) 225-34.

Corsi, M. Le 'cultura' di massa. *De Homine* 1 (62) 81-90.

Cosic, D. Culture and Revolution. In M. Markovic (ed) *Praxis*. Dordrecht: Reidel, 1979, 217-25.

Cristaldi, M. Considerazioni critiche sulla responsabilita della cultura. *Teoresi* 18 (63) 101-13.

D'Amico, R. *Marx and Philosophy of Culture*. Gainesville: University of Florida, 1981.

Derisi, O.N. Lo permanente y lo transitorio de la cultura in *Mem XIII Congr intern Filos VI* 211-19.

Derisi, O.N. Una nueva cultura para una nueva sociedad. *Sapientia* 38 (83) 232-34.

Derisi, O.N. Lo permanente y lo transitorio de la cultura. *Sapienta* 17 (62) 281-87.

Dubiel, H. Farewell to Critical Theory. *Praxis Int* 3 (83) 121-37.

Dupré, L. *Marx's Social Critique of Culture*. New Haven: Yale U, 1983.

Dupré, L. Marx's Critique of Culture and Its Interpretation. *Rev Metaph* 34 (80) 91-122.

Dussel, E. Cultura imperial, cultura ilustrada y liberacion de la cultura popular. *Stromata* 30 (74) 93-123.

Eccles, J.C. Cultural Evolution vs Biological Evolution. *Zygon* 8 (73) 282-93.

Estui, E. Liberacion y cultura. *Rev Filos la PR* 17 (66) 7-14.

Fagone, V. Umanesimo e materialismo. *Civ cat* 118 (67) 111-26.

Filiasi Carcano, P. L'esperienza della solitudine nel mondo contemporaneo. *Sapienza* 15 (62) 31-48.

Florea, M. and Smirnov, I. La Culture comme facteur de désaliénation. *Phil Log* 20 (78) 343-53.

Frank, L.K. *Society as the Patient: Essays on Culture and Personality*. New Brunswick: Rutgers, 1948.

Gay, F.T. Cultural Colonialism. *SWJ Phil* 5 (74) 153-59.

Gheorghe, E. Contradictory Aspects in the Evolution of Contemporary Culture. *Phil Log* 26 (82) 357-62.

Gulian, C. Les Crises de la culture et les "cultures de crise." *Phil Log* 27 (83) 122-27.

Gulian, C. Le Marxisme et le rôle de la conscience dans la culture. *Phil Log* 17 (73) 87-92.

Hall, D.L. *The Uncertain Phoenix: Adventures Toward a PostCultural Sensibility.* New York: Fordham University Press, 1982.

Hallen, B. Robin Horton on Critical Philosophy and Traditional Thought. *Second order* 6 (77) 81-92.

Halpern, B. The Dynamic Elements of Culture. *Ethics* 65 (55) 235-49.

Held, D. *Introduction to Critical Theory.* Berkeley: University of California Press, 1980.

Henry, J. *Culture Against Man.* New York: Vantage, 1965.

Horkheimer, M. *Critical Theory: Selected Essays.* New York: Continuum, 1982.

Jaspers, K. *The Future of Mankind.* Chicago: University of Chicago Press, 1963.

Jay, M. The Frankfurt School's Critique of Karl Mannheim and the Sociology of Knowledge. *Telos* 20 (74) 72-89.

Kahle, W. Marx' Kulturkonzeption in "Grundrisse der Kritik der Politischen Okonomie." *Deut Z Phil* 32 (84) 899-907.

Klever, W.N.A. De Kulturfilosofie van Herbert Marcuse. *Tijdschr Filosof* 32 (70) 72-85.

L'Anti-Utopie moderne. *Esprit* 29 (61) 389-86.

Lebel, M. La Culture et l'humanisme dans notre âge de transition. *Rev U Ottawa* 46 (76) 421-51.

Lilly, W. Cultural Evolution and Aesthetic Expression. *J W Vir Phil Soc* (78) 10.

MacIntyre, A.C. *Marcuse.* London: Fontana, 1970.

Markovic, M. The Idea of Critique in Social Theory. *Praxis Int* 3 (83) 108-20.

Mazzeo, J.A. Interpretation, Humanistic Culture and Cultural Change. *Thought* 51 (76) 65-81.

McDonnell, K. and Robins, K. Marxist Cultural Theory: The Althusserian Smokescreen in *One-Dimensional Marxism.* S. Clark, et al (eds). London: Allison & Busby, 1980.

Meynell, H. On Analytical Philosophy and the Critique of Culture. *Method* 1 (83) 74-81.

Moutsopoulos, E. L'idée de développement. *Rev Phil Fr* 168 (78) 79-84.

Nandy, A. Cultural Frames for Social Intervention. *Indian Phil Quart* 11 (84) 411-22.

Niel, A. Vers un humanisme de libération. *Age Nouveau* 13 (59) 50-62.

Ong, W. (ed). *Knowledge and the Future of Man.* New York: Simon & Schuster, 1968.

Opler, M.K. Cultural Evolution and Social Psychiatry. *Phil Phen Res* 27 (67) 587-96.

Paparella, B.A. Progress and Modern Man. *Thomist* 25 (62) 419-43.

Papodopoullos, T. Anthropological Criteria for a Notion of Progress. *Diogenes* (75) 32-56.

Popma, K.J. Humanisme en antihumanisme. *Philos Reform* 28 (63) 19-57.

Princay, Y. *La civilisation moderne et le progrès.* Paris: moderne des

arts et de la vie, 1937.
Prini, P. L'uomo e natura in un civilta minacciata. *Proteus* 2 (71) 3-11.
Rader, M. Toward a Definition of Cultural Crisis. *Kenyon Rev* 9 (47) 262-78.
Radhakrishnan, S. Progress and Spiritual Values. *Philos* 12 (37) 259-75.
Rasmussen, D.M. Towards Critical Cultural Theory. *Cult Herm* 1 (73) 1-2.
Redeker, H. Der Kulturprozess und die wochsende Rolle des Subjektiven Faktors. *Deut Z Phil* 22 (74) 564-83.
Regin, D. *Sources of Cultural Estrangement.* The Hague: Mouton, 1969.
Riepe, D. Subjectivist Conceptions Developed Under Imperialism. *Phil Soc Act* 2 (76) 53-65.
Ruse, M. Cultural Evolution. *Theor Decis* 5 (74) 413-40.
Sanchez Vasquez, A. Mitologia y verdad en la critica de nuestra epoca. *Revista Mexicana de Filosof* 5-6 (63) 253-62.
Sciacca, M.F. Cultura e anti-cultura. *G Meta* 24 (69) 1-39.
Searles, H.L. Progress as Value-directed Science. *The Personalist* 26 (45) n 2.
Sellon, H. The Crisis of Western Civilization. *Hibbert J* 54 (65) 161-69.
Siebert, R.J. *From Critical Theory of Society to Theology of Communicative Praxis.* Washington: UPA, 1979.
Siemek, M.J. Marxism and the Hermeneutic Tradition. *Dialec Hum* 2 (75) 87-103.
Sorokin, P.A. *Social and Cultural Dynamics: A Study of Change in Major Systems of Art, Truth, Ethics, Law and Social Relationship.* Boston: Ext. Horizons, 1957.
Sorokin, P.A. *The Crisis of Our Age: The Social and Cultural Outlook.* New York: Dutton, 1941.
Spengler, O. *The Decline of the West.* London: Allwin & Unwin, 1934.
Sreenwasa Iyengar, K.R. Progress or Perfection. *Phil Quart* 16 n 4.
Stebbing, L.S. *Ideals and Illusions.* London: Walts, 1941.
Stoikov, A. Conditions et possibilités d'un développement accéléré des cultures. *Akten XIV Intern Kongr Philos, IV*, 537-38.
Szondi, L. Thanatos et Cain, Au commencement de la culture. *Rev Philos Louvain* 68 (70) 373-84.
Thomas, G.F. Can We Believe in Progress? *Religion in Life* 6 (37) 70-82.
Toynbee, A.J. *Surviving the Future.* New York: Oxford, 1971.
Uscatescu, G. *Proceso al humanismo.* Madrid: Guadarrama, 1968.
Weaver, R.M. *Visions of Order: The Cultural Crisis of Our Time.* Baton Rouge: University of Louisiana, 1964.

REGIONAL CULTURES

Early Cultures

Babadzan, A. Remarques sur la construction d'un objet anthropologique dans l'étude des sociétés acculturées. *Comun log* 14 (81) 85-97.

Fourcher, L.A. Human Ethology and Phenomenology I. *Behaviorism* 7 (79) 23-36.

Granell, M. *La vicindad humana, fundamentacion de la ethologia.* Madrid: Revista di Occidente 1969.

Hallen, B. Robert Lithown on Philosophy and Traditional Culture. *Theor Theor* 11 (77) 215.

Keaton, A.E. Ethology: Some Philosophical Implications. *SW Phil St* 3 (78) 105-12.

Kirk, G.S. *Myth: Its Meaning and Functions in Ancient and Other Cultures.* Cambridge: Cambridge University Press., 1970.

Krolick, S.W. Gesture and Myth: A Phenomenological Reflection on Myth and Traditional Culture. *Man World* 14 (81) 201-21.

Lee, D. Being and Value in a Primitive Culture. *J Phil* 46 (49) 401-15.

Montagu, A. (ed). *The Concept of the Primitive.* New York: Free Press, 1968.

Palubicka, A. The Positivist and Instrumentalist Concepts of the So-called Archeological Culture. *Poznan Stud* 5 (79) 55-66.

Schmidt, W. *The Culture-Historical Method of Ethnology.* NY: Forlung's, 1939.

Stunkel, K.R. *Relations of Indian, Greek and Christian Thought in Antiquity.* Washington: UPA, 1979.

Von Harten, M. Religion and Culture in the Ancient American Systematics 1 (63) 35-66.

Wall, G.B. Primitive Cultures and Ethical Universals. *Int Phil Quart* 7 (67) 470-82.

Wall, G.B. Primitive Cultures and Ethical Universals. *Int Philos Quart* 7 (67) 470-82.

Winch, P. Understanding a Primitive Society. *Amer Phil Quart* 1 (64) 307-24.

Zuckerkandl, F. The Nature of the Experience of the Primitives. *Diogenes* 46 (64) 103-24..

Contemporary European and Technological Culture

Alberoni, F. Technical Progress and the Dialectics of Existence. *Hum Cont* 4 (72) 264-305.

Bahm, A.J. The American Cultural Predicament Today. *J Thought* 5 (70) 214-30.

Baier, K. & Rescher, N. *The Impact of Technological Change on American Values.* London: Collier-Macmillan, 1969.

Barnes, H.E. *An Intellectual and Cultural History of the Western World.* New York: Cordon, 1937.

Beck, R.H. Perception of Individualism in Ancient Culture and Education. *Educ Theor* 11 (61) 129-45.

Becker, C.L. *Freedom and Responsibility in the American Way of Life.* New York: Knopf, 1945.

Becker, H. Science, Culture and Society. *Phil Sci* 19 (52) 273-87.

Berdyaev, N. *The Fate of Man in the Modern World.* London: SCMP, 1935.

Bossenbrook, W.J., & Johansen, R. *Foundations of Western Civilization.* Boston: Heath, 1939.

Cernuschi, F. Harmonization of Science and Technology with Cultural Traditions. In *The Search for Absolute Values.* New York: ICF Pr, 1976. vol. 2, 889-98.

Clarke, M.E. The Shape of Modern Culture. *Hibbert J* 44 (46) 231-38.

Composta, D. La Filosofia morale di fronti all'attuale cultura Occidentale. *Doctor Communis* 35 (82) 133-59.

de Tocqueville, A. *Democracy in America.* New York: Alfred Knopf, 1945. 2 vols.

DeZan, J. La cicencia moderna y el problema de la desintegracion de la unidad del Saber. *Stromata* 39 (83) 311-49.

Dorenus, O. Note on the Coherence of the American Phenomenon. *Diogenes* 65 (99) 49-73.

Dumont-Wilder. *L'évolution de l'esprit européen.* Paris: Flammarion.

Dupré, L. Secularism and the Culture of our Culture. *Thought* 51 (76) 271-81.

Fancelli, M. Il tema della speranza nella culture contemporanea. *G Crit Filos Ital* 46 (67) 422-40.

Fischer, J.L. Science, Philosophy and the Future of Culture. In *Mem XIII Congr Filos* VI, 263-78.

Gasco Contell, E. Algunos aspectos del pensamiento europeo y su expresion actual. In *Tecnica y cultura actuales.* A. Munoz Alonso (ed). Madrid, 1962, 207-24.

Gelpi, E. Culture in the City: Institutional, Popular and Mass Culture. *Dialec Hum* 10 (83) 183-88.

Greene, T.M. *Our Cultural Heritage.* Houston: Elsevier Pr, 1957.

Hilckman, A. Natura e signficato della scienza delle civilta. *Ethica* 1 (62) 111-20.

Il'Enkov, P.V. *L'uomo e i miti della tecnica.* Roma: Riuniti, 1971.

Jennings, R.C. Truth, Rationality and the Sociology of Science. *Brit J Phil Sc* 35 (84) 201-211.

Jones, T.E. Herman Kahn and the Post Industrial Culture. *Phil Forum* 15 (77) 111-43.

Kallen, H.M. *Art and Freedom: A Historical and Biographical Interpretation of the Relations Between the Ideas of Beauty, Use and Freedom in Western Civilization from the Greeks to the Present Day.* New York: Duell, Sloan and Pearce, 1942, 2 vols.

Kelessidou-Galanos, U. Réflexions critiques sur la situation actuelle de la philosophie grecque et son apport à la culture nationale. *Philosophia* (Athens) 12 (82) 350-58.

Kimball, S.T. Social and Cultural Congruences in American Civilization. *J Aes Educ* 6 (72) 39-52.

Kloskouska, A. Development of the Conception of Culture in Polish

Sociology. *Dialec Hum* 1 (74) 19-37.

Kruks, S. Merleau-Ponty: A Phenomenological Critique of Liberalism. *Phil Phen Res* 37 (77) 394-407.

Kunz, F.L. Science as a Cultural Moral. *Main Currents* 8 (52) 113-17.

Laszlo, E. Human Dignity and the Promise of Technology. *Philos For* 9 (71) 165-200.

Levi, A.W. Modern Cultural Roots of Analytic Philosophy. *J Chin Phil* 6 (79) 15-35.

Ley, H. Geist und Technik. *Acten XIV Intern Kong Phil* VI, 52-63.

Lindsay, R.B. *The Role of Science in Civilization.* New York: Harper & Rowe, 1963.

Lotz, J.B. *Della solitudine dell'uomo, la situazione spirituale dell'epoca delle tecnica.* Alba: Ed Paoline, 1964.

Lousse, E. Les facteurs de civilisation à l'époque moderne. *Et C* 5 pp. 52- 60, 191-99, 424-32, 596-605.

Lovell, B. *Science and Civilization.* London, 1939.

Marcel, G. *La sabiduria en la edad tecnica.* Madrid: Ed Nacional, 1965.

Margolis, J. Culture and Technology in *Research in Philosophy and Technology,* V 1, P.T. Durban (ed). Greenwich: Jai Pr, 1978, 25-38.

Maritain, J. *Reflections on America.* New York: Doubleday, 1964.

McDermott, J.J. *The Culture of Experience: Philosophical Essays in the American Grain.* New York: NY Univ Pr, 1976.

Mesthene, E. G. Technology and Culture. In *The Reevaluation of Existing Values.* 2 vols., ICF (ed). New York: ICF Pr 1978, 997-1004.

Miscol, O. Tradition and Modernity in Culture in Opposition and Complementarity. *Phil Log* 25 (81) 105-12.

Moser, S. Toward a Metaphysics of Technology. *Phil Today* 15 (71) 122-28.

Moutsopoulos, E. Prolégomènes à la philosophie de la culture grecque. *Diotima* 12 (84) 17-28.

Mumford, L. *Technics and Civilization* New York: Harcourt Brace, 1934.

Nostrand, H.L. Some Elements for the Synthesis of a Contemporary Culture. *Main Currents* 7 (49) 80-86; 7 (50) 113-20.

Parkes, H.B. *Gods and Men: The Origins of Western Culture.* New York: Knopf, 1959.

Parry, C.M. *The Philosophy of American Democracy.* Chicago: Univ. of Chicago, 1943.

Percy, W. Culture: the Antinomy of Scientific Method. *New Schol* 32 (58) 443-75.

Powell, J.M. *The Civilization of the West. A Brief Interpretation.* New York: Macmillan, 1967.

Prini, P. Nacion, mundo del trabajo y formacion humana. In A. Munoz Alonso (ed), *Tecnica y cultura actuales.* Madrid: Serv-Espan del Profesorado del movimiento, 1962, 105-20.

Rintelen, F.J. Von *Humandid y espiritu occidental.* Monterrey: U

Nuevo Leon, 1962.

Robert, J.D. Conséquences tragiques du refoulement des 'symboliques' dans le monde occidentel, d'après François Lapelantine. *Tijdschr Filosof* 38 (76) 614-28.

Rostagni, A. *Classicita e spirito moderno.* Einaudi, 1939.

Rutten, A. Pour un humanisme moderne. *Synthèse* 13 (59) 109-15.

Sanfatti, D.C. Benedetto Croce e la cultura Europea. *G Crit Filosof Ital* 59 (80) 233-66.

Schaller, H. *Die europaische kulturphilosophie.* Munchen: Reinhardt, 1940.

Seibold, J.R. El nuevo desafio a la ciencia y a la culture in latinamerica: Del conflicto a la sintesi vital. *Stromata* 38 (82) 97-115.

Snow, C.P. *The Two Cultures and the Scientific Revolution.* Cambridge: Cambridge University Press, 1959.

Swabez, M.C. The Leading Myths of Our Time. *Ethics* 49 (39) 169-86.

Tanase, U.L. Les droits de l'homme et la dimension humaniste de la culture européene. *Rev Filozof* 28 (81) 97-98.

Tanase, A. Unité et tension entre culture et science dans la civilisation contemporaine. *Phil Log* 20 (78) 313-25.

Tanase, A. Die Kulturphilosophie in Rumanien. *Phil Log* 15 (71) 49-69.

Tilman-Timon, A. Du type représentatif de notre civilisation. In *Mem XIII Cong Intern Filos* VI, 155-62.

Tilman-Timon, A. La technique et le spirituel. *Et Philos* 22 (67) 301-16.

Topor, R. Romanian Contributions to Elaborating the Concept of Mass Culture. *Phil Log* 23 (79) 31-43.

Urbanski, S. Dos orientaciones culturales distintas en el hemisfero occidental. *Rev Filosof* (Costa Rica) 9 (71) 27-35.

Uscatescu, J. Existe una cultura europea? *Rev Filos* 26 (67) 199-214.

Van Melsen, A.G.M. The Impact of Science on Culture. *Int Phil Quart* 1 (61) 503-12.

Villemain, F.T. The Significance of the Democratic Ethic for Cultural Alternatives and American Civilization. *Educ Theor* 26 (76) 40-52.

Wojciechowski, J.A. Culture, Knowledge and Ecology. *Listening* 18 (83) 132-43.

Zimmerman, M. Techological Culture and the End of Philosophy. In *Research in Philosophy and Technology*, Vol. II, ed. P. Durban. Greenwich: Jai Pr, 1979, 137-46.

Hispanic Cultures

Altamira y Creva, R. Idea y estrictura de una nueva historia de la civilizacion espanola. *Filosofia y letras* (Mexico) (45).

Erassov, B. Concepts of 'Cultural Personality' in the Ideologies of the Third World. *Diogenes* 78 (72) 123-40.

Freyre, G. Americanism and Latinity in Latin America: Increasing

Interdependence and Decreasing Separateness. *Diogenes* 43 (63) 1-20.

Scannone, J.C. 'Mestizaje Cultural' y 'bautismo cultural': categoria teoricas fecundas para Interpretar la realidad Latinoamericana. *Stromata* 33 (77) 73-91.

Rivera, E. Maxima aportacion del pensamiento hispanico a la cultura: El Sentido universalista. *Rev Filos* (Mexico) 17 (84) 465-90.

Torres, C.A. Antropologia cultural Latinoamerican: Aspectos fundamentales. *Pensamiento* 34 (78) 277-97.

Valle, R.H. *La cultura en Hispano america.* New York: Nueva Democracia, 1942.

Videla, I.P. Dependencia Cultural y creacion de cultura en america latina. *Stromata* 29 (73) 525-32.

Zea, Leopoldo. The Interpenetration of Ibero-American and North American Culture. *Phil Phen Res* 9 (49) 538-44.

African Cultures

Addo, H. African Political Institutions, Their Cultural Bases and Future Prospects. *Praxis Int* 2 (82) 148-67.

Gbadegesin, O. Destiny, Personality and the Ultimate Reality of Human Existence: A Yoruba Perspective. *Ultim Real Mean* 7 (84) 173-88.

Hallen, B. A Philosopher's Approach to Traditional Culture. *Theor Theor* 9 (75) 259-72.

Lithown, R. Barry Hallen on Philosophy and Traditional Culture. *Theor Theor* 10 (76) 161-66.

Makinde, M. Akin. An African Concept of Human Personality. *Ultim Real Mean* 7 (84) 189-200.

Mendonsa, E.L. A Note on African Philosophy and Cultural Anthropology. *Second Order* 5 (76) 91-93.

Okere, T. *African Philosophy - A Historice-Hermeneutical Investigation of the Conditions of Its Possibility.* Lanham: UPA, 1983.

Roy, P.K. The Principle of Ontological Balance and Social-Ethical Ideal in African (Nigeria) Traditional Thought. *Phil Soc Act* 9 (83) 27-31.

Ruch, E.A. Is There an African Philosophy? *Second Order* 3 (74) 3-21.

Senghor, L.I. On Negrohood: Psychology of the African Negro. *Diogenes* 37 (62) 1-15.

Twumosi, P.A. The Asantes: Ancestors of the Social Meaning of Self. *Ultim Real Mean* 7 (84) 201-208.

Williams, R.C. Afro-American Folklore as Philosophical Source. *JW Vir Phil Soc* (76) 1-6.

Wiredu, J.E. On An African Orientation in Philosophy. *Second Order* 1 (72) 3-13.

Wiredu, K. *Philosophy and An African Culture.* Cambridge: Cambridge University Press, 1980.

Yangyuoro, Y. Dagon Traditional Culture Sacrifice as a Thematization of Ultimate Reality and Meaning. *Ultim Real Mean* 7 (84) 209-219.

Asian Cultures

Brunton, P. *Indian Philosophy and Modern Culture*. London: 1939.

Chang, Ching Ying. Toward Constructing a Dialectics of Harmonization: Harmony and Conflict in Chinese Philosophy. *J Chin Phil* 4 (77) 209-45.

Hall, D.L. The Width of Civilized Experience. In K. Inada (ed) *Buddhism and American Thinkers*. Albany: SUNY, 1984.

Hall, D. Nietzsche and Chuang Tzu: Resources for the Transcendence of Culture. *J Chin Phil* 11 (84) 139-52.

Lai, W.W. Once More on the Two Truths: What Does Chi-Tsang Mean by Two Truths as 'yueh-chiao'? *Relig Stud* 19 (83) 505-22.

Levenson, J.R. *Confucian China and Its Modern Fate: The Problem of Intellectual Continuity*. Berkeley, University of California, 1958.

Oomen, T.K. Traditional Values and Contemporary Dilemma: India. *Phil Soc Act* 1 (75) 61-70.

Raghunathen, N. *Reason and Intuition in Modern Culture*. Madras: University of Madras, 1969.

Rosemont, H. Jr. Notes from a Confucian Perspective: Which Acts are Moral Acts. *Int Phil Quart* 16 (76) 49-61.

Ts'ao, I.J.H. Confucius in the Middle of the New Cultural Revolution Today. *Stud Sov Tho* 15 (75) 1-33.

INDEX

THE COUNCIL FOR
RESEARCH IN VALUES AND PHILOSOPHY

PURPOSE

Today there is urgent need to attend to the nature and dignity of the person, to the quality of human life, to the purpose and goal of the physical transformation of our environment, and to the relation of all this to the development of social and political life. This, in turn, requires philosophic clarification of the basis upon which freedom is exercised, that is, of the values which provide stability and guidance to one's decisions.

Such studies must be able to reach deeply into the cultures of one's nation--and often of other parts of the world from which they derive--in order to uncover the roots of the dignity of persons and of the societies built upon their relations one with another. They must be able to identify the conceptual forms in terms of which modern industrial and technological developments are structured and how these impact human self-understanding. Above all, they must be able to bring these elements together in the creative understanding essential for setting our goals and determining our modes of our interaction. In the present complex circumstances this is a condition for growing together with trust and justice, honest dedication and mutual concern.

The Council for Studies in Values and Philosophy is a group of scholars who share the above concerns and are interested in the application thereto of existing capabilities in the field of philosophy and other disciplines. Its work is to identify areas in which study is needed, the intellectual resources which can be brought to bear thereupon, and the financial resources required. In bringing these together its goal is scientific discovery and publication which contributes to the promotion of human life in our times.

In sum, our times present both the need and the opportunity for deeper and ever more progressive understanding of the person and of the foundations of social life. The development of such understanding is the goal of the Council for Research in Values and Philosophy (RVP).

PROJECTS

A set of related research efforts are currently in process, some developed initially by the RVP and others now being carried forward by it either solely or conjointly.

1. *Cultural Heritage and Contemporary Life: Philosophical Foundations for Social Life.* Sets of focused and mutually coordinated continuing seminars in university centers, each preparing a volume as part of an integrated philosophic search for self-understanding differentiated by continent. This work focuses upon evolving a more adequate understanding of the person in society and looks to the cultural heritage of each for the resources to respond to its own specific contemporary issues.

2. *Seminars on Culture and Contemporary Issues.* This series of 10 week seminars is being coordinated by the RVP in Washington.

3. *Joint-Colloquia* with institutes of philosophy of the national Academies of Science, university philosophy departments, and societies have been underway since 1976 in Eastern Europe and, since 1987, in China concerning the person in contemporary society.

4. *The Mediation of Values to Social Life.* The development of a four volume study on the mediation of values to social life is a corporate effort of philosophers throughout the world.

5. *Foundations of Moral Education and Character Development.* A study in values and education which unites philosophers, psychologists and scholars in education in the elaboration of ways of enriching the moral content of education and character development.

The personnel for these projects consists of established scholars willing to contribute their time and research as part of their professional commitment to life in our society. The Council directly sponsors some projects and seeks support for projects sponsored by other organizations. For resources to implement this work the Council, as a nonprofit organization incorporated in the District of Colombia, looks to various private foundations, public programs, and enterprises.

PUBLICATIONS ON CULTURAL HERITAGE AND CONTEMPORARY LIFE

Series I.   *Culture and Values*
Series II.   *Africa*
Series III. *Asia*
Series IV. *W. Europe and North America*
Series IVa. *Central and Eastern Europe*
Series V.   *Latin America*
Series VI. *Foundations of Moral Education*

The volumes (except for VI.3) are published by: The Council for Research in Values and Philosophy, Cardinal Station, P.O. Box 261, Washington, D.C. 20064, Tel. 202/319-5636; Fax. 220/319-6089.